FOUNDING THE COMMUNIST INTERNATIONAL

The Communist International
in Lenin's Time

FOUNDING THE COMMUNIST INTERNATIONAL

Proceedings and Documents of the First Congress, March 1919

Edited by John Riddell

PATHFINDER

New York London Montreal Sydney

ISBN 978-0-87348-943-0
Library of Congress Catalog Card Number 87-70239
Manufactured in the United States of America

First edition, 1987
Eleventh printing, 2026

PATHFINDER
pathfinderpress.com
Email: pathfinder@pathfinderpress.com

Contents

APPENDIX

Maps

Photographs

Introduction

IN MARCH 1919, fifty-one delegates from more than two dozen countries launched the Communist International at a five-day conference in Moscow. The revolutionary working-class organizations that they represented were, for the most part, still small and inexperienced. Yet the delegates set an ambitious goal: building a world organization of Marxist parties capable of emulating the Russian Bolsheviks by leading workers and farmers to power in their countries. The program and manifesto adopted by the congress were distributed across the globe in many languages. Within two years, the new International had won the adherence of organizations on six continents and attracted hundreds of thousands of workers to its banner.

Founding the Communist International is the record of the March 1919 gathering, including its complete proceedings, its resolutions, debates, and decisions, as well as the reports received there on the work of Communists in a score of countries.

This is the third volume to be published in the series, *The Communist International in Lenin's Time,* a series of Pathfinder books that makes accessible to today's readers the example and lessons of the international communist movement in the first years after the October 1917 revolution in Russia,[1] before the death of V.I. Lenin in January 1924. The series traces the historic continuity of Marxist leadership in the workers' movement, starting with the struggle led by Lenin, following the 1905 Russian revolution, to revolutionize the Socialist (Second) International. It follows this continuity to the launching of the Communist (Third) International and through the first five years of its activity.

Those five years were the period during which the policies of the Communist International (Comintern) were shaped by Lenin and the team of Marxist revolutionaries that he led. Incorporated in the program, strategy, and organizational concepts hammered out in those years were a method and goals that provide a necessary foundation for all those seeking to chart a revolutionary course in the epoch opened by the Russian October revolution.

The volumes of *The Communist International in Lenin's Time* present the debates within this worldwide movement. They include the key exchanges between the communist leaders of the new International and the various reformist, centrist, and anarcho-syndicalist currents that reacted to its formation.

The initial volume of the series, *Lenin's Struggle for a Revolutionary International,* covers the preparatory years from 1907 through 1916. A further volume, *The German Revolution and the Debate on Soviet Power,* centers on the debates in the German workers' movement during the 1918–19 revolution, showing that revolution's role in speeding formation of the new International. A forthcoming volume, including materials from the years 1917–18, will focus on how the Russian revolution affected the prospects for forming a new, communist International.

The series will follow the Communist International's development from its foundation through the end of 1923. It will include the complete resolutions and proceedings of the first four congresses, which were held between 1919 and 1922. Companion volumes will record the decisions, debates, and activity of the Executive Committee of the Communist International between congresses and will document key developments in various Communist parties and some of the major class battles that shaped Comintern deliberations. Another volume will cover the year following the fourth congress, including the expanded executive committee plenum of 1923. The Communist International's work among trade unionists, women, anti-imperialist fighters from colonial countries, and youth will be the topics of additional books.

Building an international organization to lead the worldwide struggle for national liberation and socialism has been a goal of the communist workers' movement since its inception in the mid-nineteenth century.

The first attempt to form such an international organization was the Communist League, founded in 1847, which counted Karl Marx and Frederick Engels among its leaders. Its program, *The Manifesto of the Communist Party,* still serves as the programmatic foundation of the revolutionary workers' movement. The Communist League was dissolved in 1852 under the impact of the defeat of the 1848–49 revolutions in Europe and the subsequent restabilization of the old ruling classes.

During the twelve years that followed, Marx and Engels worked to maintain and expand international contacts and collaboration among communist revolutionaries and to promote political and programmatic clarification among them. In 1864 Marx and Engels participated in founding the International Working Men's Association (later also known as the First International), and they were its central leaders during its decade-long existence. The International Working Men's Association "laid the foundation of the proletarian, international struggle for socialism," wrote Lenin in his April 1919 article, "The Third International and its Place in History."[2] The First International succumbed to the wave of reaction that rolled across Europe in the wake of the crushing of the Paris Commune; it was dissolved in 1876. Marx died seven years later in 1883.

Engels helped found the Socialist International in 1889 and was a political leader of it until his death in 1895. In its activity before 1914, Lenin wrote in his previously quoted article, this International "marked a period in which the soil was prepared for the broad, mass spread of the movement in a number of countries." But the growth of this International, he said, "proceeded in *breadth,* at the cost of a temporary drop in the revolutionary level, a temporary strengthening of opportunism, which in the end led to the disgraceful collapse of this International."

This "disgraceful collapse" came at the outbreak of World War I in August 1914. The big majority of the International's most authoritative parties and leaders abandoned the interests of workers and peasants in their own countries and worldwide, rallying behind their respective imperialist rulers in prosecuting the war effort.[3] On August 4 the parliamentary deputies of both the French and German Social Democratic parties voted unanimously for the military appropriations ("war credits") demanded by their respective governments. The leaders of these and other major parties of the International urged the workers onward into a disastrous fratricidal slaughter.

The Bolshevik Party in Russia condemned these policies, pointing out that they served only imperialist interests. The Bolsheviks appealed to all internationalists to carry out the decisions of the Second International's pre-1914 congresses. These resolutions had called on all workers' parties in case of war to utilize the resulting social and political crisis to drive forward the revolutionary struggle to overturn capitalist rule.[4]

The chief responsibility for the collapse of the old International lay with "petty-bourgeois opportunism," Lenin wrote in September 1914; "it must be the task of the future International resolutely and irrevocably to rid itself of this bourgeois trend in socialism."[5] Here he referred to not only the outright opportunists who were in the forefront of the capitulation to patriotism. He also included centrists who initially supported "national defense" while seeking to persuade the outright chauvinists to work for a negotiated peace.

The Bolshevik Central Committee adopted Lenin's perspective, calling on November 1, 1914, for "a proletarian International, freed from opportunism." While the Bolsheviks predicted that "opportunism's present triumph will be short-lived,"[6] their position was shared at first by only a few small currents outside Russia.

On September 5–8, 1915, forty-two delegates from parties and tendencies that had dissociated themselves, to one degree or another, from the wave of national chauvinism in the International gathered in Zimmerwald, Switzerland.[7] The Zimmerwald conference adopted a manifesto denouncing the war, rejecting "national defense" in this war, and calling on workers to unite in struggle for peace, national emancipation, and socialism. This initial gathering of currents from both sides of the front lines helped inspire a revival of working-class internationalism and workers' struggles. A coordinating committee was established, and further conferences were held.

The political seed that was to blossom into the Communist International in March 1919 was not the Zimmerwald movement itself, however, but instead a revolutionary current within it initiated by the Bolsheviks.

This current, the Zimmerwald Left, proposed an uncompromising struggle against not only the overt chauvinists, but also the centrist forces—such as Karl Kautsky, then a leader of the German Social Democratic Party—who apologized for the chauvinists and strove to keep the membership yoked to them. This struggle was "the first prerequisite for . . . the restoration of the International," stated the Zimmerwald Left resolution.[8] To free humanity from the scourge of imperialist war, the Zimmerwald Left contended, a class-struggle strategy was required whose culmination was social revolution by the workers and farmers.

The majority at the Zimmerwald conference, however, rejected this revolutionary perspective, seeking instead to reassemble and revive the old International. They opposed launching a new, revolutionary International, purged of the entire class-collaborationist current in the workers' movement.

Many revolutionary currents that were to be part of the Communist International at its founding stood apart from the Zimmerwald Left. This was true, for example, of the Spartacus grouping in Germany led by Rosa Luxemburg and Karl Liebknecht, which the Bolsheviks had hailed for its courageous stand against the German government and the chauvinist leadership of the Social Democratic Party. Russian revolutionary Leon Trotsky, too, refused to support the Zimmerwald Left. Trotsky maintained sharp political differences with Lenin during the first years of the war, still seeking to reconcile the Bolsheviks with centrist elements in the Menshevik wing of the Russian Social Democracy.[9] Later, under the impact of the Bolshevik Party's course following the February 1917 revolution in Russia, Trotsky and the current he led were won to that party. Trotsky became a central leader of the Soviet republic established in October, of the Russian Communist Party, and of the Communist International.

In the two years following the Zimmerwald conference, political differences deepened among the range of currents that had signed its manifesto. The Zimmerwald Left, while supporting the manifesto, actively circulated its own views, winning growing influence as workers' consciousness changed under the blows of the war. After the Bolsheviks led the workers and peasants to power in Russia, millions of working people around the world began to look to them for leadership. The Bolsheviks' call to rebuild the International on a truly revolutionary footing won widening support.

Lenin proposed in his 1917 "April Theses" that revolutionary Marxists discard the name Social Democracy, which had traditionally designated the parties of the Socialist International, including those in its revolutionary wing. Lenin pointed out that Marx and Engels had regarded this name as unscientific and inaccurate. Furthermore, it had now been robbed of any working-class content by the betrayal by the most prominent international leaders of Social Democracy. Lenin proposed adopting the name Communist, by which the first revolutionary workers' party of 1847–52 had been known.[10] The Bolsheviks took the name Russian Communist Party (Bolsheviks) in March 1918. In 1920 the Second Congress of the Communist International decided that all its affiliated parties should adopt the name Communist Party.

In the year following the October revolution, the Soviet republic in Russia was more and more cut off from Europe and the world. The ring of counterrevolutionary armies drew increasingly tighter, a ring made up of Russian White Guards; armies of the Central Powers (Germany, Austria-Hungary, and their allies); and forces of the Allied powers (the Entente), the war alliance led by Britain, France, and the United States. Even after the March 1918 Brest-Litovsk treaty formally ended the war between the Soviet republic and the Central Powers, the German army continued to seize more territory. By the summer of 1918 the Allied powers, for their part, had launched an undeclared war against the Soviet government and landed their own armies of intervention.

Despite broad working-class enthusiasm for the October revolution, the Bolshevik Party remained largely isolated within the world workers' movement. The working people of central and western Europe, still unable to shake the grip of their imperialist warlords, were undergoing severe repression. The Bolsheviks' organized supporters outside Russia still led only small currents in the traditional workers' parties and trade unions. Moreover, the leaders of these currents had little knowledge of the Bolsheviks' political strategy or organizational methods.

Then, in late October and November 1918, revolutions erupted in Germany and across much of central Europe. The Russian revolution no longer stood alone. The German monarchy was overthrown and the Austro-Hungarian Empire was torn apart. Independent states were proclaimed in Czechoslovakia, Hungary, Poland, and German Austria (the German-speaking part of the old Austrian empire; today's Austrian republic). Insurgent workers and soldiers forced the new governments to conclude immediate armistices, ending World War I.

Workers and soldiers established revolutionary councils across Germany, Poland, and much of what had been Austria-Hungary. Revolutionary socialists in these countries proposed that the councils fight to take political power on behalf of the oppressed and exploited working people who had elected them. The revolutionaries' goal was the formation of "council republics" similar to the Soviet workers' and peasants' republic established in Russia in 1917.[11] They raised the call, "All power to the workers' and soldiers' councils."

By the end of December 1918, advocates of this revolutionary perspective had formed Communist parties in Germany, Austria, Hungary, the Netherlands, and Poland. These parties, although still very small, grew rapidly in membership and political influence, while in other countries pro-Bolshevik nuclei gained strength inside the older socialist, centrist, and anarcho-syndicalist formations.

At the end of 1918, a decisive test of strength between opposed class forces was clearly under way across Europe. Mounting unemployment, added to continuing hunger and dislocation, aggravated the suffering caused by the war. Soldiers returning to farm and city from the war joined workers in mounting a powerful offensive against their exploiters. In central and eastern Europe, the capitalist class maneuvered to stabilize its rule in conditions of revolutionary upheaval. Germany was on the verge of civil war. In Hungary bourgeois rule seemed headed for collapse. Powerful, mass-based workers' councils had emerged in Austria. Even in the countries of Europe and North America where revolution had not broken out, the Russian October revolution had given new hope and confidence to the working people, whose combativeness was growing. In addition, the October revolution gave the greatest impulse in history to fighters for national liberation in the colonies.

Meanwhile, the Allied powers were moving quickly to escalate their war against the Russian Soviet republic. They stepped up supplies to the counterrevolutionary armies while their own armed forces seized wider areas of the country. The blockade mounted against the Soviet republic during the first months of 1919 greatly increased the already substantial barriers to traveling or sending information across the Soviet frontiers.

As 1918 closed, the Allied powers were about to meet at the Paris "peace" conference to divide the spoils of victory and lay plans to safeguard imperialist rule. They did not invite the Soviet republic, continuing their war against it as the conference proceeded. The Social Democratic leaders of Britain, France, and Belgium had just issued a call for an international meeting of their own aimed at influencing the Paris conference and establishing the political continuity of their international current with the pre-1914 Socialist International. Given the ever-widening divide in the workers' movement between class-collaborationist and revolutionary currents, Social Democratic parties that had not already split were fast headed that way. In several countries the opportunist leaders were losing predominant influence over the working-class ranks. These discredited leaders and their centrist allies held their international conference February 3–10, 1919, in Bern, Switzerland.[12]

The leadership of the Russian Communist Party concluded in late December 1918 that the time had come to launch the new, revolutionary International. Both the world political situation and the crisis of the workers' movement made this an urgent necessity. Launching the new International would further clarify and sharpen the debate in the labor movement throughout Europe between working-class revolutionaries and reformist and centrist currents. It would establish a programmatic pole around which to rally the emerging international communist current and begin to build strong revolutionary workers' parties.

The Russian Communist Party broadcast a radio appeal December 24 calling on "communists of all countries" to boycott the reformists' conference and to "rally around the revolutionary Third International." Pointing to a number of revolutionary currents and newly formed Communist parties around the world, the call declared that "the Third International already exists and leads the world revolution."[13] Nonetheless, even if the Third International already existed as a world force, it had as yet no organizational expression.

On December 25, Lenin conferred with Eduard Fuchs, a representative of the German Spartacus leadership, who had just arrived in Moscow. This was the Bolshevik leaders' first opportunity for direct collaboration with the German revolutionaries. The Spartacus League in Germany had published a program and was about to found a party separate from the centrist-led Independent Social Democratic Party. After meeting with Fuchs, Lenin wrote to Georgiy Chicherin, the Soviet people's commissar of foreign affairs, urging that a conference to launch the Third International be prepared as quickly as possible and that the call be drafted in time for Fuchs to take with him back to Germany.

Lenin proposed to invite to the conference only those "1) who resolutely stand up for a break with the social-patriots (i.e., the people who, directly or indirectly, supported the bourgeois governments during the imperialist war of 1914–1918); 2) who are *for* a socialist revolution *now* and *for* the dictatorship of the proletariat; 3) who are *in principle* for 'Soviet power'" as a type of government *"higher* and *closer* to *socialism."* Lenin suggested that the conference might be convened February 1 "in Berlin (openly) or in Holland (*secretly*)."[14]

Chicherin replied on December 28, contending that Berlin was not a good location for the conference, since "surprises are possible" there.[15] Indeed, only two weeks previously the German cabinet, a coalition of right-wing and centrist Social Democrats, had barred Soviet representatives from entering the country to attend a congress of German workers' and soldiers' councils. Moreover, on Christmas Eve fierce fighting had erupted in Berlin between government troops and revolutionary sailors.

Chicherin also raised objections to holding the conference in the Netherlands and suggested that Sweden or Norway be considered. Clearly, a conference held in western Europe would have enabled many more delegates from the workers' movement in the capitalist countries to attend. This proved impossible, however, because of the hostility of the imperialist governments and the relative weakness of the new communist movements in those countries. Instead, Moscow was chosen as the conference site.

Few delegates could be expected to reach the Moscow conference from abroad. In most countries outside the Soviet republic, supporters of the new International, as a resolution of the 1920 Comintern congress noted, were not *"parties* and *organizations"* but merely "communist *trends* and *groups"*—many of them still unstructured.[16] It would not be easy to inform these currents of the planned congress; nor was it likely that many of them had the resources and connections required to slip a delegate into Russia through the ring of hostile armies.

The Communist Party of Germany, formed at the end of December, was the strongest and most authoritative of the communist groups outside Russia. The Bolsheviks regarded its formation, under the leadership of Luxemburg,

Liebknecht, and other experienced and internationally known revolutionaries, as a signal that the new International should be launched without delay.[17] The support of the German party would be a weighty factor in holding an authoritative conference.

In early January Fuchs returned to Germany, taking with him the Bolsheviks' proposal for a congress the following month to launch the new International. This plan, however, did not meet with the agreement of Luxemburg and other German party leaders. One of them, Hugo Eberlein, stated in 1924 that in Luxemburg's view, although it was "absolutely necessary" to launch a new revolutionary International, "the time to found it has not yet come," for its existence was "dependent on that of several revolutionary parties in Western Europe."[18]

Along with other Spartacus leaders, Luxemburg was committed to building a revolutionary International together with the Bolsheviks and other revolutionary forces.[19] But she had long differed with the Bolsheviks on several key questions of revolutionary policy. Although she had drawn closer to them under the impact of the Russian and German revolutions, areas of disagreement persisted.[20] She anticipated that postponing the congress would increase the weight of delegates from western Europe and make the Bolsheviks less preponderant.

Before the German Communist leadership could meet to take a stand on the proposed congress, its party came under savage attack. During the week of January 5–11, 1919, the Social Democratic government launched an armed assault in Berlin against strongholds that had been occupied by revolutionary workers and soldiers. Among the several hundreds massacred by the government's right-wing troops were Liebknecht and Luxemburg.[21] Preoccupied as it was with the consequences of this staggering blow and hard pressed by the continuing government assault, the party leadership nonetheless took up the Bolsheviks' proposal for a conference. It endorsed Luxemburg's view, delegating Eberlein to go to the conference and urge that launching the new International be postponed.

By then, all direct communication between Russia and the rest of Europe was cut off by the Allied-sponsored blockade. Receiving no word of the German Communist leaders' views, the Bolshevik leaders proceeded with congress preparations. On January 21 a meeting of about a dozen Communists from different countries resident in Russia issued a call, drafted by Trotsky, "to convoke the first congress of our new revolutionary International" in Moscow beginning February 15.[22]

The January 21 call enumerated the groups invited to the congress, starting with the Communist parties of Germany and Russia.[23] The list of thirty-nine groups included seven Communist parties organized on the territory of the former tsarist empire and four others in central and western Europe, formed through splits from the old Social Democratic parties and fusions of revolutionary forces. Fifteen other groups invited from Europe had originated in parties of the pre-1914 Socialist International; most of these currents had moved left in response to the war crisis, supported the Zimmerwald Manifesto, and then rallied to the Russian October revolution. Some had supported the Zimmerwald Left from the start; others had stood aside from it or opposed it. These currents ranged in size from small nuclei, such as the French forces led by Fernand Loriot, to mass organizations such as the Italian Socialist Party.

The list of invitations reflected the Bolsheviks' efforts to reach out to revolutionary forces that they had not previously collaborated with, including some with whom they had previously disagreed on important questions. Thus the groups invited from the United States included not only the Socialist Propaganda League, a current in the Socialist Party that had supported the Zimmerwald Left, but also that party's broader left forces whose main spokesperson was Eugene V. Debs. Also on the list was the U.S. Socialist Labor Party, which held many sectarian positions but had taken a firm stand against the imperialist war. The Industrial Workers of the World (IWW) in the United States, Britain, and Australia were invited, as were revolutionary syndicalists from the French trade unions and elsewhere.

The revolutionary workers' movement outside Europe and North America was represented on the list only by the Australian IWW and the "Socialist groups in Tokyo and Yokohama (represented by Comrade Katayama)." No group from the colonized peoples outside Europe was listed in the initial call.

The pre-1914 Second International had been almost entirely limited to the industrialized capitalist countries of Europe and North America. In the colonial countries—where there was little or no large-scale machine industry and the rural population worked largely under precapitalist conditions—the modern working class was relatively small, and there were as yet few or no trade unions or workers' parties. Modern national liberation movements among the colonized peoples, even under bourgeois or petty-bourgeois leadership, had hardly begun until the final decade before World War I. These movements received an impulse from Japan's defeat of the tsar in the war of 1904–5 and from the ensuing revolution in Russia.

The Second International had by and large failed to embrace the colonial peoples' struggles or bring their representatives into its structures and gatherings. The International's largest parties and majority leadership, increasingly oriented to a conservatized aristocratic minority of the working class, adapted to the colonial policies of their ruling classes.[24] The Bolshevik Party, on the other hand, had hailed the rise of liberation struggles in Asia. In his 1913 article, "Backward Europe and Advanced Asia," Lenin wrote that in Asia, *"Hundreds* of millions of people are awakening to life, light and freedom. What delight this world movement is arousing in the hearts of all class-conscious workers. . . !"[25]

By 1919 the national liberation, peasant, and working-class movements were making progress in China, India, and other oppressed nations in Asia. In Latin America, where the workers' movement was more developed, democratic and anti-imperialist struggles were on the rise among peasants and workers; in some countries, revolutionary socialist nuclei had begun to appear, as well. The formation in 1912 of the African National Congress in South Africa marked a new stage in the development of national consciousness among the oppressed peoples of that continent; an emerging black industrial working class in that country was beginning to wage strike struggles and was taking its first steps toward union organization.

The Bolsheviks took an uncompromising stand against every form of colonialism and for self-determination of colonial peoples, and they put these principles into practice in the Soviet republic. This record attracted militant fighters in the colonies and semicolonies, especially in Asia.

After the congress call went out in January 1919, organizations representing workers from China, Korea, Persia (Iran), and Turkey then living in the Soviet republic were invited to send delegates, as were Communist organizations of Asian peoples in Transcaucasia and inside Soviet Russia. The day after the new International was launched, Bolshevik leader Nikolai Bukharin hailed these delegates' participation, noting that this was the first international workers' congress to hear a speech delivered in Chinese. This was "a symbol of unity among revolutionary proletarian forces under capitalism with the efforts of colonial peoples who are liberating themselves," Bukharin wrote. "Under their blows the hateful capitalist system will be shattered into many pieces."[26]

Because of the imperialist blockade, the Bolshevik Party could not contact invited groups directly. By one account, two dozen messengers set out from Russia to slip through the blockade and deliver the call to different countries, but only three or four reached their destination.[27] Nonetheless, the call, first published on January 24 in the Soviet press, was printed in translation in Austria on January 29 and in Hungary on January 30. A preliminary draft of the call was published in Bremen on February 4, while the final version was printed in the German Communist Party's main daily newspaper on February 25. The call also appeared in a circular of the Italian Socialist youth in February.[28] But other invited groups never saw the call. The British Socialist Labour Party, for example, only learned of the congress one month after it had concluded.[29]

The difficulties and delays experienced by delegates coming from outside Russia forced a two-week postponement of the congress from the originally scheduled date of February 15. Even so, when the congress date arrived, key delegates expected from the parties in German Austria, Hungary, and Sweden were still absent, as were S.J.

Rutgers from the United States, who had traveled by way of Japan, and the Romanian revolutionary Christian Rakovsky, who was coming from the Ukraine. (All these delegates except those from Hungary arrived during the congress.) On March 1 only two representatives had arrived from parties outside the Soviet republic. One of them, Emil Stang of Norway, reported that he could not take a stand on launching the new International because his party had not discussed the matter. The other was Eberlein from Germany, and his view, the sole definite opinion received from a party abroad, was contrary to that of the congress organizers.

On arriving in Moscow five days before the congress was to begin, Eberlein reported the German party leadership's firm opposition to forming the new International at that gathering. He called for the meeting to be preliminary in character, to be a "conference" and not a "congress." In lengthy discussions with Lenin and other Bolshevik leaders, Eberlein held to this view, leaving the impression that he had instructions to walk out of the congress if it launched the International. The response of the Russian Communist leadership to Eberlein's stand was reported three weeks later by Bolshevik leader Gregory Zinoviev, speaking to his party's eighth congress:

"The representative of German Communism demanded almost as an ultimatum that we limit ourselves to meeting only as a conference and not proclaim ourselves a congress. The Austrian comrades had not yet arrived, nor had the delegates from the Balkans. After studying the situation, the Central Committee of our party remained unshakably convinced that we must form the Third International immediately. But at the same time we said that with the German Communists opposed, and with them posing the question as an ultimatum, we could not permit even the slightest strain in our relations with the German Spartacists. Only yesterday they had suffered severe losses. So we said: even though they are wrong, we will retreat on this question. And a statement to this effect was made in the name of our party's Central Committee."[30]

A preliminary meeting of several delegates on March 1 therefore decided to propose convening the gathering not as a congress of the new International but as a preparatory conference. This meeting also drew up proposals for the conference agenda, for reporters, and for commissions on different topics. The minutes of this meeting are printed below.

In the course of the congress, fifty-one delegates registered representing thirty-five organizations in twenty-two countries. Nine of them had recently come from seven countries outside the Soviet republic.[31] The arrival of this modest number of delegates from abroad was no small achievement, given the risks they took in getting to Russia. The danger they faced was underscored when delegates departed from Russia after the congress: two of them, Fritz Platten and Karl Steinhardt, were arrested and jailed in Finland and Romania respectively.

Eberlein, whose pseudonym at the congress was Max Albert, had been obliged to cross the front lines in Lithuania where German troops were battling the Soviet Red Army. He traversed long distances at night, sometimes on foot and sometimes by sleigh.[32] Eugen Leviné, sent by the German party to accompany Eberlein, was arrested en route by German police.

The Communist Party of German Austria was also able to send a central leader, Steinhardt, known to the congress as Gruber. He arrived late after a harrowing seventeen-day journey. His traveling companion, Karl Petin, who had been won to the Bolsheviks while an Austrian prisoner of war in Russia, was also granted delegate status.

Two delegates at the congress represented large workers' parties outside Soviet territory. The Norwegian Labor Party was a mass organization, an affiliate of the pre-1914 Second International that had not undergone a major split during the war. In 1918 it elected a left-wing leadership that sought to turn the party in a revolutionary direction. The Left Social Democratic Party of Sweden, represented by Otto Grimlund, had been formed in 1917 by a minority expelled from the opportunist-led Swedish Social Democracy. In 1919 it had 17,000 members. Leaders of these two Scandinavian parties had been among the first to rally to the Zimmerwald Left.

Another delegate from abroad, the Dutch Communist Rutgers, received credentials with consultative vote representing groups in both the United States and the Netherlands. His Dutch party, a small revolutionary organization that had been expelled from the majority Social Democracy in 1909, was part of an ultraleft international current led by Anton Pannekoek and Hermann Gorter. It had joined the Zimmerwald Left in 1915 but opposed the Bolsheviks on numerous questions. During the war, Rutgers had lived in the United States, where he was a leader of the Socialist Propaganda League.[33]

It was Boris Reinstein, however, the delegate of the U.S. Socialist Labor Party, who received credentials as the voting delegate from the United States. Reinstein had left the United States two years earlier. His party had sent him to Europe to attend a proposed conference of Social Democratic parties in Stockholm, giving him in addition a mandate to participate in the formation of a new, reconstructed International. Reinstein had traveled on to Russia in 1917, joining the staff of the Soviet foreign affairs commissariat the following year. Despite his participation in the congress, the Socialist Labor Party never joined the Third International, while Rutgers's group, the Socialist Propaganda League, became an important nucleus in launching the U.S. Communist movement.

A strong contingent of the Zimmerwald Left had also grown up in Switzerland, where it was waging a vigorous fight against the centrist leadership of the Social Democratic Party. These Swiss revolutionaries were represented at the congress by Platten, who was wanted by the Swiss police for his role in the labor upsurge of November 1918. Platten arrived in Moscow some weeks before the congress.[34] Another, smaller Swiss revolutionary current, which functioned outside the Swiss party and had taken the name Communist Party, was represented by Leonie Kascher.

In France, a small group of cadres were fighting for a revolutionary course under the banner of the Zimmerwald movement within the Socialist Party and the trade unions. They were unable to send a representative from France to the Moscow congress. On the last day of the congress, however, Henri Guilbeaux arrived from Switzerland. A controversial figure among the French Communists in Moscow, Guilbeaux, a Frenchman, had lived in Switzerland during the war, where he had published a newspaper in collaboration with the Zimmerwald Left and maintained contact with the French Zimmerwaldists.[35] He was granted credentials as the delegate of the French Zimmerwald Left.

Some important components of the developing communist movement outside Soviet territory were unable to send delegates to the congress and could be only indirectly represented. The delegates chosen by the Hungarian party, László Rudas and Gábor Mészáros (Kohn), were delayed by fighting in the Ukraine, and the party was represented by Endre Rudnyánszky, a member of its External Committee in Moscow.[36]

The Polish party, unable to send a delegate from Poland, was represented by Józef Unszlicht, a long-standing leader of the Polish Social Democracy. Like many Polish revolutionaries, Unszlicht now lived in Russia and functioned as a cadre of the Bolshevik Party.

No representative of the Italian Socialist Party was present at the congress. Nonetheless, a veteran of the Italian socialist movement was there: Angelica Balabanoff, a left-wing leader of the party before and during the war. Of Russian origin, she had joined the Bolshevik Party in September 1917 and returned to Russia from an assignment in Switzerland in the autumn of 1918. Although she still carried credentials from the Italian party, she did not consider herself in a position to act on its behalf at the congress.[37]

Instead, Balabanoff was recognized as a representative of the Zimmerwald association. During 1916 and 1917, this movement had become polarized between its revolutionary wing and its majority, which was increasingly pulled in an opportunist direction. The initial secretary, Robert Grimm, resigned in June 1917. Responsibility for the Zimmerwald movement was then assumed by a provisional committee of three leading Swedish Left Social Democrats chosen by their party; they in turn appointed Balabanoff as secretary. Although the Zimmerwald committee actively defended the Russian October revolution, it remained shackled by its refusal to break with the movement's nonrevolutionary wing and declined in importance. After September 1918 it ceased functioning.

Rakovsky, probably the most widely known revolutionary from the Balkans, was seated as a delegate of the Balkan Revolutionary Social Democratic Federation, which included parties in several countries. He had spoken for the Balkan Social Democratic federation at the Zimmerwald congress, voting in opposition to the Zimmerwald Left. Imprisoned in Romania in the latter stages of the war, he was freed by Russian troops in 1917 and became a prominent figure in the Russian revolution, a leader of the Bolshevik Party, and the head of the Soviet government of the Ukraine. No one was able to come to the congress directly from the Balkan countries. Two consultative delegates, Stojan Dyorov and Iliya Milkić, represented Communists living in Moscow from Bulgaria and Yugoslavia respectively.

The revolutionary forces in the Socialist Youth International, who held a majority in its leadership and supported the positions of the Bolsheviks, were not present at the congress. With that exception, all the major currents of the Zimmerwald Left were represented.

None of the British currents invited to the congress were represented by a delegate. The only British revolutionary present was Joseph Fineberg, who had been a member of the British Socialist Party until he came to Russia in 1918. He received credentials only as a consultative delegate representing British Communists living in Russia.

Fineberg's group was one of five affiliates of the Federation of Foreign Groups of the Russian Communist Party represented at the congress. These groups of Communists from abroad living in Russia were quite small, ranging in size from the French, with about a dozen members, to the Yugoslavs, with more than 100. Yet central leaders of several European Communist parties came from their ranks, including the leading core that founded the Hungarian party. The federation conducted active propaganda among prisoners of war from Germany and Austria-Hungary, who remained in Russia until after the November 1918 armistice. Many thousands of former prisoners of war volunteered for the Red Army, and four of them attended the congress as delegates.[38] In 1919, the federation's English and French groups were in the forefront of work to influence the soldiers of interventionist armies on Soviet territory, and the work of French Communists in Russia helped prepare the ground for the wave of mutinies that spring in France's army and navy in the Black Sea region.

Other delegates represented several Communist parties from minority nationalities within the former tsarist empire. Many of these parties had won mass support among workers and peasants in their regions following the October revolution. They had acquired experience in mass struggles and, in several cases, in revolutionary governments. With the collapse of the tsarist state structures, the Soviet government's stand for national self-determination had led to the formation of separate workers' and peasants' governments in the Ukraine, Finland, Lithuania, Belorussia, and elsewhere. These governments were linked to the Russian Soviet republic by treaties, which were regarded as first steps toward a federation of Soviet republics. It was hoped that as revolutionary upheavals mounted such a federation would expand beyond the old tsarist empire to embrace growing numbers of nations in Europe, Asia, and throughout the world.

The Communist parties in these territories had separate national structures and elected separate leadership bodies. However, with the exception of the Finnish Communist Party, they were united in the common framework of the Russian party. These parties had grappled with the distinctive problems of the class struggle of their own nations, and their policies were by no means carbon copies of those carried out in Russia. For example, the Communist Party of Lithuania and Belorussia, which was leading Soviet governments in those countries at the time of the congress, applied policies on the national and agrarian questions similar to those advocated by Luxemburg and the Polish Social Democrats, which the Bolsheviks had sharply criticized.[39] Embattled Soviet republics also existed in Latvia and in the Ukraine. The Finnish and Estonian Soviet republics had previously been overthrown with the aid of German and British forces, and the Communist leaderships from these countries had been forced into exile.

Another delegate from minority peoples in the old tsarist empire was Gustav Klinger, who was listed as representative of the Communist Party of the German Colonists in Russia. Some have tried to explain his presence as no more than an effort by the Bolsheviks to conjure up a German-speaking counterweight to Eberlein.[40] In fact, Klinger was then a central leader of the Volga Germans' Autonomous Workers' Commune, a separate Soviet government established in October 1918 among the 400,000 German speakers living on the Volga near Saratov.[41]

Several delegates from the Communist Organizations of the Peoples of the East represented the communist movement's expansion among the oppressed peoples of Asia. Their organization, which was affiliated to the Russian party, united Communists of several different Asian nationalities within the old tsarist empire. It also included Communists from Turkey, China, and Korea who led immigrant workers in Russia from their respective countries. The participation of these delegates marked a big step forward from the pattern of Socialist International congresses before 1914, and the congress devoted time to hear reports from three of them on the work of revolutionaries in these countries.

One of the organizations affiliated to the eastern peoples' group united the Chinese revolutionaries who worked among the several hundred thousand Chinese workers who had been brought into Russia during the war. These Communists led the Union of Chinese Workers in Russia, with about 50,000 members organized in branches in all the major centers of industry across Russia. Estimates of the number of Chinese workers who joined the Red Army during the civil war run up to 50,000. Their participation was bitterly denounced by anticommunist writers on the Russian civil war.[42] Although the Chinese Communists were only a small cadre in this organization, they directed an ambitious educational effort, publishing newspapers and pamphlets with press runs of 5,000 to 50,000 in different centers across the country.[43]

The most authoritative delegation, of course, was that of the Russian Communist Party. Several of the party's central leaders, including Lenin, Trotsky, Bukharin, and Zinoviev, were present as delegates and delivered key reports. Chicherin headed the Credentials Commission and was the chief congress organizer. The people's commissar of nationalities, Joseph Stalin, was listed as a delegate, although there is no indication that he participated in the congress. Other prominent Bolsheviks, such as Leon Kamenev, Alexandra Kollontai, Maxim Litvinov, and Abel Yenukidze, were present for some of the sessions.

Other observers at the congress included Marcel Body and Pierre Pascal of the French Communist Group in Moscow, Leo Karakhan and Thomas (Y.S. Reich) of the Soviet foreign affairs commissariat, the Latvian revolutionary J.A. Berzin, and the Russian Communist Party members M.M. Grusenberg (Mikhail Borodin), S. Dzerzhinskaya, and Y.M. Steklov. One non-Communist attended several sessions: the British journalist Arthur Ransome.

This was a much younger gathering than the congresses of the Socialist International: of the forty-three delegates whose age is known, twenty-four were in their thirties and five were in their twenties. Only one (Reinstein) was more than fifty years old. More than one fifth of the delegates represented Asian peoples, an unprecedented event at an international socialist congress. Three delegates and two observers were women.

Of the forty-two delegates whose political careers can be traced, seventeen had joined Social Democratic parties before the Russian revolution of 1905, while eight had become active socialists only after 1914. Most of the delegates remained prominent in the Comintern's activity during the next three years; thirty of them took part in other congresses or in executive committee meetings between 1919 and 1923. Only thirteen continued to be identified with the Comintern leadership into the 1930s when it came under Stalin's domination. After Lenin's death, at least seven joined opposition currents within the Comintern. Four of them, Trotsky, Zinoviev, Rakovsky, and Osinsky, were at different times among the leaders of the communist opposition current combating Stalin's abandonment of the revolutionary internationalist course set under Lenin's leadership. Three delegates were killed by reactionary and fascist forces. At least fifteen delegates fell victim to Stalin's frame-up purge trials of the 1930s and thereafter: executed, driven to suicide, swallowed up in prison camps in the Soviet Union, or, in Trotsky's case, assassinated in exile by Stalin's secret police. Apart from Lenin, seven leading Bolsheviks spoke at the congress; six perished in Stalin's purges.[44]

The congress was held in the Kremlin in a small hall in the Courts of Justice, a building dating from the days of Catherine the Great in the eighteenth century. The

French consultative delegate Jacques Sadoul described the setting in these words:

"The hall where the congress was held was one of the most modest in the palace. Narrow and long, it could barely hold a hundred people. The delegates took their seats on flimsy chairs at rickety tables obviously borrowed from some café. On the walls were photographs: the founders of the First International, Marx and Engels; the still-honored leaders of the Second, mostly those no longer with us, including yesterday's martyr Jaurès; and today's martyrs Karl Liebknecht and Rosa Luxemburg, together with their old companions in struggle—Franz Mehring and Clara Zetkin. At first Jules Guesde appeared in this venerated gallery. I proposed that we write under his name: 'Died in 1914,' but Lenin had the portrait removed of this old man who outlived his glory only to tarnish it.

"At one end of the hall, on a low platform, was a long table for the bureau and a high podium for the speakers. On every side were brilliant red drapes marked with traditional inscriptions. Wonderful imperial carpets covered the floor. It was cold, very cold in that hall. The carpets strove, though in vain, to make up for the heaters that blew terrible gusts of frigid air at the delegates. Morally, the congress participants were benefiting from Soviet life; physically they had to suffer the inconveniences.

"Moscow lacks fuel. The congress delegates shiver. Moscow has been on meager rations the last two years. International comrades do not always eat their fill. . . .

"They are visibly surprised by the straight-forwardness, by the total simplicity with which the Russians receive their guests—without pomp, without airs. They notice (first a little irritably, because it is very cold, and the cold sharpens the appetite, and then with pride, because they are valiant fighters) that the fare of the people's commissars is not different than that—so lamentably frugal—which is served in other Soviet eateries."[45]

In outward appearance, the congress was a modest gathering. One participant, V.V. Vorovsky, wrote March 7 in *Pravda,* "Anyone who had attended the old congresses of the Second International would have been quite disappointed if they glanced into the Mitrofan'evsky Hall of the former Courts of Justice on March 4. Instead of all the well-known 'esteemed' fathers of international Social Democracy; instead of the theoreticians, hoary with age; instead of the leaders of the workers' movement of the previous half-century; here, with a few exceptions, were gathered new people, whose names were still little known and whose young faces did not yet carry the marks of recognized leadership."[46]

Sadoul was struck by the atmosphere of the sessions. "From beginning to end the delegates were in the best of spirits—the joy of master craftsmen performing a great work. . . .

"I have already mentioned Lenin's never-ending and resonant laughter, which makes his shoulders shake and his belly quiver—the lofty, majestic laugh of a Danton or Jaurès; Trotsky's piercing irony; the sublime Bukharin's mischievous jocularity; Chicherin's mocking humor. Mixed with all these nuances of Russian joy was the boisterous gaiety of the beer drinkers—Platten, Eberlein, Gruber—and Rakovsky's subtle wit, more Parisian than Romanian."[47]

The British journalist Ransome noted that "business was conducted and speeches were made in all languages, though where possible German was used, because more of the foreigners knew German than knew French. This was unlucky for me. . . . Fineberg spoke in English, Rakovsky in French, Sadoul also. Skrypnik, who, being asked, refused to talk German and said he would speak in either

Ukrainian or Russian, and to most people's relief chose the latter. . . . Lenin sat quietly listening, speaking when necessary in almost every European language with astonishing ease."[48]

The international delegates' first plenary session on Sunday, March 2, endorsed the proposal of the planning meeting held the previous day not to found the new International yet but rather to meet only as a preparatory conference.

During the first day and a half, reports were heard on the political situation in different countries, given by delegates who in some cases (such as Switzerland and Germany) came fresh from great class battles and in other cases (such as Britain, France, and the United States) had had little contact with their homelands for a year or more. These reports, which took up half the congress, conveyed a sense of the revolutionary possibilities before the international communist movement and helped narrow the differences within the congress on launching the new International.

The business of the conference then got under way. The first discussion item was a draft platform for the Communist International. Together with the "Theses on Bourgeois Democracy and the Dictatorship of the Proletariat" and the "Manifesto of the Communist International," this resolution constituted an initial programmatic foundation for the new world movement. Discussion was interrupted, however, to hear the newly arrived delegate from German Austria, Steinhardt. He painted a vivid picture of the revolutionary upsurge in his country and the Communist movement's rapid growth there and presented the Austrian revolutionaries' motion proposing to found the new International without delay.

The draft platform was adopted in the third day's session. Lenin then delivered the report on bourgeois rule and proletarian dictatorship. This was the most important programmatic document of the congress. Refuting a central criticism of opponents of the Soviet republic, Lenin explained how the soviet system achieved a much higher level of democracy for workers and peasants than that found in parliamentary capitalist states. The report was adopted without discussion.

By this time, more delegates had arrived from abroad, and all present had been influenced by the congress reports and discussion. A number of delegates became convinced of the need to reopen the question of constituting the new International. After consultation with the congress Presiding Committee and with the Russian CP leaders, four delegates, Grimlund, Rakovsky, Rudnyánszky, and Steinhardt, moved that the conference immediately launch the Third International. Eberlein reiterated the German party's objections to this move, but many other delegates rose to support the motion, including Zinoviev, speaking for the Bolsheviks. When the vote was called, Eberlein abstained. With all other full delegates voting in favor, the new International was born. Eberlein declared he would work to win the German Communist Party to the new organization, and his party did indeed affiliate in short order.

During the final two days' sessions, the manifesto to the workers of the world drafted by Trotsky was read to the delegates and adopted. Resolutions were also approved on the Social Democratic conference in Bern, the world political situation, international counterrevolutionary terror, and Communist work among women. The congress concluded by establishing an executive committee for the new International.

Within six weeks after the congress, revolutionary republics based on workers' and soldiers' councils were established in Hungary and Bavaria. Written in this context, Lenin's "The Third International and its Place in History" stated, "The Third International has gathered the fruits of the work of the Second International, discarded its opportunist, social-chauvinist, bourgeois and petty-bourgeois dross, and *has begun to implement* the dictatorship of the proletariat. . . .

"The movement of the proletariat for the overthrow of the yoke of capital, now rests on an unprecedentedly firm base, in the shape of several *Soviet republics,* which are implementing the dictatorship of the proletariat and are the embodiment of victory over capitalism on an international scale. . . .

"A new era in world history has begun."[49]

Zinoviev reflected the enthusiasm of the moment in the May 1919 inaugural issue of the Comintern's magazine, predicting that within a year all Europe would be Communist.[50] By August, however, the counterrevolution had triumphed in both Hungary and Bavaria. The Communist movement of the time had solid grounds to anticipate that the revolutionary advance could quickly be resumed. World capitalism's postwar instability continued. Germany, especially, and other central and eastern European countries still faced economic and political crisis, while the Red Army advanced from victory to victory, forcing the imperialist armies of intervention to withdraw from Russia.

The judgment of the delegates at the March 1919 congress that launching the new International would accelerate the formation of Communist parties internationally was fully borne out during the year following the congress. Indeed, speaking on the International's first anniversary,

Lenin said, "the Communist International has been successful beyond all expectation; we may say boldly that at the time of its foundation no one expected such immense successes."[51]

Several large workers' parties joined the new International's ranks in the first three months after its founding congress: the Socialist Party of Italy, the Norwegian Labor Party, the Swedish Left Social Democratic Party, and the Bulgarian Tesnyaks. Three other mass parties broke with the reformist-led International initiated at the Bern conference (the "Bern International") and opened negotiations with the Comintern with a view to joining: the French Socialist Party, the Independent Social Democratic Party of Germany, and the British Independent Labour Party. The majority of the members of these parties in France and Germany decided in 1920 to join the Communist International. Syndicalist trade union federations in Italy and Spain also voted during 1919 to join the Comintern.

In several countries where the majority leadership of mass workers' parties declared themselves opposed to the new International, these parties' youth organizations rallied to the Comintern. Thus the Danish youth organization broke from its parent organization and in October 1919 established a rival party, which soon joined the new International. In November 1919 delegates of fourteen revolutionary youth organizations with 300,000 members united in the Communist Youth International.

Social Democratic parties in Austria, Spain, Switzerland, and the United States also broke relations with the reformist-led Bern International but still held back from joining the Comintern. In 1920, the only large parties left in the Bern International were the German Social Democratic Party, the British Labour Party, and the Social Democrats of Belgium, Denmark, and Sweden.

When the second Comintern congress convened in July 1920, the more than 200 delegates representing thirty-six countries had good reason for confidence that the anticipations of the founding congress had been realized in life. A promising world movement had come into being. While its member parties had suffered reverses in several countries, the International would, they believed, learn from its setbacks and emerge stronger.

Lenin had summed up this confidence in his closing remarks to the first congress, "No matter how the bourgeoisie of the whole world rage . . . all this will no longer help. It will only serve to enlighten the masses, help rid them of the old bourgeois-democratic prejudices and steel them in struggle. The victory of the proletarian revolution on a world scale is assured. The founding of an international Soviet republic is on the way."[52]

On this edition of the congress proceedings

No record is available describing how the congress proceedings were compiled, but the process can largely be gleaned from an examination of the editions published in 1921 and 1933.

The working language of the congress was German, and the major reports were given in that language. Some contributions were made in Russian, however, and a few delegates spoke in French or English. In general, translation into German was provided, although at least one Russian-language report was not translated. A German-language stenographic transcript was taken, which frequently failed to record remarks made in Russian. A separate transcript was made of the Russian-language contributions.

A pamphlet on the congress was published in Russia in 1919, but it contained only a limited selection of documents.[53] The resolutions adopted by the congress were published in

1920, with a few editorial changes, in a German-language edition.[54] The next year a German-language edition of the proceedings was published, which contained the resolutions in their unedited form.[55] There were many gaps in this edition, apparently because the editors lacked access to most or all of the Russian-language transcript. The Russian-language edition of the proceedings published that same year did not fill the gaps; it was merely a translation of the German-language version, with some editing to clarify obscure passages in the German text.[56]

In the early 1930s the publishing house of the Communist Party of the Soviet Union undertook a complete re-edition of the proceedings of the Comintern congresses. The volume on the first congress, published in 1933, included several items left out of the 1921 editions of the congress proceedings, along with several reports submitted to the congress in writing. This edition also falsified the record, however, by omitting favorable references to Trotsky in the report by Sadoul (see chapter 2).

During the next five years the majority of the Bolshevik leaders from Lenin's time were purged and executed as part of the bureaucratic transformation led by Stalin of the Communist Party and the Soviet state. The writings of these purged Communists and the records of their activity as working-class leaders were suppressed. As part of this falsification of history, after publication in 1934 of the record of the second congress, the Soviet edition of the Comintern congress proceedings was discontinued. It has never been resumed.

In the last thirteen years, new editions of the first congress proceedings have appeared in French, Spanish, and Serbo-Croatian.[57] The most ambitious of these is that published by the Institut za medunarodni radnički pokret (Institute on the International Workers Movement) in Yugoslavia as part of its edition of all seven Comintern congresses, the last of which took place in 1935. It restores the passages deleted from Sadoul's report in the 1933 Russian-language edition.

The congress proceedings published in 1921 were accepted by all its participants and used without challenge in the early Communist International as the record of what was said and decided there. More recently, some historians have questioned the authenticity of the published proceedings, claiming that no stenographic record was taken at the congress.[58] Yet these proceedings bear all the characteristic marks of stenographic transcriptions, including run-on sentences, grammatical incongruities (which have not been preserved in the translation), breaks, and gaps. Moreover, in three cases (the national reports of Eberlein and Platten and the report of N. Osinsky [Obolensky] on the international situation), the congress records published in 1933 contain two versions, one of which is clearly a stenographic record, while the other is an edited version.

The sole documentary basis on which to challenge the proceedings' validity appears to be a statement by Eberlein in 1929 that "the speeches were not taken in shorthand, but, as it were, reconstructed." According to Eberlein, this explained why there was no record of his having spoken out at the congress in support of immediate formation of the International.[59] Eberlein, who in 1928 had come under attack from the now-bureaucratized Comintern leadership, had good reason to attempt to escape his reputation as the one Communist who had opposed the International's formation. There is no sign from before 1929 that he claimed to have made such a statement at the congress. The accuracy of the congress proceedings on this point is borne out by the account of the British journalist Ransome.

Except as otherwise noted, the translations of congress proceedings in this book are taken from the German edition of 1921. They have been edited on the basis of a comparison with the Russian editions of 1921 and 1933. The resolutions, however, have been taken from the 1920 German edition of congress decisions. Significant differences between this text of the resolutions and that in the 1921 German edition of the proceedings have been indicated in footnotes. The congress report by Trotsky is taken from the 1924 Russian-language edition of his writings. Except for the passages by Lenin, all material has been newly translated. Lenin's articles and speeches are taken from the most recent English edition of his collected works. The spelling and punctuation have been changed to conform with current U.S. usage, and minor changes have been made on the basis of a comparison with the fifth Russian-language edition of his writings.

Of the additional material found in the 1933 Russian-language edition of the proceedings, four items have not been included in this edition. One of them, a statement by Fernand Loriot, is printed in another volume of this series.[60] Two others, the written versions of the national reports delivered by Eberlein and Platten, differ only slightly from the stenographic transcriptions of their oral reports included in chapter 2. Finally, a large portion of Osinsky's oral report on the international situation is duplicated in the resolution adopted on this topic. With these exceptions, the present edition includes all material in the 1933 edition. In addition, it contains a written report and a speech by the Polish delegate, which were not published until 1969.

Where there is evidence that a report appended to the 1933 edition was actually delivered during the congress proceedings themselves, it has been inserted by the editor at the proper point in the proceedings. In cases where such reports appear to have been submitted only in written form, they have been placed in chapter 11.

Chapters 1 to 10 correspond to the ten agenda points at the congress itself; the chapter headings and headings of individual reports are by the editor. All italicized emphasis is taken from the original text. Italicized comments in parentheses are those of the congress secretaries. The first name or initials of each speaker has been supplied. All other interpolations by the editor of this volume appear in brackets. Place names are given as they appear in the original text; modern place names are supplied in brackets at the first appearance.

The record of the congress itself has been supplemented by an article by Lenin on the significance of the Communist International, which is printed as a prologue to this volume. The editor has also supplied an appendix containing a number of brief assessments of the congress by leading Bolshevik participants published in *Pravda* the day the congress adjourned, along with two later comments by Lenin. Where relevant documents have been printed in other volumes of *The Communist International in Lenin's Time,* this is noted in footnotes. A glossary has been provided of individuals, publications, and political currents mentioned in the documents in this volume. A chronology lists important dates relating to documents in this collection.

John Riddell
AUGUST 1987

Acknowledgements

This book was produced with the assistance of a large number of collaborators who helped to collect source material, research historical questions, and translate the congress proceedings and appended reports into English.

Ronald Suny of the University of Michigan clarified many difficult questions of the history of Armenia, Georgia, and Azerbaijan. Jean-Paul Himka of the Institute of Ukrainian Studies in Edmonton gave valuable assistance in annotating the reports on the Ukraine.

Others who helped in research work while this volume was in preparation were Kate Blakeney in Australia; Fritz Keller and Raimund Löw in Austria; David Bowie, Rachel Gomme, and Mike Schlesinger in Britain; D.H. Struk of the Encyclopedia of Ukraine, Richard Day, Marlene Kadar, Kay Riddell, and Gordon Skilling in Canada; Nat London, Michel Löwy, and Rodolphe Prager in France; Wolrad Bode, Wilfried Dubois, Michal Reimann, Reiner Tosstorff, Hermann Weber, and Lüko Willms in Germany; Claudio Curatolo, Cristina Peraboni, and Fernando Visentin in Italy; Jean-Paul Andrade and Gregor Benton in the Netherlands; Gérard Donzé in Switzerland; Kjell Östberg in Sweden; Fuat Orçun, Mustafa Mersinoglu, and Semsa Yegin for Turkey; and David Abraham, Steffi Brooks, Al Campbell, Mike Italie, Deborah Jamison, Ron Richards, Nevin Siders, Mike Taber, and Bob Wilkinson in the United States.

Among the many librarians and libraries that made special efforts to help locate source material were Francesca Gori and the Fondazione Giangiacomo Feltrinelli, Milan;

Luba Hussel and the Fisher Rare Book Library, Toronto; the Slavonic Division of the New York Public Library; and Mary-Alison Farley and Ethel Lobman of the Tamiment Library, New York.

Robert Dees was responsible for much of the research for this volume and compiled the glossary and chronology. Bruce Marcus participated in the editorial preparation of this volume and organized its final production.

Bob Cantrick was staff translator for the German text of the congress proceedings; other staff translators were Robert Dees from French and Sonja Franeta from Russian and Serbo-Croatian. Other translators for this volume were as follows:

German: Regula Bürki, Al Campbell, Robert Dees, Dean Denno, Sue Hagen, Alex Koskinas, Bob Schwarz, Michael Tresidder, Walter Whalen, Duncan Williams; *Russian:* Ron Allen, Ken Eardley, Joanne Holowchak, Jeff Hamill, Jeff Jones, George Myland, Rebecca Park; *French:* Susan Wald; *Polish:* Ernest Harsch.

Rudolf Segall and his colleagues of the Association for Scholarly Research and Presentation of the Historical Heritage, Frankfurt, advised us regarding many difficult points in the translation from German.

This volume benefited greatly from the French edition of these proceedings edited by Pierre Broué and the Serbo-Croatian edition published in Yugoslavia by an editorial team headed by Pero Damjanović.

Also of great assistance was the manuscript of the Czechoslovak historians Miloš, Hajek and Hana Mejdrova on the International's formation and first years, *Vznik Tretí internacionály,* a copy of which was obtained through the courtesy of Vilém Prečan, Documentation Center for the Promotion of Independent Czechoslovak Literature, Scheinfeld, Federal Republic of Germany.

The photograph of Sebald Rutgers is published by permission of the Uitgeverij SUN, Nijmegen, the Netherlands; and the map of southern Russia, by permission of the University of Minnesota Press.

The translations, introduction, footnotes, and other annotation are the responsibility of the editor alone.

PROLOGUE

The Third International and its place in history

by V.I. Lenin

APRIL 15, 1919

The imperialists of the Entente countries are blockading Russia in an effort to cut off the Soviet republic, as a seat of infection, from the capitalist world.[1] These people, who boast about their "democratic" institutions, are so blinded by their hatred of the Soviet republic that they do not see how ridiculous they are making themselves. Just think of it: the advanced, most civilized, and "democratic" countries, armed to the teeth and enjoying undivided military sway over the whole world, are mortally afraid of the *ideological* infection coming from a ruined, starving, backward, and even, they assert, semisavage country!

This contradiction alone is opening the eyes of the working masses in all countries and helping to expose the hypocrisy of the imperialists Clemenceau, Lloyd George, Wilson, and their governments.

We are being helped, however, not only by the capitalists' blind hatred of the soviets, but also by their bickering among themselves, which induces them to put spokes in each other's wheels. They have entered into a veritable conspiracy of silence, for they are desperately afraid of the spread of true information about the Soviet republic in general and of its official documents in particular. Yet *Le Temps,* the principal organ of the French bourgeoisie, has published a report on the foundation in Moscow of the Third, Communist International.

For this we express our most respectful thanks to the principal organ of the French bourgeoisie, to this leader of French chauvinism and imperialism. We are prepared to send an illuminated address to *Le Temps* in token of our appreciation of the effective and able assistance it is giving us.

The manner in which *Le Temps* compiled its report on the basis of our wireless messages clearly and fully reveals the motive that prompted this organ of the moneybags. It wanted to have a dig at Wilson, as if to say, "Look at the people with whom you negotiate!" The wiseacres who write to the order of the moneybags do not see that their attempt to frighten Wilson with the Bolshevik bogey is becoming, in the eyes of the working people, an advertisement for the Bolsheviks. Once more, our most respectful thanks to the organ of the French millionaires!

The Third International has been founded in a world situation that does not allow prohibitions—petty and miserable devices of the Entente imperialists or of capitalist lackeys like the Scheidemanns in Germany and the Renners in Austria—to prevent news of this International and sympathy for it spreading among the working class of the world. This situation has been brought about by the growth of the proletarian revolution, which is manifestly developing everywhere by leaps and bounds. It has been brought about by the *soviet* movement among the working people, which has already achieved such strength as to become really *international*.

The First International (1864–72) laid the foundation of an international organization of the workers for the preparation of their revolutionary attack on capital. The Second International (1889–1914) was an international organization of the proletarian movement whose growth proceeded in *breadth,* at the cost of a temporary drop in the revolutionary level, a temporary strengthening of opportunism, which in the end led to the disgraceful collapse of this International.

The Third International actually emerged in 1918, when the long years of struggle against opportunism and social-chauvinism, especially during the war, led to the formation of the Communist parties in a number of countries. Officially, the Third International was founded at its first congress, in March 1919, in Moscow. And the most characteristic feature of this International, its mission of fulfilling, of implementing the precepts of Marxism, and of achieving the age-old ideals of socialism and the working-class movement—this most characteristic feature of the Third International has manifested itself immediately in the fact that the new, third "International Working Men's Association" *has already begun to develop,* to a certain extent, into a *union of Soviet socialist republics*.

The First International laid the foundation of the proletarian, international struggle for socialism.

The Second International marked a period in which the soil was prepared for the broad, mass spread of the movement in a number of countries.

The Third International has gathered the fruits of the work of the Second International, discarded its opportunist, social-chauvinist, bourgeois, and petty-bourgeois dross and *has begun to implement* the dictatorship of the proletariat.

The international alliance of the parties which are leading the most revolutionary movement in the world, the movement of the proletariat for the overthrow of the yoke of capital, now rests on an unprecedentedly firm base in the shape of several *Soviet republics,* which are implementing the dictatorship of the proletariat and are the embodiment of victory over capitalism on an international scale.

The epoch-making significance of the Third, Communist International lies in its having begun to give effect to Marx's cardinal slogan, the slogan which sums up the centuries-old development of socialism and the working-class movement, the slogan which is expressed in the concept of the dictatorship of the proletariat.

This prevision and this theory—the prevision and theory of a genius—are becoming a reality.

The Latin words have now been translated into the languages of the peoples of contemporary Europe—more, into all the languages of the world.

A new era in world history has begun.

Mankind is throwing off the last form of slavery: capitalist, or wage, slavery.

By emancipating himself from slavery, man is for the first time advancing to real freedom.

How is it that one of the most backward countries of Europe was the first country to establish the dictatorship of the proletariat and to organize a Soviet republic? We shall hardly be wrong if we say that it is this contradiction between the backwardness of Russia and the "leap" she has made over bourgeois democracy to the highest form of democracy, to soviet, or proletarian democracy—it is this contradiction that has been one of the reasons (apart from the dead weight of opportunist habits and philistine prejudices that burdened the majority of the Socialist leaders) why people in the West have had particular difficulty or have been slow in understanding the role of the soviets.

The working people all over the world have instinctively grasped the significance of the soviets as an instrument in the proletarian struggle and as a form of the proletarian state. But the "leaders," corrupted by opportunism, still continue to worship bourgeois democracy, which they call "democracy" in general.

Is it surprising that the establishment of the dictatorship of the proletariat has brought out primarily the "contradiction" between the backwardness of Russia and her "leap" *over* bourgeois democracy? It would have been surprising had history granted us the establishment of a *new* form of democracy *without* a number of contradictions.

If any Marxist, or any person, indeed, who has a general knowledge of modern science, were asked whether it is likely that the transition of the different capitalist countries to the dictatorship of the proletariat will take place in an identical or harmoniously proportionate way, his answer would undoubtedly be in the negative. There has never been and never could be even, harmonious, or proportionate development in the capitalist world. Each country has developed more strongly first one, then another aspect or feature or group of features of capitalism and of the working-class movement. This process of development has been uneven.

When France was carrying out her great bourgeois revolution and rousing the whole European continent to a historically new life, Britain proved to be at the head of the counterrevolutionary coalition, although at the same time she was much more developed capitalistically than France. The British working-class movement of that period, however, brilliantly anticipated much that was contained in the future Marxism.

When Britain gave the world Chartism, the first broad, truly mass, and politically organized proletarian revolutionary movement, bourgeois revolutions, most of them weak, were taking place on the European continent, and the first great civil war between the proletariat and the bourgeoisie had broken out in France. The bourgeoisie defeated the various national contingents of the proletariat one by one, in different ways in different countries.

Britain was the model of a country in which, as Engels put it, the bourgeoisie had produced, alongside a bourgeois aristocracy, a very bourgeois upper stratum of the proletariat.[2] For several decades this advanced capitalist country lagged behind in the revolutionary struggle of the proletariat. France seemed to have exhausted the strength of the proletariat in two heroic working-class revolts of 1848 and 1871 against the bourgeoisie, which made very considerable contributions to world-historical development.[3] Leadership in the International of the working-class movement then passed to Germany; that was in the seventies of the nineteenth century, when she lagged economically behind Britain and France. But when Germany had outstripped these two countries economically, i.e., by the second decade of the twentieth century, the Marxist workers' party of Germany, that model for the whole world, found itself headed by a handful of utter scoundrels, the most filthy blackguards—from Scheidemann and Noske to David and Legien—loathsome hangmen drawn from the workers' ranks who had sold themselves to the capitalists, who were in the service of the monarchy and the counterrevolutionary bourgeoisie.

World history is leading unswervingly toward the dictatorship of the proletariat, but is doing so by paths that are anything but smooth, simple, and straight.

When Karl Kautsky was still a Marxist and not the renegade from Marxism he became when he began to champion unity with the Scheidemanns and to support bourgeois democracy against Soviet, or proletarian democracy, he wrote an article—this was at the turn of the century—entitled "The Slavs and Revolution." In this article he traced the historical conditions that pointed to the possibility of leadership in the world revolutionary movement passing to the Slavs.

And so it has. Leadership in the revolutionary proletarian International has passed for a time—for a short time, it goes without saying—to the Russians, just as at various periods of the nineteenth century it was in the hands of the British, then of the French, then of the Germans.

I have had occasion more than once to say that it was easier for the Russians than for the advanced countries *to begin* the great proletarian revolution, but that it will be more difficult for them *to continue* it and carry it to final victory, in the sense of the complete organization of a socialist society.

It was easier for us to begin, first, because the unusual—for twentieth-century Europe—political backwardness of the tsarist monarchy gave unusual strength to the revolutionary onslaught of the masses. Second, Russia's backwardness merged in a peculiar way the proletarian revolution against the bourgeoisie with the peasant revolution against the landowners. That is what we started from in October 1917, and we would not have achieved victory so easily then if we had not. As long ago as 1856, Marx spoke, in reference to Prussia, of the possibility of a peculiar combination of proletarian revolution and peasant war.[4] From the beginning of 1905 the Bolsheviks advocated the idea of a revolutionary-democratic dictatorship of the proletariat and the peasantry.[5] Third, the 1905 revolution contributed enormously to the political education of the workers and peasant masses,[6] because it familiarized their vanguard with the "last word" of socialism in the West and also because of the revolutionary *action* of the masses. Without such a "dress rehearsal" as we had in 1905, the revolutions of 1917—both the bourgeois, February revolution, and the proletarian, October revolution—would have been impossible. Fourth, Russia's geographical conditions permitted her to hold out longer than other countries could have done against the superior military strength of the capitalist, advanced countries. Fifth, the specific attitude of the proletariat toward the peasantry facilitated the transition from the bourgeois revolution to the socialist revolution, made it easier for the urban proletarians to influence the semiproletarian, poorer sections of the rural working people. Sixth, long schooling in strike action and experience of the European mass working-class movement facilitated the emergence—in a profound and rapidly intensifying revolutionary situation—of such a unique form of proletarian revolutionary organization as the *soviets*.

This list, of course, is incomplete; but it will suffice for the time being.

Soviet, or proletarian, democracy was born in Russia. Following the Paris Commune a second epoch-making step was taken. The proletarian and peasant Soviet republic has proved to be the first stable socialist republic in the world. As a *new type of state* it cannot die. It no longer stands alone.

For the continuance and completion of the work of building socialism, much, very much is still required. Soviet republics in more developed countries, where the proletariat has greater weight and influence, have every chance of surpassing Russia once they take the path of the dictatorship of the proletariat.

The bankrupt Second International is now dying and rotting alive. Actually, it is playing the role of lackey to the world bourgeoisie. It is a truly Yellow International. Its foremost ideological leaders, such as Kautsky, laud *bourgeois* democracy and call it "democracy" in general, or—what is still more stupid and still more crude—"pure democracy."

Bourgeois democracy has outlived its day, just as the Second International has, though the International performed historically necessary and useful work when the task of the moment was to train the working-class masses within the framework of this bourgeois democracy.

No bourgeois republic, however democratic, ever was or could have been anything but a machine for the suppression of the working people by capital, an instrument of the dictatorship of the bourgeoisie, the political rule of capital. The democratic bourgeois republic promised and proclaimed majority rule, but it could never put this into effect as long as private ownership of the land and other means of production existed.

"Freedom" in the bourgeois-democratic republic was actually freedom *for the rich*. The proletarians and working peasants could and should have utilized it for the purpose of preparing their forces to overthrow capital, to overcome bourgeois democracy, but in fact the working masses were, as a general rule, unable to enjoy democracy under capitalism.

Soviet, or proletarian, democracy has for the first time in the world created *democracy* for the masses, for the working people, for the factory workers and small peasants.

Never yet has the world seen political power wielded by the *majority* of the population, power *actually* wielded by this majority, as it is in the case of Soviet rule.

It suppresses the "freedom" of the exploiters and their accomplices; it deprives them of "freedom" to exploit, "freedom" to batten on starvation, "freedom" to fight for the restoration of the rule of capital, "freedom" to compact with the foreign bourgeoisie against the workers and peasants of their own country.

Let the Kautskys champion such freedom. Only a renegade from Marxism, a renegade from socialism, can do so.

In nothing is the bankruptcy of the ideological leaders of the Second International, people like Hilferding and Kautsky, so strikingly expressed as in their utter inability to understand the significance of Soviet, or proletarian, democracy, its relation to the Paris Commune, its place in history, its necessity as a form of the dictatorship of the proletariat. The newspaper *Die Freiheit,* organ of the "Independent" (alias middle-class, philistine, petty-bourgeois) German Social Democratic Party, in its issue no. 74 of February 11, 1919, published a manifesto "To the Revolutionary Proletariat of Germany."

This manifesto is signed by the party executive and by all its members in the National Assembly, the German variety of our Constituent Assembly.

This manifesto accuses the Scheidemanns of wanting to abolish the *workers' councils,* and proposes—don't laugh!—that the councils be *combined* with the assembly, that the councils be granted certain political rights, a certain place in the constitution.

To reconcile, to unite the dictatorship of the bourgeoisie and the dictatorship of the proletariat! How simple! What a brilliantly philistine idea!

The only pity is that it was tried in Russia, under Kerensky, by the united Mensheviks and Socialist Revolutionaries, those petty-bourgeois democrats who imagine themselves socialists.

Anyone who has read Marx and failed to understand that in capitalist society, at every acute moment, in every serious class conflict, the alternative is either the dictatorship of the bourgeoisie or the dictatorship of the proletariat, has understood nothing of either the economic or the political doctrines of Marx.

But the brilliantly philistine idea of Hilferding, Kautsky, and Company of peacefully combining the dictatorship of the bourgeoisie and the dictatorship of the proletariat requires special examination, if exhaustive treatment is to be given to the economic and political absurdities with which this most remarkable and comical manifesto of February 11 is packed. That will have to be put off for another article.

V.I. Lenin, May 1, 1919.

MOSCOW

MARCH 1, 1919

Minutes of March 1 preliminary meeting

The conference will open on Sunday, March 2, at five in the afternoon.[1]

The conference will not formally be the founding congress of the Third International. It will work out a platform, elect a bureau, and issue a call for affiliation.

Name: The International Communist Conference. The opening sessions will be secret. Whether future sessions will be secret is left open.

In the proposed list of participants, numbers fifteen, sixteen, seventeen, and twenty-two are grouped together in "The United Group of Eastern Peoples of Russia" with one vote.

The Bureau Abroad of the Central Committee of the Hungarian Communist Party has three decisive votes.

If Rutgers arrives, the American Socialist Labor Party will have three votes and the Socialist Propaganda League, two.[2] The Socialist Labor Party now has five votes.

The Balkan revolutionary federation replaces the Romanian Communist Party.

Agenda: (1) Organization of the Conference; (2) Reports; (3) Platform (reporter: Albert, supplemented by Bukharin); (4) Bourgeois Democracy and the Dictatorship of the Proletariat (commission: Lenin, Reinstein, and a Finnish delegate, reporter: Lenin); (5) Election of the Bureau and Other Business (Albert, Platten, and a Finnish delegate); (6) Attitude toward the Socialist Parties and to the Bern Conference (Platten, Zinoviev); (7) The International Situation and the Policies of the Entente (reporter: Obolensky; the commission includes Albert); (8) Other Business: Polish Prisoners, White Terror (commission: Albert, Reinstein, and a Finnish delegate); (9) Manifesto (?) (Zinoviev, Bukharin, Platten).

Language: German. Russian also permitted.

The conference will be opened by Lenin.

Credentials Commission: Albert, Chicherin, Rudnyánszky, Stang.

List of congress delegates

DELEGATES WITH DECISIVE VOTE:

	Country and Party	Delegates[1]	No. of Votes
1.	**Communist Party of Germany**	Max Albert [Hugo Eberlein]	5
2.	**Russian Communist Party**	V.I. Lenin, L.D. Trotsky, G.Ye. Zinoviev, I.V. Stalin, N.I. Bukharin, G.V. Chicherin. With consultative vote: V.V. Obolensky [N. Osinsky], V.V. Vorovsky	5
3.	**Communist Party of German Austria**	I. Gruber [Karl Steinhardt], K. Petin	3
4.	**Communist Party of Hungary**	Endre Rudnyánszky	3
5.	**Swedish Left Social Democratic Party**	Otto Grimlund	3
6.	**Norwegian Social Democratic Party**	Emil Stang	3
7.	**Swiss Social Democratic Party (Opposition)**	Fritz Platten[2]	3
8.	**American Socialist Labor Party**	Boris Reinstein	5

	Country and Party	Delegates	No. of Votes
9.	**Balkan Revolutionary Social Democratic Federation (Bulgarian Tesnyaki and Romanian Communist Party)**	Christian Rakovsky	3
10.	**Communist Party of Poland**	Józef Unszlicht	3
11.	**Communist Party of Finland**	Yrjö Sirola, Kullervo Manner	3
12.	**Communist Party of the Ukraine**	N.A. Skrypnik, S.I. Gopner	3
13.	**Communist Party of Latvia**	Karl Gailis	1
14.	**Communist Party of Lithuania and Belorussia**	Kazimir Gedris	1
15.	**Communist Party of Estonia**	Hans Pögelman	1
16.	**Communist Party of Armenia**	Gurgen Haikuni	1
17.	**Communist Party of the German Colonists in Russia**	Gustav Klinger	1
18.	**United Group of the Eastern Peoples of Russia**	Gaziz Yalymov, Hussein Bekentayev, Mahomet Altimirov, Burhan Mansurov, Kasim Kasimov	1
19.	**Zimmerwald Left of France**	Henri Guilbeaux[3]	1

DELEGATES WITH CONSULTATIVE VOTE:

20.	**Czech Communist Group**	Jaroslav Handlir
21.	**Bulgarian Communist Group**	Stojan Dyorov
22.	**Yugoslav Communist Group**	Iliya Milkić
23.	**British Communist Group**	Joseph Fineberg
24.	**French Communist Group**	Jacques Sadoul
25.	**Dutch Social Democratic Group**	S.J. Rutgers
26.	**American Socialist Propaganda League Group**	S.J. Rutgers
27.	**Swiss Communist Group**	Leonie Kascher

SECTIONS OF THE CENTRAL BUREAU OF EASTERN PEOPLES:

28.	**Turkestan**	Gaziz Yalymov
29.	**Turkish**	Mustapha Subhi
30.	**Georgian**	Tengiz Zhgenti
31.	**Azerbaijani**	Mir Djafar Baguirov
32.	**Persian**	Mirza Davud Bagir-Uglu Gusseinov
33.	**Chinese Socialist Workers Party**	Liu Shauzhou, Zhang Yongkui
34.	**Korean Workers League**	Kain
35.	**Zimmerwald committee**	Angelica Balabanoff

Thirty-four delegates with decisive vote.
Eighteen delegates with consultative vote.

Presiding Committee (left to right): Gustav Klinger, Hugo Eberlein, V.I. Lenin, Fritz Platten.

MOSCOW, MARCH 2–6, 1919

Proceedings of the First Congress of the Communist International

FIRST DAY OF SESSIONS

MARCH 2, 1919

1. The congress opens

The meeting is convened on March 2, 1919, at 6:10 p.m. in the Kremlin.

OPENING REMARKS

V.I. LENIN:[1] On behalf of the Central Committee of the Russian Communist Party I declare the First Congress of the Communist International open. First I would ask all present to rise in tribute to the finest representatives of the Third International: Karl Liebknecht and Rosa Luxemburg. (*All rise*)

Comrades, our gathering has great historic significance. It testifies to the collapse of all the illusions cherished by bourgeois democrats. Not only in Russia, but in the most developed capitalist countries of Europe, Germany for example, civil war is a fact.[2]

The bourgeoisie is terror stricken at the growing workers' revolutionary movement. This is understandable if we take into account that the development of events since the imperialist war inevitably favors the workers' revolutionary movement, and that the world revolution is beginning and growing in intensity everywhere.

The people are aware of the greatness and significance of the struggle now going on. All that is needed is to find the practical form to enable the proletariat to establish its rule. Such a form is the soviet system with the dictatorship of the proletariat.[3] Dictatorship of the proletariat—until now these words were Latin to the masses. Thanks to the spread of the soviets throughout the world this Latin has been translated into all modern languages; a practical form of dictatorship has been found by the working people. The mass of workers now understands it thanks to Soviet power in Russia, thanks to the Spartacus League in Germany, and to similar organizations in other countries, such as, for example, the shop stewards committees in Britain.[4] All this shows that a revolutionary form of the dictatorship of the proletariat has been found, that the proletariat is now able to exercise its rule.

Comrades, I think that after the events in Russia and the January struggle in Germany, it is especially important to note that in other countries, too, the latest form of the workers' movement is asserting itself and getting the upper hand. Today, for example, I read in an antisocialist newspaper a report to the effect that the British government had received a deputation from the Birmingham council of workers' deputies and had expressed its readiness to recognize the councils as economic bodies.[5] The soviet system has triumphed not only in backward Russia, but also in the most developed country of Europe—in Germany and in Britain, the oldest capitalist country.

Even though the bourgeoisie is still raging, even through it may kill thousands more workers, victory will be ours, the victory of the worldwide communist revolution is assured.

Comrades, I extend hearty greetings to you on behalf of the Central Committee of the Russian Communist Party. I move that we elect a presidium. Let us have nominations.

GEORGIY CHICHERIN: I propose that three permanent members be elected to the Presiding Committee. For each session, this committee will elect a fifth member from the different national organizations.[6] As permanent members I propose Comrades Lenin, Albert, and Platten, and as permanent secretary, Comrade Klinger.[7]

(*The meeting adopts the motion unanimously. Those elected take their places at the Presiding Committee table.*)

FRITZ PLATTEN: At a preparatory meeting the question of the character of our meeting was raised. One opinion was that it should constitute itself as the *Third International*. Another position, advanced above all by a delegate from abroad, was that it would be more appropriate to designate this meeting only as the Communist Conference and leave it to a later gathering to found the Third International. The motivation given for the latter position was that this conference was called on very short notice and not all organizations could be informed of the proposal to found the Third International. It must be noted that a number of delegates were unable to reach Moscow due to technical difficulties. Therefore the proposal has been made that we should convene today only as a conference, and that this conference should set itself the task of calling, as soon as possible, a real, larger congress at which the Third International can be definitively constituted.

GREGORY ZINOVIEV: I would like to make a statement on behalf of the Central Committee of the Communist Party of Russia. Our party's position is that it is high time to formally launch the Third International. And we would move that the founding take place right now, at this first meeting. But since our friends from Germany, the Communist Party of Germany, insist that the meeting constitute itself only as a conference, we consider it necessary to support their proposal for the time being. We want to make clear, however, that we will continue to agitate for the founding of the Third International as a formal organization as soon as possible.

OTTO KUUSINEN (*Finland*): We Finnish delegates also support the position that the Third International should be constituted now. In view of the circumstances just mentioned by Comrade Zinoviev, however, we will not make that proposal today. But in our opinion, it would be very gratifying if this conference concluded with the decision to found, as a congress, the new International.

(*The assembly votes to meet as the International Communist Conference. The meeting proceeds to the matter of the Credentials Commission.*)

PLATTEN: The composition of the conference is very diverse, and it is necessary to establish a Credentials Commission that takes this many-sided makeup into account. The bureau proposes that five comrades be elected to the Credentials Commission, who will report when their work is completed. The commission will also report on the attendance from two categories: one with full voting rights and the other with consultative vote only. We have some proposals to make for the Credentials Commission.

(*Comrades Chicherin, Rudnyánszky, Sirola, Albert, and Stang are proposed.*)

LENIN: Now we come to the question of the rules of order: voting rights, apportioning of votes, decisive and consultative votes, and speaking time.

BORIS REINSTEIN: I believe it would be proper first to give the Credentials Commission a quarter of an hour so that they can report on who has full voting rights. I move that we interrupt the meeting for a quarter of an hour.

MAX ALBERT [HUGO EBERLEIN]: Comrades, in my opinion Comrade Reinstein's proposal is not acceptable because reviewing the credentials will require considerable time; longer than a quarter of an hour in any case. Therefore, I propose that we continue with the session.

(Reinstein withdraws his motion.)

PLATTEN: I believe that speaking time during the discussion must be limited from the outset, since several delegates want to return home. In view of the large number of items on the agenda, it is therefore advisable to keep the speaking time to fifteen minutes but to place no limit on the reporters' speaking time.

(Leon Trotsky moves that anyone who speaks for a second time receive five minutes speaking time.)

PLATTEN: The procedure we will follow will be to allow one speaker for and one against and then proceed to a vote.

LENIN: Is there any objection? Let us have proposals for the length of sessions.

(Jacques Sadoul moves that the conference have the right in exceptional cases to extend the allotted speaking time.)

(Lenin reads the agenda.)

AGENDA

1. Organizational.
2. Reports by Delegates.
3. Platform of the International Communist Conference; reporters: *Albert, Bukharin.*
4. Bourgeois Democracy and the Dictatorship of the Proletariat; reporters: *Lenin, Rahja.*
5. The Bern Conference and the Attitude toward the Socialist Currents; reporters: *Platten, Zinoviev.*

6. The International Situation and the Policy of the Entente; reporters: *Obolensky, Platten.*
7. Manifesto; reporter: *Trotsky.*
8. The White Terror; reporter: *Sirola.*
9. Election of the Bureau and Other Business (Organizational Questions).

LENIN (*in reference to the list of reporters*): We have received word that Comrade Rakovsky is on his way and should arrive tomorrow. Other comrades are still arriving. The list of reporters should not be regarded as final but as provisional. Three delegates of the Communist Party of Hungary have been arrested in Galicia, and it is unlikely that they will arrive at our conference. Are there other proposals for the agenda? Does anyone else wish to speak? As no one requests the floor, the agenda is adopted.

2. National reports

REPORT ON GERMANY

LENIN: Comrade Albert, the delegate from Germany, has the floor for his report.

ALBERT: Comrades, as late as November 8, 1918, even supporters of the Independent Social Democratic Party said it was excluded that Germany would ever see "Russian conditions"—in other words, the outbreak of revolution. But by November 9 the old capitalist social structure had collapsed.[1] By November 9 we confronted the exact situation for which Russia had been so harshly criticized and which was thought to be impossible in Germany.

To be sure, it initially seemed as though the whole German movement was merely a soldiers' revolt, merely a matter of military forces weary of war and discontented with their officers' draconian discipline. But overnight the council system sprang up. Even in the small towns they were formed overnight. So it is not enough to say this was just a soldiers' revolution resulting from war-weariness; rather it represented the proletariat's determination to establish the new system for which it had been struggling so long: to replace the old social system with socialism.

Of course, the hastily established workers' councils were still very unstable. The majority Socialists and Scheidemann supporters were far superior to the workers in organizational matters.[2] They knew how to worm their way into the government, take governmental posts, and gain influence in the workers' councils. The notion long held by workers that a new society could be created simply by replacing the old officials and ministers with a few Social Democrats made it possible for the Independents and majority Socialists to take posts in the government of Germany.

In the first days of the revolution, the workers' councils called on the members of what was then the Spartacus League to join the government and proposed that Comrade Liebknecht become a member of it. On the first day he stated that he would enter the cabinet only for three days, in order to conclude the armistice.[3] When the majority Socialists rejected this proposal, Comrade Liebknecht refused to enter the government, and the Spartacus League comrades followed his example. In our opinion, the moment had not yet arrived when Germany could replace the old capitalist system with the new social order. We felt it was not sufficient simply to drive out a few lackeys of the monarchs. The proletariat's primary task is to destroy the old state apparatus and create its own organs of power. Therefore, our main task is to show the working masses and explain to them that they must first build the council system, that is, the proletariat must first establish its dictatorship.

Just how correct our comrades had been in not joining the government was shown by the steps that it took only a few days later. All of the government's initial decrees were designed to deny the workers' councils any executive power.

Haase, Dittmann, Barth, and Company had also joined the government. The two tendencies had jointly issued the first decree. Just a few days later, they collided with the Executive Committee.[4] The government placed itself above the council system. The officers who had been removed were put back in their former positions and given back their military authority. It was thought to be still too soon to establish socialism, which was to be postponed until later. Workers' demands were rejected with the explanation that the existing state apparatus could not be changed because the enemy was at the door and because the Entente would not permit the government to carry through any changes.[5]

Faced with growing proletarian resistance to these conditions and with the workers' rejection of a return to the old set-up, the government of majority Socialists soon revealed its true face.

Indicative of the situation in Germany was the announcement by right-wing newspapers only three days after the revolution had broken out that it was simply an accomplished fact that could not easily be denied out of existence. The key point, they said, was for the government to ensure that democracy was really established in Germany and for this to become a reality in life. By that they meant bourgeois democracy and the convening of a national assembly. The Spartacus League promptly responded that there could be no talk of that. What we needed was the dictatorship of the proletariat, which had created its organizational structure, the council system.

Since the German proletariat had made the revolution, it was the only class in the country competent to construct the new state. We demanded that the class struggle be pressed relentlessly until the capitalist social system had been toppled.

That was not to the liking of Messrs. Scheidemann and Ebert. They went on record in favor of convening a national assembly, and with truly marvelous haste they called the elections. That determined the workers' slogan. The whole country was divided into two camps: on the one side stood the representatives of capital, who fought for the national assembly, and on the other stood the Spartacus League demanding the council system and the dictatorship of the proletariat. All struggles were waged around this axis, and you all know how they went.[6]

The comrades who joined the Spartacus League had previously belonged to the Independent Social Democrats. Until the outbreak of the war, circumstances were such that there was only one Social Democratic party, which was praised to the skies in other countries. At the beginning of the war, when the Social Democrats and their leadership went over to nationalism and joined with the bourgeoisie, shoulder to shoulder, in whipping up pro-war hysteria, the members of the Spartacus League could no longer remain in that organization. There was one other tendency within Social Democracy that disagreed with voting for war credits but supported Scheidemann and Ebert on other issues related to defense of the fatherland: the Haase-Ledebour current.[7] When they publicly opposed the leadership, they were driven out of the party and founded the Independent Social Democratic Party.

It was impossible for supporters of the Spartacus League to work or develop their activity. All of its representatives were thrown in prison or ended up in the trenches. The few who remained at large at any one time could do only limited work. When the Independent Social Democratic Party was founded in Gotha, we were ready to unite with them to form a single organization, but differences already existed and were insurmountable. After the revolution broke out, when the Independents joined the government, and after even they declared for bourgeois democracy and tried to use it to strangle the council system, we could no longer remain in their organization. On January 3, 1919,[8] at the Spartacus League conference in Berlin, we founded the Communist Party of Germany. The government led by Ebert and Scheidemann unleashed a vehement campaign against the Communists and ruthlessly employed every repressive technique of the old regime to combat the Communist Party. When the workers turned against this policy, and the proletariat showed by its strikes that it would not submit to the same old methods of repression, none other than agents of the Ebert-Scheidemann government unleashed a furious assault against the proletariat. They were the first to use machine guns and cannons against the proletariat in the streets of Berlin. On December 6, 1918, they brought machine guns and cannons to bear on the streets of Berlin against workers who were peacefully demonstrating, and many of our best comrades were killed or severely wounded. It is no accident that the soldiers who belonged to the Communist Party were singled out for the harshest treatment.[9]

What is the situation in the German armed forces today? The soldiers, who have been at war for four years, who revolted and smashed the old system on November 9, no longer want to play soldier. The old regiments have been disbanded. When the revolution broke out, they deserted, whether Scheidemann liked it or not.

The units stationed in Germany were disbanded a few days after the revolution; entire regions whose leaders supported the Communist Party carried out demobilization on their own. A few days after the revolution began the Republic of Brunswick announced that its demobilization would take place on December 23.[10] The national government protested, but the soldiers were discharged. Indeed, it made little sense for the government to restrain the soldiers any longer, since they had ceased to be reliable for its purposes anyway. The old regiments at the front had no desire to go on fighting external enemies. They had deserted, armistice or no. I should point out that Russia played a big part in the disintegration of our army. Prisoners of war returning from Russia were in a fine frame of mind. Wherever they went, the soldiers' willingness to fight rapidly melted away.

Of course, there were regiments at the front that were not receptive to agitation and remained under their officers' control, but even they soon became unfit for combat.

Lequis, the commanding general in Berlin, stated at the beginning of January that his troops, which were still under their officers' control, became completely demoralized after spending only five or six days there. Only the chance arrival from the front of units that had not yet been reached by the agitation made it possible to use troops against the workers in the streets of Berlin. That is what happened on December 6, 1918, after a meeting of the Red Soldiers' League. Acting on government orders, troops just back from Finland gunned down soldiers as they were leaving the meeting.

A few days later the sailors refused to leave Berlin. They were mostly workers who had been party members and formed the bedrock and elite corps of the revolution. Again, the government deployed a regiment from the front against the sailors, attacking them with mustard gas. Haase, Barth, and Dittmann, who were members of the government, asserted that they had not been present at the meeting where it was decided to fire upon the workers. Kicked and abused by the Scheidemanns, the Independents then withdrew from the government. They were forced out, complaining long and loud.[11]

The Spartacus League could no longer collaborate with them. It was an illusion to think that one could carry out any revolutionary work with such people. Therefore, founding our own Communist Party was a necessity. It was also necessary because the fragmentation among the Independents was proceeding apace. The majority Social Democratic Party is united, but the Independents are in sorry shape. Every leader represented a different tendency, and each was pushing for a different party. Ledebour and Däumig, in particular, were circulating the idea of founding a Germany-wide party. If this had come about there would have been yet another Independent Social Democratic Party, oriented neither to the right nor the left. It would not have shared the views of the far left, the Spartacus League, nor stood for the dictatorship of the proletariat. This prompted us to make an immediate break with these people and thus block the foundation of such a mishmash party.

The Communist group's task was not just to found a new party but above all to educate the masses and prepare them to establish the socialist order, a task that requires everyone's active participation. This is important because the idea continually surfaces among the workers that their work is done when they have replaced a few ministers with Social Democrats. Our job was to point out that the decisive battles with the bourgeoisie could be waged only through mass action. It was clear to us from the beginning that the November 9 revolution was no more than a halfway attempt to destroy the old social system and that the real German revolution still lay ahead.

It was precisely in these weeks that it became evident that transforming society will require even more difficult struggles and that civil war will erupt with a fury such as world history has never known. It is necessary to show the masses that this objective can be reached only through the council system. The goal of all our agitation is to explain councils to the workers and inspire them to create their own.

What is the situation of the councils today? At the beginning of the revolution, councils were organized everywhere. Workers met in the factories and workshops and formed councils whose task was to improve conditions for the work force in each factory. What is significant for us is that these factory councils completely eclipsed the trade unions, which until then had been highly influential in Germany, but had been in league with the scab unions, had forbidden the workers to strike, consistently opposed their public actions, and stabbed them in the back at every opportunity.[12] Since November 9 these trade unions have been completely bypassed. Since then, all struggles for better wages have been led without and even against the trade unions, which had not won a single one of the workers' wage demands. Only recently did the retail clerks' union wage an open struggle. But that was because there were Communist Party members in its leadership.

What are the prospects for the struggle in Germany? To judge by the number of votes received in National Assembly elections, you would have to say that the majority Socialists have the broad masses in Germany behind them: eleven million voted for the Scheidemanns and two million for the Independent Socialists. But if you examine the workers' movement, you will see that the workers are not as solidly behind the government as it claims. On the contrary, it is becoming clear that whenever the workers try to fight the government and win something for themselves by using independent, socialist forms of struggle, they always turn to the Communists' slogans. In Rhineland-Westphalia a mass movement of the miners arose. They elected a central council that gained control over all the coal mines. The workers were not the only ones involved in socializing the mines—the office staff also declared their readiness to carry through socialization without the capitalists and to run the socialized operation together with the miners without sabotage. It is not possible to carry out socialization in only part of a country. Nevertheless, it is significant that the workers realize the old economic system can only be done away with by socializing the factories and all aspects of life.

The outlook for future struggles is good since the whole German economy is in steep decline. Less favorable is the fact that the government is moving harshly against the workers. But the workers are not intimidated. As I reported earlier, every time struggles broke out in Germany, the old army units always said, "We will not fight against the workers." A neutral army was of no use to the government, and so it had to follow the Russian example and create White Guard units from volunteer regiments. New regiments were put together for "defense of the east." This was done under the twin pretexts of suppressing the rebellious Poles—who were oppressed by a dictatorship of the bourgeoisie and today remain as mistreated as before—and of stemming the onslaught of Bolshevik Red Guards.[13] That is a story in itself. In Germany the Red Guards are portrayed as robber bands that loot and kill. This propaganda is vigorously promoted in order to recruit soldiers to fight the Bolsheviks.

But the soldiers are used against the workers in the streets of Berlin to crush their revolutionary struggles. The first such struggle occurred in Berlin in January 1919. The government had dismissed the chief of police and in his place had appointed a majority party member who had earned the workers' hatred for his previous betrayal of them. Therefore the proletariat had reason to fear that he would once more use extremely brutal measures against them. On January 19, with no slogan and no directive from the party, let alone from the Spartacus League, workers occupied several printing plants, above all that of *Vorwärts,* which they had hated for so long.[14] After several days of struggle and occupation, the majority Socialists, through the government, sent the White Guards into battle for the first time to restore order in Berlin. The first of those to emerge from the *Vorwärts* building under the flag of truce were simply beaten to death by the soldiers. Seven people were killed. That gives some idea of their dreadful brutality and ruthlessness. When the White Guards had crushed the revolutionary movement, they began arresting all supporters of the Spartacus League and throwing them into jail. In this way, our best leaders, Karl Liebknecht and Rosa Luxemburg, fell into the hands of these murderers and were killed on the street. All the fairy tales about Liebknecht attempting to escape and Luxemburg being dragged away by the workers are transparent lies. Statements by eyewitnesses are already available proving that Liebknecht was clubbed over the head by the White Guard soldiers and, gravely wounded, was taken away in an automobile and shot; and that Rosa Luxemburg was murdered by two blows from a rifle butt and her body carted away. The murderers and their officers have been identified, and the statements have been published, but the killers still roam the streets. The government has no intention of prosecuting them.[15]

Many other Spartacists have met the same fate as Liebknecht and Luxemburg: murdered and buried in shallow graves by fanatical soldiers and officers. Similarly, our Russian comrade Karl Radek was arrested, laid in heavy iron chains, and placed in a damp, cold cellar, in a cell for murderers in a former prison.[16] As you can see, the terror is in full swing in Berlin, and the struggle of the proletariat against the bourgeoisie is now no longer being waged with leaflets and pamphlets but with bullets and guns. The frightened bourgeoisie has no solution other than crushing the proletariat by force. They have no other methods.

The economic outlook in Germany is dismal. Factories are closing everywhere. The workers have struggled and gone on strike for wage increases, winning gains such that the capitalists regard the enterprises as unprofitable. Simply because they cannot make a sufficient profit, they close up shop. But in addition, the workers in the factories have less and less desire to work. It is no wonder that the workers, who could themselves take over the factories today, are reluctant to keep on filling the pockets of the capitalists. This reluctance is increasing all the time. Raw materials are scarce, and where they are available, they end up being traded on the black market. So the capitalists close their factories. The number of unemployed in Berlin had reached 260,000 when I left. Economic collapse in Germany is imminent.

The transportation system is in poor condition. In Germany I was told: "When you go to Russia, you are in for a rough ride." Comrades, my trip from the border to Moscow was splendid compared to Germany. The British and the French took our best locomotives. A trip from Berlin to Leipzig that used to take only two hours now often takes nine or ten, and where before there was an express train every hour, now there are only one or two local trains a day. Here too, it is evident that the system cannot go on being run as it was before.

The problem of providing food is becoming ever more complex. Food is becoming more expensive and cannot be obtained. Rations are not enough to live on, so that people are dependent on the black market. Workers are unable to get food. Consequently, there are revolts everywhere. The White Guards are waiting for the right moment to move against the proletariat; violent clashes are therefore inevitable.

All of these problems, especially the added factor of the peace with the Entente, make us optimistic that the battles the proletariat will have to fight can be waged with high hopes of victory. The government continually puts the workers off by saying, "We don't dare do anything, because we are on the verge of making peace with the Entente." But the working class is no longer taken in by these lame excuses. For months we have been told that we must fight against Russia in order to curry favor with the Entente. But we have received nothing from them and we are not going to, either. The few cans of condensed milk we have received are being sold at prices that only capitalists can afford to pay, not workers. The Scheidemanns, who four years ago applauded and supported going to war against the Entente countries, are now groveling before them, whining and begging for mercy. They are terrified of the peace terms. The German government—the Scheidemanns and their friends—demonstrated to the Entente how peace is made with the vanquished.[17] Now the British and French can point to Brest-Litovsk and say, "You taught us how to negotiate peace treaties." If their terms are bad, it is because the Entente's representatives—the Wilsons and Clemenceaus—are nothing but managers of the capitalist states that they represent, and they view concluding peace as a business transaction from which maximum advantage is to be extracted. We will gain nothing from the government's whimpering and crawling on its belly before this gang; we will gain if the proletariat carries the revolution forward energetically and passionately. We must win the confidence of the proletariat of England and France so that we can struggle side by side with them for the world revolution.

That is the Communist Party's opinion. Wherever the German proletariat has not yet come over to the Communist Party, it can be won to our views by our agitation. I do not believe I am being too optimistic when I say that the German Communist Party, like the Russian party, will continue the struggle with complete confidence that the time has come when the German proletariat will carry the revolution through to a successful conclusion; when, despite national assemblies, Scheidemanns, and bourgeois nationalism, proletarian dictatorship can be established in Germany. To win this struggle the German workers must join forces with the proletariat of other countries. In view of this I was pleased to accept your invitation, confident that we would soon be fighting for the world revolution shoulder to shoulder with workers everywhere, especially with the British and French workers, and in this way realize the goals of the revolution in Germany as well.

LENIN: The representative from Switzerland, Comrade Platten, has the floor.

REPORT ON SWITZERLAND (PLATTEN)

PLATTEN: Comrades, Switzerland is a small country with a modest revolutionary movement. As its representative, I cannot make as extensive a presentation about struggles there as the reporters from other countries can, although it should be noted that we have tried to fulfill our duty of solidarity to the Russian comrades.

We were spared the scourge of the war. Our living conditions were not as harsh, and our workers' movement proceeded at a different pace than those in the warring states. But even Switzerland felt the political repercussions of the war. The Swiss party adhered to Zimmerwald from the start. I want to touch on the split only briefly to tell you that the fight for Zimmerwald got rid of the most extreme nationalist forces in the party,[18] leaving an internationalist party, which developed vigorously. But despite the division in our ranks it was not possible to force out all the right-wing elements. All comrades remained in the party because of the need to preserve unity.

To give a brief idea of the party's development, suffice it to say that when we selected delegates to the Zimmerwald conference, it turned out that even this united party contained not two, but three tendencies. The right-wingers, such as Studer, Müller, and Greulich, were not part of the delegation, although Comrade Naine was, and afterwards he veered sharply to the right and formed part of the right wing. Those who later formed the center and left wings of the party, however, were represented, and the vote was split on every question. I joined the Zimmerwald Left. Grimm voted against the left and explained his stance by saying that as chairman he had to keep the tendencies together by remaining neutral. Later it became apparent that deeper political differences underlay his position.

The struggle inside the party that was required after Zimmerwald was conducted by the left wing together with the party centrists. The Grütli forces split away, and that determined the party's course. It evolved rapidly to the left. Judging from all the party's convention resolutions it should be counted as part of the left in the International, and by rights should be represented here today. However, the social structure of the country leads to big contradictions between theory and practice.

Comrade Grimm's mission to Russia was not without political repercussions in the Swiss party.[19] When we learned by telegraph about his conduct in Petersburg, the most farsighted, especially the left-wing forces in Zurich, recognized that Grimm's attitude and position in the International as well as in the Swiss party could not be the same as before. But at the time many of our co-thinkers still clung to the hope that it was only a personal blunder. I took the position that we should have publicly repudiated his politics, but I was alone in this opinion. He returned and at first displayed a pseudoradicalism. Soon he drew the logical conclusions of his positions, and we had to carry out a hard fight against him. At the next party congress the fight will become even sharper, as that is where the party will definitively decide its course. Whether there will be a split, I cannot yet say.

The Swiss trade union movement suffers the same diseases as the German. A staff of functionaries controlled the trade union movement, and it was in danger of becoming permanently ossified. The poverty that workers faced due to the high cost of living forced them into struggle, without authorization from headquarters. The unions had to consent to assuming the leadership. The Swiss workers recognized early on that they could better their material conditions only by proceeding directly into struggle, regardless of the union statutes, under the direction not of the old trade union federation but of leadership they elected themselves. A workers' congress was held and a workers' council formed.[20] The latter, however, like the Russian soviets at the beginning of the Russian revolution, did not have a revolutionary perspective. The workers' committee had to take all the power into its own hands.

The workers' congress was founded despite the opposition of the trade union federation and was immediately faced with learning to organize mass strikes. Preparations were made for battles that lay ahead. Against the will of the leading committee of this workers' congress, a massive fight developed that posed a great challenge to Swiss workers. This was the most recent upsurge, which swept more than 400,000 workers into struggle.[21]

Once again, because of the central leadership's hesitant policy, Zurich had to take the lead. Two days after the Zurich strike had begun, the central leadership issued a belated call for a general strike, and then only to salvage its dwindling prestige. That made it possible to extend the fight to the rest of the country. But there was still no sign of any arming of the workers. The Swiss proletariat believed it could wage this fight without arms, just by stopping work and sticking it out. The strike lasted five days. On the fifth day the central leadership gave the order to break it off, much to the workers' dismay. Once again, the workers' cause had been betrayed. The [Olten] committee, which consisted partly of functionaries, had shown that it was not up to the situation. It justified terminating the fight by saying that to continue striking would have led to a bloody civil war. That led to fierce disagreements. The defeat also resulted in lockouts. The battle had been lost.

The struggle made great demands on the workers' courage, because a well-armed force of approximately 40,000 soldiers was mobilized. Workers gained a much better understanding of what future struggles would be like. After the strike ended and the workers started to evaluate the situation, they began to realize that the struggles to come could no longer take the same form, but would be bloody revolts.

A frightful reaction followed the defeat. Almost all the leadership comrades were put on trial and now await sentencing. Similarly, hundreds of railroad workers are also being tried by the war tribunals for refusing to carry out their duties.

After this action, the next major event was the expulsion of the Russian mission from Switzerland. Incidentally, the mere rumor that it was going to be expelled from the country helped provoke the workers' outrage. Various other demands were raised in the course of this fight later on. We explained that the struggle was taking place because steps had been taken against the Soviet government that we considered to be a provocation. The expulsion was doubly painful for us because the Russian embassy had provided us with an invaluable service by setting up a special bureau to bring news from Russia, which enabled us to refute the dishonest rumors that the bourgeoisie was spreading.

As soon as we had regrouped, we set to work publishing a number of new documents and circulating that excellent material as broadly as possible. We circulated articles by Lenin and Trotsky among the masses, which helped not only to raise the workers' revolutionary spirit, but also to give them the opportunity to gain a profound insight into the proletarian movement in Russia and the different forms of proletarian dictatorship. Our own propaganda work has become much more comprehensive lately. We have tried to use leaflets, pamphlets, and meetings to revolutionize the proletariat and give it a clear set of goals.

I would like to mention one group in particular with which we had differences on certain questions.[22] This group deserves special credit for its educational work in the army. We will have to discuss seriously how our groups can join forces to do common work. That will be possible once the [Social Democratic] party has taken a clear position. An important consideration here is the need to make absolutely sure that in this struggle we do not lose our powerful weapon—our press. If we are careful and make sure we hold onto our press, we will have nothing to worry about.

The party convention that preceded the workers' congress was a surprise attack.[23] I played a role there, since as party secretary I was able to throw my weight into the balance. At this congress the right wing launched an attack. With help from the center they managed to relocate the headquarters from Zurich to Bern. I declared that I would oppose any attempt to transfer the headquarters from the radicals in charge in Zurich to the Bern comrades, for that would mean centrist politics. Comrade Grimm condescended at this congress to allow himself to be elected to the leadership. This former Zimmerwald president was not elected chairman, but he was ready to serve under a social-patriotic chairman, who so proudly declared in parliament: "I am not a Bolshevik, nor even a Zimmerwaldist!"

These comrades helped to elect this outspoken opportunist as chairman, and thereby committed a vile act against our wing and contributed to discrediting themselves in the eyes of the masses. Relocating the headquarters did not make as much difference as had been hoped, because a subsequent party congress unseated the chairman and proved that two-thirds of the comrades stood with the far left.

The idea of sending a delegation to the social-patriotic conference in Bern was rejected. The results of the vote illustrate this graphically: 198 votes for and 154 against my resolution, which opposed sending a delegation to the conference. Our solidarity with our Russian comrades had been expressed. Everyone from the center and the right voted against the resolution, but in the final vote we were still the majority. In this country, which has been the favorite meeting place of the social-patriots, the resolution caused a huge sensation.

LENIN: Comrade Zinoviev, representing Russia, has the floor.

REPORT ON RUSSIA

GREGORY ZINOVIEV: Comrades, as you will appreciate, I can discuss only a few points chosen from the wealth of material at my disposal. For the first time, we are now able to hold an international conference on *Russian* soil and to present comrades with a vast quantity of information about our movement. We are no longer forced to participate as emigrants, able to present only a feeble echo of the Russian workers' movement.

We could recount many experiences out of our own past similar to what you have heard from Comrade Albert of Germany. His report reminds us of the Kerensky period that we underwent in Russia around August 1917.[24]

Our party, as you know, was the only one that called for proletarian revolution in Russia. All other parties opposed the October revolution, and it was clear that the Communist vanguard of the Russian proletariat had to bear the entire weight of the struggle, not only without any help, but in the face of many obstacles.

Before the October revolution our party had about ten thousand members. Now, on the eve of the eighth regular congress of the Communist Party, we number about five hundred thousand members in Russia. That may not be many, but you must understand that we do not simply throw open the gates to all elements that now wish to join our party. Of course, the best elements of the working class and its youth are coming to us, and they are welcome. However, because our party stands at the helm of the state, it is understandable that a considerable number of careerists and wavering petty-bourgeois elements also seek admission. But we have made a firm and clear decision to put obstacles in their way. Our Central Committee even decided to deny voting rights for the party congress to some categories of party members. It is, of course, unusual that we had to take the step of restricting voting rights even within the party, but I emphasize that the whole party approved of this measure because we want the party to be cast in the same mold. We want only genuine communists admitted into our party. This decision on voting rights affects only our half million members—who hold in their hands the entire state apparatus, from top to bottom.

Workers form the core of our party, while intellectuals are very scarce in our ranks. Only recently has this changed. A number of intellectuals are now willing to work with us in the Soviet institutions, but it is difficult for them to gain admission into the party.

The second form of workers' organization in Russia is the trade unions. They developed differently here than in Germany: they played an important revolutionary role in the years 1904–1905, and today they are marching side by side with us in the struggle for socialism. The Russian trade unions now have 3.5 million members, a number confirmed by the last trade union congress.

A large majority of trade union members support our party's positions, and all decisions of the unions are made in the spirit of those positions. Only a very small minority in the unions advocate that the unions be "neutral" and "independent." The majority consider that the unions must work hand in hand with the Communists. A fairly large current demands incorporation of the trade unions into the state; that is, that the unions formally be part of the Soviet government.[25]

In practice, the unions are functioning as a part of our state machinery. On the question of wage scales, strictly speaking the Council of People's Commissars makes the decisions, but in fact the unions have the final word. The same is true of many questions such as workers' insurance and other issues affecting their lives.

The third form of organization is the consumer cooperative societies. We now have twenty-five thousand such cooperatives: in the cities there are 2 million members of workers' cooperatives; in the countryside, 10 million members of rural cooperatives. If you include family members, about 50 million people belong to these organizations.

But the main organizations, as everyone knows, are our soviets. It is somewhat difficult to say how many people—workers and peasants—are organized in the soviets. One thing is certain: after we had drawn up our Soviet constitution, we saw that the right to vote could gradually be broadened to include even some middle layers. That is what the elections to the Petrograd Soviet indicated, for example. In Petrograd there are approximately 650,000 eligible voters. More than two-thirds of them voted, and more than nine-tenths of the population have the right to vote. I believe that the situation in Petrograd is more or less typical of all of our cities, and that more than 100 million people in our Soviet republic have the right to vote and exercise it.[26]

In the soviets, of course, ordinary workers carry the entire burden. This fact is significant for comrades in other countries as well. Once we too were intimidated, and even the workers themselves believed we could not carry out such a complex task by ourselves. Even today we still make many mistakes, but the Russian working class, which of course does not have the highest cultural level in the world, has shown that when it has political power in its hands and an organized party to lead it, it can accomplish these complex tasks.

Until recently, our party was primarily a party of the urban proletariat. That is understandable, since its first members came from the factories, and since it was born in the workers' districts. Now our party is becoming a party of the toiling masses in both the city and the countryside. We have not worked in the rural areas as long as in the cities, nor perhaps as intensively. But we can report that a year's work there has attracted many new forces to our Communist Party, and we have supplanted all other parties. The Communist Party enjoys widespread and steadily growing popularity in the countryside. Rural youth, army veterans, and urban workers (mainly from Petrograd and Moscow) have all contributed greatly to this work. The Petrograd workers have been particularly outstanding. In the past year, 280,000 workers left Petrograd for the front and the countryside. Of course, the departure of the Russian workers' best battalions was bad for Petrograd, but it was a good thing for our revolution that they left and continued their productive work in the rural areas. In the last few months the communist revolution has permeated the countryside. Now even the poorest Russian peasant is experiencing his October revolution, and from this source will flow a great many new forces for the communist revolution.

Our party and our proletariat are the first to be able to utilize the state to propagandize for communism. And we have made good use of it. Our work here has just begun, and although much has been done, much remains to be done. Our party has thirty-five newspapers. In Russia more than one hundred soviets publish newspapers for the peasants and soldiers; that is genuine freedom of the press. In the villages we are now in a position to publish newspapers for the peasants that are for the most part written by peasants themselves. That is true freedom of the press, the kind the working class needs.

The circulation of our newspapers is rather large. *Izvestia,* the central organ of the Soviet government, has a circulation of 400,000. *Krasnaya Gazeta,* published in Petrograd, has a circulation of 280,000, which would be increased except for the paper shortage. *Pravda,* the central organ of our party, has a circulation of 150,000, and it could be more. We have founded many proletarian and peasant universities, which are doing very successful work and are drawing many educational workers to the countryside to work in the interests of communism. Our soviets in the big cities have organized large publishing houses. The Petrograd Soviet's publishing house, for example, printed 11.5 million pamphlets and books last year; our Central Publishing House in Moscow published even more.

The People's Commissariat of Education deserves special attention in this respect. It is devoting some of its resources to communist propaganda, and our party is now calling on the commissariat to organize its work from top to bottom on a communist basis. Here are just a few figures. During 1917 the expenses of the Ministry of Public Education totaled 300,000 rubles; during 1918, three billion; and for the first *half* of 1919 four billion are budgeted. From this you can see the scope of what the commissariat must do. You have also been able to follow in the French and German bourgeois press how even many bourgeois authorities must acknowledge the astonishing work accomplished by the Soviet government in this area.

Economic conditions here have been the subject of considerable discussion abroad. Kautsky spoke of the "socialism of poverty" in Russia. The country is indeed poor. When we took it over, it was bleeding from every pore. We faced a truly difficult situation, and still do. But in one year we achieved something: we have the economic institutions in our hands; we have a system that is functioning more or less satisfactorily, and although it has to be perfected, at least it works. For next year ten billion rubles have been budgeted for the work of the Supreme People's Economic Council and other economic institutions. You can see from this figure how great the work is and how much there is to do.

As regards housing, we have not achieved all of our goals, but we have taken important initial steps. In the large cities, especially Petrograd and Moscow, but also a number of others, the housing question is on the road to solution. The working class, the core of the proletariat, considers that we have done what we could on this; we could immediately carry out many improvements that were meaningful, if not fundamental. We expropriated the bourgeois residences and partly distributed them; we confiscated the most needed furniture and distributed it among the working class. Entire streets, formerly bourgeois neighborhoods, are now proletarian, communist, working-class neighborhoods, because communist workers have moved in—whole factory work forces and so on.

I will not speak on the Red Army as that is a topic in itself. Comrades more knowledgeable in military matters, perhaps Comrade Trotsky, can say a few words on that.

We have also viewed it as not only our highest duty but also an honor and privilege to give as much material aid as possible to the workers' movement of other countries. Thus, the bourgeoisie of all countries does not rage against us without reason. We have fulfilled our obligations in this respect and will continue to view it as our duty to aid every communist workers' movement.

Our party has never before been so united as it is today, on the eve of its eighth party congress. Some comrades left the party at the beginning of the revolution, and we had especially heated discussions during the Brest-Litovsk peace negotiations. The main argument then was that by signing the Brest-Litovsk peace treaty we might weaken the position of the German comrades internationally.[27] That was also our primary consideration. More than anything else, we feared taking a false step that could make the situation more difficult for the workers in Germany or other countries. Fortunately, that did not happen. The working class of every country understood us. I hope that the measures we took made the position of the working class easier rather than more difficult. If we ever have to deal with this sort of problem again—for example, if we have to sign a peace treaty with the Entente—I believe our party would unanimously approve the decision of the Central Committee and the Soviet government. Furthermore, the French, British, and American workers will understand what we are doing and will completely solidarize with us.

It is accurate to say that our working class yearns for international ties. That was true earlier. At the beginning of the revolution, when the Mensheviks were at the helm, the Moscow and Petrograd workers were happy to see even such gentlemen as Albert Thomas, Henderson, and the like.[28] When they came to Petrograd to hobnob with Tsereteli, Kerensky, and others, our working class took them seriously at first. Now our working class understands that they are pseudosocialists, and the least sophisticated worker in Petrograd and Moscow is thoroughly acquainted with the three main currents in the international movement.

Now I would like to say a few words about the so-called Red Terror. I know from accounts by supporters of our party in other countries that this is the main argument used against us and that occasionally we do not enjoy the wholehearted solidarity of some on this point. Now that we have lived through the experiences in Germany, seen that the civil war there is much more acute than it is here, and after the murders of Liebknecht and Luxemburg, I believe that even those of our friends who have lived too long under peaceful conditions and do not understand everything that happened in Russia will be able to appreciate why we have to wield the sharp weapon of Red Terror. Impartial socialist historians will fault us not for applying too much terror but for being far too forgiving at times. It is a fact that we freed nearly all the ministers of Kerensky's government. Many fled and now lead the struggle against us. We had in our hands Konovalov, Maklakov, and all the gentlemen in Paris who currently are fighting us. We let them all go. We released the former minister of war, General Verkhovsky. Previously opposed to us, within the last few days he has offered to work with us. And even Alexinsky, who in July 1917 was the main organizer of the whole Dreyfus affair against Comrades Lenin, Trotsky, Zinoviev, and others,[29] was released by the Moscow Soviet and is now working in Moscow. When you get to know the concrete circumstances, you find that the Red Terror our party used was historically necessary.

You all know that the parties calling themselves socialist that opposed us and led the struggle against us became bankrupt and have dwindled to a tiny minority. The right-wing Socialist Revolutionaries, who were on the presiding committee of the Constituent Assembly, capitulated to our party.[30] I mentioned the results of the recent elections in Petrograd. Out of 150 delegates there are eight Left Socialist Revolutionaries, five or six from the right, and approximately ten Mensheviks. All the rest are Communists or candidates for membership in the Communist Party and are implementing its platform. The elections were conducted mostly by secret ballot, and no power in the world could have prevented the workers at, say, the Putilov factory from voting for members of other parties if they had wanted to. But they did not.

Because of the acute shortage of food, especially of bread, there are some dissatisfied elements within the working class. But in the elections, which involve expressing where their confidence lies, the core of the working class, its great majority, placed their total confidence in our party. That is the best testimony that we have fulfilled our duty to Russia despite the great difficulties. We endeavored from the start to understand all the lessons of the Paris Commune;[31] we made it our business to understand what the Paris workers taught the world in 1871 and to apply it to the new situation. Of course, a rather large share of the credit for our accomplishments must go to the pioneers of the French working class.

Comrades, it may be that we are at a crossroads and can now breathe somewhat more easily. We believe the odds are good that the bourgeoisie of the Entente will not and cannot attack us. An indication of this is Lloyd George's statement to the bourgeois parties.[32] He said that if they had known how many soldiers would be needed to defeat Russia, they probably would not have prosecuted the war so confidently. He whispers in their ears that the number required would amount to a million or more. It is not easy to find that many White Guards, and it will be difficult to use workers against our party. Once we were surrounded by enemies. But the vanguard of Russia's Communists believed that the majority of the workers of the world would be with us. And we have now already seen that the most advanced working-class forces in all countries consider it an honor to build Communist organizations and follow in our footsteps.

Comrades, all of our work is based on the legacy of the heroic Paris Commune of 1871. Our great teacher, Karl Marx, taught us to love the Commune. Its heritage is sacred to us. We take great pride in bringing that legacy to life and making our contribution to the international working class's victory over the bourgeoisie.

(A motion by Platten to adjourn the session for three-quarters of an hour is carried. When the session resumes, Lenin recognizes Sirola to deliver a report on Finland.)

REPORT ON FINLAND

YRJÖ SIROLA: Comrades, it has now been a year since the Finnish proletariat fought the bourgeoisie's bands of mass murderers in life-and-death combat.[33] Courageously, Finnish workers rose up to defend their freedom and their lives and to beat back the reactionary White Guard attack. Although not adequately prepared politically or militarily for such a struggle, the workers held their ground at the front for three months, while at the same time doing a great deal behind the lines to organize social and economic life.

That first revolution by the Finnish proletariat was defeated. The willingness to sacrifice and courage of the comrades, men and women, who fought in the Red Guard and the invaluable aid given by our Russian comrades were not enough to repel the onslaught launched by the international gangs of White Guards led by Finnish, Swedish, German, and Russian officers. At the end of April, German imperialism tipped the balance by committing regular army troops to the fight. The White Guards were then able to block the plan to evacuate the revolution's best surviving forces to Russia. The White tyranny's barbaric thirst for revenge is known the world over. For months these butchers raged against proletarian men, women, and children. Along with Finnish proletarians, hundreds of Russian comrades and Red Guard instructors were shot down. According to recent reports in Finnish newspapers, more than 13,000 were massacred in all; additional reports are still appearing of the execution of 100, 300, or more proletarians in this or that locality. Another 15,500 have perished of starvation, illness, and deprivation in concentration camps.

These bloody facts are not at all exaggerated; they should serve as a warning to all workers who have illusions about peacefully coexisting with the bourgeoisie on a democratic basis. We hope the comrades of the Third International will impress the lessons of the Finnish experience upon workers in their own countries. These lessons can be briefly summarized: The proletariat must carefully define its principled position as quickly as possible. It must not delay in breaking from elements and groups who either have already shown themselves to be betrayers of the workers or who may desert them at the decisive moment. The question of democracy versus dictatorship cannot be glossed over; the existence of a revolutionary situation must be clearly spelled out. The proletariat must not give the enemy any chance to seize the initiative; rather it must go on the attack, insofar as possible at a time of its own choosing, and smash the bourgeoisie's instrument of power, the state machine.

For too long, we also were imbued with the ideology of a "united" workers' movement.[34] Only after the revolution did the split become unavoidable. There was a sharp polarization. The bourgeois dictatorship in Finland gave the extreme right wing of the old Social Democracy "freedom" of organization and of the press for the express purpose of pacifying the workers. These traitors did their best to defeat the revolution the Finnish proletariat had made the previous year and to propagandize for a peaceful workers' movement functioning through parliament, trade unions, and cooperatives. They gained a hearing in a few petty-bourgeois circles, and will receive a number of votes in the political elections, both now and in the future. But the admonitions of those bourgeois lackeys are alien to the masses, who are tormented by prison, hunger, and poverty. The workers' memories of the White Terror are still fresh, and they can see the living example of proletarian dictatorship in Russia. The revolutionary proletariat of Finland has nothing in common with these comrades of the Scheidemanns and Branting, who are fraternizing in Bern with every social traitor in the world. This proletariat is now more revolutionary than ever. Evidence that it hails the founding of the Communist Party is amply provided by even the bourgeois papers. There is no lack of evidence of that.

The Finnish Communist Party was founded at a Moscow congress at the end of August by exiles. But we are living in a completely new type of exile: one in a socialist country. We, who were radicals and left radicals, acquired our communist beliefs by studying our own revolutionary experiences, by getting to know the theoretical work of the Russian comrades, and particularly through the living example of the communist organizational work being carried out here on Russian soil. In an open letter from our party to Comrade Lenin, we reported on this and outlined our experiences more fully.

From Petrograd, where our Central Committee works, we have conducted agitation among the Finnish workers and peasants living in Russia. We have founded some twenty-five Communist organizations in Russia, published over forty pamphlets, and launched a daily paper and two magazines, one in Finnish and one in Swedish. Joint work with the Russian comrades has been organized in the party, in the Soviet institutions, and in the economic and cultural spheres. Military preparations are, of course, important. Our military organization provides further training for Finnish soldiers in the Red Army. Some fifteen translations of books for the army have been published.

In Finland many secret Communist organizations are at work. They distribute literature and periodicals, conduct propaganda, and, despite prison, torture, and death, are doing preparatory work for insurrection. Our conference at the end of January, attended by delegates from Finland, adopted several resolutions on the immediate tasks facing the Finnish revolution.[35]

We are firmly convinced that soon we will be fighting beside our comrades in Finland. This conviction is based not only on our ardent desire, but on an analysis of the situation in Finland. The effects of overripe, rotting imperialist capitalism are visible even in little Finland. The Finnish bourgeoisie has fashioned its little world in its own image. Decay and demoralization are the rule. Speculation and fraud are flourishing. Cases of starvation are becoming ever more common. The state budget has risen from 100 million to well over a billion, and taxes and the national debt have gone up accordingly. There is a widespread system of bribery, and culture has been prostituted. They created an army complete with a shabbily pretentious officer corps and a dictator living in regal splendor. Reaction is triumphant everywhere. As an example of the generalized state of decay, I would point out that while the patriots indulge in dreams of conquest, the Swedish-speaking population of the Aaland [Ahvenanmaa] Islands and other localities is building a separatist movement. This pretty picture is rounded out, of course, by the activity of the police, along with the violence of the bourgeois White Guards, the persecution of revolutionaries, massive house-to-house searches, arrests, torture modeled on the Spanish Inquisition, the shooting of prisoners "suspected" of planning to escape, and so forth.

Such a system cannot survive for long. All it takes is a spark, and the revolutionary tensions will explode. That event will be connected to developments in the international situation. To be sure, ever since their German adventure ended in an utter fiasco,[36] the Finnish bourgeoisie is disposed to friendly relations with the Entente, and the latter expect their new servant to give good service in world imperialism's struggle against Bolshevism. That is clear from the Finnish expedition against Estonia and by the organization of armed, counterrevolutionary Russian groups in Finland, willing to fight even against Finnish independence.

Clearly the whole adventure will come crashing down, and that will be the signal for struggle. This time it will follow the example set by our loyal and courageous precursors, the Russian proletariat. It will result in the establishment of the iron dictatorship of the proletariat. We put our trust in the solidarity of the world proletariat with the international Soviet republic of Russia. The Finnish proletariat, too, will fight under the banner of the Communist, Third International and the worldwide federation of workers' soviet republics.

LENIN: Comrade Stang, representing Norway, has the floor.

REPORT ON NORWAY

EMIL STANG: The Norwegian Labor Party is the only socialist party in Norway and therefore includes today among its members adherents of all socialist currents. It is a legal party and works in parliament; however, it has always considered itself a revolutionary Social Democratic party.

In the winter of 1916–17 we had very great food and fuel problems in Norway, and the workers' mood was quite revolutionary. The Central Executive Committee of the party, together with the trade unions, declared that if the government did not meet the workers' demands, the workers would use more forceful methods of struggle against the state and that a congress of the party and the union organizations would be convened immediately. Neither the congress nor the more forceful methods materialized, which greatly outraged the workers.

During the winter of 1917–18 the first workers' and soldiers' councils were formed, and in the spring of 1918 they held their congress.[37] In its proclamation the congress of workers' councils declared that the councils should immediately implement certain demands such as the eight-hour day and that they intended to take over the entire administration of Norway.

Meanwhile, the various party publications and workers' associations had discussed the party's position very intensively. The Central Executive Committee and the party's main publication, edited by Vidnes, were decidedly against the workers' and soldiers' councils, against Bolshevism, and against the revolutionary tendencies in general. They wanted not a dictatorship of the proletariat, but rather a further development of democracy. They were fought by the great majority of the various local party publications.

At the Easter 1918 party conference the revolutionary minority of the central committee proposed that the party declare itself a revolutionary party. However, the party would primarily do parliamentary work, while at the same time enthusiastically greeting the workers' and soldiers' councils. The conference adopted this proposal by a vote of 159 to 126.[38] The party, which formerly belonged to the [Second] International, also decided to join the Zimmerwald International. Since the right wing did not want to participate in the Central Executive Committee, the entire committee was made up of members of the left wing. Under the new leadership, the central party organ, *Social-Demokraten,* sided decisively with Russian Bolshevism, the Spartacus League, and the other left Social Democratic parties.

As you can see, the party is a legal, parliamentary party that at the same time also wants to employ revolutionary methods of struggle. Even though it has recognized the workers' and soldiers' councils as revolutionary organs of struggle, it has not come out against democratic parliamentarism and for a council system. However, the constitutional question is being discussed in all the newspapers and workers' associations with great interest.

The trade union organizations used to be entirely in the hands of the right wing, and all important proposals of the so-called union opposition were rejected by a large majority at the autumn 1917 union congress. But the mood in the union organizations as well shifted considerably, and in 1918 the Laborers Union, a large federation of mine, construction, and other workers,[39] and also the Iron and Metalworkers' Association went over to the left wing.

In Norway, as elsewhere, the workers' revolutionary mood was heightened after the German revolution. Both wings of the party were then able to join together in common revolutionary work. The central executive committees of the party and the trade unions are now in agreement first, to work with all available means to implement the Social Democratic program; second, to prepare the way for the formation of workers' councils but not to set them up yet; and third, to organize soldiers' councils at once as organs of agitation in the army.

As you can see, it is a question of the greatest significance for the Norwegian Labor Party whether or not it should completely abandon the democratic perspective and declare itself for the dictatorship of the proletariat based on the workers' council system. Personally, I am convinced that the party, influenced by the development of the world revolution, will reach a clear position on this question.

However, the party's Central Executive Committee has not yet had the opportunity to adopt a position on this question, just as it did not see the invitation to this congress prior to my departure from Christiania [Oslo]. For that reason, without consultation with my colleagues in the Central Executive Committee, I cannot take a position on the new Communist International. However, I am very eager to participate in the preparatory work and to present the results of our work to the Norwegian Labor Party. I hope that the Norwegian Labor Party as well, which has developed so far in a revolutionary direction, will be able to make an effective contribution to the victory of the international revolution.

LENIN: Comrade Reinstein, representing the American Socialist Labor Party, has the floor.

REPORT ON THE UNITED STATES

BORIS REINSTEIN: Comrades, because it will soon be nearly two years since I left America to live here, I, unlike some other comrades, am not in a position to bring you new information about the movement in America. Consequently, I cannot tell you much on current conditions in the United States. However, I do believe I can say that the movement in America has developed very rapidly to the left, especially since the entry of the United States into the World War.

Even before the war America was looked upon, and rightly so, as the classic land of bourgeois democracy and at the same time of financial and industrial autocracy. This is the country where democracy is most mature and fully developed. I am sure I can say without exaggeration that as far as the objective basis for a real socialist revolution is concerned, America is the country that is most ripe.

Here I want to present a few more facts that will explain why I can say that despite the apparent backwardness of the workers' movement in general, as far as the number of socialist votes is concerned, the United States of America is at least as ripe for the world socialist revolution as are the European countries, if not more so. In the first place, a public commission appointed by President Wilson and made up of nonsocialists and antisocialists determined that the impoverishment of the American people has progressed so rapidly in the last few decades that nearly 37 percent of the peasantry, America's farmers, who until recently could lead an independent existence, now no longer own their own land and can eke out their living only as tenant farmers. Of the remaining two-thirds, approximately half, although the nominal owners of their farms, have mortgaged them to the banks. The farmers, in short, that backbone of the middle class, have been very rapidly pauperized and ruined in the last few years.

As another commission learned, the entire population has been so rapidly proletarianized that, a few years before the war, there were thirty-two and a half million men, women, and children in America over the age of fifteen who depended upon wages or salaries for their sustenance. If we add to that the small children and the citizens who are too old and "worn out"—in many branches of industry in America persons over the age of forty are no longer considered good objects of exploitation—you will see that these thirty-two and a half million people who are dependent upon wages represent almost two-thirds of the total population of the country. That is the picture of modern-day social conditions in America.

At the same time that this process of proletarianization of the masses was going on, a process of concentration of capital was developing at the opposite pole, the likes of which cannot be observed in any other country. A few years before the war one economist reported that the capital holdings not of the entire American capitalist class but of the Morgan Bank alone, which is probably the largest bank in the world today, already amounted to more than $527 million in stocks and bonds. But that was back in 1892 when old Morgan was not yet an old man. Since then this Morgan Bank capital has absorbed property in land, industry, and commerce as a sponge soaks up water. By 1912 the sum of the capital controlled by the Morgan Bank no longer came to $527 million, but to more than $26 billion.

That is why I say that America is at one and the same time the classic land of bourgeois democracy and also of financial and industrial autocracy. This process of concentration of capital in the hands of a few has gone so far in America that you really can say without exaggeration that a handful of billionaires have the power to employ hundreds of thousands or even millions of workers or to let them starve, as they please. They have the lives of vast armies of wage workers in their power.

These are the facts on which we may base the conclusion that social conditions in America are a veritable powder keg for capitalist rule. And you need not be too much of an optimist to say that in America even before this war, any major strike, industrial crisis, or wave of unemployment could touch off a social explosion. I would only stress here that the American capitalist class was practical and shrewd enough to create for itself a useful and efficient lightning rod by developing a large antisocialist union organization under the leadership of Gompers.

It is not correct to consider Gompers the American Scheidemann. It is true that Scheidemann is a social patriot and not really a socialist, but he did do something for socialism in his past. Gompers, by contrast, is more like an American Zubatov. He was and remains a determined opponent of the socialist perspective and of socialist goals. And yet he passes for a representative of a large workers' organization, the American Federation of Labor, which is founded upon the myth of harmony between capital and labor and which cripples the power of the working class and thus prevents it from successfully fighting back against capitalism in America.

The other lightning rod, which worked like chloroform on the proletariat, was the opportunist character of the most influential leaders of the American Socialist Party. Like their counterparts in other countries, they have seen to it that the Socialist movement in America stayed on an opportunist course and was not led in a genuinely revolutionary Marxist manner. These two factors sufficed during the past few decades to prevent the proletariat in America from rallying in a truly revolutionary struggle.

Fortunately, the facts and the recent evolution of the Socialist movement and workers' movement as a whole now permit us to say with confidence that these lightning rods of the capitalist system are quite rapidly losing their power and effectiveness. There has been a powerful ferment in the American trade unions in recent years despite all the efforts of antisocialist trade union leaders influenced by the capitalists and the clergy. In 1916 we experienced one of the most heartening examples of this ferment and swing to the left. Four of the largest railroad workers' organizations—the brotherhoods of locomotive engineers, firemen, conductors, and trainmen—decided to jointly demand the eight-hour day for railroad workers. Before that time, organized into separate brotherhoods, they had been unwilling to coordinate their struggles. They also took another step: they staunchly and bluntly refused to let their struggle be settled through arbitration. They insisted that their demands be met immediately; otherwise they would paralyze transportation. They thereby forced the government to set everything else aside, and for several days the entire governmental apparatus in Washington worked day and night to head off the threatened strike. The pressure of the four railway brotherhoods forced the government to enact the eight-hour day for railroad workers immediately. What happened then showed just how cleverly the whole bourgeois-democratic governmental apparatus in America is constructed. After the eight-hour day became law, they contrived to have the United States Supreme Court decide whether or not the law was constitutional. The court ruled that it was indeed constitutional, but it added that in the future railroad workers would no longer have the right to strike and disrupt transportation. In other words, they took away the right to strike. This case illustrates how in the developed capitalist countries bourgeois "democracy" is rendered not only illusory but downright detrimental to the workers. On the other hand, the uncompromising methods of struggle used by these four large rail workers' organizations, which until then had been very "moderate and reasonable," showed that even within the conservative trade unions a new mood is asserting itself and that these unions will increasingly resort to revolutionary weapons in their struggles. What is still lacking, however, is practical reorganization of the workers' movement, embracing both their political and their trade union organizations. The job of practical reorganization was given a boost when the American government in turn plunged its country into the war.

The growing influence of different revolutionary socialists in America is very refreshing indeed. It was evident that the war was unpopular from the day it was declared. The masses showed no enthusiasm for it. To be sure, the capitalist press did everything it could to rekindle patriotism, but with a few exceptions the factory proletariat showed no enthusiasm. Furthermore, as the war became more unpopular, many of the previously very influential unions lost popularity. In the last eighteen or twenty months we have seen a considerable shift to the left in the American socialist workers' movement. The organizations belonging to the IWW, the Industrial Workers of the World, which a few years ago still had a strong anarcho-syndicalist orientation and were heavily influenced by the anarchists, became somewhat more rational and less anarchistic. They also launched an energetic struggle against the war, militarism, social patriotism, and the capitalist wage system in general. There was also a noticeable swing to the left inside the Socialist Party, which only three years earlier had still been led almost entirely by social-patriotic or purely parliamentary figures. When the 1917 emergency party convention in St. Louis took place, for the first time a truly revolutionary spirit in the party could be clearly seen. The mood was so revolutionary that many former leaders were either thrown overboard or were backed against the wall and deprived of their influence. Leaders of the Hillquit type were obliged to strike a revolutionary pose in order to avoid losing their influence.[40] They were shrewd enough to see the need for this and react accordingly. Many others did not do so and lost out. The bulk of the party's real leaders from the ranks exhibited a much bolder spirit and character, at least on the war question, and the party has hewed to this revolutionary position until the present. Distinct organized tendencies developed inside the party. Debs, one of the most popular agitators in America, won more and more influence in the Socialist Party. As for the Socialist Labor Party, from the first day of the war until today it has firmly based its program and tactics on Marxist doctrine.

A process is under way in America today in both trade union and political organizations that gives us every reason to anticipate a transformation there soon through which the separate revolutionary forces in the Socialist parties will finally fuse, making a common stand against those who have acted as lightning rods protecting capitalist democracy. Then we will be able to say that when the hour strikes to extend the world socialist revolution, the American proletariat will be at its post, ready to carry out its duty.

In this battle between the world proletariat and world capitalism, I am convinced that the American proletariat will be as decisive for the victory of the world proletariat as American capital was in this imperialist war against the Central European powers. There can be no doubt that the Russian revolution has exerted an enormous influence upon the proletarian masses in America. Nor can there be any doubt that the Soviet government, and the Bolsheviks in particular, are gaining in popularity every day among the rapidly awakening masses. I maintain therefore that the American proletariat has already had a very significant impact upon the American government. If Wilson has changed his tune in the last few months and assumed a different posture toward the Russian revolution and government, that is most definitely due fundamentally to pressure from below, the pressure of the awakening proletarian masses of America.[41]

I would like to say in closing that the step which we are taking here will lay the cornerstone for the Third, the Communist and Soviet International. There can be no doubt that our laying this cornerstone will be hailed and unanimously approved not only by the members of my party; it will also be cheered by large masses, numbering in the millions. We may rest assured that in the not too distant future, a large number of American proletarians will join the struggle under our banner, the banner of the Third, the Communist International.

LENIN: Comrade Rudnyánszky, the delegate from the Communist Party of Hungary, has the floor.

REPORT ON HUNGARY

Endre Rudnyánszky reads the following report: Since the delegates sent from Hungary by the Communist Party were detained on their way here and consequently cannot take part in the congress, the following report on the development of the Communist movement in Hungary is based on reports the party bureau here received from Hungary before February 15.

The Communist Party of Hungary—composed of Communists returning from Russia, the most radical left-wing forces, and a small group of left-radical intellectuals—quit the Social Democratic Party at the end of November.[42] The metalworkers provided the Communists' first mass base. When the Communist Party was founded, conditions were favorable for a revolutionary proletarian movement.

Although Hungary was proclaimed a republic on November 16, the real power remained in the hands of the same government that had been appointed by Archduke Joseph.[43] The only difference was that the Prime Minister, Count Károlyi, and his followers designated themselves the "Peoples' Government" and subordinated themselves to the National Council, which had assumed all functions formerly exercised by the parliament. This National Council consisted of Independents, Radicals, and Social Democrats and was supposed to function until the election of a National Assembly with legislative powers.

But the further course of the revolution could be foreseen from the very first weeks. The peasants expected land from the new "Peoples' Government"; the proletariat hoped to be liberated from exploitation; the masses of soldiers, streaming home from the disintegrating army, clamored for jobs and compensation; but the government could not satisfy all of these demands, and the discontent of the masses grew steadily.

At that point, the Communists who had returned from Russia went into action. The Social Democratic Party, which had initially regarded the Communist movement as insignificant, was quickly forced to recognize that the masses were in solidarity not with the governmental Socialists but with the Communists. After the Communists' first rapid successes, the Social Democratic Party tried everything it could to defeat the movement.

The Communists explained to the proletariat that the Social Democracy in alliance with the bourgeoisie could not carry through a genuine revolution. Daily they reiterated that the "revolutionary" Social Democracy was compelled to defend private property and to oppose the interests of the working masses. The Social Democrats, for their part, had only one counterargument at hand, and that was the charge that if the Communists ever got a base in Hungary, it would spell the end of unity for the Hungarian proletariat. The Social Democrats' counteragitation met with very little success, but it gave them the opportunity—with the approval of several union organizations—to persecute the Communist movement ruthlessly.

The Communist movement gained a base primarily among the urban working masses. Whole factories and industries joined its ranks. A vigorous Communist ferment could also be seen among the soldiers, above all in the special forces.

A special feature of the Communist movement among the peasants was that Communist organizations sprang up there quite spontaneously among the poor peasants. After the Social Democrats announced an agrarian reform, peasants—especially those returning home from wartime imprisonment in Russia—began establishing Communist organizations and offered to help the Communist Party. The same phenomena could be observed in the soviets, as well.

In general, the movement for councils in Hungary is weak. Since the urban proletariat is under the influence of both the Social Democrats and the Communists, those few workers' councils that were formed by the leadership of the Social Democratic Party are almost entirely in their hands and serve the Communists only as a battleground.

The Communists have already fought this battle to its conclusion in the soldiers' councils and are the majority in some of them. But the peasants' councils, which of course are not very strong or numerous, are entirely Communist. The growing size and strength of the Communist Party and the Communists' growing influence in the councils permit us to predict that communism will play the decisive role in Hungary as elsewhere.

LENIN: Comrade Kascher, the delegate of the Communist Group of Switzerland, has the floor.

REPORT ON SWITZERLAND (KASCHER)

LEONIE KASCHER: Comrades, in addition to the Socialist Party and the Socialist Youth Organization, there is also a small but determined Communist movement in Switzerland. It originated in and was taught by the Zimmerwald Left, whose ideas circulated among us in Switzerland, as elsewhere.

What we learned from the Zimmerwald Left is to demand mass action, not just in the distant future, but right now—in the present. I must confess that we were unable at that time to acquire either clear principles or a clear program from the Zimmerwald Left. We wanted to draft a clear communist program, but lacked time as well as written material and traditions.

In 1917 Comrade Itschner, together with a few other comrades in Switzerland, launched a newspaper called *Die Forderung* [The challenge], and it began to print very sharp criticisms of the [Social Democratic] party and to propagandize in the working class for communism. In addition, in the summer of 1917 Comrade Herzog founded a soldiers' organization to carry out socialist propaganda among soldiers in the army and to make preparations for the approaching revolutionary movement. The Central Executive Committee of the youth organization and Comrade Platten wanted to use this organization for the time being to improve the soldiers' conditions. The Communists resisted these efforts, and the organization retained its purely revolutionary character, developing very rapidly.

The appearance of the Communists in public, on the streets, coincided with the October revolution. Our leaflets advanced almost all of the programmatic points later put into practice by the Soviet government. Even then, at the beginning of Soviet rule, we took to the masses the call to form workers' councils in Switzerland. As comrades have read, this movement had very serious consequences. There was shooting for two days and two nights.[44] We saw a spectacle in free Switzerland that had been seen in Russia only in 1905—the use of machine guns. The reaction that set in after two days was terrifying: state of siege, mass arrests, house-to-house searches, and so forth. Our newspaper, which we had published under different titles, was suppressed.

What the Communists had achieved was that—under the pressure of the conditions, the inflation, the discontent, and under the influence of the contagious, inspiring movement in Russia—the Swiss working class proclaimed its complete solidarity with the Russian revolution. But a determined program with clear goals was missing. As a result of this experience, a new tendency emerged in the Communist movement, too.

We knew of course that there is but one goal—the conquest of power. The Swiss working class, however, is not content with such general objectives. It seeks a clearly defined slogan. It is practical; it wants to know what it is going into battle for. The masses were concerned first with winning the eight-hour day and second with inflation and the unsatisfactory economic conditions. We formulated the slogan "Seize the food supplies; distribute them under workers' control, not according to wealth, but according to need." These two slogans seemed to us to be suited to the Swiss workers, decisive, and different from others that had been put forward. They bore a socialist stamp, especially the second one, and to realize them meant a fight against the capitalist social order.

This positive work was continued in 1918. In this period sentiment for communism also emerged in the trade unions. The Swiss unions are no different from unions in other capitalist countries. In the metalworkers union the Communist comrades formed a special group, whose program had as its main point the formation of workers' councils.

In the summer of 1918 a congress of all Communist groups and soldiers' organizations took place in Olten with twenty-six delegates representing thirteen Swiss towns. This congress was needed because we kept hearing from all sides that it was finally time to break from the Social Democratic Party and establish an independent Communist Party. The congress decided not to split from the party yet but to function as an opposition within it. The influence of the party leaders and of the two tendencies was rather significant. The most important thing was, as before, to place the main emphasis on the formation of workers' councils.

We set about founding workers' councils with redoubled energy. This we counterposed to another project that was being advanced in the working class, namely, uniting the party and the unions in a common committee, a slogan that originated in the party's left wing. We foresaw the wretched collapse of the Olten committee, and we fought against the committee from the first day. A significant section of the working class stood with us. It was then that we declared that the time for parliamentarism was over and that nothing more could be expected from this bourgeois institution. At that time we lost any further opportunity to collaborate on the party press. Even announcements of meetings were no longer accepted by *Das Volksrecht* [The people's justice], and we had to distribute leaflets personally in the factories. The soldiers' organizations were persecuted, too. We had to work clandestinely; we were spied upon.

The Communist groups felt mounting pressure to carry out the split. Then a moment arrived when the split actually became necessary. That was in October 1918, after the bank employees' strike in Zurich.[45] The solid sympathy strike by the Zurich workers was certainly not aimed solely at corralling the few outstanding—or shall we say tardy—signatures from bank directors. Rather, it was an elemental release of the tension that had prevailed in Zurich for months and that had fueled the movement for a cantonwide strike for the eight-hour day.

However, for the Zurich Workers' Union and the strike leaders—Comrades Platten and Küng—the movement was a vehicle to bring the bank employees into that organization. In this they failed completely, since the bank employees did not take part in the general strike. The outraged, aroused masses unanimously endorsed Comrade Herzog's proposal to continue the strike for the slogan of the eight-hour day. However, because of sharp opposition from a meeting of delegates and from the Workers' Union, the strike stopped the following day. This separate action by the *Forderung* supporters was publicly condemned, Comrade Herzog and others were expelled from the party, and the groups were sharply rebuked.

This stand by the party authorities showed that further collaboration with them was no longer possible. A large public meeting was held, which resolved to found a Communist Party. Mass arrests followed soon after, and the organizations were broken up. From then on it was necessary to work clandestinely.

The general strike grew out of this climate. On its second day we could already see how it was going to end. The strike leaders' instructions to the workers to "remain calm" and the leaders' fearful avoidance of demonstrations and rallies enabled the bourgeoisie and their excellently organized militia calmly to weather the days of the strike. From a purely economic standpoint the strike could not have been effective. Only with a revolutionary approach could the workers have achieved anything, but that is precisely what the leadership and the party, without exception, fearfully avoided. The Olten committee's betrayal was the inevitable outcome of this movement's entire course. Once again, as has so often been the case in Switzerland, the movement's direction was not in the hands of the masses but in those of individual leaders, all of whom saw a short, "calm" general strike as a necessary safety valve.

The betrayal by the strike leadership had an unexpected impact on the public. After the masses learned of it, the cry went up: "We want workers' councils! The Communists are right!" In other words, the masses understood that this betrayal was possible because they had entrusted everything to a few people instead of taking the leadership into their own hands through workers' councils. After this strike, the metalworkers' group got the metalworkers' delegates to form a council. Other branches of industry followed suit, and soon a Zurich workers' council was formed. At first it had to work in secret as it was watched closely by the police. A frightful reaction followed the strike. The government justified the huge military mobilization as a necessary measure against an anticipated Communist armed uprising. In a word, they sought to blame the Communist Party for everything, and therefore it is no surprise that the most terrible reaction was directed at the Communists.

The crafty leaders gave the despondent working class yet another opportunity to vent their outrage in a large congress of labor. We demanded abolition of the Olten committee and all other committees; immediate election throughout Switzerland of delegates to workers' councils; establishment of soldiers' councils (they had already been formed in the soldiers' organizations during the general strike); arming of the workers; and above all, calling of a revolutionary, armed general strike in the near future to demand the eight-hour day and workers' control of production and distribution. Moreover, we called for a different peasant policy than the one that had been followed up until then.

Our slogans and demands were well received among the workers; the manifesto was distributed by the thousands and touched off a lively discussion in the working class. The bourgeois press raged, writing whole columns on the manifesto; the last of the comrades were arrested and accused of high treason; and more troops were mobilized. But the party press and top leadership bodies continued their head-in-the-sand policies and remained silent on the burning questions of the day.

The workers' council adopted the Communist program as its platform, and the metalworkers' group made a motion to establish workers' councils. But after the defeat of a motion by the party left wing (Comrades Platten and Rüegg) to elect a new committee, the motion by the metalworkers' group was not even put to a vote. At a metalworkers' congress that was convoked expressly for the purpose, the group was reprimanded for founding the workers' council and for their separatist leanings, and the delegates to the workers' councils were threatened with expulsion from the union for "breaking the rules."

The movement of the soldiers' councils developed too, and progress was made in arming the soldiers and workers.

In conclusion a few words should be devoted to our relationship to the party left wing. Recently, these comrades have changed their minds on the question of arming the workers and soldiers and on antiparliamentarism and have come to support these concepts. In the realm of theory, the Communist program of the Russian party has been fully acknowledged. In practice, too, the comrades of the left wing have defended the Bolsheviks and the policies of the Russians very vigorously in press and propaganda.

The left wing behaved no differently toward us than did the rest of the party. Their swing to the left, however, justifies the hope that they will leave the party altogether and pursue a purely Communist policy for Switzerland as well. Then and only then would their unification with the existing Communists be possible, and our long efforts and struggles would result in a strong, large Communist Party of Switzerland.

(*Albert proposes hearing the supplementary report on the Russian Communist Party, especially on the Red Army. The proposal is adopted with loud applause.*)

REPORT ON THE RED ARMY

LEON TROTSKY *(Russia)*: It is clear from Comrade Albert's report that the question of the Red Guard has become the talk of the town in Germany, and if I understood him correctly, the thought of a possible incursion of our Red Guard into the territory of East Prussia is causing Messrs. Ebert and Scheidemann to suffer nightmares and sleepless nights.[46] On this score Comrade Albert may reassure the rulers of Germany: they have nothing to fear. Fortunately or unfortunately—and this is, of course, a matter of taste—affairs have not yet reached that stage. On the other hand, as far as the threat of intervention against us is concerned, we can say boldly that we are in an incomparably better position than the one we were in last year at the time of the conclusion of the Brest-Litovsk Treaty.[47] It is hardly necessary to dwell on that.

At that time we were still wearing diapers so far as the construction of both the Red Army and the Soviet government as a whole was concerned. The Red Army was then actually called the Red Guard, but that name has long since dropped out of circulation among us. The Red Guard was the name given to the first partisan detachments, improvised groups of revolutionary workers who, prompted by revolutionary zeal, spread the proletarian revolution from Petrograd and Moscow throughout the country. This phase lasted until the first clash between the Red Guard and the regular German regiments, when it became quite obvious that such improvised detachments, while able to conquer the Russian counterrevolution, were impotent before a disciplined army and in consequence could not serve as the real shield of the revolutionary socialist republic.

That moment was the turning point in the attitude of the working masses toward the army. From that time on, we began to scrap the old methods of army organization. Under the pressure of events we proceeded to the creation of a healthy army, organized on principles dictated by military science. It is true that our program calls for a "people's militia." But it is impossible even to talk of a people's militia—this demand of political democracy—in a country where the dictatorship of the proletariat is in power, for an army is always intimately bound up with the character of the reigning power. War, as old Clausewitz says, is the continuation of politics by other means. The army is the instrument of war, and it must therefore correspond to politics. Since the government is proletarian, therefore the army, too, must be proletarian in its social composition.

For this reason we introduced a set of restrictions into the army. Since May of last year, we passed from a volunteer army, from the Red Guard, to an army based on compulsory military service, but we accept into our army only workers and peasants who do not exploit the labor of others.

The impossibility of seriously considering a people's militia in Russia becomes even clearer if we take into account that within the boundaries of the former tsarist empire there were and still are to be found simultaneously several armies from classes hostile to us. In the Don region there is even a monarchist army consisting of bourgeois elements and rich Cossacks, commanded by Cossack officers. Furthermore, in the Volga and Ural regions, there was the army of the Constituent Assembly.[48] Now, this army was also designed as a "people's army" and took this name, but it quickly fell apart. The honorable members of the Constituent Assembly were left with empty hands. They found it necessary—entirely against their will—to leave the Volga province and to accept the hospitality of our Soviet government. Admiral Kolchak simply placed the government of the Constituent Assembly under arrest, and the army was converted into a monarchist army.

We thus observe that in a country involved in a civil war, the army can be built only according to class principle; we did exactly that, and we got results.

The formation of a commanding staff presented us with great difficulties. Our primary concern, naturally, was to train Red officers from among the workers and the most-advanced peasant youth. This is a job we tackled from the outset, and here at the doors of this hall you can see not a few Red cadets who will shortly enter the army as Red officers. We have quite a number of them. I do not want to specify the exact figure, since military secrets should always remain military secrets. This number, I repeat, is rather large. But we could not bide our time until Red generals arose out of our Red cadets; the enemy did not give us such a breathing spell. We had to turn to the old commanding personnel and find capable people among these reserves; this too was crowned with success. Naturally, we did not seek our officers amid the glittering salons of military courtesans, but we did find in more modest circles people who were quite capable and who are now helping us in the struggle against their own former colleagues. On the one hand, we have the best and the most honest elements among the old officer corps, whom we surround with sensible Communists in the capacity of commissars; and on the other, the best elements from among the soldiers, workers, and peasants in the lower commanding posts. This is the way we formed our Red commanding staff.

From the moment the Soviet republic arose in our country, it was compelled to wage war, and it is waging war to this very hour. Our front extends more than 8,000 kilometers—from the south to the north, from the east to the west—everywhere the struggle is being waged against us arms in hand, and we must defend ourselves. Why, Kautsky has even accused us of cultivating militarism! But it seems to me that if we wish to preserve the power in the hands of the workers, then we must show them how to use the weapons they themselves forge. We began by disarming the bourgeoisie and by arming the workers. If that is called militarism, so be it. We have created our own socialist militarism, and we shall not renounce it.

Our military position in August of last year was extremely precarious; not only were we caught in a ring of steel, but this ring surrounded Moscow rather tightly. Since then we have widened this ring more and more, and in the course of the last six months the Red Army has reconquered for the Soviet republic an area of not less than 700,000 square kilometers, with a population of some 42,000,000—sixteen provinces with sixteen large cities, the workers of which conducted and continue to conduct an energetic struggle. Even today, if you draw a straight line on the map radiating from Moscow in any direction, you will find everywhere at the front a Russian peasant, a Russian worker standing in this cold night, gun in hand, at the frontiers of the socialist republic and defending it. And I can assure you that the worker-Communists who comprise the hard core of this army feel that they are not only the elite troops of the Russian socialist republic, but also the Red Army of the Third International.

And if we are today given the opportunity to extend hospitality to this socialist conference and in this way repay our western European brothers for their many years of friendship, then we in our turn owe this to the efforts and sacrifices of the Red Army, in which the best comrades from the worker-Communist milieu are serving as ordinary soldiers, as Red officers, or as commissars, that is, as direct representatives of our party, of the Soviet power. In every regiment, in every division, they set the political and moral tone, showing the Red soldiers by their example how to fight and die for socialism. And these are not the empty words of our comrades; accompanying these words are deeds: in this struggle we have lost hundreds and thousands of our best socialist workers. I believe they have fallen not only for the Soviet republic but also for the Third International.

And although it does not even enter our minds at present to attack East Prussia—on the contrary, we would be extremely satisfied if Messrs. Ebert and Scheidemann left us in peace—one thing is nonetheless unquestionable: should the hour strike and our Western brothers call upon us for aid, we shall reply:

"We are here! We have in the meantime become skilled in the use of arms; we are ready to struggle and die for the world revolution!"

(After Trotsky's presentation, Comrade Rutgers describes the enthusiasm with which propaganda for the Red Army of Russia was conducted in workers' circles in America. At meetings, women and children donated jewelry for the benefit of the Red Army.)

LENIN: Comrade Rutgers, the delegate of the Communist Party of Holland, has the floor to give his report.

REPORT ON THE NETHERLANDS

S.J. RUTGERS: In reporting on Holland, I must stress that a formal split between the Second International and the new ideas of the Third International already took place there more than ten years ago.[49]

The revolutionary movement in Holland is a child of the Russian revolution—but born before its time, from the bloody wedding of 1905. At that time we founded our organ, *De Tribune* [The tribune], whose agitation was the reason for our expulsion from the old Social Democratic Workers Party. That is what was then called "freedom of the press." Since then we have always kept in close contact with our Russian comrades. In those days we already hoped that the Russian methods of struggle would be transmitted via Germany to western Europe—a hope reinforced by the huge demonstrations in Berlin.[50] But the party bureaucrats under Kautsky's leadership succeeded in discrediting the tactic of mass action and converting it into a mere defensive tactic. Thus was the road opened not to revolution but to world war. Understandably, the victory of reaction in Germany also affected Holland.

To be sure, the young Social Democratic Party—now called the Communist Party—did not let itself be led astray, but it was unable to become a large mass movement.

On a theoretical and a practical level, however, the Dutch movement has contributed to greater clarity on imperialist relations and future communist policy. The writings and speeches of Lenin, Zinoviev, and Kamenev have become well known to the readers of the *Tribune,* and in turn Dutch comrades such as Roland-Holst, Gorter, Pannekoek, van Ravesteyn, Wijnkoop, and others are already old acquaintances to many Russian comrades.

In Holland itself the young revolutionary party had to wage a hard struggle against the opportunists led by Troelstra, and our chairman, Wijnkoop, was even forcibly ejected from meetings. However, the syndicalist dock workers came to our defense and formed a bodyguard for him of six-foot-tall giants.

Theoretically as well there was steadily increasing agreement between us and the syndicalist forces in the Dutch workers' movement. When the World War broke out, our party, the syndicalists, and an anarchist group formed a revolutionary committee, which came out for immediate demobilization and against the banditry the government was pursuing with its food policy.[51] Gradually our party won great influence over the masses and could try to give a revolutionary direction to the mass actions that broke out as a consequence of hunger and poverty.

As you know, several such mass demonstrations occurred in Holland, during which there were clashes with the troops, causing casualties. At the celebration of the anniversary of the Russian revolution, a women's demonstration was broken up by the police, at which time Comrade Henriette Roland-Holst and others were wounded.

After the outbreak of the first German revolution, there were dead and wounded at demonstrations in Holland.[52] In those days a terrible fear gripped the bourgeoisie. Public buildings were barricaded with sand bags, and at night the army stood by. It seemed at first that even Troelstra's party would join the revolutionary movement, but a hastily convened special congress of the social traitors decided that all the desired improvements could be obtained just as well by peaceful means. That interrupted the movement temporarily.

However, it has now become clear that some army units refused to shoot at the workers, and the army may already be regarded as unreliable for the capitalists. The Communist Party has formed underground soldiers' councils in different army detachments.

Holland is now in a difficult position because it has become entirely a vassal state of Britain. The Dutch bourgeoisie used to place their hopes for continued exploitation of their colonies on Germany.[53] But since Germany has been eliminated as an imperialist power, only one hope remains for the Dutch capitalists: to show such servility toward Britain that John Bull will prefer to use the Dutch exploiters' services in the colonies and let them have a piece of the booty. Of course, from now on, the lion's share of the booty from the Dutch colonies will go to the British capitalists. But I fear the Dutch bourgeoisie is prepared to commit any vile act to get hold of a share. That will lead to a period of severe reaction for Holland. Just as they drove Finland and Poland to attack the Russian proletariat, so they will set Holland against the proletarians of the East. Moreover, Holland will be so dependent on Britain and the Entente that it could become an invasion route into revolutionary Germany.

This gives the Dutch proletariat a very difficult job and our Communist Party is fully aware of the problems we face. We urgently need international support, and we wholeheartedly welcome the first Communist congress. Our best propaganda material is always the factual reports of revolutionary developments in other countries, and for that reason our primary concern is to maintain international ties.

It would also be a good thing for this congress to adopt practical resolutions on the struggle we have to wage in the colonies hand in hand with the brown and yellow proletarians. That is another major task requiring considerable strength. Only if we harness all of our strength can we hope for an early victory.

LENIN: Are there any further supplementary matters to come before the body?

PLATTEN: We wish to submit the following motion: "The International Communist Congress, meeting on March 2, 1919, in Moscow sends greetings to the Red Army." This will show that during our meeting we are mindful of their glorious deeds. (*It is approved with tumultuous enthusiasm.*)[54]

ZINOVIEV: The question has arisen of whether to make any statement at this time to the press about our meeting. A number of comrades have discussed this and decided to treat the sessions as secret for now. In other words, we will make no statements to the press or to individual comrades and will leave it up to the Presiding Committee to determine the proper moment to announce our work.

LENIN: We have just received word that Comrade Rakovsky and the Swedish delegate are on their way. We must now decide at what time the session should begin tomorrow. Are there any proposals? At five o'clock in the evening. But Comrade Stang must depart at seven o'clock. Other proposals? At noon.

GUSTAV KLINGER: I move that the session begin at 5:00 p.m. both because comrades are still arriving and also for purely technical reasons since the bureau must prepare for the session. It would make a difference of only two or three hours in the departure time of the Norwegian comrades. Therefore, five o'clock would be best, especially for the secretariat.

LENIN: I must point out that Comrade Rakovsky will be here for only one day. Therefore, it would be best to begin tomorrow at noon.

TROTSKY: I believe we will be unable to fix the time now. Let us leave it to the bureau to set according to circumstances.

(*This proposal is adopted. The session ends at 12 midnight.*)

SECOND DAY OF SESSIONS
NOON, MARCH 3, 1919

National reports (continued)

PLATTEN: We are scheduled to hear reports from Rakovsky, from the Ukrainian comrade, from France, and possibly from German Austria. These points will take up the morning session.

CREDENTIALS COMMISSION REPORT

GEORGIY CHICHERIN: Our report can be only provisional because, as of yesterday evening, all delegates were not yet present.[55] That is still the case. However, we did have to decide several basic questions. In addition to the credentials of voting delegates, our commission reviewed those of consultative delegates. The following participants will be considered as consultative delegates: those who have ties to their home countries but do not represent them directly; those who came from their home countries but were not officially mandated for this conference; and those who are prominent figures in their movement and therefore have the moral authority to speak for that movement here, although they cannot produce official mandates.

As for voting delegates, the commission reviewed the rather complicated question of apportioning votes and makes the following recommendation to the conference.

Since it is not possible to put the large and small countries on the same level, and since on the other hand it is not possible to take over the excessively complex ranking system devised by the Second International, the Credentials Commission proposes adopting a simplified method. Under this system, it is not the strength of the parties but the importance of the countries that is taken into account. We view the revolutionary parties as the representatives of the revolutionary proletariat in their countries, even in cases where they are at the moment not very large in purely numerical terms. Thus, the votes will be distributed according to the importance of the country.

We propose that three categories be adopted: large, medium-sized, and small countries—the first receiving five votes; the second, three votes; and the third, one vote each. The countries that are counted as large are Germany, Russia, and America. Should a delegate from Italy arrive, Italy will also be considered a large country and receive five votes. The same will apply to France. The following will be considered medium-sized countries and receive three votes: the Ukraine, Finland, Poland, Norway, Sweden, Switzerland, and the fragments of what was formerly Austria-Hungary. At the moment, the last mentioned are represented here only by Hungary. The remaining countries, those that receive one vote each, are Lithuania and Belorussia, which are now unified and have established the Lithuanian-Belorussian Communist Party; Latvia; Estonia; the German colonists' region, which is a separate area; Armenia; and finally, the peoples of the east of Russia: the Tatars, the Bashkirs, the Kirghizes, and the Caucasian Mountain Peoples. Since these Eastern peoples all share certain cultural similarities, inhabit distinct territories, and also have Communist movements in their homelands, they will be viewed collectively as a single country with one vote. The question of the Balkans was left open because Comrade Rakovsky had not arrived as of yesterday.

Thus, there are three countries with five votes each, four countries with three votes each, and six countries with one vote each, making thirteen countries in all. Five countries were still expected; some have arrived in the meantime, and others are still on the way. Yesterday we had twelve countries with consultative votes; we are expecting three more and we hear they are underway. As of yesterday, the following countries with consultative votes were represented: Bohemia, that is, the Czech group residing here in Russia; Bulgaria; the Yugoslav and South Slavonian group, which comprises Serbia, Croatia, and Slavonia; Holland; the French group; the American Socialist Propaganda League; the Swiss Communists; Turkestan; Turkey; Georgia; Azerbaijan; and Persia. We received the credentials for the British group only today. We still expect China and Korea, that is, the emigrant groups living in Russia who represent the Chinese and Korean workers.

Yesterday evening we counted a total of twenty-six delegates with decisive votes representing thirteen countries, and thirteen delegates with consultative votes.

In reviewing the credentials we had to take into account the fact that the conference has convened under highly abnormal circumstances. First there was the necessity of maintaining secrecy, which made it impossible to hold elections or to take any other steps that might have advertised the fact that the conference was going to take place. Second there were the difficulties of the journey. As you know, the Hungarian delegates were arrested on their way here. Other delegates had to expect the same problems, and as a result some were unable to furnish written credentials; thus their mandates had to be verified by the testimony of witnesses. For the parties that function in Russia and the neighboring Soviet republics only the first circumstance was a factor, the need for secrecy. Thus, many can present credentials only from their central leadership bodies. For the peoples of the East, the mandate is from the Central Bureau of Eastern Peoples of Russia. The need for secrecy applies with particular force to the delegates of the western European countries.

Among the delegates listed in the initial program,[56] the Japanese Socialist Group was named, with consultative vote. However, after the commission heard the report by Comrade Rutgers, it no longer seemed possible to keep the Japanese group on the list. Comrade Rutgers represents Holland with a consultative vote. He is not mandated, but he can speak for the party. In addition, he has a consultative vote for the American Socialist Propaganda League. However, since he stopped in Japan only briefly as he was passing through, he can be considered neither a prominent member in that movement nor as a delegate with consultative vote. Consequently, it was necessary to remove the Japanese group from the list. The question of representation from Romania will remain open until the Credentials Commission can consult Comrade Rakovsky.

Those are the results of the work of the Credentials Commission so far. When we have reviewed the remaining credentials, we will present the final list to all delegates here.

LENIN: Does anyone wish to speak on the Credentials Commission report? As there are no speakers, the credentials are approved. We will continue with the reports. Comrade Rakovsky has the floor.

REPORT ON THE BALKAN REVOLUTIONARY SOCIAL DEMOCRATIC FEDERATION

CHRISTIAN RAKOVSKY: On behalf of the Balkan revolutionary federation, I would like to make a few supplementary remarks. The federation was founded in 1915 and includes the Romanian, Serbian, and Greek parties and the Tesnyaki, a part of the Bulgarian party. From the very beginning, even before the Zimmerwald conference, the federation declared its support for the struggle against the war and it has acted accordingly ever since.

The Romanian party has gradually developed into a Communist party and therefore refers to itself as Communist.[57] Conditions there are developing in a way that bodes well for the revolution. Much depends on the advance of the Red Army, and contact with it will undoubtedly encourage a strong revolutionary movement. However, some significant events have already taken place, especially in recent weeks.[58] The soldiers have refused to take part in monarchist rallies, which has led to armed clashes. Even though it is not possible to predict the precise moment at which the revolution will break out, there can be no doubt that conditions in Romania are developing in a distinctly revolutionary direction.

The Bulgarian party, that is, the revolutionary current known as the Tesnyaki, has remained loyal to its internationalist class position since the outbreak of the war. Its agitation and propaganda helped to hasten the defeat of German imperialism. Its influence has been aided by the economic conditions in Bulgaria, and it is growing steadily.

The Serbian party, unfortunately, has abandoned the class position it adopted at the beginning of the war. Everyone remembers its courageous and resolute stand when its delegates refused to vote for war credits and how, at an extremely difficult moment, the Serbian party issued a completely uncompromising statement and was subsequently guided by it. Everyone also remembers Comrade Kaclerović's position at Kienthal.[59] However, both Kaclerović and Popović, the party's official and authoritative representatives, eventually went over to social patriotism, particularly after their sojourn in Stockholm. It is a shame that a party that took such a flawlessly courageous position at the beginning of the war has veered onto a social-patriotic course.

(Iliya Milkić requests the floor to make a correction.)[60]

(Rakovsky reads a number of greetings he has received from participants in the opposition at the Bern conference. These all show a strong left orientation; they show that previously vacillating elements are becoming convinced that a crossroads has been reached. One must either break completely from the Second International or be prepared to be considered an enemy of the working class. No middle ground remains for the hesitant.)

REPORT ON THE UKRAINE

N.A. SKRYPNIK: Speaking here as the representative of the Communist Party of the Ukraine, I must say first of all that I cannot briefly present a detailed picture of my party's situation. This is especially so since we are now waging the struggle arms in hand.[61] In addition, our third party congress is still in session.

Today our party has nearly 30,000 members. I must add that we have always tried as much as possible to restrict the admission to our party of less than fully reliable individuals. Furthermore, because of the extremely difficult conditions of underground work in the parts of the Ukraine that have not yet been liberated, our membership is significantly smaller there than in the liberated areas.

The best indicator of the steady growth in our party's influence are the soviet congresses that were held at both the provincial and district levels. Provincial congresses have already taken place in Kharkov, Poltava, Ekaterinoslav [Dnepropetrovsk], and Kiev provinces. As for the districts, soviet congresses have been held in them all. All of the districts have already held their party congresses. Between 75 and 90 percent of those attending these congresses were members of the Communist Party. The remaining 10 to 25 percent were from other parties.

Our party's activity today consists chiefly of broadening our influence and of organizing party schools, which now exist and function in all provinces and larger district capitals.

We publish eight or ten party newspapers and also twenty or more soviet newspapers, which are controlled by Communists.

One of our party's major projects today is to institute political commissars in every part of the Red Army. An equally extensive and vigorous revolutionary propaganda campaign is being conducted, as well as a recruitment drive for the army. An aggressive propaganda campaign is also being carried out among foreign troops in the occupied areas. Especially noteworthy is the newspaper that the Communist group in Odessa is publishing in French and English with the help of soldiers from the French occupation forces, which has a circulation of 10,000 copies.

Similarly, with the able assistance of Spartacus comrades, a very intense propaganda campaign is now being waged in Nikolayev among the German occupation army of approximately 20,000 still stationed there.

Of course, the party's main activity is organizing soviets and organizational work in the army. Even before the Ukraine was free of the occupying army, our party had organized two revolutionary divisions stationed for the most part near the demarcation line. When our party called for an uprising, they launched an offensive in that region in August. Later, after the German revolution broke out, the revolutionary divisions broadened the geographic range of their activity and attacked first Hetman Skoropadsky's regime, then the Ukrainian Directory.

Internally we were organized as an extensive network of military revolutionary committees. These were composed mostly of our party workers and headed by a military revolutionary central committee set up by the Central Committee of our party. This activity was unable to prevent the collapse of the revolutionary district committee in Odessa and the executions in Kiev and in many other places that claimed the lives of many comrades. Among those executed were Comrades Klochko, Gruzman, and Berg in Ekaterinoslav; Isaak Kreitsberg in Poltava; Vrublevsky, Gali Timofeyevna, and others in Kiev. I could name many more comrades in other cities. But no amount of bloody executions by the bourgeoisie and social traitors could halt the steady growth and widening influence of our party.

The opportunists' parties, led by the Directory, had to assume an outward appearance of Bolshevism in order to gain influence over the masses, who were still not fully conscious politically. While the hetman's regime was still in power, Vinnichenko officially announced in Vinnitsa that the Ukrainian Social Democratic Party supported the Soviet government. Later, however, when the Ukrainian social traitors' party got into power, they initiated a bitter struggle against the Communist Party and against the proletariat and poor peasants, who in the meantime had become conscious of their own real interests.

An open revolutionary movement then began against the hetman and the Directory, and from then on revolutionary armed forces extended their struggle to the whole country, fighting with extraordinary self-sacrifice. They received the enthusiastic support of broad layers of the working masses throughout the Ukraine. We built our two revolutionary divisions, the foundation of our military organization, into a massive and powerful Red Army of almost 180,000.[62] I am sure of this figure, as it has been frequently cited.

I will say no more about our army's heroism and victories, as they are well known. I will just say that the fundamental concept behind our work is to train both our own revolutionary forces and also the troops from Petlyura's army that are constantly coming over to our side and transform them from isolated, poorly disciplined units into a fully disciplined Red Army. Our well-trained army with its centralized command and coordinated operations serves as a model for us.

Our party's influence cannot be measured solely by the size of our membership or the activity of the government, which is made up of party comrades and administered by the party's Central Committee. The Communist Party's impact has also caused a significant shift in the other Ukrainian parties.

The Ukrainian Socialist Revolutionary Party, which until very recently fought under the banner of nationalism, has been affected by the struggles it went through with us and by the prevailing mood among the masses, as well as by our propaganda, and has completely come over to our side. It now supports social revolution and the dictatorship of the proletariat. It understands and acknowledges the need to unify fully with our Communist Party.

The overwhelming majority of the Ukrainian Socialist Revolutionary Party and its smaller organizations in the provinces are simply coming over as a whole to our party. A similar thing is happening with the Bund—it is already working with us, and the question of their completely coming over to communism has already been posed. The Left Socialist Revolutionary Party—as you know it functions separately from the Ukrainian Socialist Revolutionary Party—the party that played such a hostile and ruinous role against the Soviet government and the social revolution in Russia, has no influence at all in the Ukraine. The delegation from their Central Committee in Russia, which was sent to the Ukraine to try to push through the same policies they used in Russia, failed miserably.

Even the Ukrainian Social Democratic Party, to which belong the heads of the Directory, Vinnichenko and Petlyura, was affected by the Communist struggles. Moreover, a faction of Independent Social Democrats split away from them under the impact of the Communist-led struggles. Although these Independent Socialists differ from the Communists on fundamentals, they are nevertheless working harmoniously with our party today and participate in the soviets.[63]

Precisely the same thing happened to the Right Socialist Revolutionaries. They too now take part in the soviets and completely renounce any form of accommodation with the Entente.

Finally, a realignment is occurring in the right wing of the Ukrainian Social Democratic Party, to which Messrs. Shvets and Andriyevsky belong. It too is falling apart, but at the same time a process of differentiation and redefinition is taking place. Specifically there was a split in the Ukrainian Right Social Democratic Party that, on the one hand, resulted in Vinnichenko and others leaving the government and, on the other, Petlyura, Shvets, and their followers leaving this party.[64] In a related development, a purely military dictatorship emerged headed by Grekov, a former tsarist general and a clearly avowed monarchist. Hence we now have to contend with a military dictatorship. The Directory is totally bankrupt and has lost all influence over the masses. The only forces that back it now are Ukrainian officers' groups and Galician National Democrats,[65] who have nothing to do with socialism.

Our Communist government issued a strongly worded statement saying that the Ukrainian masses wanted a social revolution and proposing that the Directory halt the unnecessary and senseless bloodshed, which served only the enemies of the working class. If our appeal is ignored by the Directory, it will nonetheless strike a powerful chord among the masses, who were swinging over to our side because they wanted to fight not against us but against their rulers.

Before ending this brief report, I must stress one other point: the international character of our movement. Although the Ukraine endured an extremely cruel occupation under the Germans, there is no nationalist movement among the workers and farmers.[66] The Red Terror, by means of which the Ukrainian workers and peasants ward off the White Terror of international capital, is directed not against the German and French soldiers but against their officers. It is wielded in a joint effort with German, French, Greek, and Romanian soldiers, workers, and peasants against the bourgeoisie of all nations and against international capital. That is our approach.

Our movement has gone through many ordeals. But despite the threat from Krasnov in the south and from the Entente troops, the Third Ukrainian Soviet Congress, which will convene tomorrow, will demonstrate that the Ukrainian workers and peasants, who are rallying to the red banner of the Communist Party, are invincible.

Since my time is almost up, I cannot detail our party's activities, so I will say one thing very briefly:

Last year, when the Ukrainian workers and peasants rose up, the revolutionary wave swept over the borders of the former Russian empire and spilled into Galicia as far as Stanislav [Ivano-Frankovsk]. We were occupied first by the Germans, then by the French, then by Galician troops being transported to Russia. But the consequence was that all those soldiers from different countries rubbed shoulders with us, and so we can expect that our revolutionary movement will spread even wider. It will engulf Galicia and form a bridge for the revolution to cross from Russia to Hungary. That in turn will be an important step forward for the world revolution.

REPORT ON FRANCE

SADOUL: Comrades, I deeply regret that I speak neither German, which Comrade Zinoviev yesterday called the "language of international socialism," nor Russian, which will be the language of international communism tomorrow.[67] I must address you in French, the only language in which I am reasonably fluent, a language that for now, at least, can unfortunately be referred to only as the language of a revolution of long ago.

Comrade Lenin has asked me to describe the political situation in France. But first I want to answer a question several comrades from abroad have asked me. That is, what do I, as a French officer, think of the Russian Red Army.

Comrades, a few weeks ago I had the opportunity to visit the northern front, on which is focused the anguished gaze of the young, bloodied Soviet republic. With pleasure I now take the opportunity afforded by this first international Communist congress to express before the whole world the deep feelings that the great Russian Communist Party, the torch of the world revolution, inspires in every true revolutionary. Despite the many great obstacles this party has faced, it has nevertheless found enough inner strength to construct this unquestioned military power, this Red Army, in whose ranks I have the honor to serve.

We are deeply indebted to the leaders of this army, but most of all to Comrade Trotsky. His ceaseless energy, combined with superior intelligence and true genius, succeeded in breathing new life into the Russian army, which had been in a state of complete disintegration.[68]

Hardly six months have passed since the Allies, with contemptuous arrogance and out of profound hatred for the Russian revolution, claimed that two Czech divisions supported by a single Anglo-French detachment would be enough to topple the Soviet government and conquer Russia.[69] The first weeks following these events seemed to support their predictions, for hostile attacks were launched with lightning speed around the White Sea and Volga basin.

Faced by this mortal danger, the revolutionary army was trained with equal speed. Now even the Allies acknowledge that the "contemptible" Red Army is well developed enough to hold its own against the hostile armies criminally hurled against the citadels of Bolshevism. They acknowledge its merits, organization, and military power. Indeed, they fear it.

Despite their hypocritical declarations, they long to strangle the Russian revolution, which poses a constant revolutionary threat to all Europe. They long to restore the political power of this or that tsar and help the Russian bourgeoisie regain economic power. But the Allies fear the Red Army—so much so that they have been forced, despite a year of shameless threats, to forego military intervention against the Soviet government. What the Allies are unable to accomplish with their own forces is now supposed to be achieved by the White Guards of Kolchak, Denikin, Krasnov, Petlyura, Mannerheim, and Paderewski, in league against Soviet Russia.

However, forcing the Russian Red Army into new battles only prepares it for new victories: at Petrograd, on the Volga, in the Urals, in the South—everywhere.

And that is why I call upon the Communist conference to send a message of appreciation to the first international army.[70] This army frustrated the Allies' machinations and their punitive expedition and assured the security of the Russian revolution, thereby giving the western European proletariat the time to organize and prepare for struggle.

Comrades, I left France eighteen and a half months ago. Therefore, of course, I am not an eyewitness to what has happened there. But for an active political fighter very familiar with the thinking of his compatriots, following the French newspapers closely is enough to gauge accurately political events. Moreover, it permits an evaluation of the role of two such significant and large organizations as the Socialist Party and the General Confederation of Labor.

It is very interesting to follow the evolution of the moods of the French masses. When I left Paris in September of 1917, just a few weeks before the October revolution, public perception of Bolshevism in France was that of a hideous caricature of socialism. Bolshevik leaders were viewed as criminals or madmen; their army was depicted as a horde of several thousand fanatics or outlaws.

That was the opinion of all of France. I am ashamed to confess that nine-tenths of both the majority and the minority Socialists held the same view.[71] In our defense we can only point to mitigating circumstances: we were not the least bit informed about the situation in Russia and, further, newspapers of every stripe printed fabrications and falsified documents to prove the corruption, cruelty, and unscrupulousness of the Bolsheviks.

The seizure of power by this "gang of bandits" had a wrenching impact in France. The slanders hiding the true face of Russian communism became even more vicious with the signing of the Brest-Litovsk peace. Anti-Bolshevik agitation reached a fever pitch. Despite all this, a few unbiased accounts managed to penetrate into France. Some of us began to see the light and asked if it was possible for a party that had cleared away so many obstacles to be based exclusively on terrorism. Rather, was it not known, loved, and supported by the majority of the Russian people?

The vile slander campaign in the bourgeois press continued. The social-patriotic papers stopped shouting, it is true, but aimed fierce attacks against the Bolshevik leaders. In the social patriots' view, the Bolsheviks' "utopian schemes" plainly threatened to destroy the Russian revolution and to compromise the world revolution forever.

The newspapers of the Socialists of the center (the Longuet group) were more moderate in their indignation and contempt. They even began to expose the intrigues of the bourgeois Entente and protested against armed intervention. But their policy was not based on a sense of socialist solidarity; rather it appealed instead to the right of self-determination of nations. Wavering and cowardly in their orthodoxy, they refrained from any judgment on the merit of the Bolsheviks' program from a socialist point of view. They were startled and frightened by the radical nature of the gigantic social upheaval being carried out with iron conviction by the Soviet power, and they watched this meteoric revolution without comprehending its power or its necessity. But they lacked the nerve to condemn it. Their indecision, like that of any bourgeois confronted with a new idea, demonstrates their complete lack of will as socialists. However, I should not judge them too harshly. It was not so very long ago that I myself was in their ranks, and I might still be as blind as they if I had not gone through the great school of Russian communism here.

The first sign of sympathy, the first evidence of fraternal reconciliation, appeared in October 1918 at the national conference of the Socialist Party of France. Suddenly, in the middle of Longuet's speech on the military intervention, enthusiastic shouts of "Long live the Soviet republic!" broke out, surprising most leaders of not only the majority but the minority as well. Even Longuet, elevated by this conference to the position of leader of the Socialist Party, was completely astonished. It was the first warning to the leadership from the little-known but far-sighted rank-and-file fighters.

After that, the leaders began openly to support the party's leftward evolution.[72] This has steadily deepened in the last six months. It has become apparent, however, that the masses' leftward evolution has outstripped that of their leaders.

The proletariat's immediate interest in material, real things, its well-developed political sense, the deeply rooted and healthy instincts characteristic of the French people, all naturally lead the proletariat to sensible conclusions. In other words, although the proletariat has no scientific grounding in socialism, it nevertheless instinctively moves toward communism. Although we lack specific details, we may nevertheless assume that this natural tendency is somewhat influenced by syndicalism. I do not wish to dwell here on the official leaders of the General Confederation of Labor, like Jouhaux, who flirted with the militarist government during the war, or Merrheim, whose revolutionary activity has slackened considerably. I much prefer to speak about the syndicalist fighters who, though less well known, are also less affected by the process of decay. Shielded from the spirit of innumerable parliamentary commissions and negotiations with governmental representatives, they have preserved syndicalism's principles undiminished. Although poorly informed about Bolshevik communism, these men seem to have an intuitive grasp of its real power and vitality. For the most part they belong to the lower social classes and their cultural level is frequently none too high. But they possess a strong will, and one day, when history drives the people of France to make the revolution, they will be found in the front ranks.

Comrades, I see no revolutionary leaders in the French Socialist Party today. At its head stand chiefly people who, like bureaucrats, have no integral connection with the broad masses. Bourgeois parliamentarism has devoured their souls and narrowed their horizons. The demoralizing influence of the legislative chamber, with its gentlemanly public debates on the one hand and secret machinations on the other, is quite powerful. No one withstands this. Worthy comrades of strong temperament and sound political convictions such as Cachin, Lafont, and, you may be surprised to hear, even Renaudel, succumb to opportunism after serving only a few months there. Many of them will surely come to their senses, but not in time to light the fire of revolution with their own hands.

While many of them will surely join the revolution twenty-four hours after it begins, they are quite unable to foresee it even twenty-four hours in advance; their judgment is dulled and their actions lack courage and conviction. Whether they will attempt to prevent the outbreak of revolution, divert it, or try to hold it back by repression I cannot yet say. Nor would I ascribe any such intentions to them. I hope it is not so, for they could be extremely valuable collaborators if swept along by the proletariat and brought under its supervision.

So, we see that the French revolution has not as yet produced either its own Lenin or its own Trotsky. Nature is none too prodigal with men of their kind. In the last analysis, the fact that these two powerful leaders direct the world revolution is enough to assure the proletarian victory. These two leaders are fully equal to their monumental task. They were the first to show the road and they will continue to lead the way. And should the French revolution one day require their aid, then surely you will loan them to us for a few weeks, won't you, comrades?

For the moment, at least, French communism lacks not only the commander but also the outstanding revolutionary generals that Russia has in such great abundance. They are, in essence, a Russian phenomenon, molded by the nature of the country—its harsh climatic contrasts and immeasurable geographic expanse. They are authentic Russian figures whose powerful will was hardened in tsarist prisons and in long years of exile and who are ready to endure any suffering and sacrifice.

The leaders of the French left Socialists, Longuet and his friends, who worship reformism and opportunism, are incapable of revolutionary valor. By that I do not mean that they will fail to do their duty when the hour strikes. But they lack the necessary valor to speed that hour.

The Bolshevik leaders are, in fact, leaders in the highest sense of the word. They knew how to lead the proletariat into revolution on the road ordained by history. They are like a beacon lighting the way for the popular masses. Our French leaders, I fear, will turn out to be nothing more than their disciples.

The French proletariat will certainly take the first step and begin its first battle on its own. We place all our hopes on it. It has rested on the laurels of its illustrious forefathers long enough. But now it is beginning to awaken. Conscious of its great historic destiny it reaches out hungrily with clumsy but powerful hands toward power. For the last six months the echo of the cry that first resounded at the October conference has been heard everywhere in France.

Most public rallies in France today end with the new slogans, "Long live Lenin!" "Long live Trotsky!" "Long live the dictatorship of the proletariat!" "Long live the Soviets!" These cries must be distressing to the powers that be, and the bourgeois press reports them with indignation. Unfortunately the lack of leaders is felt strongly. The movement lacks a centralized organization and is all too easily suppressed by brute force whenever it flickers up in isolated areas.

By and large, however, events are moving in a direction favorable for revolution. The collapse of the capitalist order—its inability to resolve the problems of peace or of war, its tendency to work out illusory compromises, the hatred it feels for the popular masses—only fuels the people's anger and bitterness.

The outdated notion of an agreement with the bourgeoisie appears pointless to the workers. The social patriots, convinced proponents of that monstrous pact, are objects of deep proletarian scorn. The indecisive resolutions by the Socialists of the center, whose verbosity inspires no confidence at all, satisfy no one.

At last the inner workings of Russian events have been made plain. The Bolshevik Party's honest, forthright policy is much more in accord with the French temperament than are the unclear, muddy formulations of the first German revolution.[73]

I am firmly convinced that in the near future the program of the Russian Communist Party will be adopted by the French proletariat, with only a few minor changes required by French conditions, particularly on the agrarian question.

There is only one road to this goal: propaganda and more propaganda. The ground for agitation is well prepared. The inexcusable delay in demobilizing the army; the imperialist aspirations of the capitalist oligarchy that governs the republic; the bourgeoisie's harsh policy against the Russian and German revolutions; the disintegration of the state; the economic chaos; the unemployment crisis; the food problem—all this contributes to the collapse of the predatory social order.

When will the freedom movement begin? Well, who can predict the course of events? Grave obstacles can always retard even that which is inevitable.

Even before the capitalists of the Entente had organized their mutual assistance pact called the League of Nations, the French ruling classes understood this. They stationed special armed forces made up of colored and black troops, of Senegalese and Indochinese, in all the industrial centers, poised to strike at the working masses.

Finally, the government threatens the future revolution with an economic blockade that would cut off the supply of American grain to France and condemn the French population to starvation.

The dangers and tasks we face must be carefully thought out, for the responsibility we assume is gigantic.

Nevertheless, I am confident that once demobilization has brought several million citizens back into the country and precipitated a crisis of food and employment, the workers will surely come into action. Its outcome will undoubtedly be the construction of a Soviet republic, and the victory of the Communist Party.

Therefore, let us continue our work and await the blessed hour, the sacred union of the German, French, and Russian revolutions, which will make the world social revolution invincible.

I will conclude on that note.

But allow me one more thing. I would like to read here statements of two fighters from the ranks of the left Socialists—Verfeuil and Loriot—which strikingly illustrate the thinking of the truly viable and courageous forces in the French Socialist Party.[74]

Comrades, in closing I repeat yet again: barely six months ago the majority of the French Socialist Party was crying: "Down with the Bolsheviks!" Now the same Socialists exclaim: "Long live the Soviet republic!" The official party newspapers are carefully studying the possibility of a dictatorship of the proletariat in France. Do these facts require any comment? And can we not now justifiably hope that we no longer have long to wait?

REPORT ON BRITAIN

JOSEPH FINEBERG: The hopes of revolutionary countries are directed toward Britain. In the last two months, events there have heightened these hopes. The strike movement is spreading throughout Britain and is affecting every branch of industry. Discipline in the army has been considerably undermined, and in other countries that was the first symptom of revolution.

The strike movement in Britain did not begin when the war ended. Rather it is the continuation of a movement that arose and continued during the entire war. Even before the war, it had reached a very high level of development, especially in 1911 and 1912. A great many strikes occurred in those years, affecting the railroads, shipyards, and docks. The government felt that the railroad workers' strike was so serious that it occupied all railroads with troops, and in Liverpool soldiers were called in to suppress the strike. The workers were fired upon, and many were killed or wounded.[75]

As for the wartime strike movement, we should note that it was strongest when the Allies scored successes.[76] As soon as they suffered setbacks, however, the movement subsided. Nevertheless, there were moments when we Socialists believed we were on the eve of revolution.

What interests us Communists the most is the form and character of the movement, and when we examine these aspects, we find that the British workers' movement has changed completely since 1914. When war broke out, the British labor movement, like that in every country, was swept along with the tide of chauvinism. The trade unions relinquished gains won in long years of struggle, and the General Council of the Trades Union Congress [TUC] concluded a "civil peace" with the bourgeoisie.[77] But life—the intensified exploitation, the food price increases—forced the workers to defend themselves against the capitalists, who were taking advantage of the "civil peace" to further their own exploitative ends. The workers had no choice but to demand higher wages and to back up this demand with strikes. The TUC General Council and the leaders (until then) of the movement, who had promised the government that they would keep the workers in check, sought to restrain the movement and disavowed the strikes. But the strikes went ahead "unofficially." In the press and through its officials, the government lectured the workers on discipline and respect for their leaders. When pleading and cajoling no longer sufficed, it turned to threats. Nevertheless, despite the severe punishment dealt to strikers or to those persuading others to strike, one strike followed another.

Naturally, a movement like that could not arise or continue without some kind of organization. In fact, such an organization exists: the shop stewards committees. The shop stewards had long been part of the life of the trade unions. They represent the unions in the factories, see to it that the unions' terms are met, and handle negotiations with the factory management. In large factories with many departments there is a shop stewards committee for each department, and owing to the way the unions are currently organized, it sometimes happens that there are several unions in the same factory.

Changing organizational and production techniques in industry made clear to the younger and more advanced forces in the labor movement that craft organizations could no longer serve as a weapon in the class struggle. Agitation was begun in favor of amalgamating all unions within a particular branch of industry. In Britain this movement is regarded as industrial utopianism. The executive committees of the unions and the former leaders fought against it. The shop stewards committees, on the other hand, got organized. When the trade union executive boards, acting as tools of the government, tried to defeat the workers' movement, its leadership was assumed by the shop stewards committees. In the industrial districts, local workers' committees were formed, such as the Clyde workers' committee, the London workers' committee, the Sheffield workers' committee, and others, which included representatives of the shop stewards' bodies. These committees became the hub of the organization, acting as the representatives of the organized workers in each locality.

For a time the employers and the government refused to recognize the shop stewards committees at all, but in the end they were forced to negotiate with these "unofficial" committees. The fact that Lloyd George agreed to recognize the Birmingham committee as an economic organization proves that these committees have become a permanent factor in the British labor movement.

In the shop stewards committees, their national conferences, and the workers' committees, we already have an organization similar to that on which the Soviet republic is based. This organization was not created artificially by spreading a new idea; rather it grew naturally out of the labor movement, fresh evidence that the principles of the Communist Party are correct. This organization entails a complete change in the form and structure of the British labor movement, and there is every reason to believe that it will play a most outstanding role in the further history of that movement.

The workers, especially the metalworkers, recognized that the changes in industrial and production techniques seriously jeopardized their situation. Jobs that formerly required great skill were now performed by unskilled workers: men, women, and children. The older and more conservative workers thought that this would be the case only for the duration of the war, but the younger workers perceived that a return to the old way was neither possible nor desirable. The workers, the metalworkers in particular, emphatically demanded control of industry, and the government had to pay attention to this demand. A commission established to determine the cause of workers' discontent proposed granting partial control of industry to the workers in order to pacify them.[78] When implemented, however, this plan gave the workers no control at all, but only tightened discipline and introduced arbitration courts. The "Whitley Report" had little impact on the workers; the demand for control of industry became ever more insistent.

The Russian revolution undoubtedly had a great influence on the British labor movement. As in every other country, the war divided the movement into a majority and a minority. But as a result of the peculiar structure of the Labour Party conferences, the minority was unable to organize its forces as effectively as did the minorities on the continent. That is why the Socialist parties internationally could not accurately assess its strength.

When the Russian revolution broke out, however, we mounted a major effort to rally our forces for an offensive against the majority. We decided to convene a conference of all organizations or parts of organizations that would join us in opposing the war and championing internationalism, to be held in June 1917 in Leeds.[79] The main objective was to publicize the working class's attitude toward the Russian revolution. We were much more successful than we had expected. Over 1,200 delegates attended, mostly representatives of the shop stewards committees, and the enthusiasm and genuine revolutionary fervor were truly remarkable. Both our friends and our enemies declared it the most impressive conference in Britain since the Chartists' convention; it made a deep impression on the country.

The conference decided to establish national and local soviets of soldiers' and workers' deputies and to conduct revolutionary propaganda against the war. Steps were taken to form local soldiers' and workers' soviets, and numerous trade union organizations expressed a desire to affiliate. The fact that we received a great many requests from the army to form soldiers' soviets under our aegis was extremely significant. The government became apprehensive and, although it did not repress us with legal means, used methods that it had undoubtedly learned from its tsarist ally. Our local meetings were broken up by bands of thugs and drunken soldiers.

The idea of soldiers' and workers' soviets is not new to the British labor movement; this is shown by the way this organizational form evolved naturally within the labor movement itself. That portion of the labor movement in Britain represented by the shop stewards committees understands the importance of the Russian revolution, of the October revolution in particular, and sees the Soviet republic as a model on which to pattern itself.

When the war ended, a mighty strike movement unfolded in which the shop stewards committees played the central role.[80] At the same time, the troops openly voiced their opinions of the government, undeterred by harsh disciplinary penalties. The soldiers' movement is essentially the natural expression of the desire to return home. But when the possibility of another invasion of Russia arose, there were visible signs of a revolutionary awakening.[81] At soldiers' demonstrations in the streets, immediate demobilization was demanded, and in Aldershot, one of the largest military bases in Britain, the soldiers marched through the streets chanting, "You want to send us to Russia?" All throughout the war the soldiers used to say, "Wait till the war is over; we won't go back to the old, intolerable conditions." And there can be no doubt that the demonstrating soldiers had this in mind.

The main goal of the strike movement is to shorten the hours of work. In the branches of industry where the eight-hour day has not yet been introduced, the workers demand it; where it is already in effect, the workers demand a 40-hour workweek. The issue is how to create work for the soldiers returning home without throwing those already employed in the factories and mines out of work. In addition, there is a powerful movement against intervention in Russia. This arose for two reasons: first, out of sheer war-weariness and a desire to have done with the hostilities once and for all; and second, because the working class is aware that an Allied invasion of Russia would be an attack on the working class of the whole world.

It cannot yet be said that the shop stewards movement is fully conscious of its task. It demands control of industry, but it does not yet seem to realize that workers' control of industry is unattainable so long as industry is owned by the capitalists. But this is beginning to be understood, as shown by the demand by several important unions for the nationalization of the railroads, mines, land, and so forth. The movement has not yet reached the stage where it can demand that power be transferred to the shop stewards committees. But Lloyd George was forced to recognize the Birmingham shop stewards conference, and that shows that the movement has made enormous strides.

The enormous number of social and economic problems produced by the war will compel the British working class to take the one and only radical action that can make possible the solution of these problems. Even if the hours of work are shortened, a certain amount of unemployment is inevitable; and the necessity of paying the costs of the war will intensify the exploitation of the workers and have a revolutionizing effect on them. Furthermore, the situation in Ireland will help to accelerate the accumulation of revolutionary tensions—all of which must lead toward revolution.[82]

The movement in Ireland will also contribute to revolutionizing the working masses in Britain. The Sinn Fein movement is purely nationalist or revolutionary nationalist, and it has influenced the Irish working class. On the other hand, however, the Irish labor movement, especially the large transportation workers union, the largest in Ireland, has shown a revolutionary and internationalist side. It was precisely this union, led by Connolly, that was behind the Dublin uprising of 1916.[83] Although Connolly is dead, his influence on the Irish labor movement lives on, as demonstrated by the enthusiasm the Irish workers have for the Russian Bolshevik revolution. At present, the Irish labor movement is having an important effect on the Sinn Fein movement; thus every attempt by the government to suppress Sinn Fein will lead the workers to take a more active interest in the Irish struggle.

I expect that the outcome of the elections has taught the workers that no lasting improvement can be expected from parliamentary action.[84] And although it would be incorrect for the Russian Soviet government to base its policies on the prospects of immediate revolution in Britain, still there is no doubt that events are moving in a revolutionary direction. Organizations are being created with whose aid the proletariat will seize power and proclaim the dictatorship of the proletariat.

ALBERT: Comrades, we must impose certain limitations on the presentation of reports. If we want to finish this morning, then a restriction is necessary. It has been proposed that the comrades deliver a short report here and submit the rest of their report in writing, thus reducing the time spent on oral statements.

ZINOVIEV: I would like to propose that the remaining reports be entered into the minutes and that we make an exception only for Comrade Grimlund, who has come from Sweden. We will never finish if we continue like this.

(*The proposal is adopted. The session ends at 3:30.*)

Top: Leon Trotsky addresses Red Army unit; below left: Gregory Zinoviev; below right: Nikolai Bukharin.

3. The platform for the International

(The session is reconvened at 5 p.m.)

LENIN: Next is the report from Sweden. The Swedish comrade is not here. We propose to end the presentation of reports. Do the comrades agree that the Swedish report be submitted in written form?[1]

We will proceed to the next point on the agenda: Platform of the International Communist Conference. The reporters are Comrades *Albert* and *Bukharin*. Comrade Albert has the floor.

REPORT ON THE PLATFORM (ALBERT)

ALBERT *(Germany)*: Comrades, yesterday's statements by the Russian and Finnish delegates could give the impression that the comrades from Germany oppose founding the Third International. We harbor no principled objections to founding it. However, we do feel that in approaching the creation of a new International, some consideration should be given to moods among the workers, particularly the workers in the western countries. Over time, they have developed a mistrust toward the notion of founding such organizations. Out of respect for this sentiment among workers in western countries, the German comrades declared that we do not want to proceed to founding the International just yet. Instead, we want to hold a preparatory conference first to take stock of the forces we have now and to see what political basis we have for unity.

Everyone who knows the history of the last International will concede that the misgivings workers in the West have about establishing this sort of organization are well-founded. We are familiar with the pomp and circumstance at those conferences, where resounding resolutions were drawn up and plans were hatched for great actions. And then, when the critical hour arrived to translate all of this into deeds, all those resolutions were ignominiously abandoned and all the International's work was wrecked. All the resolutions were trampled underfoot, and the actions taken were in direct contradiction to what had been resolved. That is why workers are mistrustful. They do not want to see the Third International patched together in the same old way by a group of comrades who, because of the difficult conditions under which we assembled here for this conference, were selected by chance.

And in fact, very few delegates representing the various organizations from different countries are present. The workers do not want us to hold another pompous founding congress and adopt resolutions that will exist only on paper. The first thing they want to know is who stands with them, who stands behind us, and whom they can rely on in the coming struggles. They want to know that the activity of the Third International will be different from that of its predecessor. We all agree on that.

At conferences nowadays it is no longer a question of arguing over socialist theory. It is no longer a question of proclaiming future struggles, concocting plans, and passing resolutions. It is a question of leading the world proletariat into action. Today the proletariat everywhere is fighting for its emancipation with more than leaflets, pamphlets, and speeches. Today it is a life-and-death struggle. Today, workers want to know whether or not the Third International that must be founded has the strength required to support their struggles, and if not, whether it can acquire it. Workers therefore believe that we must first state what we want and what basis there is for further struggle; then they will say whether they are ready to found the new International and join it. That will also be the simplest and most correct course and will lead to the objective we all desire.

I can tell you categorically that the German workers do not oppose founding a third International. But they want it to be equipped from the start with the strength and power required to support proletarian struggles in all countries. To do that, we believe we must first present our platform to the world, explaining clearly and exactly the tasks of the proletariat and pointing out its objective and line of march; we must create a banner that can lead the way in struggle against the bourgeoisie. To do that we must be as clear and precise as possible from the very beginning. We cannot go on thinking that all we have to do is gather to deliver as many speeches as possible, as they did before, decorating the International with figureheads who have no more substance than soap bubbles. We must unite all who completely identify with us and exclude all who are half-hearted, weak, and unreliable.

Comrade Bukharin and I have prepared basic theses for such a platform, which you have before you. Our job is to explain it briefly; yours is to take a position on it, to say whether you agree with our reports, and to say whether you will accept responsibility for translating its provisions into action. You must get your organizations to support it and, based on that program, see to it that the proletariat itself decides whether it is ready to unite behind a third International.

The first part of this platform is a preface, which analyzes the bourgeoisie and capitalism. It describes how capitalism's imperialist tendencies transformed nations into predator states. It describes the policy that capitalism pursues in its constant quest for new markets, sources of raw materials, and new colonial territories and how the entire world came to be divided up among the capitalist nations. It describes how the capitalist nations partitioned the world. Yet even then, capitalism's tendencies still did not go away. The need to expand and aggrandize still existed, and the greed of the capitalist classes was not satisfied. These nations are at each other's throats, seeking to tear one market after another away from each other. Without regard for the needs of the working class in different countries, capital was impelled by its very nature, by its greed and its need to increase profits and enlarge its own wealth, to create conflict and enmity among nations.

The platform describes how capitalism attempted to recruit the working class for its selfish ends; that is, how it tried to overcome the contradictions inherent in the national social structure so that it could use workers in wars against neighboring states to fill the capitalists' pockets. It tried to use workers to further each country's individual colonial policy. Capitalism and the bourgeoisie in each country were able to convince the working class that labor and capital have the same interests. They sowed the idea of the "fatherland" in workers' minds and hearts and exploited that sense of commonality to start war against their neighbors. The platform thus explains the origin of "civil peace."

The imperialist tendencies of capitalism led to the World War in which each large capitalist nation set out to devour the others. Workers obediently served the desires and the needs of the ruling classes, thus trampling their own interests into the ground and harnessing themselves completely to the ruling classes. The fact that the great majority of workers followed the dictates of capitalism was possible only because our predecessor, the Second International, failed so utterly and completely. As recently as its last congress,[2] the Second International still resolved that in the event of war, the proletariat should employ *all* possible means to prevent it. When war did break out, the leaders did *everything possible* to promote it. The same leaders who had attended all the earlier conferences tried with all their strength and influence to convince the workers that the class struggle had ceased and that workers had to unite with the ruling class; they utilized their influence to lead the entire proletariat to the slaughtering block.

In the course of the war and the "civil peace" it became clear that the ends that the proletariat had been conned into serving could not be achieved. Instead of bettering its circumstances by helping the war effort, the working class had done the opposite; instead of improving living standards, the wartime "civil peace" almost led to general physical destruction of the proletariat. Poverty, misery, and the enslavement of the proletariat worsened. "Civil peace" led the proletariat not to gains but to worldwide famine.

After the war ended, more and more workers began to understand this. It began to dawn on the working class that it had committed a colossal blunder by hurling itself, side by side with the bourgeoisie, at workers in neighboring countries. As workers saw that the theory of "civil peace" had led to a fiasco, the imperialist war turned into civil war in one country after another. In the larger countries we are witnessing the outbreak of revolution. In Russia and other countries, the workers have turned their rifles around and are aiming them at their real enemies, the capitalists of their own countries. We saw that this generated unrest in the other countries as well as revolt among the colonial peoples, who until now have suffered the worst exploitation at the hands of the capitalist states. Workers' rebellions multiplied in every country.

In the aftermath of the "civil peace," the conflict between labor and capital sharpened and class antagonism intensified. In many countries today, the struggle is no longer being waged with leaflets, pamphlets, and rallies but with machine guns and poison gas grenades. The capitalist class can find no way out of this situation. It led us further and further down the road to the abyss; it reduced the citadels of European civilization to rubble; and it is incapable of constructing a new social order upon the ruins. We know that unless a change finally takes place, we can look forward to the complete destruction of European civilization. The workers are searching for a way out of this dilemma.

If we begin by asking whether the ruling class is capable of rebuilding this shattered society, we must reply that it will not and cannot rebuild what is destroyed. The capitalist system has shown that it is unfit to continue to rule; it is not competent to control the destiny of humanity any longer. There is no other way out than for the proletariat, by far the largest of the productive classes, to take power into its own hands. It has already done so in some countries; in Russia the last, decisive battle has already begun and has proceeded successfully a good part of the way; in Germany the bourgeoisie and the proletariat are arming for the bitter showdown battle, and the ruling class is gathering all the resources that it still commands. The League of Nations idea and the establishment of White Guards and White Terror will not and must not prevent the proletariat from going into battle. That is what we say in this platform, in order to lay bare the contradictions, open the workers' eyes, and show them where we stand today.

Then of course the platform must say how we propose to realize our objectives; it must plainly tell the workers what they must do and analyze what road they must follow in order to attain the goal of socialist revolution and make the new social system a reality. That is extraordinarily difficult, because the requirements of the struggle vary widely from one country to the next, and some have made more progress than others along the road to the socialist revolution. What we are presenting to you today will be behind the times for some and too advanced for others. We will see that in countries that are furthest along the road to socialist revolution the workers will say, "We have already done most of the things you call for," while others will tell us, "We are far from being able to carry out what you call for in this platform; we have not progressed to that point yet."

Yet we must find a way to work together; we must define some kind of middle road that can serve as a basis for our common work. It is important and necessary that the countries further ahead in development vigorously support those that lag behind—not only with advice, but materially as well. We must be able to work together, and I hope that any objections to the platform we have proposed will be brought up in the discussion and resolved. What we call for, in line with what I have said, is that the proletariat work toward taking political power; the proletariat must set to work building international understanding and unity with working people in all other countries.

In order to take political power, the proletariat will have to wage a relentless struggle against the bourgeoisie and destroy its political power. It is not possible to first rebuild the old political system and then later try to introduce socialism, as the centrists maintain. We dare not delay now, when the bourgeoisie's power is vulnerable. We must throw all our energy in every country into an effort to seize political power and smash that of the bourgeoisie. However, that must not be done simply by making a pseudorevolution, that is, by eliminating a few princes and their lackeys and putting a few other men in their places, as events in Germany have shown us. You must not topple an emperor and replace him with an Ebert—that is not enough. Not only must the proletariat change the personnel of government; it must also destroy the whole state apparatus in capitalist countries. Not individuals, but the system must be done away with, and the socialist system must replace the capitalist one.

In Germany, in the first days of the revolution, we called for disarming the entire bourgeoisie, especially the officer corps. The workers must take physical power out of the hands of the bourgeoisie and place it into the hands of the proletariat; they must disarm the agents of the enemy class and sweep aside the whole state apparatus: the government bureaucracy, judges, and the administrators of the educational system. In their place they must put men and organizations that will rebuild the machinery of state in the spirit and interests of socialism. Comrade Bukharin will go into this in greater detail.

After the proletariat and its organizations have seized political power their first priority is to destroy the state apparatus of the bourgeoisie and the ruling classes. Our slogan is: either bourgeois democracy or dictatorship of the proletariat. Socialist measures cannot be carried out together with the ruling classes. In every country where a revolution has taken place, the bourgeoisie's first slogan is, "Now that you have made a revolution, your task is to take your stand for democracy." Our reply must be, "The proletariat never demanded your kind of democracy." Wherever the proletariat has been for socialism, it has always taken a class-struggle position. It has always advocated relentless class struggle by the proletarian classes against the bourgeoisie, so it is out of the question to ask the proletariat to renounce the class struggle once it gets in power. That is precisely when the proletariat must begin using class-struggle methods to totally dismantle the old social system. But that can be done only if the proletariat rejects bourgeois democracy, rejects rebuilding society shoulder to shoulder with the bourgeoisie, and rejects preserving the old state apparatus. It can happen only if the proletariat ignores the howls of the bourgeoisie, continues to struggle, and proclaims the dictatorship of the proletariat.

For this, the new system of proletarian mass organization, the council system, must replace the old state apparatus. Among the key questions, therefore, that the delegates assembled here must pose to the proletariat is: "Do you support bourgeois democracy or do you stand for the dictatorship of the proletariat, that is, the council system?"

We cannot possibly found the Third International together with those who continue to defend bourgeois democracy and refuse to unite with us in calling for the council system. Therefore, we cannot unite with that left wing of the old International that gave enthusiastic support to bourgeois democracy from the start and thereby strangled the development of the council system. We cannot join forces with people who cling to the coattails of the bourgeoisie, who believe preserving this class is a prerequisite for future development, and who in that way stifled the council system and slipped power back into the hands of the bourgeoisie. Now they tearfully explain that they want a system of workers' councils *as well* and are looking for a way to combine bourgeois democracy and proletarian dictatorship; they want to combine parliament and the council system. We cannot and dare not unite with such weak and indecisive people. They will not strengthen the proletarian front; on the contrary, they will be a brake slowing our progress along the road of proletarian class struggle. One of the main tasks in each country will be to get rid of those elements and help Communists everywhere begin to stand on their own feet, champion the dictatorship of the proletariat and the council system, and rally only those workers who firmly support the dictatorship of the proletariat and the class struggle. Workers in every country must begin to smash the existing organizational forms and create their own mass organizations. The masses must fight against bourgeois democracy, which is designed to take back the proletariat's power. Their task will be to keep the power in their own hands and introduce self-government through the council system. Comrade Bukharin will discuss this as well, in detail.

If we want to lead the proletariat in struggle for its dictatorship, however, we will have to tell the workers what tasks are involved in taking power. I refer to the fact that along with the political dictatorship, an economic dictatorship must be established. The proletariat must immediately begin to expropriate the bourgeoisie and socialize production. I explained earlier that it is not possible to reconstruct each nation's economic life. Workers increased their wages during the war, sometimes substantially. Now, in large-scale enterprises, the employers no longer want to produce because, as they see it, successful wage struggles have made their businesses unprofitable. At the same time, the workers have less and less desire to work. They have no interest in working to put money in the capitalists' pockets. They want the mode of production transformed so that they too can have the use of what their labor creates. It is thus necessary for the proletariat, wherever it has taken power, to begin expropriating the big capitalists and big landowners, in order to pave the way for socialization. Its first order of business is to break the back of the bourgeoisie so they will not be able to strike back and regain power. That is what is needed, not the Kautskyite view that socialism should be postponed to a later time and the old mode of production restored until the damage caused by the war has been repaired.

We must also tell workers how socialization will take place. We must explain that a general redistribution of goods, as they frequently imagine it, is out of the question. Workers must not believe that socialization can be accomplished by throwing the capitalists out and dividing up the available raw materials, as has happened for example in some regions in Germany. We must tell them that this approach is wrong. The workers may not socialize the economy for themselves alone. Socialization must be carried out in the interests of society as a whole. We must see to it that the capitalists' possessions are cut off, taken from them, that national debts and war loans are annulled, and that landlords' buildings are expropriated and handed over to the workers. When it comes to expropriations we can draw powerful lessons from Russia, for we can see how the big capitalists have been chased out of their palaces and replaced there by the rightful owners, the workers—for only those whose labor maintains society are entitled to a decent life.

We can and must also show workers how to attain all the objectives outlined in this platform. We will show them the way to victory and tell them that the proletariat must wage its struggle primarily through mass action. It is no longer enough to attack the bourgeoisie only with fine speeches, nor for workers to make common cause with those who are weak and indecisive. Breaking with the agents of capital is our first demand here. It is intolerable for the proletariat to be led astray by or be dragged along behind the Yellow International.

All of these considerations argue strongly for preparing to found the Third International and need to be explained in this document. We have nothing more in common with the representatives of the Yellow International of Bern. Henceforth we must not only declare a life-and-death struggle against the bourgeoisie; we must also declare war on the traitors to the proletariat, such as the Scheidemanns and the weak and cowardly elements everywhere. Then we will be able to say with good reason that we are fulfilling the historic mission of the Third, the Communist International.

REPORT ON THE PLATFORM (BUKHARIN)

NIKOLAI BUKHARIN *(Russia)*: Comrades, it is my task to analyze the theses that we have proposed. Their general character must necessarily be somewhat abstract, since we can present here only positions that apply to all the countries that will be represented in the Third International, not just to one or another individual country. On the other hand, these theses must contain the entire experience of the countries where the movement has already developed, especially the enormous experience of the Russian communist workers' revolution.

I believe the comrades are already acquainted with the text of the theses. First comes the theoretical introduction. It gives a characterization of the whole present epoch from a particular point of view, namely, one that takes the bankruptcy of the capitalist system as its starting point. Previously, when introductions of this sort were composed, they simply gave a general description of the capitalist system. In the most recent period, in my opinion, this has become insufficient. Here we must not only give a general characterization of the capitalist and imperialist system, but also show the process of disintegration and collapse of this system. *That is the first aspect of the question. The second* is that we must examine the capitalist system not just in its abstract form, but concretely in its character as *world* capitalism, and we should examine it as something that is a single entity, as an economic whole. And if we look at this *world* capitalist economic system from the standpoint of its *collapse,* then we have to ask ourselves: How was this collapse possible? And that is why we must analyze, first of all, the contradictions of the capitalist system.

The two most important contradictions of capitalism are to be found, first, in the anarchy of production, and second, in the anarchy of its social structure. In the first instance we have before us the purely economic contradictions, and in the second, the social contradictions—and we are considering these contradictions not in their general form, but in the form in which they manifest themselves at the present time. In the first part of the introduction we show that the economic contradictions of the capitalist system result from its anarchic nature. Everywhere, capital has to some extent decided to initiate a process of organizing itself. As everyone knows, the previous form of capital—dispersed, unorganized capital—has almost disappeared. This process had already begun before the war and strengthened while it was underway. The war played a great organizing role. Under its pressure, finance capitalism was transformed into an even higher form, the form of state capitalism.[3] And in this way, previously unorganized capitalism was replaced, in certain countries, by its organized, state capitalist form.

Various bourgeois scholars assert that the anarchic nature of capitalism Marxists write about is an illusion, and that all the conclusions Marxists draw from the premise of capitalist anarchy are also illusory. But these good bourgeois scholars fail to notice the other side of that development. As economic contradictions gradually disappeared and capitalism went from being dispersed through various countries to being organized, that very process—the development of a world-wide system of production—led to an enormous intensification of economic anarchy on a *world* scale. It is a general law of capitalist development that competition is the expression of the anarchy in the capitalist system. This competition has been reproduced on an ever greater scale. What bourgeois scholars have not noticed is that in our time the anarchic nature of capitalism is manifesting itself in gigantic proportions, that is, in the framework of the whole world capitalist economy; its internal contradictions have led it to complete collapse. That is one aspect of the question.

The matter stands exactly the same with the *social* anarchy of capitalist production. Capitalism wanted to overcome that, too. By what means? Precisely by means of imperialist policy, however paradoxical this may sound. The capitalists of the most developed countries have tried to do this by plundering other countries and by accumulating superprofits through robbing the population of the colonies. The capitalists wanted to distribute a portion of these superprofits to the European worker and thereby establish uninterrupted "civil peace." We all know now how the plunder of the colonial population was used to awaken patriotic sentiments among the workers, especially among the skilled layers of the working class, who received the greatest share of these superprofits. But precisely because this method of establishing "civil peace" was imperialist in character, it too contained a contradiction. This method of establishing "civil peace" led inevitably to a powerful collision between the capitalist forces of the robber states. But in addition, these means, by which capitalism sought to overcome the inner contradictions of its social structure, led in reality to an unexpected sharpening of social contradictions and thereby to the beginning of civil war, to a grandiose collapse in various countries. We describe this in the theoretical introduction.

In this introduction we thought it necessary to consider the latest instrument fashioned to overcome these contradictions—the League of Nations. It is world capital's latest attempt at surmounting its contradictions. But this instrument is being used in a situation where capitalism no longer has sufficient strength to stop the process of social ferment and communist revolution. Such is the theoretical background of our program, our projected theses.

Now, comrades, I would like to briefly review the separate points of our theses. The first point concerns the *conquest of political power*. Here we must frankly declare that we are returning to Marxism's previous teachings. As we know, the old Social Democracy, which calls itself Marxist, bases itself almost everywhere on an emasculated version of Marxism. According to Marx's teachings, the state is an apparatus of oppression. In communist society there is no state at all; since there are no classes in communist society, it follows that there are no class organizations, either. We say here that after the conquest of political power by the proletariat and the complete destruction of the bourgeoisie as a class struggling against the proletariat, the state itself, together with all social classes and class organizations, will inevitably "wither away." Here we used the expression that Marx and Engels often employed to designate this process.[4]

So you see, comrades, we had to include a fairly detailed discussion of the conquest of political power. The old Social Democratic Party had absolutely no idea what the seizure of political power really meant. They thought of political power as some kind of neutral object. That idea of state power is completely false. State power does not exist in the abstract; every state power is concrete. If the bourgeoisie stands at its helm, then the state is a bourgeois organization. And if the proletariat conquers state power, then it does not appropriate that state power, but organizes its own, and in this process it must necessarily destroy the old state organizations. This is especially clear now, after the experience of the Russian and German revolutions.

Take the best support of the old state—the army. Can you imagine a situation where the proletariat seized state power without disorganizing the imperialist army? Of course not. The conquest of state power is bound together with the disorganization of the imperialist army. The same thing can be said about the whole state apparatus in general. By seizing state power, by taking the power into its own hands, the proletariat destroys the bourgeois state apparatus. This is a revolutionary truth, and to Marx and Engels, the founders of communist doctrine, it was well known.[5] It was only in the later period of peaceful development that this basic idea was completely forgotten. Now we are returning to this old and tested Marxist doctrine when we say, first, in communist society no type of state whatsoever can exist and, second, the conquest of political power by the proletariat must necessarily lead to the destruction of the old state organizations. That is all I will say on the conquest of political power.

Next follows the point on bourgeois democracy or the dictatorship of the proletariat. I will not dwell on this point in any particular detail. Not because it is not important, but because a special discussion of it has been placed on the agenda, and Comrade Lenin will make a report on this question. I will explain only a few of the basic ideas contained in the theses.

First, a few words about the structure of the theses. The propositions are constructed in the form of contrasts. When discussing the question of bourgeois democracy or the dictatorship of the proletariat, it is necessary to underline two things: first, bourgeois democracy signifies nothing other than the dictatorship of the bourgeoisie; and second, it is based entirely on a fiction, namely, the fiction of the so-called will of the people. This fetish, this false concept of the will of the people is the slogan of all parties. If we take any leaflet of the old Social Democratic Party, we will find these hallowed words "will of the people" innumerable times. But in reality, this will of the people is an absurdity. Capitalist society does not in any way constitute some sort of unified whole. Capitalist society consists not of one, but *two* societies. The will of the exploiting minority is in sharp opposition to the will of the exploited majority. Therefore, a unified will of the people, embracing all classes, cannot exist. It is also impossible to say that there exists a resultant of the will of various classes. In reality, such a resultant is impossible, since one class tries to force its will on the other with the aid of various measures of brute force or ideological deception. In reality, only a single will prevails. It is no accident that it is precisely under bourgeois democracy that this fiction, the "will of the people," is pushed especially to the forefront. Precisely under bourgeois democracy it is clear that only the will of the bourgeoisie is realized and not the will of the proletariat, which is, on the contrary, completely suppressed.

The second basic idea in our theses is the contrast between *formal* freedom under bourgeois democracy and the *material realization* of freedom through the medium of the proletarian dictatorship. The former proclaims various freedoms for the whole people and, therefore, for the workers as well. But as long as the material basis of society remains in the hands of the capitalist class, these freedoms cannot be realized by the workers. The situation is like that of freedom of the press in the United States: American censorship did not prohibit proletarian newspapers, but it refused to distribute them through the mails.[6] In fact, therefore, the formal existence of freedom of the press had no significance for the proletariat. Exactly the same situation exists with all freedoms under bourgeois democracy. Since buildings, paper, print shops, in a word everything, belongs to the bourgeoisie, the proletariat might formally possess various freedoms, but it is not in a position to exercise them. Under the proletarian dictatorship it is just the opposite. Here we do not hold forth at great length about various freedoms. We guarantee their realization by taking the material basis of capitalist society—property, material means—away from the bourgeoisie, and putting them into the hands of the workers and poor peasants, that is, the actual people.

Third, our theses contain one more contrast between bourgeois and proletarian democracy: participation in the exercise of state power. Although there is a lot of talk about the rule of the people under bourgeois democracy ("democracy" even means "rule of the people"), the real people—above all, the proletariat—are completely excluded from the state apparatus. In bourgeois-democratic republics such as Switzerland and the United States the "participation" of the proletariat in the direction of the state consists only in this: once every four years the proletarian drops a piece of paper in a ballot box and thereby fulfills his "civic duty." All the work is delegated to a representative, very often a member of the bourgeoisie, and the worker usually has no idea of what kind of "work" his representative is doing. He himself is never allowed access to the state apparatus. It is otherwise under the proletarian dictatorship. Here the proletariat not only takes part in elections, but rather is an active part of the whole state apparatus, of that massive mechanism that holds the whole life of the country in its hands and determines its fate. All the mass organizations of the working class are transformed into auxiliary organs of the proletarian state power and are thereby given the opportunity to participate continuously in its direction.

Following this, comrades, we take up the expropriation of the bourgeoisie—the economic side of the dictatorship of the proletariat. This aspect of the proletarian dictatorship is as important as the conquest of political power. For us, the political dictatorship, the dictatorship of the proletariat, is only an instrument we use to bring about an economic revolution. The transformation of capitalist society into communist society is accomplished on the basis of a change in the economic structure of contemporary society, and this change in productive relations is the main goal of the proletarian dictatorship.

Here we must first of all engage in a polemic with our political opponents. As you know, they object that the war has produced such extreme exhaustion that it would be ridiculous to undertake any kind of socialist measures. The Scheidemanns, our Mensheviks, Kautsky—all those who merely flirt with socialism—affirm, of course, that socialism is in itself a very good thing but, given the low level of the productive forces that exist now, after such destruction, given the impoverishment of the working class and the whole society, it would be laughable to move forward to socialism. Kautsky has even said that to socialize Germany today would mean turning the whole country into a madhouse. We, on the contrary, assert in our theses that with the present state of class relations and productive forces it is not only mistaken, but even utopian, to think that it is possible to rehabilitate the capitalist system at all. The capitalist system is cracking at all its seams.

Let us take the economic aspect of the question. It is true that everything is destroyed—but what is destroyed cannot be stuck together again on the old basis. Let us look at the relationship between the worker and the capitalist. The previous capitalist society presupposed a special type of relationship between the employer and the worker. This system rested on continuous "civil peace," not only in a political sense, but in a much broader sense. This "civil peace" had to be observed in every factory for capitalist society to function at all. But once these ties binding the capitalists and workers are ruptured, it is impossible to restore them on the old basis. Since the workers' movement for higher wages cannot be stopped, it will continue to grow. But as a consequence of this, various branches of production will stop being profitable for the capitalist class, and under these circumstances the capitalists will sabotage production and close down enterprises, as happened in Russia. Nowhere do we see the possibility of further development of capitalist relations. Only a utopian could think of demanding that. The Kautskyites have already shown themselves to be utopians in the way they dealt with the questions of imperialism and the further development of proletarian struggle. Now they are showing themselves to be utopians in their strivings to reestablish capitalist productive relations. There are only two possible outcomes: either the complete destruction of all economic life or socialist production. To reestablish capitalist productive relations would mean only prolonging the agony of the old society. It would protract the anarchy and the process of decomposition and at the same time obstruct the possibility of restoring economic life on new foundations.

A further question is connected with this. Not only Russian, but also German Socialists of the Kautsky type claim that we are bringing about some sort of special kind of communism. That instead of communism of production, we are practicing some special kind of lumpen communism, a communism of distribution, which has nothing in common with the genuine tasks of the working class. To this we must object that these Socialists have forgotten the fundamentals of Marxist doctrine. According to Marx, the most important productive force of capitalist society is its labor force. From a strictly economic point of view the *proletariat* is the most important productive force of the whole society. Now, after the immense destruction produced by the war, the task of anyone who is in any way striving for social progress consists in preserving this most important productive force—the working class. But all the burdens of the war and the whole process of destruction that was connected with the war lie especially heavily on the working class, so that this productive force is on the verge of disappearing. On this score, one of the bourgeois economists correctly noted that even if all material wealth were destroyed, but the labor force still existed, hope would still be preserved. There would still be confidence that with the help of this labor force the material wealth would again be produced. But if it too disappears, if the proletariat itself is destroyed, then the last hope for the further existence of human society in general will vanish along with it. Therefore, it is clear to every reasonable person that all efforts must be directed to the preservation of this force. And the so-called consumer communism that we practice, this "communism of distribution," that is, the transfer of what was previously in the hands of the capitalists into the hands of the proletariat, is the only way to save the workers from complete destruction. It is literally creating the possibility of further developing the productive forces and productive communism.

In this way, we are approaching the problem along a new path that also leads us, in the final analysis, only to the development of society's productive forces. We have explained this idea not only in theory, but in terms of practice.

As far as the concrete measures that we propose are concerned, they are known to all the comrades. Almost all of them have been expressed in the program of the radicals, in the program of the Dutch Tribunists during the war, in the pamphlet "What the Spartacus League Wants," and in works published by the Communist Party.[7] I will note in this connection that we have emphasized certain points that deserve special attention. First of all, a point concerning the various state capitalist agencies in the more developed countries. It is said that we must expropriate banks and large-scale enterprises, socialize corporations, and so on, but at the same time it is forgotten that state capitalism itself has created new institutions that we can use for our ends. I have in mind the different municipal bureaus of distribution, as well as the state capitalist institutions that have arisen in great numbers during the war, especially in Germany, but also in Britain, America, and France. Although these agencies in particular are closely bound to the state, it is very difficult to preserve them during a revolution. Nonetheless, we should be able to use some of their physical components for our ends. That is why we particularly emphasized this point.

Further on, in a special point, we consider the question of the petty bourgeoisie and the small peasantry. This question can be raised only in a general way here, since agrarian relations in different countries vary so greatly that it is impossible to work out anything concrete on this subject. But here, too, we have set down a basic principle: first, the petty bourgeoisie and the small peasantry must never be expropriated by the working class; second, these classes will be drawn peacefully, through a gradual process, into the general socialist organization of society; and third, the proletariat will not struggle against these classes, but will rather give them something positive by freeing them from the oppression of usury capital, tax burdens, and state debts. This last financial question, which is also closely tied to the cancellation of state debts, is very important.

If we were writing only for Russians, we would take up the role of the trade unions in the process of revolutionary reconstruction. However, judging by the experience of the German Communists, this is impossible, for the comrades there tell us that the position occupied by their trade unions is the complete opposite of the one taken by ours. In our country, the trade unions play a vital role in the organization of useful work and are a pillar of Soviet power. In Germany, however, it is just the opposite. This was brought about, evidently, by the fact that the German trade unions were in the hands of the Yellow Socialists—Legien and Company. Their activity was directed against the interests of the German proletariat. That continues even today, and the proletariat is already dissolving these old trade unions. In place of them, new organizations have arisen in Germany—the factory and plant committees, which are trying to take production into their own hands. The trade unions there no longer play any kind of positive role. We cannot work out any kind of concrete line on this, and therefore we say only that, in general terms, to manage the enterprises, institutions must be created that the proletariat can rely on, that are closely bound to production and embedded in the productive process. If in Britain, for example, there are shop stewards committees or some kind of other organizations that stand close to the productive process, then they, like our trade unions or the German factory and plant committees, will serve as a basis of administration in socialist society.

Two more questions remain to be considered: first, the cooperative movement, and second, technicians and specialists. As the Russian revolution has shown, the question of cooperatives is very important. In organizing an apparatus of distribution, we must say that we would have been able to do next to nothing in Russia without these cooperatives. Therefore we must take them into account and fully use them for our ends. In our conversation with Comrade Albert, we did not hear a single argument that could invalidate our experience in Russia. Therefore, we are including this Russian experience in our theses so that it can be applied in other countries as well.

As you know, the problem of technicians and specialists is now immensely important in Russia. All of these people want to work with us now. We know very well that some of them are our opponents. But because these people represent the accumulated practical experience of the previous order, we cannot get along without them in the sphere of economic technique. In Germany, in Britain, and even more, in America, the first phase of struggle with these forces will be much sharper than in our country. For *us,* this stage is already in the past. The two basic thoughts in this paragraph are the following: first, as long as these strata conduct an open or hidden struggle against us, we must deal with them accordingly; and second, once the resistance of these strata and the bourgeoisie as a whole is broken, we must fully utilize these technical forces and gradually assimilate them.

The concluding section is called, "The Road to Victory." Here we point to the possibility of making revolutionary use of bourgeois parliamentary institutions. We included this possibility in our theses, since it would be theoretically incorrect to say that it is impossible in principle for us to enter any parliament. The question of a boycott of a bourgeois-democratic parliament is purely tactical. It is determined exclusively by the given situation, that is, the relationship of class forces, the strength and maturity of the proletariat, and its readiness for a final, victorious struggle.

Only one thing remains to be said: We stand for armed insurrection. It is the highest form of revolutionary mass struggle. But the concrete date of this insurrection, the time of the final clash, depends on the given situation and the relationship of class forces. We say that it is not our business to force the pace of historical developments but first to organize our forces, even utilizing bourgeois parliamentary organizations, so that once we are organized, we can go into the final conflict at full strength.

As for the opportunists and the Kautskyites, we do not have anything to add about them.

In concluding our theses, we express the thought that the international proletariat is not the attacking, but the defending side. This formulation has great agitational value. The bourgeoisie is screaming that we are the ones who are breaking the peace, that we represent Red imperialism, that we are the aggressors. All the facts of the Russian revolution, as well as the German revolution, contradict this. We know that a White Terror already exists, and that the bourgeoisie is using barbarous methods of struggle against us. We also know very well that the League of Nations signifies nothing other than the preparation for the last battle of capitalism against the international proletariat—and against this, the proletariat must defend itself. It finds itself in a defensive situation. However, when it is defending itself against a bourgeoisie that is moving against it with all its resources, the proletariat must also respond to the attack in kind.

Such are our theses. I would like to express the wish that most of the comrades take part in the discussion of these theses. As you see, they touch on almost all the questions that concern the current tasks of the proletariat under present circumstances, and almost all the problems that face the proletariat and that it must strive to solve. That is the situation. Of course, we still have a number of questions on the agenda to discuss, but in general and on the whole these theses of ours represent our program and are the foundation for the program of the Third, Communist International. And if the comrades show a lively interest in them, Comrade Albert and I will consider that we have done our duty well.

(*Five minute recess.*)

DISCUSSION ON THE PLATFORM

LENIN: We are back in session. Comrade Rutgers has requested the floor. Each speaker has fifteen minutes speaking time.

RUTGERS *(Holland)*: I would like to raise the general question of whether or not the platform adequately stresses the role of the middle layers—the intellectuals and better-off workers. It does point out that the higher wage scale in the imperialist countries comes at the expense of the colonial peoples. But it fails to note the fact that this gives officials, intellectuals, and better-off workers a privileged position, especially in America. This makes it possible for the finance capitalists to build a sufficient base of support.

Comrades, we now find that these middle layers are our strongest opponents. We must now see how the possibility of their taking control of production will affect them. The proletariat is not yet mature and needs support. Only if the workers succeed in reconstructing all economic life with their own forces will they be able to accomplish this task. More emphasis should be placed on the great practical importance of this for the ultimate victory of the proletariat.

The platform says: "The proletarian dictatorship will be able to accomplish its economic task only to the degree that the proletariat can establish a centralized administration."[8] But the situation is more complicated than that, because it is not possible to reorganize the economy only partially. The workers must organize and control the entire system or they will be controlled by other layers. Clearly, the road to victory cannot lead to success unless workers' control can be instituted. Perhaps greater emphasis should be placed on that.

A further comment on the colonies: It would be good to expand the passage on colonial policy in order to make quite clear to the colonial peoples that we seek to work actively with them, regardless of whether or not they have their own ideology and religion. We are prepared to go forward together with them on the basis of opposition to imperialism, and if, for example, a rebellion were to erupt in India, that would be of enormous importance for us. I therefore propose specifically that where the resolution reads, "in order to hasten the final collapse of the world imperialist system"[9] we insert the phrase "active collaboration" to contrast our position with that of the Yellow International.

I have some reservations about a subsequent formulation. The first thing it says there is, "But the bloody deeds of German imperialism . . . soon showed its actual predatory nature. Now the Entente countries are being exposed as international bandits."[10] That is certain to make a strange impression on the colonial peoples, who have been robbed and oppressed for centuries, especially by Britain. Now we announce that these countries are finally showing their true face as world bandits. This is an unfortunate choice of words, and perhaps it could be modified.

Nor should we make special reference here to the "barbaric colonial troops."[11] Anyone familiar with the colonial adventures that the Dutch and others waged against our brown brothers before the war will find it unnecessary to accuse those colonial soldiers of barbarism here. To modify this formulation, I have a proposal. After "predatory nature" reword the sentence as follows: "The Entente countries too are now revealing their true nature as global bandits and murderers of the proletariat. Together with the German bourgeoisie, they will now condemn the Russian and German workers to starvation with the same ruthlessness with which they proceeded against the colonial peoples. . . ."

One final comment. The resolution states that living conditions cannot improve because of the automatically increasing prices of all consumer goods, and so on.[12] In my opinion, the word "automatically" ought to be deleted. Rising prices prevent an improvement in living conditions in any case, but I believe that fundamental objections could be made to "automatically."

KUUSINEN *(FINLAND)*: Comrades, the Finnish delegation agrees with the draft resolution's main points. The platform that the comrades have read to us has already been tested by revolutionary experience, and I believe that the task here is only to formulate it in the best possible way. Of course, finding the right wording for such a document is very difficult, and I am certain that the conference can make it even more precise.

I want to direct your attention to a few places that in our opinion are not formulated as we might wish. An objection could be raised to the passage where revolutionary unions and cooperatives are discussed.[13] In Finland we have neither revolutionary unions nor revolutionary cooperatives, and we very much doubt even the possibility of there being any in our country. The structure of unions and cooperatives there convinces us that after the revolution the new social order could be better established without these unions than with them, even if they were founded on a new basis. Perhaps this is the case in other countries as well.

The formulation at the end of the draft on taking a defensive approach, which Comrade Bukharin particularly emphasized, is also not so well chosen in our opinion. We once fought a defensive revolution in Finland, and we would not want to go through that experience again under any circumstances. That, we believe, would be an error. From an agitational standpoint it is much more useful to draw attention to the offensive carried out by the proletarian revolution.

Above all, I want to stress that the draft contains many very worthwhile new ideas, including an underlying concept which I feel should be stressed more strongly and stated more concretely. The last section, "The road to victory," says that the rise of the revolutionary movement in all countries and many other recent events must lead to the founding of a genuinely revolutionary and genuinely proletarian Communist International. Earlier the German comrade expressed doubts as to whether the international movement is mature enough for this step. In that context, of course, no decision to found the new International can be adopted. But I believe that historical development must lead to founding the revolutionary proletarian International now, and if possible, to founding it before the end of this conference. In our opinion, the German comrade's arguments against such a decision were not convincing. On the other hand, his statement was also a great relief. Yesterday when we listened to his objections, we thought he might have principled reasons to oppose founding the new International; now we hear that is not so. He merely believes the working class today looks upon such action with some suspicion. I think this is a mistake. There is distrust of Internationals such as the Second, which, in fact, only passed resolutions and never acted on them. The Third International will be quite different in that respect. It will not simply adopt resolutions on paper but will be an International of the deed, of revolutionary action, of struggle.

Frankly, comrades, if we passed no resolution, no decision other than this platform, it would be rather reminiscent of the resolutions of the old International. The platform's content is good. It is revolutionary and communist. But we should not fail to draw the practical conclusion that flows from it, because the international revolutionary movement needs the Third International now. The time has come to create it.

The only somewhat convincing objection that could be made against this is that the founding of the Third International is not so urgent because, in reality, we now already have one—namely great, revolutionary Russia. Comrades, you know that for over a year now revolutionary Russia has in effect constituted the new International. It has served the international revolutionary proletarian movement very well—not so much directly by agitation, as the bourgeoisie claims, as indirectly by its great example, as a model for the great social revolution. Nevertheless, there is a practical need in struggle for the new International.

The German comrade also said that this gathering may not be large enough to make that decision. That is true, but it is not the fault of the revolutionary workers' parties of Europe or America. In my opinion this meeting is not so weak compared to a previous gathering that founded the First International on a day over a half century ago.[14] That meeting also had few representatives from different countries. Perhaps our gathering is reminiscent of that earlier one in that there, as here, there were very few great revolutionary thinkers, and many more individuals who were only halfway along in their development. Yet Marx and his comrades had no misgivings about founding the First International under those circumstances. Even Wilhelm Liebknecht, the delegate from Germany,[15] had no objections to founding the new International at that time. I am convinced that his illustrious son, Karl Liebknecht, would have no second thoughts either, if he were here. I believe that the power of the new International will be proportionate to the power of the revolutionary proletariat and not to that of this small assembly.

Comrades, it was said that no decision on founding the new International could be made here; but now, as yesterday, I must state my desire to make that decision before our meeting adjourns. The situation is ripe, the international revolution has already begun, and therefore the revolutionary International should be constituted now.

The decision to found the Third International will draw the line and show the world working-class movement where to take its stand: on the one side or the other, on the side of the fighting proletariat or on the side of its hangmen. Therefore I would ask the comrades to add at the end of the draft the great idea that the Third International is hereby founded.

REPORT ON GERMAN AUSTRIA

J. GRUBER [KARL STEINHARDT]:[16] My dear comrades, we, the delegates from German Austria, cannot find words to express the sentiments that we feel today in your midst. We arrived here an hour ago after a seventeen-day trip of incredible difficulties, and we bring you the greetings and warmest good wishes of our revolutionary comrades in German Austria. Comrades, we bring greetings for you all, but most of all we must thank our Russian comrades, because through the great revolution of more than a year ago, they gave the revolutionary forces in Austria a tremendous impetus. It is thanks to them alone that we have today a strong, youthful Communist Party in German Austria. History will erect a lasting monument to the Russian comrades for having helped the world revolution achieve this breakthrough.

Now I would like to report on the events that led to the founding of the Communist Party of German Austria and describe its development.

The peace of Brest-Litovsk was in preparation. In Austria famine reigned, aggravated by the dictatorship of unbridled military abuse. The proletariat urgently and tumultuously demanded that Austria quit the World War once and for all. But it was put off by the promises of the criminal government, which said that peace would be concluded very soon. But that did not happen. The proletariat saw that it had been duped again. The standard of living deteriorated enormously. This led in January 1918 to a very strong movement that originated in the industrial centers south of Vienna and spread to Vienna within hours.[17] The wheels of industry stopped turning. The parliamentary representatives of the party of social traitors were speechless.[18] The proletariat did not want to have anything to do with the leaders of either the unions or the Social Democratic Party.

After the movement had lasted several days and extended into all sectors of industry, both the union leaders and the party bosses roused themselves and tried to divert it. That caused the whole movement to bog down. Messrs. Seitz, Renner, and Leuthner from the Social Democrats, and Tomschik, Domes, and others from the unions took the leadership and promised to represent the workers' interests. They contended, however, that Austria had no right to withdraw from the ranks of the warring countries as that would cause the collapse of the economic basis for the Austrian proletariat's existence. Once again, the workers let themselves be deluded by their political and union representatives. Placing themselves between the government and the workers, they formulated some radical-sounding demands and received a prepared statement from the government—and after an industrial shutdown of barely a week, the workers went back to work.[19]

The inevitable happened. The government, recognizing that the workers' representatives were a pliant tool in its hands, refused to even consider implementing the demands it had agreed to. It also broke its promise not to punish the leaders of the movement. It sent them to the front or buried them behind prison walls—they were wiped out of existence. Our comrades, who had worked in the movement as Left Radical Social Democrats, were accused by the party leaders of high treason, and a number of leading comrades were expelled from the party.[20]

The collapse of the fronts in Italy and Bulgaria, the countrywide famine, the destruction of the food distribution system, and the flood of soldiers returning from the front all hastened the final disintegration of the Austro-Hungarian monarchy.[21] Out of it several states were formed along ethnic lines: the Czechoslovak and Hungarian republics were established, and the Yugoslav, Italian, and Romanian peoples joined their respective mother countries. Nothing was left of the "glorious empire" but a rump state, German Austria, with about nine million inhabitants. Only at the last minute did the Social Democracy in German Austria decide to assume leadership of the "revolution" and to declare German Austria a republic.

Today the Social Democracy's stuffed-shirt heroes still speak of a revolution in Austria. But there was no real revolution. Just when the proletariat could indeed have taken power without a fight, the representatives of the Social Democracy placed themselves protectively in front of the bourgeoisie and said, "This is not yet the time to take power; we must form a coalition with the bourgeoisie." A presidency was formed consisting of a most archclerical of clerics, a German Nationalist, and a Social Democrat. When this triumvirate took over the government,[22] the hour had struck for a defensive struggle by the Austrian proletariat. Not even in Stürgkh's time was reaction more brutal than under the reign of the workers' representatives. Dr. Renner became chancellor; Dr. Bauer, that onetime radical, became secretary of state for foreign affairs; the army was put under Comrade Deutsch; and Social Democrats sat side by side with bourgeois in all posts.

Earlier, in May 1918 the Left Radicals and various opposition groups had come closer together and sought to define a common platform. That is when the first proposal was made to form a Communist Party in Austria.[23] We did not know at the time that the Russian comrades would also one day call themselves Communists; we didn't know that our comrades in Germany, the Spartacist League, would also take the name Communist Party. We conceived the idea while we were still a small group; we aimed to put it into practice and begin a new epoch in the revolutionary workers' movement in Austria.

There were only a few of us who began the struggle. Many of our best comrades were behind bars, and a dozen people had to provide all the energy for our struggle. We decided then to put out a paper called *Weckruf; Kommunistisches Wochenblatt* [Reveille; a communist newsweekly]. For the first time the name "Communism" was inscribed on our banner. However, the entire newspaper, from the first to the last line, was confiscated, and we therefore could not accomplish our goal of distributing copies of the *Weckruf* among the masses of workers celebrating on the first of May.[24] But when Austria's military collapse led to a partial restoration of bourgeois civil liberties, and when after nine months of imprisonment our brave comrades were released, we acquired a new and stronger foundation. On November 3, 1918, we constituted ourselves as the Communist Party of German Austria. The central organ of the party was *Weckruf.*

The republic was due to be publicly proclaimed on November 12, 1918. Aware that the Austrian proletariat was in a thoroughly revolutionary mood, we resolved to speak to them about communism. Innumerable red banners bore the words: "Forward to the socialist republic." Several of our comrades jumped up on the ramp in front of the parliament building and proclaimed the principles of communism to the people. Then we selected several Communists who tried to go inside and tell the government representatives that the proletariat demanded not a bourgeois but a socialist republic, but they slammed the door in our faces. Our comrades from the Red Guard banged against the door with the butts of their rifles, meaning to get us inside. At that point the widely reported shooting incident began. The Red Guard and the people's militia returned the fire, which came from inside the parliament building, and the so beautifully arranged celebration of the bourgeois republic ended in the temporary occupation of the parliament by the proletariat.[25]

In retaliation the agrarian deputies decided to send the Communist ringleaders to the wall. They threatened to stop food deliveries to Vienna if that were not done. The Social Democratic representatives thought that was going too far, although they agreed that the villains should be severely punished. They also arrested Comrades Steinhardt and Friedländer on charges of rioting, but they were released after two weeks, mostly because of pressure by the councils of the people's militia. Many of our Russian friends were also detained and deported.[26] The Social Democrats in the government not only approved these measures but helped to initiate them.

War was declared on the Communist movement. The government applied all its power against us. The hardest struggle we had to undergo was with the governmental Social Democrats. We could not get hold of a meeting hall in Vienna. When we tried to hold meetings as the Communist Party in some parts of Vienna, they took the halls away from us, seeking to paralyze us. In the provinces the governmental Socialists were able to show their strength even more forcefully. In Graz, the industrial center of Styria, we were unable for four weeks to hold a meeting. The Social Democrat Resel, the district military commander there, organized a reign of terror against the Communists.

Only because we took to the streets and held meetings in public squares can we hold meetings today in any hall we choose. Now there are Communist organizations in all of northern Styria, and the workers come to us, discuss with us, and support our platform. Today no one would dare prevent us from holding meetings and building our organization.

So we prevailed. But history will record, to the eternal historic shame of the Social Democratic Party, that it tried to destroy our movement using the most crude and violent means.

In our agitation we never said that the Social Democratic workers were our enemies, but rather that they had been led onto the wrong track. We endeavor to win over the revolutionary layers of the working class, and indeed everywhere the Left Radicals joined up with us.

On February 9 of this year we finally had the opportunity to hold a full review of our forces from all over German Austria. Whereas at our first convention on November 3, 1918, only a small handful of comrades had come together, on February 9, 1919, there was representation from groups in all of German Austria.[27] We put forward a clear, precisely formulated Communist platform. As for the National Assembly, we declared that we wanted no part of the elections to it, because it was a tool to sidetrack the revolution. For the Social Democracy elections were the very culmination of its political existence. We counterposed the idea of the dictatorship of the proletariat and called for workers' and soldiers' councils.

That is how things stood when we left German Austria. We now have four months of organizational work behind us. Rather than making a point of the quite large number of members we have signed up, we stress that they embody the revolutionary will to action and that a revolutionary force exists that will prove itself when the decisive moment comes.

So the Communist Party in German Austria is consolidated and ready to fight—persecuted by the government and hated by the Social Democrats. Unfortunately, Fritz Adler is not in our ranks. When he killed Prime Minister Stürgkh and Austria's working class united to energetically demand his release from prison, he was a revolutionary symbol for us. But what happened when Fritz Adler was released? To those who were devoted to him and were ready to sacrifice everything for him he was no longer a friend, but had become their opponent. He placed himself at the disposal of the Social Democratic Party, the very party that had condemned him and that would have expelled him had he not been the son of a famous father. He was nominated for deputy to the National Assembly, and his name, associated with the reactionary workers' leaders, served as bait to lure many workers into voting in the parliamentary elections. He declared himself against any attempt to split the workers movement and especially opposed the work of the Communist Party.

Ours is a movement of the masses. Every day we are told, "You Communists have no prominent leaders. Ah, yes, the Russian Communists have a Lenin, a Trotsky, a Bukharin, who have been fighting for many years for the ideas of communism and for the dictatorship of the proletariat; but you haven't a single outstanding, internationally known leader." Yet the working class took us seriously nevertheless, because they saw that having a big-name leader is not the only thing that counts.

We workers in German Austria have been told that destruction, pillage, and sabotage reign in Russia and that before long all the Bolsheviks' glory would come tumbling down. But we see that that glory is now firm and that the Communist Party of Russia today has opened up a new epoch in world history. Moscow used to be the center of reaction; today it is the center of the Communist movement, and that can never be destroyed. That is why the workers of German Austria support the Russian comrades' movement so passionately. For they know that if the communist regime in the East is destroyed, it will be impossible to build a society on communist foundations in the West for a long time to come.

The conference of the Second International in Bern is the death agony of an era; today's congress is the revolutionary proletariat's first gathering to organize action.

Therefore we greet you, hoping that this gathering inaugurates a new era. For seventeen days we have been under way from Vienna to Moscow. We traveled the whole way like hoboes; on coal cars, locomotives, couplings, in cattle cars, on foot through the lines of Ukrainian and Polish robber bands, our lives constantly in danger, always driven by the single burning desire: we want to get to Moscow, we must get to Moscow, and nothing will stop us from getting there!

We have reached our goal. We are with you, comrades! And we must and will reach our common goal, the Communist Federal World Republic—let it be in the not all too distant future!

THIRD DAY OF SESSIONS
MARCH 4, 1919

Discussion on the platform (continued)

(*Lenin opens the session at twelve noon.*)

ALBERT *(Germany)*: Comrades, the bureau moves that we meet publicly from now on, since it can no longer be kept secret that our meeting is taking place. Also we want to let you know that the remaining delegates have now arrived.

(*The motion is adopted unanimously. The discussion on the platform continues; Comrade Reinstein takes the floor.*)

REINSTEIN *(Socialist Labor Party of America)*: I want to discuss two points that in my opinion should either be incorporated into the declaration of principles or given more emphasis there. The first point is that in regard to militarism and war, the Third International rejects the concept of defense of the fatherland. In every country the representatives of the Second International adopted resolutions against militarism, against supporting the government's various war expenditures, and so forth. But most of them also took the position that if their country was attacked, that is, if it was not the attacker but the object of the attack; if in other words it was a "defensive" war—then the proletariat and the entire labor and socialist movement would have not only the right but the duty to support their government.

The consequences of this position are only too well known to the proletariat of all countries. Therefore, I am in favor of the Third International clearly spelling out here, in a few sentences, that in our century there can be no wars that are not rooted in capitalist competition. As long as capitalist society exists there will be wars over markets. In light of the purely commercial causes of modern wars, the proletariat not only does not have the duty, it does not even have the right to support its government, even in so-called defensive wars. There is only one war that the proletariat is duty-bound to support, and that is social war, the social revolution.

The other idea that in my view is not correctly presented is the role of the economic organizations, the trade union movement. We in America have a position on this question that is the opposite of that of our Finnish comrades. We are not inclined to ascribe an insignificant or subordinate role to the trade union movement. Our successes in the most highly developed capitalist country, the United States, teach us something else. The entire membership of the Socialist Labor Party, a big part of the Socialist Party led by Debs, and those workers grouped around the IWW and other industrial unions see the trade union organizations as the most important institutions, whose role in the revolutionary struggle will be not only prominent but decisive. Thus our position is that the Third International should more sharply stress the need for revolutionizing and transforming the trade union movement. Our experience leads us to conclude that those who carry the banner under which the masses of organized workers march—such union leaders as Gompers in America, Carl Legien in Germany, Henderson in England—actually hold the key to the overall situation and can have a determining influence. The problem is to free the union movement from the disastrous influence of these capitalist flunkies.

When I speak of reorganizing the trade union movement, what I mean is that Communists in every country must see to it that the unions take consistent class-struggle positions, not merely in words but in deeds as well. We must strive to organize the unions so their form is suitable for the present-day struggle.

I can well imagine the objections that can be made to this. It will probably be said that it is too great a task and will consume too much time. I grant that it is easier to criticize capitalist or social-patriotic leaders than it is to criticize the leaders of economic struggles—the union leaders—or the unions themselves: their goals, methods, and mentality. To be sure, that is a difficult job. But we believe that it is a necessary one.

We regard as absolutely indispensable the liberation of the international trade union movement from the influence of the capitalist lackeys in their leadership. Therefore I move that we instruct the committee to revise the relevant sentences in the document so that the union organizations receive more than the present passing mention and to call on the proletariat of all countries in the name of the Third International, with the prestige of the Third International, to set about, with redoubled energy, the task of building the union movement into what it really ought to be. If a call like that goes out from the Third International, I can assure you, at least as far as the American movement is concerned, it will give the revolutionary forces in the union and political movements the moral support they need. Thus our work will be made all the more successful and we will be able to break the traitors' grip.

If the Third International takes the position that the union movement is useful but of no great significance, that is grist for the mill of Gompers and Henderson. The Gomperses and Hendersons are already hard at work founding a Yellow international union movement whose task will be to function as an international lightning rod.[28] We must work against them.

KASCHER *(Communist Group of Switzerland)*: Comrades, I wholeheartedly endorse the previous speaker's views. I too feel that this draft, which the Third International will distribute to the workers of all countries, should actually offer the proletariat something completely positive and more practical. The workers need support in this difficult fight, not only against the bourgeoisie but also against the social patriots and centrists of every variety. Precisely in this respect, I feel, the section of the draft on the road to victory is inadequate. This section, in contrast to all the drafts and appeals that have appeared until now, ought to be based upon the experiences of the Russian and German revolutions.

This part of the draft clearly addresses two challenges to the international working class: the need for mass struggle and the need to found Communist parties. I can find nothing else concrete under this point. I would like to see the tasks of the world proletariat defined more precisely.

The first of the two points is on the council system. The platform deals with this, but in its broadest sense, where the council system already holds political power. I am speaking about the kind of council structure that does not represent the final stage of the revolution but is possible in countries where the proletariat has yet to take political power. I am speaking of the workers' councils.

It seems strange that these workers' councils, which are forming everywhere, are not mentioned in the platform. Perhaps this seemed self-evident to the authors because these councils are arising spontaneously in all countries. But comrades, those who have had to work in countries where the revolution has not yet occurred know that we have a hard fight to wage for these councils, against not only the social patriots but also radicals who for reasons of principle cannot yet resolve to take a stand for the councils. In order to support these revolutionary efforts and support the proletariat against the social patriots, the International must say in its platform that to prepare the best and most correct road to victory right away, workers' councils should be formed now.

The second point I wish to raise, which I regard as a factor on the road to victory, is the concept of control of production. This should be included in part three of the draft, which takes up socialization. In countries where the revolution has not yet taken place, the broad masses see nationalization and socialization as something monstrous, something that reminds them of the "Russian chaos." Hence, in those countries there is a struggle going on between workers who favor socialization, on the one hand, and on the other, the various leaders and tendencies—even the radical ones—who wish to block this idea from spreading and taking root. As I see it, we must also formulate a slogan on this. The intermediate goal of workers' control of production and consumption must be posed as a stage on the road to socialization. We should not forget that the employers thought of this long ago and tried to use it to play games with the workers. We know their motives; but it will be a different story when the workers are the ones raising this slogan.

The third point I want to emphasize is preparing for the seizure of economic power. I know how difficult it was to find people, even one or two comrades, who could explain to the workers what taking over production and economic power really means, how to fight sabotage, how to govern and administer countryside and factory.

I urge this gathering and the authors of the platform to discuss these questions. If anything put forward by the Third International is not truly based on the experiences of the revolution or is not truly capable of moving the proletariat of the Entente nations into action, then our whole conference will have been a failure.

In conclusion I wish to emphasize that I also share the opinion that the founding of the Third International should not be postponed. It is awaited everywhere, in every country. There are small groups everywhere that need such a center, and the German proletariat as well wants it unreservedly.

PLATTEN: Comrades, the resolutions commission had to consider quite a number of motions.[29] We decided to make a few minor alterations in the draft.

The commission would like to incorporate the motion by Rutgers by rewriting the sentence as follows: "Now the Entente countries are being exposed, even before the backward layers of the population, as international bandits and murderers of the proletariat."[30] In other words, the phrase "even before the backward layers" was inserted. While Comrade Rutgers went into greater detail, the commission believes it quite sufficient to insert only that phrase. We can assume that before and during the war there was no doubt that the Entente countries too were pursuing a policy of robbery, and that only backward elements could still harbor the misconception that these governments were really fighting for freedom, justice, and so on. In this context, adding that phrase should bring clarity.

(Lenin moves that there be two speakers on amendments, one for and one against. The motion is carried.)

(No one wishes to speak.)

SUMMARY

ALBERT *(Germany)*: Comrades, when Comrade Bukharin and I set out to draft the platform, we did not think it would be possible to reach agreement on the different questions so painlessly. After all, it appeared from the outset that, given the completely different development of each country—especially today—there would be a large number of conflicts and differences. We are greatly encouraged that this was not the case and that the platform was by and large accepted by the conference.

In drafting it, our main problem was how to summarize the level of the revolution's development, which differs from country to country, and come up with a coherent whole. You will agree that this was no easy job. On the one hand, in countries with the most advanced revolutionary development, demands and wishes of a far-reaching nature could be put forward. On the other hand, the countries that lag behind could say: Our country is not yet ready for the demands in your platform; we cannot begin to attempt such things. However, it turns out that the delegates agreed with what was proposed here.

Last evening, the editing commission, with both authors participating, considered the amendments to the platform proposed during yesterday's discussion. There too we achieved complete unanimity. The changes presented to you today by Comrade Platten as chairman of the editing commission were agreed upon in consultation with the authors. No fundamental changes were made, only editorial ones. It must be said that it would be quite easy to expand the platform. But from the outset we set ourselves very strict limits to make it possible to unite the widest possible array of forces and the greatest number of organizations around this platform.

I now come to a very important question that the platform does not deal with, that of the trade union movement. We spent a lot of time on this question. We interviewed delegates from each country about their trade union movement, and concluded that since the proletariat's situation in each country is completely different, it is impossible at this time to include in the platform an international position on this question. There is no one solution to this problem that we could present as a single, overall policy toward the trade unions.[31]

We were told that in Russia the trade union movement, because of its revolutionary character, plays a very important role in the Soviet system, and that Soviet power relies in part on the unions to distribute goods and manage the factories.

Elsewhere, the situation is quite different. The Finnish comrades told us that it is impossible to utilize the unions for the revolution. In Britain, on the other hand, the unions play a quite different role. We in Germany see that since the revolution began, the unions have been completely shoved aside and that all economic struggles are being waged without the unions and indeed against them. It would be easy to say they must be revolutionized, with revolutionary leaders replacing the Yellow ones. But that is not so easy to do, because all organizational structures in the unions are adapted to the old state apparatus and because a council system cannot be established on the basis of craft unions. We in Germany transferred the leadership of economic struggles to the workers' councils. Since the revolution began, the workers' councils in the factories have taken over the entire job, and the unions in Germany are in effect nothing but support organizations. At present, no one can predict how they will develop or whether they can be revolutionized and transformed into industrial unions.

These are all conditions that vary from one country to the next, and we therefore believe it is impossible to offer the workers a clear international policy. For that reason we cannot resolve the question today. We must leave it up to each national organization to develop a position on it. We therefore state very simply that revolutionary unions should be utilized for the struggle wherever possible.

It was requested that the concept of "fatherland" be defined more precisely in the draft, and that we tell the workers that as Communists we have no interest in defending the fatherland. A qualification is necessary—we should say that we have no interest in defending the *bourgeois* fatherland, but we look at the question differently when it concerns a socialist fatherland. Comrades, we see what a keen interest the workers of Russia take in defending their fatherland. However, since the platform is aimed at destroying the bourgeois state apparatus, it is obvious that with the collapse of the bourgeois social order the bourgeois concept of the fatherland will also collapse. For this reason, I would ask you not to accept this proposal.

Comrade Kascher wishes to have the council system discussed in greater detail. I would like to point out to her that we have yet to discuss the question of the council system and that a position will be outlined in separate resolutions.

In conclusion we ask you to adopt the changes proposed here by the resolutions commission and then the platform in its entirety. If we do that, and if possible do so unanimously, then we can go before the world with confidence and tell the proletariat of all countries: It is up to you to create the organizations that will struggle relentlessly in each country and that will unite to create the great, new Third International.

Only then, in my opinion, will it be possible to found the Third International. Today opinions vary so widely about what Communists in different countries want, and there is such widespread ignorance—not only because of the malicious slanders of the bourgeoisie—that it is impossible to educate those groups of workers who already consider themselves Communist about the thinking and activities of their fraternal parties in other countries.

PLATTEN: The discussion is closed. No new motions may be introduced.

Now, Comrade Reinstein has made the following motion:

"The Communist Third International calls upon revolutionists of all countries to work with redoubled energy and determination to set the trade union movements of their countries on a truly revolutionary course and to transform them into movements whose structure, goals, policies, and spirit are equal to the revolutionary objectives of communism."

It would seem most appropriate to vote on whether or not this body wishes to refer the Reinstein motion to the commission for a final decision on how an amendment can be entertained.

ALBERT: In my opinion, the motion by Comrade Reinstein should not be linked to the platform. Each delegate is free to present separate resolutions to be discussed and voted on at the end of the agenda together with other resolutions and not be associated with the platform.

I therefore move that we vote on Comrade Reinstein's motion under the agenda point "Other Business."

(*Reinstein moves that the vote be taken at once.*)

LENIN: We must vote on the procedural motion.

Comrade Albert's motion is adopted with sixteen voting for and eleven against. No amendments are proposed, so we will now proceed to the vote on the text as a whole.

KLINGER: All those in favor of adopting the text as a whole.

Communist Party of Germany ....yes
Communist Party of Russia ....yes
Communist Party of German Austria..........................yes
Communist Party of Hungary ....yes
Communist Party of Sweden ....yes
Norway...abstains
Switzerland...yes
American Socialist Labor Party .... yes,
on the condition that the statement
is adopted. [See statement by Reinstein below.]
Balkan revolutionary federation..................................yes
Polish Communist Party..yes
Finnish party..yes
Ukrainian Communist Party..yes
Latvian Communist Party..yes
Lithuanian/Belorussian Communist Party..................yes
Estonian Communist Party..yes
Armenian Communist Party..yes
Communist Party of the German colonists.................yes

ALBERT: The platform is adopted unanimously with one abstention.

REINSTEIN: I state for the record that I am *for* adopting the platform *in the expectation* that what it lacks—stress on the need to work for revolutionizing the trade union movement—will be made good by adopting the resolution I submitted for that purpose.

Left: Alexandra Kollontai; middle: Georgiy Chicherin; right: Christian Rakovsky.

4. Theses and report on bourgeois democracy and the dictatorship of the proletariat

ALBERT: We come to the next point on the agenda: "Bourgeois Democracy and the Dictatorship of the Proletariat."

LENIN: Theses have been drafted on this question. Everyone present has copies of them in German and Russian, and the English and French comrades will receive English and French translations later on. Consequently I consider it unnecessary to read the theses aloud again.

ALBERT: We have heard a motion to distribute the theses only and not read them aloud.

REINSTEIN: I move that we proceed to another point and return to the theses at a later time, after comrades have had an opportunity to read them.

PLATTEN: We must proceed with the agenda. The resolutions commission has discussed its position on the theses very thoroughly and decided to recommend no discussion on their details. Instead it recommends taking only motions pertaining to printing and international distribution. It might therefore be best to read the theses and take no discussion on their details.

ALBERT: I support that motion and ask whether there are any further proposals along these lines. A motion has been made that we not await printing but proceed to read them aloud. Is there any opposition?

The motion to read the theses passes with one dissenting vote.

(*Lenin reads the following theses:*[1])

THESES ON BOURGEOIS DEMOCRACY AND THE DICTATORSHIP OF THE PROLETARIAT

1. Faced with the growth of the revolutionary workers' movement in every country, the bourgeoisie and their agents in the workers' organizations are making desperate attempts to find ideological and political arguments in defense of the rule of the exploiters. Condemnation of dictatorship and defense of democracy are particularly prominent among these arguments. The falsity and hypocrisy of this argument, repeated in a thousand strains by the capitalist press and the Bern Yellow International conference in February 1919, are obvious to all who refuse to betray the fundamental principles of socialism.

2. First, this argument employs the concepts of "democracy in general" and "dictatorship in general," without posing the question of the class concerned. This nonclass or above-class presentation, which supposedly is popular, is an outright travesty of the basic tenet of socialism, namely, its theory of class struggle, which Socialists who have sided with the bourgeoisie recognize in words but disregard in practice. For in no civilized capitalist country does "democracy in general" exist. All that exists is

bourgeois democracy, and it is not a question of "dictatorship in general," but of the dictatorship of the oppressed class, i.e., the proletariat, over its oppressors and exploiters, i.e., the bourgeoisie, in order to overcome the resistance offered by the exploiters in their fight to maintain their domination.

3. History teaches us that no oppressed class ever did, or could, achieve power without going through a period of dictatorship, i.e., the conquest of political power and forcible suppression of the resistance always offered by the exploiters—a resistance that is most desperate, most furious, and that stops at nothing. The bourgeoisie, whose domination is now defended by the Socialists who denounce "dictatorship in general" and extol "democracy in general," won power in the advanced countries through a series of insurrections, civil wars, and the forcible suppression of kings, feudal lords, slaveowners, and their attempts at restoration. In books, pamphlets, congress resolutions, and propaganda speeches socialists everywhere have thousands and millions of times explained to the people the class nature of these bourgeois revolutions and this bourgeois dictatorship. That is why the present defense of bourgeois democracy under cover of talk about "democracy in general" and the present howls and shouts against proletarian dictatorship under cover of shouts about "dictatorship in general" are an outright betrayal of socialism. They are, in fact, desertion to the bourgeoisie, denial of the proletariat's right to its own, proletarian revolution, and defense of bourgeois reformism at the very historical juncture when bourgeois reformism throughout the world has collapsed and the war has created a revolutionary situation.

4. In explaining the class nature of bourgeois civilization, bourgeois democracy, and the bourgeois parliamen-

tary system, all socialists have expressed the idea formulated with the greatest scientific precision by Marx and Engels, namely, that the most democratic bourgeois republic is no more than a machine for the suppression of the working class by the bourgeoisie, for the suppression of the working people by a handful of capitalists.[2] There is not a single revolutionary, not a single Marxist among those now shouting against dictatorship and for democracy who has not sworn and vowed to the workers that he accepts this basic truth of socialism. But now, when the revolutionary proletariat is in a fighting mood and taking action to destroy this machine of oppression and to establish proletarian dictatorship, these traitors to socialism claim that the bourgeoisie have granted the working people "pure democracy," have abandoned resistance, and are prepared to yield to the majority of the working people. They assert that in a democratic republic there is not and never has been any such thing as a state machine for the oppression of labor by capital.

5. The Paris Commune—to which all who parade as socialists pay lip service, for they know that the workers ardently and sincerely sympathize with the Commune—showed very clearly the historically conventional nature and limited value of the bourgeois parliamentary system and bourgeois democracy—institutions which, though highly progressive compared with medieval times, inevitably require a radical alteration in the era of proletarian revolution. It was Marx who best appraised the historical significance of the Commune. In his analysis, he revealed the exploiting nature of bourgeois democracy and the bourgeois parliamentary system under which the oppressed classes enjoy the right to decide once in several years which representative of the propertied classes shall "represent and suppress" (*ver- und zertreten*) the people in

parliament.[3] And it is now, when the soviet movement is embracing the entire world and continuing the work of the Commune for all to see, that the traitors to socialism are forgetting the concrete experience and concrete lessons of the Paris Commune and repeating the old bourgeois rubbish about "democracy in general." The Commune was not a parliamentary institution.

6. The significance of the Commune, furthermore, lies in the fact that it endeavored to crush, to smash to its very foundations, the bourgeois state apparatus, the bureaucratic, judicial, military, and police machine, and to replace it by a self-governing, mass workers' organization in which there was no division between legislative and executive power. All contemporary bourgeois-democratic republics, including the German republic, which the traitors to socialism, in mockery of the truth, describe as a proletarian republic, retain this state apparatus. We therefore again get quite clear confirmation of the point that shouting in defense of "democracy in general" is actually defense of the bourgeoisie and their privileges as exploiters.

7. "Freedom of assembly" can be taken as a sample of the requisites of "pure democracy." Every class-conscious worker who has not broken with his class will readily appreciate the absurdity of promising freedom of assembly to the exploiters at a time and in a situation when the exploiters are resisting the overthrow of their rule and are fighting to retain their privileges. When the bourgeoisie was revolutionary, they did not, either in England in 1649 or in France in 1793, grant "freedom of assembly" to the monarchists and nobles, who summoned foreign troops and "assembled" to organize attempts at restoration. If the present-day bourgeoisie, who have long since become reactionary, demand from the proletariat advance guarantees of "freedom of assembly" for the exploiters, what-

ever the resistance offered by the capitalists to being expropriated, the workers will only laugh at their hypocrisy.

The workers know perfectly well, too, that even in the most democratic bourgeois republic "freedom of assembly" is a hollow phrase, for the rich have the best public and private buildings at their disposal and enough leisure to assemble at meetings, which are protected by the bourgeois machine of power. The rural and urban workers and the small peasants—the overwhelming majority of the population—are denied all these things. As long as that state of affairs prevails, "equality," i.e., "pure democracy," is a fraud. The first thing to do to win genuine equality and enable the working people to enjoy democracy in practice is to deprive the exploiters of all the public and sumptuous private buildings, to give the working people leisure, and to see to it that their freedom of assembly is protected by armed workers, not by scions of the nobility or capitalist officers in command of downtrodden soldiers.

Only when that change is effected can we speak of freedom of assembly and of equality without mocking at the workers, at working people in general, at the poor. And this change can be effected only by the vanguard of the working people, the proletariat, which overthrows the exploiters, the bourgeoisie.

8. "Freedom of the press" is another of the principal slogans of "pure democracy." And here, too, the workers know—and socialists everywhere have admitted it millions of times—that this freedom is a deception while the best printing presses and the biggest stocks of paper are appropriated by the capitalists and while capitalist rule over the press remains, a rule that is manifested throughout the world all the more strikingly, sharply, and cynically the more democracy and the republican system are developed, as in America for example. The first thing to

do to win real equality and genuine democracy for the working people, for the workers and peasants, is to deprive capital of the possibility of hiring writers, buying up publishing houses, and bribing newspapers. And to do that the capitalists and exploiters have to be overthrown and their resistance suppressed. The capitalists have always used the term "freedom" to mean freedom for the rich to get richer and for the workers to starve to death. In capitalist usage, freedom of the press means freedom of the rich to bribe the press, freedom to use their wealth to shape and fabricate so-called public opinion. In this respect, too, the defenders of "pure democracy" prove to be defenders of an utterly foul and venal system that gives the rich control over the mass media. They prove to be deceivers of the people who, with the aid of plausible, fine-sounding, but thoroughly false phrases, divert them from the concrete historical task of liberating the press from capitalist enslavement. Genuine freedom and equality will be embodied in the system which the communists are building and in which there will be no opportunity for amassing wealth at the expense of others, no objective opportunities for putting the press under the direct or indirect power of money, and no impediments in the way of any workingman (or groups of workingmen, in any numbers) for enjoying and practicing equal rights in the use of public printing presses and public stocks of paper.

9. The history of the nineteenth and twentieth centuries demonstrated, even before the war, what this celebrated "pure democracy" really is under capitalism. Marxists have always maintained that the more developed, the "purer" democracy is, the more naked, acute, and merciless the class struggle becomes, and the "purer" the capitalist oppression and bourgeois dictatorship. The Dreyfus case in republican France, the massacre of strikers by hired bands

armed by the capitalists in the free and democratic American republic—these and thousands of similar facts illustrate the truth which the bourgeoisie is vainly seeking to conceal, namely, that actually terror and bourgeois dictatorship prevail in the most democratic of republics and are openly displayed every time the exploiters think the power of capital is being shaken.

10. The imperialist war of 1914–18 conclusively revealed even to backward workers the true nature of bourgeois democracy, even in the freest republics, as being a dictatorship of the bourgeoisie. Tens of millions were killed for the sake of enriching the German or the British group of millionaires and multimillionaires, and bourgeois military dictatorships were established in the freest republics. This military dictatorship continues to exist in the Allied countries even after Germany's defeat. It was mostly the war that opened the eyes of the working people, that stripped bourgeois democracy of its camouflage, and showed the people the abyss of speculation and profiteering that existed during and because of the war. It was in the name of "freedom and equality" that the bourgeoisie waged the war and in the name of "freedom and equality" that the munition manufacturers piled up fabulous fortunes. Nothing that the Yellow Bern International does can conceal from the people the now thoroughly exposed exploiting character of bourgeois freedom, bourgeois equality, and bourgeois democracy.

11. In Germany, the most developed capitalist country of continental Europe, the very first months of full republican freedom, established as a result of imperialist Germany's defeat, have shown the German workers and the whole world the true class substance of the bourgeois-democratic republic. The murder of Karl Liebknecht and Rosa Luxemburg is an event of epoch-making

significance not only because of the tragic death of these finest people and leaders of the truly proletarian, Communist International, but also because the class nature of an advanced European state—it can be said, without exaggeration, of an advanced state on a worldwide scale—has been conclusively exposed. If those arrested, i.e., those placed under state protection, could be assassinated by officers and capitalists with impunity, and this under a government headed by social patriots, then the democratic republic where such a thing was possible is a bourgeois dictatorship. Those who voice their indignation at the murder of Karl Liebknecht and Rosa Luxemburg but fail to understand this fact are demonstrating only their stupidity or hypocrisy. "Freedom" in the German republic, one of the freest and most advanced republics of the world, is freedom to murder arrested leaders of the proletariat with impunity. Nor can it be otherwise as long as capitalism remains, for the development of democracy sharpens rather than dampens the class struggle, which, by virtue of all the results and influences of the war and of its consequences, has been brought to boiling point.

Throughout the civilized world we see Bolsheviks being exiled, persecuted, and thrown into prison. This is the case, for example, in Switzerland, one of the freest bourgeois republics, and in America, where there have been anti-Bolshevik pogroms, etc. From the standpoint of "democracy in general," or "pure democracy," it is really ridiculous that advanced, civilized, and democratic countries, which are armed to the teeth, should fear the presence of a few score men from backward, famine-stricken, and ruined Russia, which the bourgeois papers, in tens of millions of copies, describe as savage, criminal, etc. Clearly, the social situation that could produce this crying contradiction is in fact a dictatorship of the bourgeoisie.

12. In these circumstances, proletarian dictatorship is not only an absolutely legitimate means of overthrowing the exploiters and suppressing their resistance, but also absolutely necessary to the entire mass of working people, being their only defense against the bourgeois dictatorship which led to the war and is preparing new wars.

The main thing that Socialists fail to understand and that constitutes their shortsightedness in matters of theory, their subservience to bourgeois prejudices, and their political betrayal of the proletariat is that in capitalist society, whenever there is any serious aggravation of the class struggle intrinsic to that society, there can be no alternative but the dictatorship of the bourgeoisie or the dictatorship of the proletariat. Dreams of some third way are reactionary, petty-bourgeois lamentations. That is borne out by more than a century of development of bourgeois democracy and the working-class movement in all the advanced countries and notably by the experience of the past five years. This is also borne out by the whole science of political economy, by the entire content of Marxism, which reveals the economic inevitability, wherever commodity economy prevails, of the dictatorship of the bourgeoisie that can only be replaced by the class which the very growth of capitalism develops, multiplies, welds together, and strengthens, that is, the proletarian class.

13. Another theoretical and political error of the Socialists is their failure to understand that ever since the rudiments of democracy first appeared in antiquity, its forms inevitably changed over the centuries as one ruling class replaced another. Democracy assumed different forms and was applied in different degrees in the ancient republics of Greece, the medieval cities, and the advanced capitalist countries. It would be sheer nonsense to think that the most profound revolution in human history, the

first case in the world of power being transferred from the exploiting minority to the exploited majority, could take place within the timeworn framework of the old, bourgeois parliamentary democracy without drastic changes, without the creation of new forms of democracy, new institutions that embody the new conditions for applying democracy, etc.

14. Proletarian dictatorship is similar to the dictatorship of other classes in that it arises out of the need, as every other dictatorship does, to suppress forcibly the resistance of the class that is losing its political sway. The fundamental distinction between the dictatorship of the proletariat and the dictatorship of other classes—landlord dictatorship in the Middle Ages and bourgeois dictatorship in all the civilized capitalist countries—consists in the fact that the dictatorship of the landowners and bourgeoisie was the forcible suppression of the resistance offered by the vast majority of the population, namely, the working people. In contrast, proletarian dictatorship is the forcible suppression of the resistance of the exploiters, i.e., an insignificant minority of the population, the landowners and capitalists.

It follows that proletarian dictatorship must inevitably entail not only a change in democratic forms and institutions, generally speaking, but precisely such a change as provides an unparalleled extension of the actual enjoyment of democracy by those oppressed by capitalism—the toiling classes.

And indeed, the form of proletarian dictatorship that has already taken shape, i.e., Soviet power in Russia, the *Räte* [council] system in Germany, the shop stewards committees in Britain, and similar soviet institutions in other countries, all this implies and presents to the toiling classes, i.e., the vast majority of the population, greater practical opportunities for enjoying democratic rights and liberties than ever existed before, even approximately, in the best and the most democratic bourgeois republics.

The substance of Soviet government is that the permanent and only foundation of state power, the entire machinery of state, is the mass-scale organization of the classes oppressed by capitalism, i.e., the workers and the semiproletarians (peasants who do not exploit the labor of others and regularly resort to the sale of at least a part of their own labor power). It is the people, who even in the most democratic bourgeois republics, while possessing equal rights by law, have in fact been debarred by thousands of devices and subterfuges from participation in political life and enjoyment of democratic rights and liberties, that are now drawn into constant and unfailing, moreover, decisive, participation in the democratic administration of the state.

15. The equality of citizens, irrespective of sex, religion, race, or nationality, which bourgeois democracy everywhere has always promised but never effected and never could effect because of the domination of capital, is given immediate and full effect by the soviet system, or dictatorship of the proletariat. The fact is that this can only be done by a government of the workers, who are not interested in the means of production being privately owned and in the fight for their division and redivision.

16. The old, i.e., bourgeois, democracy and the parliamentary system were so organized that it was the mass of working people who were kept farthest away from the machinery of government. Soviet power, i.e., the dictatorship of the proletariat, on the other hand, is so organized as to bring the working people close to the machinery of government. That, too, is the purpose of combining the legislative and executive authority under the soviet orga-

nization of the state and of replacing territorial constituencies by production units—the factory.

17. The army was a machine of oppression under not only the monarchy. It remains as such in all bourgeois republics, even the most democratic ones. Only the soviets, the permanent organizations of government authority of the classes that were oppressed by capitalism, are in a position to destroy the army's subordination to bourgeois commanders and really merge the proletariat with the army; only the soviets can effectively arm the proletariat and disarm the bourgeoisie. Unless this is done, the victory of socialism is impossible.

18. The soviet organization of the state is suited to the leading role of the proletariat as a class most concentrated and enlightened by capitalism. The experience of all revolutions and all movements of the oppressed classes, the experience of the world socialist movement teaches us that only the proletariat is in a position to unite and lead the scattered and backward sections of the working and exploited population.

19. Only the soviet organization of the state can really effect the immediate breakup and total destruction of the old, i.e., bourgeois, bureaucratic and judicial machinery, which has been, and has inevitably had to be, retained under capitalism even in the most democratic republics, and which is, in actual fact, the greatest obstacle to the practical implementation of democracy for the workers and the working people generally. The Paris Commune took the first epoch-making step along this path. The soviet system has taken the second.

20. Destruction of state power is the aim set by all socialists, including Marx above all. Genuine democracy, i.e., liberty and equality, is unrealizable unless this aim is achieved. But its practical achievement is possible only

through soviet, or proletarian democracy, for by enlisting the mass organizations of the working people in constant and unfailing participation in the administration of the state, it immediately begins to prepare the complete withering away of any state.

21. The complete bankruptcy of the Socialists who assembled in Bern, their complete failure to understand the new, i.e., proletarian democracy is especially apparent from the following. On February 10, 1919, Branting delivered the concluding speech at the international conference of the Yellow International in Bern. In Berlin, on February 11, 1919, *Freiheit,* published by affiliates of the International, printed an appeal from the party of "Independents" to the proletariat. The appeal acknowledged the bourgeois character of the Scheidemann government, rebuked it for wanting to abolish the soviets, which it described as *Träger und Schützer der Revolution*—vehicles and guardians of the revolution—and proposed that the soviets be legalized, invested with government authority, and given the right to suspend the operation of National Assembly decisions pending a popular referendum.

That proposal indicates the complete ideological bankruptcy of the theorists who defended democracy and failed to see its bourgeois character. This ludicrous attempt to combine the soviet system, i.e., proletarian dictatorship, with the National Assembly, i.e., bourgeois dictatorship, utterly exposes the paucity of thought of the Yellow Socialists and Social Democrats, their reactionary petty-bourgeois political outlook, and their cowardly concessions to the irresistibly growing strength of the new, proletarian democracy.

22. From the class standpoint, the Bern Yellow International majority, which did not dare to adopt a formal resolution out of fear of the mass of workers, was right in

condemning Bolshevism. This majority is in full agreement with the Russian Mensheviks and Socialist Revolutionaries and the Scheidemanns in Germany. In complaining of persecution by the Bolsheviks, the Russian Mensheviks and Socialist Revolutionaries try to conceal the fact that they are persecuted for participating in the civil war on the side of the bourgeoisie against the proletariat. Similarly, the Scheidemanns and their party have already demonstrated in Germany that they too are participating in the civil war on the side of the bourgeoisie against the workers.

It is therefore quite natural that the Bern Yellow International should be in favor of condemning the Bolsheviks. This was not an expression of the defense of "pure democracy," but of the self-defense of people who know and feel that in the civil war they stand with the bourgeoisie against the proletariat.

That is why, from the class point of view, the decision of the Yellow International majority must be considered correct. The proletariat must not fear the truth, it must face it squarely and draw all the necessary political conclusions.

REPORT ON THE THESES ON BOURGEOIS DEMOCRACY AND THE DICTATORSHIP OF THE PROLETARIAT

LENIN: Comrades, I would like to add a word or two to the last two points. I think that the comrades who are to report to us on the Bern conference will deal with it in greater detail.[4]

Not a word was said at the Bern conference about the significance of Soviet power. We in Russia have been discussing this question for two years now. At our party conference in April 1917 we raised the following question, theoretically and politically: "What is Soviet power, what is its substance, and what is its historical significance?" We have been discussing it for almost two years and at our party congress we adopted a resolution on it.[5]

On February 11 the Berlin *Freiheit* published an appeal to the German proletariat signed not only by the leaders of the Independent Social Democratic Party of Germany, but also by all the members of the Independent Social Democratic group in the Reichstag. In August 1918, Kautsky, one of the leading theorists of these Independents, wrote a pamphlet entitled *The Dictatorship of the Proletariat,*[6] in which he declared that he was a supporter of democracy *and* of soviet bodies, but that the soviets must be bodies merely of an economic character and that they must not by any means be recognized as state organizations. Kautsky says the same thing in *Freiheit* of November 11 and January 12. On February 9 an article appeared by Rudolf Hilferding, who is also regarded as one of the leading and authoritative theorists of the Second International, in which he proposed that the soviet system be united with the National Assembly juridically, by state legislation. That was on February 9. On February 11 this proposal was adopted by the whole of the Independent party and published in the form of an appeal.

There is vacillation again, despite the fact that the National Assembly already exists, even after "pure democracy" has been embodied in reality, after the leading theorists of the Independent Social Democratic Party have declared that the soviet organizations must not be state organizations! This proves that these gentlemen really understand nothing about the new movement and about its conditions of struggle. But it goes to prove something else, namely, that there must be conditions, causes, for this vacillation! When, after all these events, after nearly two years of victorious revolution in Russia, we are offered resolutions like those adopted at the Bern conference, which say nothing about the soviets and their significance, about which not a single delegate uttered a single word, we have a perfect right to say that all these gentlemen are dead as socialists and theorists.

However, comrades, from the practical side, from the political point of view, the fact that these Independents, who in theory and on principle have been opposed to these state organizations, suddenly make the stupid proposal to "peacefully" unite the National Assembly with the soviet system, i.e., to unite the dictatorship of the bourgeoisie with the dictatorship of the proletariat, shows that a great change is taking place among the masses. We see the Independents are all bankrupt in the socialist and theoretical sense and that an enormous change is taking place among the masses. The backward masses among the German workers are coming to us, have come to us! So, the significance of the Independent Social Democratic Party of Germany, the best section of the Bern conference, is nil from the theoretical and socialist standpoint. Still it has some significance, which is that these waverers serve as an index to us of the mood of the backward sections of the proletariat. This, in my opinion, is the great historical significance of this conference. We experienced something of the kind in our own revolution. Our Mensheviks traversed almost exactly the same path as that of the theorists of the Independents in Germany. At first, when they had a majority in the soviets, they were in favor of the soviets. All we heard then was: "Long live the soviets!" "For the soviets!" "The soviets are revolutionary democracy!" When, however, we Bolsheviks secured a majority in the soviets, they changed their tune; they said: the soviets must not exist side by side with the Constituent Assembly. And various Menshevik theorists made practically the same proposals, like the one to unite the soviet system with the Constituent Assembly and to incorporate the soviets in the state structure. Once again it is here revealed that the general course of the proletarian revolution is the same throughout the world. First the spontaneous formation of soviets, then their spread and development, and then the appearance of the practical problem: soviets or National Assembly or Constituent Assembly or the bourgeois parliamentary system; utter confusion among the leaders; and finally—the proletarian revolution. But I think we should not present the problem in this way after nearly two years of revolution; we should rather adopt concrete decisions because for us, and particularly for the majority of the western European countries, spreading of the soviet system is a most important task.

I would like to quote here just one Menshevik resolution. I asked Comrade Obolensky to translate it into German. He promised to do so but, unfortunately, he is not here. I shall try to render it from memory, as I have not the full text of it with me.

It is very difficult for a foreigner who has not heard anything about Bolshevism to arrive at an independent opinion about our controversial questions. Everything the Bolsheviks assert is challenged by the Mensheviks, and vice versa. Of course, it cannot be otherwise in the middle of a struggle, and that is why it is so important that the last Menshevik Party conference, held in December 1918, adopted the long and detailed resolution published in full in the Menshevik *Gazeta Pechatnikov* [Printers' newspaper].[7] In this resolution the Mensheviks themselves briefly outline the history of the class struggle and of the civil war.

The resolution states that they condemn those groups in their party which are allied with the propertied classes in the Urals, in the South, in the Crimea, and in Georgia—all these regions are enumerated. Those groups of the Menshevik Party which, in alliance with the propertied classes, fought against the soviets are now condemned in the resolution; but the last point of the resolution also condemns those who joined the communists. It follows that the Mensheviks were compelled to admit that there was no unity in their party, and that its members were either on the side of the bourgeoisie or on the side of the proletariat. The majority of the Mensheviks went over to the bourgeoisie and fought against us during the civil war. We, of course, persecute Mensheviks, we even shoot them when they wage war against us, fight against our Red Army, and shoot our Red commanders. We responded to the bourgeois war with the proletarian war—there can be no other way. Therefore, from the political point of view, all this is sheer Menshevik hypocrisy. Historically it is incomprehensible how people who have not been officially certified as mad could talk at the Bern conference, on the instructions of the Mensheviks and Socialist Revolutionaries, about the Bolsheviks fighting the latter, yet keep silent about their own struggle, in alliance with the bourgeoisie against the proletariat.

All of them furiously attack us for persecuting them. This is true. But they do not say a word about the part they themselves have taken in the civil war! I think that I shall have to provide the full text of the resolution to be recorded in the minutes, and I shall ask the foreign comrades to study it because it is a historical document in which the issue is raised correctly and which provides excellent material for appraising the controversy between the "socialist" trends in Russia. In between the proletariat and the bourgeoisie there is another class of people, who incline first this way and then the other. This has always been the case in all revolutions, and it is absolutely impossible in capitalist society, in which the proletariat and the bourgeoisie form two hostile camps, for intermediary sections not to exist between them. The existence of these waverers is historically inevitable, and, unfortunately, these elements, who do not know themselves on whose side they will fight tomorrow, will exist for quite some time.

I want to make the practical proposal that a resolution be adopted in which three points shall be specifically mentioned.

First: One of the most important tasks confronting the western European comrades is to explain to the people the meaning, importance, and necessity of the soviet system. There is a sort of misunderstanding on this question. Although Kautsky and Hilferding are bankrupt as theorists, their recent articles in *Freiheit* show that they correctly reflect the mood of the backward sections of the German proletariat. The same thing took place in our country: during the first eight months of the Russian revolution the question of the soviet organization was very much discussed, and the workers did not understand what the new system was and whether the soviets could be transformed into a state machine. In our revolution we advanced along the path of practice and not of theory. For example, formerly we did not raise the question of the Constituent Assembly from the theoretical side, and we did not say we did not recognize the Constituent Assembly. It was only later, when the soviet organizations had spread throughout the country and had captured political power, that we decided to dissolve the Constituent Assembly. Now we see that in Hungary and Switzerland the question is much more acute.[8] On the one hand, this is very good: it gives us the firm conviction that in the western European states the revolution is advancing more quickly and will yield great victories. On the other hand, a certain danger is concealed in it, namely, that the struggle will be so precipitous that the minds of the masses of workers will not keep pace with this development. Even now the significance of the soviet system is not clear to a large mass of the politically educated German workers, because they have been trained in the spirit of the parliamentary system and amid bourgeois prejudices.

Second: About the spread of the soviet system. When we hear how quickly the idea of soviets is spreading in Germany, and even in Britain, it is very important evidence that the proletarian revolution will be victorious. Its progress can be retarded only for a short time. It is quite another thing, however, when Comrades Albert and Platten tell us that in the rural districts in their countries there are hardly any soviets among the farm laborers and small peasants. In *Rote Fahne* [Red flag] I read an article opposing peasant soviets, but quite properly supporting soviets of farm laborers and of poor peasants.[9] The bourgeoisie and their lackeys, like Scheidemann and Company, have already issued the slogan of peasant soviets. All we need, however, is soviets of farm laborers and poor peasants. Unfortunately, from the reports of Comrades Albert, Platten, and others, we see that, with the exception of Hungary, very little is being done to spread the soviet system in the countryside. In this, perhaps, lies the real and quite serious danger threatening the achievement of certain victory by the German proletariat. Victory can be considered assured only when not only the urban workers, but also the rural proletarians are organized, and organized not as before—in trade unions and cooperative societies—but in soviets. Our victory was made easier by the fact that in October

1917 we marched with the peasants, with all the peasants. In that sense, our revolution at that time was a bourgeois revolution. The first step taken by our proletarian government was to embody in a law promulgated on October 26 (old style), 1917, on the next day after the revolution, the old demands of all the peasants which peasant soviets and village assemblies had put forward under Kerensky.[10] That is where our strength lay; that is why we were able to win the overwhelming majority so easily. As far as the countryside was concerned, our revolution continued to be a bourgeois revolution, and only later, after a lapse of six months, were we compelled within the framework of the state organization to start the class struggle in the countryside, to establish Committees of Poor Peasants, of semiproletarians, in every village, and to carry on a methodical fight against the rural bourgeoisie. This was inevitable in Russia owing to the backwardness of the country. In western Europe things will proceed differently, and that is why we must emphasize the absolute necessity of spreading the soviet system also to the rural population in proper, perhaps new, forms.

Third: We must say that winning a communist majority in the soviets is the principal task in all countries in which Soviet government is not yet victorious. Our resolutions commission discussed this question yesterday. Perhaps other comrades will express their opinion on it; but I would like to propose that these three points be adopted as a special resolution. Of course, we are not in a position to prescribe the path of development. It is quite likely that the revolution will come very soon in many western European countries; but we, as the organized section of the working class, as a party, strive and must strive to gain a majority in the soviets. Then our victory will be assured and no power on earth will be able to do anything against the communist revolution. If we do not, victory will not be secured so easily, and it will not be durable. And so, I would like to propose that these three points be adopted as a special resolution.

ALBERT: The resolution that Comrade Lenin mentioned can be read to you this afternoon.[11]

Resolution on the theses on bourgeois democracy and the dictatorship of the proletariat

by V.I. Lenin

On the basis of these theses and the reports made by the delegates from the different countries, the congress of the Communist International declares that the chief task of the Communist parties in all countries where Soviet government has not yet been established is as follows:[12]

1. to explain to the broad mass of the workers the historic significance and the political and historical necessity of the new, proletarian democracy which must replace bourgeois democracy and the parliamentary system;
2. to extend the organization of soviets among the workers in all branches of industry, among the soldiers in the army and sailors in the navy, and also among farm laborers and poor peasants;
3. to build a stable Communist majority inside the soviets.

DISCUSSION ON PLATFORM (CONTINUED)

ALBERT: We now come to the discussion of the draft platform. Would you rather open that discussion or refer the platform to the bureau for publication? Does anyone request discussion on it? Do you agree with turning it over to the bureau for distribution?

ZINOVIEV: The commission's decision was somewhat broader. It voted unanimously not only to refer the platform to the bureau, but also, on behalf of the conference, to express solidarity with its general line.

ALBERT: That is essentially the same thing as having the platform printed and distributed in each country in the name of the conference.

PLATTEN: Comrades, the bureau would like to present several motions for discussion today. First of all, we note that two statements have been submitted pertaining to the platform. One is by Comrade Reinstein, and the other by Comrade Kascher. Then there is a motion to take up the founding of the Third International. After that we will hear a statement by participants in the Zimmerwald and Kienthal conferences. Third, if we constitute ourselves as a congress, we will have to decide whether to permit voting by delegates who cannot act officially here in the name of their parties. Next will follow a report on the Bern conference, and, if we are able to name a reporter without delay, we will proceed to the point "Motivation of the Resolution"[13] and after that to a discussion on "The Policy of the Entente." Does anyone wish to raise any objections or request further clarification about this procedure?

STATEMENT BY KASCHER

I feel that my position on the platform was not presented as I had wished. I must therefore make the following statement:

I am in *complete and total agreement* with the platform and all principles expressed in it. However, I believed it imperative to have the extremely important section, "The road to victory," expanded to reflect the experiences of the Russian and German revolutions. The platform therefore remained incomplete, in my view, and I could not vote for it.

AMENDMENT TO THE PLATFORM BY REINSTEIN

The Communist Third International calls upon revolutionary proletarians of all countries to work with redoubled energy and determination to set the trade union movements of their countries on a truly revolutionary course and to transform them into movements whose structure, goals, policies, and spirit are equal to the revolutionary objectives of communism.

Delegates to the first Comintern congress.

5. The decision to found the International

PLATTEN: I will now inform you of a motion submitted by delegates Rakovsky, Gruber, Grimlund, and Rudnyánszky. It reads as follows:

"The delegates of the Communist Party of German Austria, the Left Social Democratic Party of Sweden, the Balkan Revolutionary Social Democratic Federation, and the Communist Party of Hungary propose a motion to found the Communist International.

"I. The necessary struggle for the dictatorship of the proletariat requires a homogeneous and united international organization of all Communist forces that stand on this platform.

"II. Founding it is all the more necessary because an attempt is now being made in Bern, which may be repeated elsewhere in the future, to revive the old, opportunist International and to bring back together all the confused, undecided forces among the proletariat. A sharp break is therefore required between the revolutionary proletarian forces and the social traitors.

"III. If the conference meeting in Moscow were not to found the Third International, the impression would arise that the Communist parties were divided. That would weaken our position and increase the confusion in the undecided forces among the proletariat of all countries.

"IV. Therefore, constituting the Third International is an absolute historical necessity and the International Communist Conference meeting in Moscow must make it a reality."

This motion assumes that we will reopen discussion on the question of conference versus congress. The motion has been made to constitute the Third International. The discussion is open.

ALBERT: Comrades, we already had lengthy debates at the beginning of our deliberations on whether this conference should become a congress to found the Third International or whether we first had to make preparations to launch it. At the request of the German delegation, which felt bound by its mandate and unable to vote for an immediate founding, we agreed that this conference would prepare the launching of the Third International but that the actual founding would take place later. Despite that decision, some delegates are nevertheless making another attempt today to launch the Third International here immediately. I am therefore obliged to outline briefly the considerations that led us to advise against doing so.

We venture to contest the view expressed here that founding the Third International is absolutely necessary. To those who say that the proletarian struggle requires before all else an intellectual center, we answer that such a center already exists. All the forces that have converged in supporting the council system show by that very action that they have already broken with all other forces in the workers' movement who still lean toward bourgeois democracy. We see that split being prepared and carried out everywhere.

But a Third International should not be simply an intellectual center, an institution where theoreticians hold forth in heated discussion. It must be the basis for an organizational power. If we want to make the Third International a useful tool and forge it into a weapon of struggle, then certain conditions must be present. Therefore, as we see it, the question ought not be discussed and evaluated solely in the realm of ideas. Rather, we must ask objectively whether the organizational prerequisites for it are present.

I cannot help feeling that the comrades who are so intent upon founding the International are letting themselves be greatly influenced by the evolution of the Second International, so that now, after the Bern conference, they want to set up a rival operation. That does not seem so important to us. Some say that clarification is needed because otherwise all the undecided forces might go over to the Yellow International. I reply that the forces that are headed there even today will not be stopped by the Third International, and if that is where they go nevertheless, then that is where they belong.

But surely the most important question to be resolved in founding the Third International is to know what we want, on what basis unity between us is possible. The reports by comrades from different countries showed that our views on action and on the methods to reach our goal were not known to them; and when delegates arrived from different countries it was not at all with the intention of taking part in founding the Third International. Their task must be first to inform their membership. Even the invitation to the conference indicates that on the first page, where it says, "All these factors compel us to take the initiative in placing on the agenda for discussion the calling of an international congress of revolutionary proletarian parties."[1] The invitation itself thus said we must first weigh here the feasibility of calling the comrades together for a founding congress.

How little we knew about each party's methods and goals before our discussion began here is shown by the letter from Longuet,[2] a politically active comrade who adheres to the center and still believes we could take part in the deliberations of the Bern conference.

In Germany we also had no idea how great the differences among the parties here would be. When I left Germany I was braced for difficult debates on the various questions. I can see now that we concur on most questions, but we did not know that in advance.

If we want to launch the Third International, we must first let the world know what we want; we must first explain what road lies ahead of us that we can agree and unite upon.

It is irrelevant to say that the Third International was already founded at Zimmerwald. Zimmerwald fell apart long ago, and only a small part of the left wing can be considered for subsequent collaboration.

On the one hand, these factors present sufficient grounds to advise against founding the Third International at this time. However, there are also organizational problems that should hold us back. What is the situation? Real Communist parties exist in only a few countries, and most of these were created only within the last few weeks. In several countries today where there are communists, they have as yet no organization.

It astounds me that the Swedish delegate moves to found the Third International and yet has to admit that there is no purely Communist organization in Sweden—only a large Communist grouping within the Swedish Social Democratic Party.[3] As we know, there are no real parties in Switzerland and other countries; parties have yet to be founded, and the comrades here can therefore speak only in the name of groupings. Can you really say who stands with you today? Finland, Russia, Sweden, and Austria-Hungary. As for the Balkans we do not even have the whole federation, for the Greek and Serbian delegates do not regard Rakovsky as their representative.[4] Missing is all of western Europe; Belgium and Italy are not represented; the Swiss delegate cannot speak for a party; France, Britain, Spain, and Portugal are missing. Nor can the American delegate say which parties would be behind us. So few organizations are involved in founding the Third International that it is difficult to go before the public. Therefore, before we proceed to founding the International, we must announce our program to the world and call upon Communist organizations to declare whether they are ready to found the Third International with us.

The formation of Communist organizations must be promoted because it is no longer possible to make common cause with Kautsky and Scheidemann. Yet I strongly warn against founding the Third International at this time. I ask you not to act hastily. Instead, convene a congress as soon as possible at which we can found the new International—but one that will have real power behind it.

Those are my organization's reservations against launching the Third International immediately, and I urge you to consider most carefully whether it is advisable to found it on such a weak basis.

ZINOVIEV: Comrades, as you know, from the beginning of our work our party has favored launching the Third

International immediately. In the name of our Central Committee we stated our opinion that the interests of the Russian proletariat as well as those of the world working class imperatively require this. But as we explained, our German friends insist upon postponing the founding a while longer. So, as we said at the start, we were willing to meet as a conference. Later, however, comrades from Austria, the Balkan countries, and Sweden arrived and told us—as we had expected—that further delay would harm the revolutionary movement in their countries. The question was thoroughly discussed yesterday in the resolutions commission, and we voted unanimously to propose that this body constitute itself as the Third International.[5]

Comrade Albert says, "Why are we in such a hurry?" What is so urgent about founding the Third International now? I believe we can turn the question around and ask him to give the reasons why the workers of the world should postpone founding the Third International any longer. We have a victorious proletarian revolution in a large country and a powerful revolution marching toward victory in two other countries. Yet we are supposed to say we are still too weak! No one calls it utopian when we advance the slogan of the international council republic as our motto. If we believe that is an immediate prospect, how can we shrink from founding what is after all only an instrument for achieving it, the Third International? Everyone must agree that if we launch the Third International, the broadest layers of the world's working masses will enthusiastically hail our action. But if we hesitate, we will lose our credibility.

You want to see Communist parties formally launched everywhere first? You have a victorious revolution; that is more than a formal launching. In Germany you have a party that is striding toward power and that in a few months will form a proletarian government. And we are supposed to hesitate? No one will understand us. From Longuet's point of view, postponement could seem right; we should wait until the appropriate venerable congress bigwigs have congregated. But that is just the kind of delay that is indefensible from a communist point of view.

Let me remind you that the intellectual clarification began back at Zimmerwald in 1915. Now we have not only intellectual clarity but an organization as well. And the party of today's German Communists took an active part in that process. Let me remind you that the Zimmerwald Left worked out a program and that some of the German Communists were part of that process. At that time we took as our basis the theses worked out by the Internationale Group.[6] Three years have elapsed. Now we are back together again for the first time, and our task is to move forward to an international organization. I think it follows that we should do it. We are confident that the German workers will say, "You did the right thing."

We should not work under the assumption that we are too weak. Rather let us be inspired by a great sense of strength and by the conviction that the immediate future belongs to the Third International. If we work in that spirit, we will take this necessary step without wavering. After careful consideration, therefore, our party recommends the immediate formation of the Third International. That will show the whole world that we are theoretically and organizationally armed. Look at the spectacle of the Bern conference. The important thing is to confront these weaklings decisively. Their theoretical poverty comes through in every line of the Bern resolutions. They have not dared to draw the logical conclusions. We have good reason to courageously proclaim all that we believe in.

ANGELICA BALABANOFF *(Zimmerwald commission):* I take this occasion to carry out my duty to extend warmest greetings to this gathering from the great majority of the parties and organizations of the Zimmerwald movement and from all those who rallied to its banner.

I have the moral right to assume that had political and technical obstacles not prevented the representatives of those parties from attending this conference, they would have not been content simply to bring you platonic greetings. Rather, they would have personally welcomed and advocated the founding of the Communist Third International.

I would like to discuss Comrade Albert's objections in this context. Although his remarks sound logical, he misses the main point. The conflict between word and deed was often sharply posed in the Second International too, especially in the final phase of its existence. But there are times in history when the word is the deed, and when the word not spoken at the right time obstructs the deed. Nowadays, not only the proletariat but all public opinion—everyone who thinks or feels politically—is aware that we face a showdown battle between the power of the bourgeoisie and that of the proletariat.

I had the responsibility of upholding the banner of the Zimmerwald movement and maintaining contact with its affiliated organizations, insofar as political conditions then permitted. I did this until events—the German revolution on the one hand, and the insane reaction of the Entente nations, drunk with victory, on the other—destroyed the framework of that international organization. Therefore, I feel qualified to point out here as well that ever since Russia's second, proletarian revolution, revolutionary class-conscious public opinion has completely come over to the side of Soviet power and supports the fundamental ideas it embodies.

As for Zimmerwald, I must stress that it was established as a provisional organization, essentially formed to wage a defensive struggle against the imperialist war and the disgraceful conduct of the social-patriotic majority. It did not represent the definitive establishment of a new international center. We knew that once political life resumed its normal course, the class-conscious proletariat and its revolutionary vanguard would not hesitate to settle accounts with those who had betrayed the proletariat so disgracefully in its most difficult and decisive hour. In the meantime, it was up to those forces around the world that had remained loyal to socialism to maintain theoretical and practical contact with one another, to explain to the masses, from a scientific socialist viewpoint, the overwhelming events that had taken place, and to draw the appropriate theoretical conclusions.

Comrades, just as it would be childish and arrogant to try to claim that the world-shaking events in Russia and Germany are taking place according to some specific directive from Zimmerwald, it would be equally unfair to blame Zimmerwald for the errors made by its affiliated parties or minorities.

On the second day of the proletarian uprising in Russia, when no one could yet say whether it would go down within hours to bloody defeat, the leaders of the Zimmerwald organizations considered it their duty and their right to declare their solidarity with this uprising. Applying the decisions of the third Zimmerwald conference, they called for an international mass strike, appealing to the masses of class-conscious workers to support the cause of the Russian proletariat with all their might.[7]

Today, in exactly the same way—and I do not underestimate the burden I assume in saying this—I feel I have the right and the duty to state that most of the parties that united at Zimmerwald advocate founding the Third International immediately.

I see that in a resolution to be presented to today's session, the executive committee of the Zimmerwald commission will be asked to turn over its archives to the newly formed organization. I would like to add that quite apart from the degree to which as secretary of the International Socialist Commission I have the legal authority to take actions without consulting other commission members; and quite apart from the fact I am also not in a position to comply with this request due to the police and the material circumstances of my expulsion from Switzerland, because I could not bring the archives with me, and so forth; I am convinced that if police obstacles were not keeping broad layers of the world revolutionary socialist movement and the broad masses from attending this gathering, we would not only be able to incorporate into the International being formed here the material legacy of Zimmerwald; we would also be enlisting the most active solidarity, heartfelt congratulations, and active collaboration of millions of proletarian hearts and minds.[8]

OTTO GRIMLUND: In reply to Comrade Albert I wish to point out that he did not understand me quite correctly. I speak for the Swedish left party, which split from the social-patriotic party. Our party vigorously defended the Zimmerwald program and the Russian proletarian revolution. It is certainly true that complete unity does not prevail in our party, and that it includes forces that do not entirely agree with that perspective. But there is no doubt whatsoever that at the first party conference we will formally affiliate as the Communist Party.[9] It surprises me that Comrade Albert, who comes from Germany, can have doubts, and that he will not or cannot see that only by founding the Communist International can the proletariat hope to find a firm footing. I welcome the Third International and believe it our duty and obligation to constitute it immediately.

JÓZEF UNSZLICHT:[10] Comrades, on behalf of the Communist Workers Party of Poland, allow me to point out that the doubts voiced by the German Communist Party delegate about whether to form the Third International immediately are purely formal. Comrades, we cannot accept his point of view at the revolutionary juncture we now confront. It also sounds odd coming from a representative of the German Communists.

How can the question be posed in such a way as to require us to suspend the further development of the revolution? Why? Because of certain formal considerations: Communist parties have not been created everywhere, and all representatives are not here in person. In my opinion that is the wrong way to pose the problem. We should rather say that in spite of very great difficulties a good number of Communist Party representatives have indeed managed to arrive at this conference.

The task of this conference is not only to make decisions but also to translate them into reality. Therefore, it would be completely appropriate if we did no more than found the Third International. Such a central body would unite the efforts of all Communist parties, cement the revolutionary movement of different countries, and prompt the already existing Communist parties in different countries to move toward uniting with us. It is thus of paramount importance to resolve immediately to form such a central body. And since Russia and Germany, the countries that have already experienced revolutions, have the decisive say on this question, the representatives from these countries should be the first to announce publicly that they favor founding the Third International.

On behalf of the Communist Party of Poland and in the name of the moral authority represented by the founding of the Third International as a unifying central body, I appeal to the delegate of the German proletariat, the German revolutionary proletariat, to set aside his earlier position. I urge him to join us, the overwhelming majority of the conference, in advocating that the Third International be launched immediately. I urge him to concede that this is not a formal question but one of necessity and that it must be resolved.

On behalf of the Communist Party of Poland, permit me to hail the proposed founding of the Third International with complete confidence that these first steps will produce fruitful results in the near future. Even those countries with no delegates here will soon rally around, recognizing that there is a central body that can offer direction and leadership. In the near future, we will see in our ranks proletarian representatives of those countries that have not participated in this conference.

JUKKA RAHJA *(Communist Party of Finland):* Comrades, the delegation from the Communist Party of Finland, which I represent, attended the preliminary meeting mentioned by Comrade Albert. When the question came up whether it would be possible and beneficial to found the Third International at this conference, our delegation decided to make a statement to the conference as a whole, which I shall now read.

"Since the party we represent sent us here for the clearly stated purpose of attending the founding conference of the Third International, we wish to make the following brief statement to this gathering:

"The Communist Party of Finland believes that the time has come to found the Third International. The need to found it is dictated by the world situation in general as well as by the tasks facing the international revolutionary proletarian movement.

"The Second International, whose leaders betrayed the proletarian cause at the beginning of the World War, is to all intents and purposes dead as far as the revolutionary proletariat is concerned. It can therefore no longer serve as a connecting link in the future struggles for working-class emancipation.

"The main goal of the social patriots' Bern conference was to revitalize already outlived formulas and create a center around which the social-patriotic and vacillating forces of the Second International could regroup in the guise of fighting for the liberation of the oppressed classes. It is particularly important to note that the Bern conference concluded that the Second International *has continued* and *will continue* to exist.

"The absence of an ideologically and organizationally tightly knit Communist organization on an international scale leaves open the possibility that under the banner of the Second International, international deception will continue to be practiced successfully behind the facade of international unity.

"The break with the social traitors and social patriots is already a reality in a number of major countries.

"In fighting against the imperialist bourgeoisie, the revolutionary proletariat of Russia, Germany, Italy, Britain, Austria-Hungary, America, France, Sweden, and many other countries is also combating the social traitors and social patriots, who continue to hide under the cloak of the Second International.

"Establishing the Third International will concretely pose the question to the existing parties and groupings in a great many countries: to which International do they wish to affiliate, and for what objective? This will necessarily draw a sharp line of demarcation and promote clarity in relations among the individual currents. There is no doubt that this will in short order bring together the revolutionary forces of the whole world.

"The elaboration by this conference of a theoretically sound and tactically feasible program will, in our party's view, resolve in life the question of founding the Third International. However, formally refusing to establish the International would weaken the power of the proletariat internationally in its struggle against capitalism and its prop, the social-patriotic Yellow International."

This statement originated when the preliminary conference amounted in essence to no more than an exchange of views between our delegation and that of Spartacus. When we spoke in favor of founding the Third International there, Comrade Albert raised a few objections, which I will take the liberty of repeating.

Comrade Albert says we must know what we are striving for before establishing the Third International. Allow me to ask him a question: Does the German proletariat, which fought so heroically against not only the imperialist bourgeoisie but also against Scheidemann and Noske, know what it wants? I am completely convinced that the German proletariat, which has suffered a temporary setback, will nevertheless resume its struggle with the same slogans, whether or not the Third International is founded here.

The question posed around the world today is not one of propaganda or of creating an apparatus for educating the masses. The problem is that in every country a struggle between two dictatorships is under way: the dictatorship of the bourgeoisie and the dictatorship of the proletariat. So far there has been no international center to unify this struggle, so it is waged haphazardly.

Comrade Albert says that, for now, we do not know what attitudes the individual parties in the various countries take toward the founding of the Third International. In our view, that of the Communist Party of Finland, the answer to that question lies in the titanic revolutionary movement unfolding throughout the world. That answer tells us very clearly what the proletariat is striving for. This revolutionary movement of the proletariat in the West clearly shows that if the proletariat of the whole world had such a unifying center, the struggle would be significantly easier and more effective.

Comrade Albert tells us that the revolutionary proletariat in Germany would not object in principle to founding the Third International. He is only raising purely formal considerations. However, it would be an error to postpone founding the Third International for purely formal reasons or for want of a mandate or a representative from one country or another whose proletariat was unable to send one. After all, it is perfectly understandable why a sufficient number of representatives could not attend.

Founding the Third International is also vital because it would have tremendous importance now as the center of the worldwide revolutionary labor movement. Had such a center existed yesterday, a week ago, a month ago, we can be sure that the revolutionary proletariat in every country, which continues to wage a heroic struggle, would have been able to fight far more vigorously and correctly. The first news that the Third International has been founded will be hailed around the world.

RAKOVSKY: An analogy can be drawn between the position of the present German Communist delegates and that of Ledebour. Back when the issue was whether to authorize war credits, Ledebour said he was opposed to voting for them. He just did not want to be bound by a decision that would be seen as having been made under pressure from abroad.[11] Prejudices like this fear of what public opinion might say about foreign pressures were prevalent in the Second International. It is time to rid ourselves of these prejudices.

Immediately founding the Third International is necessary for other reasons as well. Failure to do so now would arouse the suspicion in the rest of the world that the Communists cannot agree among themselves. Besides, many would be justified in interpreting it as a vote of no confidence in the Soviet republic, and that would have far-reaching moral and political consequences.

As to the practical matter that not all parties are represented here, it should be pointed out that in this respect the situation was no better when the historic First International was founded. The parties were no more completely represented then than they are now. The important thing is to give direction to the International. For the most part, that is with respect to the class struggle and the direct expropriation of land and capital, everyone is in agreement. It would therefore be ill-advised to forego on formal grounds founding the Third International immediately.

RUDNYÁNSZKY: Comrades, the Hungarian Communists have united behind the motion to formally organize the Third International here, for in reality it has already existed for a long time. The International was born in the struggle of the Russian proletariat against the Russian bourgeoisie. The Communist Party of Hungary strongly supports this position. We must not merely repeat endlessly that the Second International has died, that the voices of the participants in Bern are dead, and that we here in Moscow are participants of a living International, just born in struggle.

Can it be that we are afraid to formally recognize the founding of the Third International, when objectively it has been won in struggle by the Russian proletariat? The German Communist proletariat has begun the same kind of fight, and the revolutionary Communist proletariat of Hungary is in the midst of one today. Comrades, we hope that this conference will turn itself into a congress, as Comrade Zinoviev has moved we do, and formally launch the Third International.

SADOUL *(translated by Comrade Balabanoff):* I would just like to raise a few arguments to refute Comrade Albert's objections. Above all, Comrade Albert said that this gathering is not fully representative. But could a more representative one have been expected? Do not forget, the parties that still face big political obstacles in their own countries are not in a position to be here at a specified time.

Secondly, what situation would the national parties face if our efforts were unsuccessful? Without a center the contradictions will deepen. If a center is established, the movement can be directed by a tighter organization, whose permanent representatives should reside in Russia.

I appeal to Comrade Albert's sense of internationalism and ask him to change his position. The struggles in each and every country would gain prestige if they were led by an international center.

GRUBER *(German Austria):* Comrades, as one of those making the motion I would like to add a few words in its support.

From the movement's inception, the Austrian Communists thought about building a new International. We worked hard for it, unaware that parties had been formed in other countries on the basis of the *Communist Manifesto* and the dictatorship of the proletariat. Now, to our astonishment, the delegate from the Communist Party of

Germany announces that for formal reasons he cannot decide to vote for the motion.

We know that what they are forging in Paris is similar to the Holy Alliance.[12] Supposedly it is going to utterly demolish every revolutionary proletarian movement in the world. Simultaneously, a scheme is being devised in Bern whose purpose is to divert the proletariat's revolutionary energy. A commission was set up there that is to come to Russia and see how Bolshevism is doing. We hope those gentlemen—Bauer, Renner, Adler, and Kautsky—will find here in Moscow not only a new program but also a new international proletarian organization.[13] They should not find us waiting around until every last detail about Bolshevism has been worked out. Those beacons of scientific socialism should see that we are looking much further into the future than they are.

For these reasons, I urge Comrade Albert to renounce his abstentionist attitude. We live in a state of permanent civil war. We must confront the bourgeois coalition right now with a solid coalition of the revolutionary proletariat, and that means we must dispel any doubts that individual sections of the proletariat may have.

I would wager my own head that if I were to go to Munich or Bremen or anywhere else and ask: "Comrades, do you support what we did in Moscow when we founded the International?" the response would be, "You did the right thing."

And even if one of us has instructions not to vote for this, what he has helped to achieve here is much greater and more important than any formal discipline he thinks he must observe.

As Communists we want to work efficiently and not waste time and energy. That can be accomplished only with the aid of a center that has the authority to give clear direction to all sections. If we have a bureau, it must include delegates from every section, and it absolutely must be in contact with all sections of the proletariat.

Now, Comrade Albert wants to report back to his party comrades before he votes to found the International. But it may not be possible to reconvene for months. That is why we favor founding the International now. Russia has been the intellectual center for the Communist movement of the whole world from the beginning of the Russian revolution. A physical center should now also be created, and that requires an organization. It is not our fault that all countries are not represented here. The very purpose of the Third International is to make it possible to create Communist organizations in countries where none exist.

Additional reasons for immediately establishing the International could also be given. In conclusion, I appeal to you: adopt the motion unanimously. Then the Moscow conference will embody the revolutionary proletariat's will to struggle and its confidence in victory to an even greater degree than did the founding of the First or Second Internationals.

(Platten announces that four speakers remain on the speakers' list and moves that the list be closed. The motion carries.)

FINEBERG *(translated by Reinstein):* I would like to say that I disagree with Comrade Albert's objections. It is true that I am not authorized to speak for the British Socialist Party, as I represent only a local organization.[14] Nevertheless, everything that has happened in the British movement justifies the assumption that the workers there will, without a doubt, be in favor of founding the Third International. My party was recognized as a member of Zimmerwald even though it could not send representatives, and I believe we could do the same now for parties that for technical reasons are unable to be here. The British Socialist

Labour Party broke with the Second International long ago, and there is no reason to doubt that it would welcome the founding of the Third International.

PLATTEN: A motion has been made to close the discussion. Are there speakers for or against? The motion carries. The discussion has been closed, so we will now come to a vote. We will vote on the motion to found the Third International signed by Rakovsky, Gruber, Grimlund, and Rudnyánszky.

(*The motion is read aloud.*)

This motion has been put forward to bring about a decision on whether to proceed to the founding of the Third International. All in favor of the motion say "yes"; all opposed, say "no."

Decisive votes:

Communist Party of Germany ....abstains
Russia..yes
German Austria...yes
Hungary ....yes
Sweden ....yes
Norway..yes
Switzerland..yes
America...yes
Balkan federation ....yes
Poland ....yes
Finland ....yes
Ukraine...yes
Latvia...yes
Lithuania ....yes
Estonia...yes
Armenia ....yes
Colonists' region ....yes
United Group of the Eastern Peoples of Russia ....yes

Approved unanimously with five abstentions.[15]

Consultative votes:

Czechoslovakia....................yes
Bulgaria....................yes
Yugoslavia....................yes
Britain....................yes
France....................yes
Holland....................yes
American Socialist Propaganda League....................yes
Switzerland....................yes
Turkestan....................yes
Turkey....................yes
Georgia....................yes
Azerbaijan....................yes
Persia....................yes
China....................yes
Korea....................yes

Final result: consultative votes unanimous;[16] decisive votes unanimous with five abstentions.

(*Lively applause. The "Internationale" is sung enthusiastically.*)

PLATTEN: Comrades, we continue the proceedings under the designation, "Congress of the Communist International."

We must first decide on the right to vote. Clearly, given the circumstances under which some of the delegates received their invitation, the question must be asked whether they are still entitled to vote following the decision just taken. The resolutions commission unanimously moves that the comrades retain their right to vote.

Are there any objections? Apparently not. You have decided to make no change in the voting procedure.

The Ukrainian delegates must leave us now and return home to take part in a congress in their country. It is appropriate to give the comrades greetings to take back with them. The greetings read as follows:

"The Congress of the Communist International sends the Ukrainian comrades warmest greetings on the occasion of the third conference of the Ukrainian soviets. The Ukrainian comrades have finally succeeded in toppling the enemies within their own borders. They have made the Entente interventionists understand that the workers and poor peasants of the Ukraine will fight for the Soviet republic and not for the rule of any bourgeoisie.

"Long live the dictatorship of the proletariat!

"Long live the social revolution!"

All those wishing to show their approval of these greetings please raise your hands. We present these greetings to the Ukrainian comrades.

And now Comrade Albert has requested the floor to make a statement.

ALBERT: Comrades, as requested by my party and in accord with my personal convictions I have done my utmost to postpone the founding of the Third International. It has now been founded nevertheless. I cannot conceal my grave doubts and deep concern when I consider that the International does not yet have the strength and power we want it to have. But I assure you that when I return to Germany I will do all in my power to convince my comrades to declare as soon as possible that they too belong to the Third International.

PLATTEN: It is late, but we must still deal briefly with one point on the agenda and leave the remaining time for the commission's work.

The Zimmerwald comrades, represented here by Comrades Balabanoff, Zinoviev, Lenin, Trotsky, Platten, etc., have submitted the following declaration:

DECLARATION BY ZIMMERWALD PARTICIPANTS

(Delivered at the Congress of the Communist International in Moscow, March 2–6, 1919.)[17]

The Zimmerwald and Kienthal conferences were important at a time when it was vital to unify all the forces of the proletariat who were prepared to protest in any way against the imperialist slaughter. But along with the clearly Communist forces, forces that were centrist, pacifist, and vacillating also entered the Zimmerwald Association. These centrist forces, as the Bern conference has shown, are now allying themselves with the social patriots in the struggle against the revolutionary proletariat. Thus, they are exploiting Zimmerwald in the interests of reaction.

At the same time, the communist movement is gaining strength in a number of countries. The struggle against the centrist forces, who obstruct the development of the social revolution, has become one of the most urgent tasks of the revolutionary proletariat.

The Zimmerwald Association has outlived its usefulness. Everything that was truly revolutionary in the Zimmerwald Association is passing over to the Communist International.

The undersigned participants in the Zimmerwald movement declare that they regard the Zimmerwald Association as dissolved and call on the bureau of the Zimmerwald conference to turn over all its documents to the executive committee of the Third International.

(Signed:) *Ch. Rakovsky,*
N. Lenin, G. Zinoviev,
L. Trotsky, Fr. Platten.

PLATTEN: Comrade Bukharin has submitted the following resolution.

RESOLUTION ON THE ZIMMERWALD ASSOCIATION

(*Adopted by the Congress of the Communist International in Moscow, March 2–6, 1919.*)[18]

Having received the report of Comrade Balabanoff,[19] secretary of the Zimmerwald International Socialist Committee, and the declaration of Comrades Rakovsky, Platten, Lenin, Trotsky, and Zinoviev, participants in the Zimmerwald Association, the First Congress of the Communist International resolves that the Zimmerwald Association be considered disbanded.

(*Adopted unanimously. Comrade Platten ends the session at* 9:30 *p.m.*)

Top: Iliya Milkić,Fritz Platten, Karl Steinhardt, Gregory Zinoviev; middle: Red Army commander M.N. Tukhachevsky, (unidentified), French Communist Group of Moscow—Robert Petit, Georges Guellfer, Pierre Pascal, Jacques Sadoul, Marcel Body; bottom left: S.J. Rutgers; right: Hugo Eberlein.

FOURTH DAY OF SESSIONS
MARCH 5, 1919

6. The Bern conference and the socialist currents

(Lenin opens the session at 12:30 *p.m. and recognizes Platten.)*

REPORT ON BERN CONFERENCE (PLATTEN)

PLATTEN *(Switzerland):* Comrades, when the war broke out, the Second International proved to be a fellowship of those Social Democrats unwilling to abide by previous decisions or do revolutionary proletarian work. The bureau and its supporters swung over into the camp of the social patriots,[1] those who like cowards tried to use their influence in workers' organizations to place them too at the service of the governments of their respective countries. During the war we repeatedly appealed to these people to remember their internationalist duty and, in keeping with the Stuttgart resolutions,[2] to begin to take action that could disarm the international bourgeoisie. The bureau did not respond to this appeal, and it is characteristic that the war in Europe could be settled without the bureau ever having lifted a finger to call the proletariat of the world into action. That made it easier for the ruling classes to wage the war for their enrichment.

The bureau was full of social patriots, who did their best at fraud and deception. As socialists with a revolutionary communist perspective we understood very clearly that we could not tolerate any further relations with such people, who are as bound to their governments as a lost soul is to the devil. For us the Second International is dead. Let them gather for a congress to refurbish their image and justify their existence to their governments by proclaiming their willingness to go on betraying the workers: still they will not succeed in restoring the old International.

I will explain how the Bern international conference was organized in order to illustrate the great effort we made to get our Zimmerwald comrades to reject it. Clearly this conference aimed to furnish proof that the proletariat still did have some kind of International. The underlying reason for it was that the gentlemen of the Entente felt it would be desirable to secure the blessing of the "Socialist International" for their policies. These people could convene in Bern and set up shop as bourgeois tools of the Entente powers without seeming out of character, for they are loyal servants of their national governments. By reviving the Second International, this congress may have also aimed at breaching the revolutionary front, breaking up the Zimmerwald group as previously composed, and, if possible, isolating the revolutionary Communists.

We should acknowledge here that since Zimmerwald was made up of different political groups, it lacked the strength to call itself an International inspired by a common thought and by the will to act. The Zimmerwald conference was an alliance of parties willing to wage a fight against continuation of the war. The existence of serious differences among its components became clear the minute the question was broached of revolutionizing the masses and of violent overthrow. By calling the Bern conference, the Social Democrats were in fact able to induce a few former Zimmerwald comrades to participate, which demonstrates how poorly grounded in revolutionary ideology was a layer of the Zimmerwald participants.

As revolutionary internationalists in Switzerland, we had served as a connecting link between the western European countries and the Central Powers. We now had to solve a difficult problem: persuading our own national party not to participate in the Bern conference. Clearly, if the Swiss party had decided to participate, it would have been advertised amid great fanfare. But we, the Zurich leadership, did all we could to prevent that.[3]

It should also be noted here that we had to carry out a task given me by Comrade Longuet in France. He asked us to inform the Russian comrades that the French party was sending a delegation to the Bern conference, and they would be very pleased if the Russian comrades would attend as well. I gave this telegram to Comrade Vorovsky in the hope that doing so might help you gain entry into Switzerland, since we had heard you were unable to come to Bern for technical reasons.[4] I knew perfectly well that you would not take part as an opposition in a social-patriotic conference.

Naturally, the former Zimmerwald parties attending this conference were from its far right wing—that is, people who still hoped somehow to convince the representatives of the old International to take on the role of a revolutionary International. Nearly all the French delegates—except Loriot and Frossard—believed it was an exceptionally grave error that no Swiss, Russian, or Spartacus comrades came to Bern, thinking that together they could have routed the right-wing forces there.[5] We correctly understood the situation from the outset and regretted that the French comrades stooped to attending this conference instead of, from the beginning, separating themselves from the avowed social patriots.

Several other comrades and I came up with the idea of immediately inviting the former Zimmerwald participants at this conference to a meeting in order to do what we could to help clarify their position. There I presented to those assembled the position taken by the Swiss party, the Italian comrades, the Russians, and—as best I could—that of comrades in other countries. We had to try to persuade the former Zimmerwald comrades to decide to boycott the conference and to refuse to meet with social patriots. A number of comrades were invited to this meeting, including Comrades Fritz Adler, Petrov, Paul Faure, Frossard, Loriot, Morgari, Rappoport, Herzfeld, Verfeuil, Burian, Scheflo, Besteiro, Betritos, and Marnus.[6] We proposed to these comrades that they state publicly they would not attend the Bern conference. We would then have agreed to hold special meetings with them on reorganizing the International, and most important, perhaps we could have normalized relations for our present gathering. In short order, however, all except Loriot and Morgari cited formalities and declared they had been specifically mandated to attend the conference and would constitute the opposition there.

After we heard their explanation, we turned to helping them at least organize an opposition. We said to them, "If, as you say, you want to participate in the congress only as an opposition, then you will have to agree upon a program." So we proposed that they organize themselves as a left wing, present a resolution under every point on the agenda different from that proposed by the bureau, and denounce, from the standpoint of Zimmerwald, the bureau's efforts for what they are—a policy that serves the bourgeoisie.[7]

We explained that as former Zimmerwald members they could not avoid recognizing the fundamental contradictions between social-patriotic positions and their own. It was necessary to counterpose the Zimmerwald declarations to the bureau's resolutions. We spent a great deal of time attempting to influence these people in this direction, but in the end they explained they did not want to split their respective national delegations; rather they wanted to appear as part of united national sections. That made any organized intervention impossible, and the comrades became nothing more than a rudderless boat drifting down the river.

The discussion of responsibility for the war promptly revealed that in the commission meetings the Zimmerwald delegates were pressing for the best resolution possible in the framework of seeking a unanimous decision. You can well imagine how difficult it was to combine the politics of a Renaudel, of the German social patriot Wels, or of Grumbach and Huysmans in particular with the viewpoint of former Zimmerwald members. The fact that unity was achieved does not speak well for this resolution. It should have brought the disagreements to the surface.

Thus the comrades we had called together ended up completely isolated. All of them acted on their own initiative as part of their respective national delegations. They stuck by that approach in the discussions on the territorial question and on the League of Nations.[8] It was touching to see how energetically some comrades, including Comrade Adler from Austria, tried to find something that the extreme right, the center, and the left could agree on.

Their role at the conference became important when one grouping made a concerted effort to pass a resolution on Soviet Russia. Its real purpose was to try to push through a strong condemnation of Bolshevik policies and of the Soviet government. I suspect this was done not so much to gain a statement that would help their parties as it was to lend the blessing of the social-patriotic conference to a possible Entente invasion. Passing such a resolution would have been a public announcement that the social patriots were backhandedly instructing their governments to "bring order to the chaos" in Russia. That was the primary intention. A second was that adopting such a resolution would decisively discredit the Russian party and the revolutionary movement in the eyes of workers abroad.

This time the efforts of the oppositionists, the former Zimmerwald members, met with success. By the third day individuals such as Grumbach already wanted to introduce this resolution. We owe it to Comrade Adler's efforts that it was decided not to take up the question.[9] Adler argued that not enough was known about the situation in Russia and that there was insufficient information on the Bolsheviks' policies. The resolution should be withheld, he said, until an appropriate commission could observe the situation in Russia first-hand and evaluate the Russian Soviet government's policy.

Two days later, Grumbach made another thrust. The French delegate Renaudel declared they could not return to France unless the congress took such a position on this very important question. They also had in mind that condemnation of Bolshevik policies would erect a wall, a barrier, against the ever-widening sympathy for the Russian revolution among the western European working class.

The workers' movement in western Europe is already concerned almost exclusively with the questions of the revolutionary movement in Russia, and it is safe to say that, as a rule, the workers in almost every country have no interest whatsoever in the eight-day social-patriotic conference in Bern. The capitalists made a great fuss over it. They tried very hard to show what fine work the conference had done and what great politicians it took to find the course that the bourgeoisie itself might have chosen. The workers, in contrast, recognized that the real revolutionaries were not represented there, and the only thing that caused any confusion was Adler's presence.

A few comrades actually played a role that was very supportive for us. For example, Comrade Morgari from Italy made quite clear that he was not there as a participant in the conference but essentially as a reporter for the Italian press. He tried repeatedly to get the left-wing forces to repudiate the conference. Comrade Loriot's declaration accurately exposed the character of the Bern conference. Furthermore, it should be noted that the Norwegian comrades also submitted a statement explaining that although they had been instructed to attend the conference, they had been insufficiently informed about its character. Consequently they were abstaining on the votes and restricting their work to gathering information. They would refuse to accept any responsibility for the conference and said its decisions were in no way binding on them. They would return home and inform their party of the conference's real character. These delegates declared that they aimed to persuade their party to make a definitive break with the Second International and to propose that it turn toward the Third International.

Another task of the Swiss comrades was to try to engage individual delegates at the Bern conference in private conversations to learn about the state of the movement in each country. Here I would like to share with you a few of the things our comrades reported, even at the risk of putting a damper on some high hopes.

The first comrades to give us a detailed report were the Italians. Morgari explained his opinion that revolution is not yet at the doorstep in Italy because the government is artificially delaying demobilization and is still holding troops on foreign territory. Only after demobilization will the situation change. Then, driven by hunger and by the discontent sown in the population by the returning soldiers, he said, the proletariat will give the signal for revolution.

Morgari was more pessimistic about when the revolution will break out than were the other comrades in Italy. However, one significant comment was made: the development of both the party and the unions has caused them to turn toward the most radical perspective within the revolutionary International. We learned that the Italian party has spoken out for the dictatorship of the proletariat.[10] That comes as no surprise if you know that conditions down there are such that when the proletariat rises up, there will be no stopping until the dictatorship of the proletariat is proclaimed. Thus, the Italian comrades believe that a movement will arise in Italy akin to the Russian revolution.

We learned from a report by Comrade Loriot that four-fifths of the French workers very strongly oppose intervention against Russia. He told us that the workers will not quietly tolerate such action by the French government; rather this will trigger a revolutionary struggle. Intervention in Russia can no longer be carried out with French soldiers, he said; it can be done only with colonial peoples.

It is true, he said, that demobilization has heightened the masses' revolutionary mood, and that the returning soldiers' outlook is such that incidents are likely. Nonetheless, more time is needed before these moods solidify enough to be expressed politically. This is true primarily in the Seine [Paris] district, Loriot said. He cannot claim a large following, nor can he say that a party with tens of thousands of comrades stands behind him, but his influence on the working class as a whole is much greater than the numerical strength of his party would indicate. Now, after the trip to Bern, the propaganda activity can be stepped up because the outcome there was not encouraging for the social patriots, and the differences in the French party will only get deeper with time.

A conversation with another comrade from the trade unions revealed that unionists have already formed a firm opinion on the social patriots in France. He believes that very soon the socialist ministers and their followers will be driven out of the party.[11] Now that censorship has diminished, the syndicalists are also able to conduct more extensive revolutionary propaganda than they could previously.[12]

Everyone—from Loriot to Longuet—agreed that they would stand by the Russian comrades. Whatever shortcomings the movement in the East may have, they say, it is clearly genuinely proletarian, and it is not the business of comrades in western Europe to criticize these comrades.

Little could be learned from the British delegates. As far as we know, the parties in Britain have agreed that the majority at conferences where all workers' parties are represented selects the delegates to be sent abroad.[13] The British delegates conceded that a powerful movement exists among the workers there, as elsewhere, and that many workers had strongly opposed participation in the social patriots' conference and had declared their sympathy for the revolutionary Russian comrades. However, they said that the struggle in Britain does not have the character of a revolutionary struggle for socialism.

Rather, it is purely an economic movement of immense proportions. We may assume that this economic workers' movement in Britain will soon develop into a truly revolutionary one.

The final comrade that we questioned about the situation in his country was Adler, from Austria. His answers made quite clear to us his attitude toward the Communist Party in German Austria. He explained that first he had needed time to get his political bearings, and then he had had to try to regain full legal rights. Next we asked him why he had not assumed leadership of the Communists. He responded that it was impossible for him to participate in that movement, because he hoped to organize a left-wing current in the [Social Democratic] party powerful enough to lead the Austrian proletariat in a united struggle against the bourgeoisie. Further inquiry into the situation in Austria and into Adler's attitude toward the Viennese working class revealed that he was also frightened by the growing chaos. He wanted to commit himself to construction. He stated flatly that giving in to Communist policies would definitely result in the complete depopulation of Vienna, because the class struggle between peasants and city dwellers would lead to a cutoff of the food supply. His line of reasoning is highly significant because it helps us to understand the reasons why he is so hesitant.

You can see from this report that these comrades' efforts to intercede for us were not overly successful. I am sure of one thing—the movement in each of their countries will open the eyes of some of them, who will later break with the social-patriotic Second International and join the Communist Third International. "With or against the workers?" That is the moral question that has been posed to the leaders. Class-conscious workers will join the new Communist International with or without those who have been their leaders until now.

LENIN: The second reporter, Comrade Zinoviev, has the floor.

REPORT ON THE BERN CONFERENCE (ZINOVIEV)

ZINOVIEV: Comrades, we have two questions to discuss: first, our attitude toward the social patriots' Bern conference, and second, our attitude toward the principal currents in the workers' movement today. I drew the basic material on the first question from the reputable bourgeois newspaper, the *Neue zürcher Zeitung*. This newspaper was very favorably disposed toward the Bern conference and featured very detailed, almost stenographic, reports on it.[14]

What happened at the opening session is itself significant. The conference was convened by Branting. His opening remarks were dedicated to the founding of the International and to its chairman, Jaurès, in whose memory all those present briefly stood. After this, the report continues, Branting proposed to salute a second great man, one still among the living—Mr. Wilson. So you can see, comrades, that the very first words of the chairman were highly significant: on the left wing is our deceased Jaurès, and on the right, Wilson—very much alive! Nothing more need be said.

Next to take the floor was Albert Thomas, the former French war minister. His speech brought the apathetic audience to life. To quote Thomas: "The conference must pass resolutions. But what effect will they have? An International existed before the war and now it has convened once more. But is everyone the same as they were before? And does mutual trust still exist as before? That is the question. And that is why Belgium refused to take part in the conference."

Thomas, one of the most influential participants at this conference, told the truth. He had the same message as the Russian proverb: "Once a liar, always a liar!" Behind Thomas's remarks lay the question: After you have lied for four entire years, who will believe you now? Thomas aimed his question at the German social patriots. But they could just as well have put the same question to Thomas, and *both* sides would have been right.

At the second session, Henderson, one of the most influential leaders of the Second International, proposed the following resolution: "This conference resolves that its work must henceforth be conducted so as to attain at the Paris conference the greatest influence for the interests of the working class and the Socialist movement of the countries represented here."

These words outline the main task of the Bern conference, and we encounter them often in the speeches of Henderson and the others. They see their task exclusively in exerting the greatest possible influence over the Paris conference. So much for the political task of the Bern conference.

Further in the resolution Henderson says: "This conference also recognizes that the war provoked misunderstandings and strong disagreements over what attitude to take toward it." It would seem that the workers' movement in the last four and a half years has experienced merely some small misunderstandings.

Henderson's resolution goes no further than the demands that were advanced by Wibaut and Kautsky, namely, that the League of Nations question be decided not by governmental, but by parliamentary representatives. That is, by representatives of bourgeois layers, since governments and bourgeois layers are really one and the same thing, and not by representatives of the workers and soldiers.

Although Wilson was not present at the conference, his spirit hovered above it. At the fourth session of the conference, Huysmans introduced a resolution to form a commission including Henderson, Branting, Huysmans, and two delegates from each country, to exert the greatest possible influence on the Paris conference and to monitor how its decisions are carried out. When one of the centrists made some remarks against Wilson, Milhaud rose to declare that if Wilson's policies were not approved, he would walk out of the conference in protest. Huysmans quickly took the floor to calm him, saying it was excluded that Wilson's policies would not be approved.

The first question before the conference was the question of "blame" for the war, which was closely connected with the "territorial" question. During the discussion of whom to hold responsible for the war, they examined in minute detail each step taken by respective bourgeois ministers before the war. The idea was to conceal from the proletariat the central fact that it was finance capital of both coalitions and the social patriots themselves who were responsible for the war.

It was on territorial questions and on the League of Nations that the duplicity of the Bern conference reached its climax. But Thomas and Henderson nevertheless knew how to attain almost complete clarity in the interests of the bourgeoisie. They decided to implement the so-called right of nations to self-determination through referendum. But the two previous resolutions on the territorial question at the conference required that: "Possession of contested regions shall be decided by a referendum under the supervision of the League of Nations, which shall make the final decision."[15]

The key point here, clearly, is the supervisory role of the League of Nations, an alliance made up of the bourgeois imperialists.

Incidentally, they also touched upon the colonial question, but did not dare subject it to a detailed examination. The German social patriots begged the conference to preserve Germany's colonies, that is, to leave them to the exploitation by German capital. They received no direct answer on this. It goes without saying that the French and British felt that the colonies ought to be handed over to exploitation by French and British capital. In the fifth point of the previously mentioned resolution the conference demands: "The League of Nations must safeguard the population in dependent regions and colonies and establish a protectorate over them, which must see to it that measures are taken to promote the quickest possible development of the native population toward national self-determination."[16]

One can imagine how the League of Nations might safeguard the colonies. Thus, in the resolution there is not even a hint that colonial slavery as a whole must cease, no words like Kautsky once wrote: "Hands off the colonies, down with bourgeois colonial exploitation,"[17] but rather a whitewash of bourgeois colonial policies. Such are the basic features of the majority's policy at the Bern conference.

Later on, a small group of pacifists and former centrists was organized by Wibaut, Kautsky, and Bernstein. These gentlemen did no more than coat the imperialist politics of the majority with sugary phrases. For example, Wibaut proposed this resolution: "The unification of all peoples into a harmonious society has been from the very start among the noblest ideals of the Socialist International. This ideal is rooted in the solidarity of proletarians of all countries and in the final goal of socialism."[18]

But, it may be asked, what kind of "society"? One like the League of Nations? That was hardly an ideal of the Socialist International! Some empty phrases were uttered to the effect that this society would prevent the outbreak of new wars. But no one said a word on how this could be done. Troelstra, a leader of the Dutch social patriots, also played the pacifist role, declaring that we, the Russian Bolsheviks, are to blame that the war did not end at the beginning of 1917. Bolshevism began with the Brusilov offensive, and if only the Stockholm conference had been held, then surely the events in Russia would have had a different outcome.[19] It was essential, he said, that Paris do nothing that would lead to Bolshevism's artificial extension into Germany. I believe we can reply that whatever steps they may take, they can only further the growth of Bolshevism in Germany and around the world. History leaves them no other way out.

The most important question before the Bern conference was the evaluation of the Russian situation, that is, the condemnation of Bolshevism. We can ascertain with satisfaction that here a whole number of our French comrades spoke brilliantly against the majority, and in the name of the party we must thank them. Even though it was an error from the start to take part in the conference, here they carried out their proletarian duty. Paul Faure and Loriot were the only ones to speak the truth to the faces of the social patriots.

The most remarkable speech was made by Kautsky, the leader of the centrists. In his opinion it is necessary to struggle even now against Bolshevism, because you cannot identify it with the Russian revolution. Of course, he thinks that the Russian revolution should be identified with the Mensheviks, that is, with the counterrevolution. Kautsky holds that the most important task today consists of enriching an impoverished humanity and restoring production. He is not interested in the economic basis upon which such production should be restored. Humanity should be enriched, capitalist production must be restored, and only then should the struggle for socialism be begun. Turning to a critique of the Bolsheviks' activities during the last year, Kautsky declared: "The Russian revolution destroyed large-scale industry, wrecked proletarian organization, and forced the surviving workers to return again to the countryside. The Bolsheviks are trying to implement socialism. But the reality is that their single positive result will be a new militarism."[20] This brought him a storm of applause. Of course, our Red Army does not appeal to such gentlemen, and everyone who has a rather strong reason to fear its appearance in his own country ought to join the applause. Kautsky continued: "We must take a clear position toward Bolshevism in order not to lose the trust of the masses." We can reply that you can't lose what you don't possess! And by taking a definite position, a counterrevolutionary position toward Bolshevism, these gentlemen will win the trust only of the imperialists.

Comrades Faure and Loriot replied to this speech. Loriot said: "Let us concern ourselves first of all with the question of the dictatorship of the bourgeoisie," and further explained that even in the bourgeois republics the bourgeois dictatorship is just as much a reality as in a monarchy. These remarks seemed to have grabbed Bernstein by the scruff of the neck, and he rose to deliver a bloodthirsty tirade against Bolshevism.

Take note that the conference was not able to pass any resolution against Bolshevism. The small opposition that had formed there managed to prevent the conference from coming to any kind of conclusion. We should not see in this a diplomatic victory of one group over another. Instead we view it as direct proof that the authentic masses of the western European proletariat have not only refused to condemn us, but in fact have some sympathy toward us. The conference simply sidestepped the most important questions that today interest the broad masses of the working class. It did not dare to speak its clearly defined opinion about the system of soviets of workers' deputies. Thus, they only displayed their spiritual poverty and theoretical bankruptcy, as Comrade Lenin showed yesterday. They did not say even one word about what we have accomplished. They might condemn it, but at the very least they should have taken a definite position toward us. But they could not say anything. Their conduct reminds me of the December 9, 1918, congress of the Swiss metalworkers' union. It was compelled to discuss councils of workers' deputies because many metalworkers were demanding that their trade unions, as an educational slogan, call for their formation. The trade union hacks then took up this question and drafted a resolution opposing councils of workers' deputies on the grounds that these councils and their activities undermine workers' national organizations and, above all, that forming them was against the bylaws. The old-time social-patriotic leaders have nothing to say about this historic movement other than that it is—against the rules. That shows their intellectual poverty better than anything.

Such were the proceedings of the conference. When it finished, a delegation set out for Paris,[21] where it was received by none other than Clemenceau, the most reactionary bourgeois leader today. Clemenceau declared that the Bern conference had taken the same general course as the Paris conference was taking and invited the delegation to take part in the relevant commissions of the Paris conference. He thereby openly confirmed that the Bern conference was really only a tool of the imperialists' meeting in Paris. That describes the conference perfectly. I hope that the vast majority of the world working class sees the essence of the conference just as we do. The initial universal lie, on defense of the fatherland, is well understood by workers. So the first task that Paris gave to the Bern conference was to convince the working masses to approve the methods to settle the war now proposed by the bourgeoisie: laying the whole burden of debts and taxes on the backs of the working masses, retaining the same old armies unchanged, and taking a stand against the soviets, against the dictatorship of the proletariat.

Comrades, I believe that if we study the work of the Bern conference closely we will have to say that it flows naturally from the entire evolution before and during the war. Even before the war it was very clear that a tendency had formed within the Second International, a majority whose position was bourgeois patriotism and social chauvinism rather than the viewpoint of Marx and Engels. Let me remind you of the discussion at the Stuttgart congress. The revisionist gentlemen, led by van Kol of Holland and Bernstein, openly proposed that the Second International approve a colonialist policy, specifying only that it should be conducted in a more humane way. Further let me remind you that this proposal of the revisionists was voted down in the commission by only a narrow majority. Decisive forces in the Second International had already then taken the viewpoint of the bourgeoisie on colonial policy, that is, the question of imperialism.

Let me remind you further of the most important point of the Stuttgart resolution: "In case war should break out anyway, it is [the Socialists'] duty to intervene for its speedy termination and to strive with all their power to utilize the economic and political crisis created by the war to rouse the masses and thereby hasten the downfall of capitalist class rule." This point was proposed by the leaders of the left, Lenin and Rosa Luxemburg, and was adopted only under pressure from the left. As we can see, the basic traits of the Second International were already apparent at Stuttgart, seven years before the war began. You are all familiar with the resolution adopted unanimously at Basel. Let me therefore remind you of what Marcel Sembat wrote only a few months after Basel. He dubbed it the "grand pardon de Bâle" [the general absolution of Basel]. Resolutions may be adopted, but no one will stand by them. He foresaw this even before the war, and he was right.

Further, let me remind you of the positions taken by the parties, at least on paper, before the war began. It can be said that up until twenty-four hours before the declaration of war in 1914 these gentlemen spoke entirely differently than today. Professor Carl Grünberg of Vienna has published a book of materials he collected on the weeks just before and just after the war; it is the best indictment of the Second International, and we should make wide use of it.[22] Twenty-four hours before the war began *L'Humanité,* the central organ of the French party, declared that the war was imperialist in nature and would be conducted in the interests of the bourgeoisie. The very same thing was said by the Scheidemannite official newspaper, *Vorwärts,* by the Italian party organ, and by the party press of almost all countries.[23] When the first shot was fired, they all did an about-face and on August 4 called white what they had called black on August 2.

This situation did not come about suddenly; it was a logical end result. The bankruptcy of the Second International was prepared by twenty-five years of peaceful development. We discern three main tendencies. They did not spring up in a day, but were formed over the years. Of the three tendencies at hand, the first, the social patriots, have carried out one and the same political line both during and after the war—the line of imperialism and bourgeois democracy. The second tendency is the center current, represented before the war by Kautsky's grouping in particular. It put forward the very same policies, although under different circumstances. Before the war they spoke against the Left Radicals and called them anarchists. When the war broke out, however, Kautsky published a pamphlet with his remarkable formula "Struggle for peace, class struggle in peacetime";[24] that is, no class struggle whatsoever during a war. Then came his propaganda of unity with the social patriots who bore both moral and physical responsibility for the murders of proletarian leaders Karl Liebknecht and Rosa Luxemburg. Indeed, the very same Kautsky who proposed that the Bern conference stand to honor the memory of Karl Liebknecht and Rosa Luxemburg still calls on us to unite with their murderers. Kautsky and some of the delegates to the Bern conference demanded a mutual amnesty,[25] which they had also called for at the beginning of the war. In fact, in 1915 Kautsky had worked out a complete theory of mutual amnesty. And it goes without saying that in 1919, when the war had ended and the proletarian revolution had begun, they exchanged mutual assurances and, thus united, granted each other an amnesty.

There is still the question, will the proletariat ever grant them an amnesty? No, that will never happen. The proletariat will not permit any cover-up on the collapse of the Second International. It will discuss and resolve this great problem posed by the 1914–18 imperialist war. And we should try to interest every ordinary worker in this. We should inspire each one to study and understand the central question of socialism today: why the Second International became a tool of the international bourgeoisie, what caused its downfall, and why we must found a Third International.

The Yellow International of Bern and the Red International that we founded yesterday are now locked in single combat. There can be no doubt that the Red International will prevail over the Yellow International and, moreover, prevail in the very near future.

LENIN: Who wishes to take the floor for discussion?

We will hand the resolution on this question to the resolutions commission.

(*Zinoviev reads the resolution.*)

OUR ATTITUDE TOWARD THE SOCIALIST CURRENTS AND THE BERN CONFERENCE

I

As early as 1907, when the Second International took up the question of colonial policy and imperialist wars at the International Socialist Congress in Stuttgart, it was revealed that more than half of the International—and most of its leaders—stood much closer to the views of the bourgeoisie on these questions than to the communist standpoint of Marx and Engels.[26]

Nevertheless, the Stuttgart congress adopted an amendment proposed by the representatives of the revolutionary wing, N. Lenin and Rosa Luxemburg, which said: "In case war should break out anyway, it is Socialists' duty to intervene for its speedy termination and *to strive with all their power to utilize the economic and political crisis created by the war to rouse the masses and thereby hasten the downfall of capitalist class rule."*

At the Basel congress, called in November 1912 during the Balkan War, the Second International declared:

"Let [the bourgeois governments] remember that the Franco-German War was followed by the revolutionary outbreak of the Commune; that the Russo-Japanese War set into motion the revolutionary energies of the peoples of the Russian Empire. . . . Proletarians consider it a crime to fire at each other for the profits of the capitalists, the ambitions of dynasties, or the greater glory of secret diplomatic treaties."[27]

As late as the end of July and beginning of August 1914, twenty-four hours before the outbreak of the World War, official publications and institutions of the Second International were denouncing the approaching war as the bourgeoisie's greatest crime.[28] The statements issued during those days by the Second International's leading parties constitute the most eloquent indictment of the leaders of the Second International.

At the first shot fired on the battlefields of the imperialist mass slaughter, the leading parties of the Second International betrayed the international working class. Under the guise of "defending the fatherland," each party went over to the side of "its own" bourgeoisie. Scheidemann and Ebert in Germany, Thomas and Renaudel in France, Henderson and Hyndman in Britain, Vandervelde and de Brouckère in Belgium, Renner and Pernerstorfer in Austria, Plekhanov and Rubanovitch in Russia, Branting and his party in Sweden, Gompers and his co-thinkers in America, Mussolini and Company in Italy—all called upon the proletariat to conclude "civil peace" with the bourgeoisie of "their own" country, abandon the war against the war, and become in fact cannon-fodder for the imperialists.

That was the moment of the definitive bankruptcy and demise of the Second International.

The general course of economic development enabled the bourgeoisies of the wealthiest countries to bribe and seduce the upper layer of the working class, the labor aristocracy, with a few crumbs from their enormous profits. The petty-bourgeois "camp-followers" of socialism streamed into the ranks of the official Social Democratic parties and gradually swung those parties' policies toward the side of the bourgeoisie. An entire caste, a labor bureaucracy, arose from the leadership of the peacetime parliamentary workers' movement, from the union leadership and from the secretaries, editors, and officials of the Social Democracy. This caste had its own selfish group interests and was in reality hostile to socialism.[29]

For all these reasons, official Social Democracy degenerated into an antisocialist and chauvinist party.

Three basic tendencies began to form in the womb of the Second International. Their outlines emerged with complete clarity between the start of the war and the beginning of the proletarian revolution in Europe.

1. *The social-chauvinist current* (the "majority" current). Its most typical representatives are the German Social Democrats, who currently share power with the German bourgeoisie and have become the murderers of leaders of the Communist International: Karl Liebknecht and Rosa Luxemburg.

The social chauvinists now stand completely exposed as class enemies of the proletariat. They are pursuing the program of "liquidating" the war written for them by the bourgeoisie: shift the burden of taxation onto the toiling masses; maintain the inviolability of private property; leave the army in the hands of the bourgeoisie; dissolve the workers' councils that are springing up everywhere; leave political power in the hands of the bourgeoisie; promote bourgeois "democracy" against socialism.

Although the Communists have been waging a vigorous struggle against the "majority Social Democrats," the workers still do not clearly grasp the extent of the danger posed to the international proletariat by these traitors. Opening the eyes of all toilers to the social chauvinists' Judas-like role and, arms in hand, rendering this counterrevolutionary party harmless is one of the most important tasks of the international proletarian revolution.

2. *The centrist current* (social pacifists, Kautskyites, Independents). This current began to form even before the war, primarily in Germany. At the beginning of the war, the center was almost everywhere in agreement with social chauvinism on the main points. Kautsky, the theoretical leader of the center, came forward with a defense of the policy being followed by the German and French social chauvinists: the International was only a "peacetime instrument." Kautsky's slogan was "struggle for peace, class struggle in peacetime."

Since the beginning of the war, the center has insisted on "unity" with the social chauvinists. After the murder of Liebknecht and Rosa Luxemburg, the center goes right on preaching the same unity, which means unity between Communist workers and those who murdered the Communist leaders Liebknecht and Rosa Luxemburg.

From the very beginning of the war the center (Kautsky, Victor Adler, Turati, MacDonald) began preaching for a "mutual amnesty," which was to apply to the leaders of the social-chauvinist parties of Germany and Austria on the one hand and to the social-chauvinist leaders in France and Britain on the other. Even today, after the end of the war, the center still preaches this amnesty and thereby prevents the workers from clearly understanding the reasons for the Second International's collapse.

The center sent representatives to the international conference of compromise Socialists in Bern, thereby making it easier for the Scheidemanns and Renaudels to deceive the workers.

It is absolutely necessary to split the most revolutionary forces away from the center, a task that can be achieved only through pitiless criticism and exposure of the centrist leaders. The organizational split from the center is an absolute historical necessity. The task of the Communists in every single country is to determine the moment for this break according to the level of development of the movement in their country.

3. *The Communists.* This current remained a minority in the Second International, where it defended the Marxist-communist viewpoint on the war and the tasks of the proletariat (resolution by Lenin and Luxemburg, Stuttgart congress, 1907). The Left Radical group in Germany (which later became the Spartacus group), the Bolsheviks in Russia, the Tribunists in Holland, the youth organization in Sweden, and the left wing of the youth International in several countries together formed the first nucleus of the new International.

This tendency remained loyal to the interests of the working class and proclaimed from the beginning of the war the slogan: "transform the imperialist war into a civil war."[30] This current has now constituted itself as the Third International.

II

The Bern Socialist conference of February 1919 was an attempt to galvanize the corpse of the Second International.

The composition of the Bern conference clearly reveals that the revolutionary proletariat of the world has nothing in common with it.

The victorious proletariat of Russia; the heroic proletariat of Germany; the Italian proletariat; the Communist part of the Austrian and Hungarian proletariat; the proletariat of Switzerland; the working class of Bulgaria, Romania, and Serbia; the left-wing workers' parties of Sweden, Norway, and Finland; the Ukrainian, Latvian, and Polish proletariat; the best currents of the organized proletariat of Britain; the youth International; and the women's International have demonstratively refused to participate in the social-patriotic conference in Bern.[31]

Those attending the Bern conference who still have some contact with the real workers' movement of our time formed an opposition group that countered the efforts of the social patriots, at least on the main question: appraisal of the Russian revolution. The statement by the French comrade Loriot, who castigated the majority at the Bern conference as henchmen of the bourgeoisie, represents the real opinion of all class-conscious workers of the entire world.

On the so-called war-guilt question, the Bern conference remained within the framework of bourgeois ideology. The German and French social patriots leveled the same accusations against each other that the German and

French bourgeoisies had hurled at one another. The Bern conference got lost in the petty details of this or that step taken by one or another bourgeois minister prior to the war. It refused to see that primary guilt for the war rests with capitalism, finance capital of both coalitions, and their social-patriotic lackeys. The social-patriotic majority in Bern wanted to identify the main culprit for the war. But to recognize some of the guilty parties they had only to glance in the mirror.

What the Bern conference had to say on the territorial question is full of ambiguities. The bourgeoisie requires this ambiguity. Mr. Clemenceau, the most reactionary representative of the imperialist bourgeoisie, acknowledged the services to imperialist reaction rendered by the Bern social-patriotic conference by receiving its delegation and proposing it participate in all relevant commission meetings at the imperialist conference in Paris.

The discussion on the colonial question clearly revealed that the Bern conference is treading the same path as the bourgeois-liberal colonial politicians, who believe the imperialist bourgeoisie's policy of colonial exploitation and subjugation is justified and only wish to dress it up with humanitarian and philanthropic phrases. The German social patriots demanded that the German colonies remain the property of the German state. In other words, they advocate continued subjugation of those colonies by German capital. The disagreements that emerged at Bern in this discussion demonstrate that the social patriots of the Entente take the same position as the slaveholders: they regard continued subjugation of the French and British colonies by domestic capital as self-evident. Thus did the Bern conference show that it has completely forgotten the slogan, "withdraw from the colonies."

In its stand on the "League of Nations," the Bern conference showed that it followed in the footsteps of those bourgeois forces who want to exorcise the growing worldwide proletarian revolution with the illusion of the so-called League of Nations. Instead of exposing the dealings at the Allies' Paris conference as horse trading in nations and economic regions, the Bern conference stooped to becoming an instrument to promote them.

The Bern conference left it up to a conference of bourgeois governments in Paris to resolve the problem of workers' protective legislation. This servile attitude demonstrates that the social patriots have consciously taken their stand for continued capitalist wage slavery and are willing to let the working class be put off with petty reforms.

Efforts were made to get the Bern conference to pass a resolution lending the cover of the Second International to possible armed intervention against Russia. These efforts—inspired by bourgeois policies—were thwarted only by the work of the opposition. This success by the Bern opposition over the flagrantly chauvinist elements shows us indirectly that the western European proletariat sympathizes with the Russian proletarian revolution and is ready to struggle against the imperialist bourgeoisie.

The timid refusal of these lackeys of the bourgeoisie to pay even the slightest attention to the workers' councils betrays their fear of the inevitable spread of this world-historic phenomenon. The workers' councils are the most important event since the Paris Commune. By ignoring the question, the Bern conference has openly proclaimed its intellectual poverty and its theoretical bankruptcy.

The congress of the Communist International regards the "International" that the Bern conference seeks to resurrect as a Yellow, strike-breaking International, which is and remains nothing but a tool of the bourgeoisie.

The congress calls upon the workers of all countries to take up a determined struggle against the Yellow International and protect the broad masses of the people from this International of lies and deception.[32]

LENIN: We have this resolution, then the draft resolution on tactics will be read, and then a draft of Comrade Sadoul's resolution, which is being translated into German. We propose turning all of these resolutions over to the editing commission. Is there any objection? The proposal is therefore adopted. This point on the agenda is finished.

We now give the floor to the delegate from China.

REPORT ON CHINA

LIU SHAOZHOU: (*The Chinese delegate speaks in Chinese, then continues in Russian.*)[33] This is the first time the Chinese democratic movement has ever been represented at a congress of an International that declared war on world imperialism and capitalism.

The yoke of this imperialism weighs especially heavily on China's five hundred million people. After a thousand years of isolation, their entry onto the world stage is marked by an unprecedented hostile campaign by the European powers, America, and Japan. Although these imperialist powers claimed to be bringing Western civilization to China, their real goal was clear. All were intent on enslaving China and reducing it to a colony in order to extract its wealth for the profit of the European bourgeoisie.

After a great many wars the different European countries triumphed because of their technical superiority. They then accepted the "Open Door" policy and seemed to be willing to leave China in peace.[34] But this was in reality merely an agreement among a flock of vultures, feebly restraining each other as they encircled their prey, each of them worried about a greedier rival. It was a tacit understanding among the powers, each of which had partitioned off for itself a section of China's huge territory for exploitation on behalf of its own bankers and capitalists.

The Chinese people have understood the Western powers' actions and can feel only the pain of helplessness as they watch the gradual enslavement of their homeland. In addition they have the bitter memories of Manchu despotism, which led the Chinese people to ruin. The more advanced sectors of the Chinese people united in a national movement against the Manchu dynasty. Thanks to the energy of these forces, headed by their outstanding leader, Sun Yat-sen, the Manchu monarchy was overthrown in that great act of Chinese history, the 1911 revolution.

The events that followed showed even more clearly the true face of European imperialism, whose agents did all they could to restrict the national movement in China to a narrow framework favorable to them.[35] Their backing of the reactionary Yuan Shikai and of Zhang Xun's insane attempt to restore the monarchy demonstrated better than anything else just how sincere the European powers were in their professed sympathy for young progressive China.

Then came the European war. The European bourgeoisie vastly increased its pressure and forced China into the war. The Chinese proletariat was utilized both as cannon fodder and as a submissive labor force in the tundras and swamps of northern Russia, in the mines, and for other labor services supplying the front lines of the European war. The European bourgeoisie could hardly have acted otherwise, since they had exterminated millions of European proletarians for the glory of the gods of war and capital.

In 1917 another revolution broke out in the south of China demanding the overthrow of the reactionary government. Even then the majority of the Chinese parliament, assembled in Shanghai, sent greetings to the Russian provisional government. Their salutations and proposal for joint struggle against imperialism could receive no response, of course, from the Kerensky government. So you can imagine the joy among Chinese revolutionaries when through the fiery circle of war and revolution was heard the voice of Russia's Soviet government in its address to the peoples of the East, and especially in Comrade Chicherin's letter to China's highly esteemed Sun Yat-sen. In these statements China first heard foreign comrades express understanding for its cherished aspirations.[36] It heard the Russian people, through their workers' and peasants' government, resolve to struggle resolutely for the very goals that the best forces of the Chinese democratic movement, despite their isolation from the world, are fighting for.

The struggle of Chinese revolutionaries in the south of China is extremely difficult. Perhaps it is their lot to fall in unequal combat. But the voice of Russia with its fraternal appeal will serve as a most inspiring call to battle.

This International was founded by the Russian Communist Party, which leads a government that has declared war on world imperialism on behalf of the world's toilers and for the freedom of its peoples. This party enjoys the liveliest sympathy among the Chinese people.

It is a great honor for me to represent the Chinese organization at this International congress. On behalf of not only the group I represent and the many thousands of Chinese proletarians scattered across Russia, but also the many millions of long-suffering Chinese people, I bring fervent greetings to the Third International. Its banner marks out the course of our relentless battle against the monster of world imperialism.

REPORT ON TURKEY

MUSTAFA SUBHI: How fortunate I am to be here in Moscow—the center of the great Third International that must change the whole world's future—speaking in the name of freedom, equality, and brotherhood on behalf of the proletariat, of the oppressed Turkish peasantry and working class, of the oppressed people who have suffered so much from oppressive and rapacious imperialism and who are perishing in the tenacious claws of capitalism, perishing from the violence of Western civilization.[37]

The truth is that in Turkey and also in other states there are many barbarians and traitors committing murder and sucking the people's lifeblood. There are our Turkish sultans, who suck the blood not only of the Armenians,[38] but also of the Turkish poor, of the workers and peasants. These barbarians are not the masses of the oppressed people, but rather the Turkish pashas and sultans. Comrades, the workers' and peasants' representatives in Russia after the October revolution decided to join battle against capital and above all to crush and destroy these predatory barbarians, who call themselves rulers.

A full year ago, when the Turkish generals intended to send their army to occupy the shores of the Caspian Sea, Persia, and Turkestan, the Turkish revolutionists in Moscow—this center of revolution, which promises happiness to the whole world—boldly raised a Turkish banner to counter the generals' adventuristic aspirations.[39] The Turkish ambassador in Moscow tried to drown out our voice by constantly bombarding the Russian government with notes demanding our immediate expulsion from Russia. He propagandized against us in Tashkent, Orenburg, and Kazan, centers of the Muslim peoples, and attempted with all his might to destroy our work.

The bourgeois newspapers directed articles against us, with questions like: "What kind of people are these, who mock the faith and most sacred duty of the Turkish-Tatar nation, at a time when the Muslim world is celebrating the victory of the Turkish army in the depths of Asia? Where is these people's religion? Where is their nationality?" And when the embassy tried to dupe the whole eastern Muslim world with these wily questions, we, the Turkish Communists, solemnly declared the whole earthly realm to be our homeland and humanity itself to be our nation. And so, boldly raising the red banner of revolution, we decided to go against the stream, against the groups united around Turkish imperialism. For a time we remained alone on the road to the realization of our ideas. But now all the East is with us. Comrades, when the Anglo-French predators occupied Constantinople [Istanbul], all the lying voices speaking against us vanished along with the Turkish imperialists.[40] It became clear to everyone that the oppressed and the unfortunate had no better friend than the great Russian revolution.

Back in 1908 some Turkish youth already understood that the only salvation for the people was in socialist revolution. But at that time the work of socialists was suppressed, and the resounding voice of the unforgettable Jaurès, coming to the defense of the oppressed people, remained a voice in the wilderness.[41] Only the friends of Jaurès did not turn back from the process he started, and now they have organized a Turkish revolutionary center here in Russia. Their confidence that the economic and social transformation in the East can be accomplished through the world socialist revolution was further strengthened by the great October events.

An interesting example shows that this confidence exists today among the Turkish proletariat and intelligentsia. After the October revolution, the awarding of the Nobel prize was discussed at the University of Constantinople. Despite the pressure of their professors, the Turkish youth awarded it to Comrade Lenin, and thus showed once more that the ideas of socialist revolution have firmly taken root in the East. By his ideas, aspirations, and work, our respected and great teacher, Comrade Lenin, represents the entire revolutionary world. By their choice the Turkish youth have shown that they are part of that world.

I do not believe it necessary to say more about the Turkish people's sympathy for the Russian revolution. But let the heroes of the Russian social revolution, who have made so many sacrifices to the altar of the world social revolution, know that they are not alone on the field of battle. The mass of the Turkish proletariat together with the entire intelligentsia is joined together with them heart and soul.

Let these heroes be confident that under the southern sun the profound indignation of the Turkish proletariat is growing. It too is caught in the trap and thus awaits only a call to arms from its elders, the Russian comrades, to join in the struggle.

Comrades, I say this to show you that in the Near East true revolutionaries live among the Turkish people and sympathize with the Russian revolution with all their heart.

Now I will touch very briefly on how the movement in the East relates to the world revolution. I am deeply convinced that the revolution in the East is directly related to the revolution in the West. We, the Turkish revolutionaries working in the ranks of the Russian revolution, firmly believe that the revolution in the East is indispensable not only to liberate the East from European imperialism, but also to support the Russian revolution.

Comrades, you all know that if the head of Anglo-French imperialism is located in Europe, then its belly rests on the rich fields of Asia. And for us, the Turkish socialists, the first and main task is to tear out capitalism by the roots in the East. Only in this way will Anglo-French production be deprived of raw materials. If Turkey, Persia, India, China, and others close their doors to Anglo-French industry, they will prevent it from selling its stocks on the European exchanges and thus provoke an unavoidable crisis. Through this crisis power will pass to the proletariat, and the socialist order will be established. That can be achieved only by arousing a revolutionary movement in these countries, by an uprising of the Eastern peoples against Anglo-French imperialism.

But how are we to revolutionize the East?

I have often been present at meetings where the Eastern question and the religious life of the Eastern peoples was discussed and a desire was expressed to learn more about these peoples. Even under the tsarist regime the East was studied. But then the goal was to find better ways to exploit these nationalities. Nowadays this question is studied in order to liberate the oppressed East. While scholars pursue the study of the East, we must grasp our weapons firmly and not let our goal slip from view—that is, the organization of a revolutionary center in the East. The uprising of the peoples of the East against European capital that is necessary for Russia is just as essential for the young German revolution, whose existence is now exciting the proletariat of the world. The German revolution is under the constant threat of Anglo-American violence, and it awaits help from us, from the East.

That is why the next task of the Third International must be the creation of revolutionary centers among the Eastern peoples.

In the midst of the powerful young Red Army of Russia, cells of Turkish military revolutionary organizations are being created and strengthened. Thousands of Turkish Red Army men are now active on the different battlefields, fighting to defend Soviet power.

Through its geographical position Turkey always connected Asia with Europe. Moreover, it has fallen under the immediate yoke of capitalism. It is therefore safe to assume that the Turkish proletariat will occupy an honorable place in the future course of the world revolution.

We are sure that the Turkish proletariat will muster all its forces to support and develop the world social revolution.

Top: U.S. intervention troops under British command at Murmansk; bottom left: Yrjö Sirola; bottom right: Jukka Rahja.

7. The international situation and the policy of the Entente

LENIN: We now come to point seven on the agenda: "The International Situation and the Policy of the Entente." The reporter is Comrade Obolensky [N. Osinsky].

[Osinsky presents the draft resolution.[1]]

THESES ON THE INTERNATIONAL SITUATION AND THE POLICIES OF THE ENTENTE

The experience of the World War exposed the imperialist policy of the bourgeois "democracies" as the great powers' battle plan to divide the world and consolidate finance capital's economic and political dictatorship over the exploited and oppressed masses.[2] The war has killed and maimed millions of people, pauperized and enslaved the proletariat, destroyed intermediate social layers,[3] and enriched the upper layers of the bourgeoisie as never before through war production, loans, and so on. Military reaction triumphed in every country. All these factors began to destroy illusions in "defense of the fatherland," "civil peace," and "democracy." The "peace policy" of imperialists of all countries is unveiling their true ambitions and leading to their complete exposure.

The Brest-Litovsk peace and the unmasking of German imperialism

Both the treaty of Brest-Litovsk and the subsequent Treaty of Bucharest revealed the predatory and reactionary character of the imperialism of the Central Powers.[4] The victors extorted both reparations and annexations from defenseless Russia. They converted the right of nations to self-determination into a disguise for annexationism by creating vassal states whose reactionary governments have promoted a policy of plunder and suppressed the revolutionary movement of the toiling masses. Since German imperialism had not won a complete victory in the international conflict, it was not then in a position to show its true intentions with complete candor. It was compelled to live in phony peace with Soviet Russia and to cloak its predatory and reactionary policies in hypocritical rhetoric.

The Entente powers, however, once they had won world victory, dropped their masks and revealed the true face of world imperialism for all to see.

The victory of the Entente and the alignment of states

The victory of the Entente has divided the so-called civilized nations of the world into the following groupings. The first consists of the ruling powers of the capitalist world—the victorious imperialist great powers (Britain, America, France, Japan, Italy). Opposite them stand the vanquished imperialist powers, broken by the war and shaken to their foundations by the onset of the proletarian revolution (Germany and Austria-Hungary with their former vassals). The vassal states of the Entente powers form the third grouping. It is made up of small capitalist states that took part in the war on the side of the Entente (Belgium, Serbia, Portugal, etc.) and of the newly created "national" republics and buffer states (the Czechoslovak republic, Poland, the counterrevolutionary Russian republics, and so on). The position of the neutral states is close to that of the vassal states; however, they suffer severe political and economic pressure, which at times reduces their situation to that of the vanquished nations. The Russian socialist republic is a workers' and peasants' state that stands outside of the capitalist world and poses a tremendous social danger to victorious imperialism—the danger that all the spoils of victory will be lost under the onslaught of world revolution.

The 'peace policy' reveals Entente imperialism's true nature

Taken as a whole, the "peace policy" of the world's five ruling powers has exposed its true nature and continues to do so.

Despite all the hollow rhetoric about "democratic foreign policy," it represents the complete triumph of *secret diplomacy,* which settles the fate of the world through deals by agents of the financial trusts, behind the backs of the millions of toilers of all countries and at their expense. Every important question without exception is decided by the committee of the five great powers in Paris behind closed doors and in the absence of representatives of the conquered, the neutral, or even the vassal states.

The need for *annexations* and *reparations* is openly proclaimed and defended in the speeches of Lloyd George, Clemenceau, Sonnino, and others.

Despite the lying rhetoric about the "war for universal disarmament," they openly declare the need for *further armament* and, in particular, for maintaining British naval power in order to "safeguard freedom of the seas."

The right of nations to self-determination proclaimed by the Entente is publicly trampled on and replaced by *apportionment of the disputed territories* among the ruling nations and their vassals.

Alsace-Lorraine was annexed to France without consulting its population; Ireland, Egypt, and India are denied the right of self-determination; the Yugoslav state and the Czechoslovak republic were established by armed force; shameless haggling is going on over the partition of European and Asiatic Turkey; redivision of the German colonies has actually already begun; and so on.

The policy of *reparations* has been pursued to the point of complete *plundering* of the vanquished nations. Not only are they presented with bills running into the billions; not only are they stripped of all weapons of war; the Entente nations also take away their locomotives, railway cars, ships, agricultural equipment, gold supplies, and so on. On top of that, prisoners of war are to be made into the conquerors' slaves. Plans are under discussion to impose compulsory labor service upon the German workers. The Allied powers intend to turn them into abject and hungry slaves of Entente capital.

The policy of inflaming extreme *national chauvinism* finds its expression in ongoing hysterical campaigns against the vanquished nations carried out by the Entente press and the occupation authorities and in the hunger blockade, which condemns the peoples of Germany and Austria to extinction. This policy leads to pogroms organized by the Entente's accomplices, the Czech and Polish chauvinists, against the Germans as well as anti-Jewish pogroms that surpass all the heroic exploits of Russian tsarism.

The "democratic" states of the Entente are pursuing a policy of *extreme reaction.*

Reaction is triumphant not only within the Entente countries themselves (France has reverted to the worst days of Napoleon III), but also throughout all parts of the capitalist world under Entente influence. The Allies are strangling the revolution in the occupied territories of Germany, Hungary, Bulgaria, and elsewhere. They are inciting the bourgeois-opportunist governments of the vanquished countries against the revolutionary workers by threatening to withhold food supplies. The Allies have declared they will sink every German ship that dares to hoist the red flag of revolution; they have refused to recognize the German workers' councils; and they have abolished the eight-hour day in the occupied parts of Germany.[5] Besides supporting reactionary policies in the neutral countries and fostering these measures in the vassal states (like the Paderewski regime in Poland), they are whipping up reactionary elements in those countries (in Finland, Poland, Sweden, and elsewhere) against revolutionary Russia and demanding that the German armed forces intervene.

Antagonisms among the Entente states

A number of deep antagonisms are evident among the great powers that rule the capitalist world, even though their fundamental imperialist policies are the same.

These antagonisms center primarily around American finance capital's peace program (the so-called Wilson program).[6] The most important points in this program are "freedom of the seas," the "League of Nations," and "internationalization of the colonies." Stripped of its hypocritical disguise, the slogan "freedom of the seas" really means abolishing the naval supremacy of individual great powers (Britain above all) and opening all sea-lanes to American trade. "League of Nations" means denying the right of the European great powers (France above all) to directly annex weaker states and peoples. "Internationalization of the colonies" establishes the same rule for the colonial territories.

This program is determined by the following factors: American capital does not have the world's largest navy. Since it is unable to annex European countries directly, it aspires to exploit the weaker states and peoples through trade and capital investment. Thus, it wants to force the other powers to form a cartel of state trusts, divide up shares in exploiting the world "equitably" among them, and transform the struggle among the state trusts into an exclusively economic struggle. America's highly developed finance capital can win effective hegemony in the domain of economic exploitation, thereby assuring itself a predominant economic and political position in the world.

"Freedom of the seas" stands in sharp conflict with the interests of Britain, Japan, and to some extent, Italy as well (on the Adriatic Sea). The "League of Nations" and "internationalizing the colonies" comes decidedly into conflict with the interests of France and Japan and to a lesser degree with those of the other imperialist powers.

In France, where industry is not well-developed and the productive forces were completely destroyed by the war, imperialist policy is resorting to the most desperate measures to preserve the capitalist system. Such measures include barbaric plunder of Germany; direct subjugation and predatory exploitation of the vassal states (proposals for a Danubian federation and a Yugoslav state); and forcible extortion of the debts incurred by the Russian tsar from the French shylock. As continental countries, France and Italy are also able to pursue a policy of direct annexations, as can Japan in a different form.

While the interests of the great powers clash with American interests, they also conflict with each other. Britain fears any strengthening of France on the continent, since it has interests in Asia Minor and Africa that are at odds with those of France. Italian interests in the Balkan peninsula and Tyrol clash with French interests. Japan quarrels with British Australia over islands in the Pacific, and so on.

Groupings and currents within the Entente

These antagonisms among the great powers make possible a number of groupings within the Entente. Two major combinations have begun to emerge: the French-British-Japanese combination, which is directed against America and Italy; and the Anglo-American combination, which stands opposed to the other great powers.

The first combination predominated until the beginning of January 1919, that is, until President Wilson relinquished his demand for an end to British naval hegemony. The development of the revolutionary workers' and soldiers' movement in Britain impels the various imperialist countries to come to an agreement, liquidate the Russian adventure, and rapidly conclude peace. It has also increased Britain's inclination toward the Anglo-American combination, which from 1919 has become the dominant one.

The Anglo-American bloc opposes France's preferential right to plunder Germany, as well as the exaggerated intensity of it. This bloc partially limits the excessive annexationist demands made by France, Italy, and Japan and prevents them from directly subjugating the newly created vassal states. On the Russian question, the Anglo-American bloc is more peaceably inclined: it wants a free hand so that it can finish dividing the world, stifle the European revolution, and then crush the Russian revolution as well.

These two great-power combinations reflect two currents that exist among them: an extreme annexationist current and a more moderate one. The latter supports the Wilson–Lloyd George combination.

The 'League of Nations'

In view of the irreconcilable antagonisms finding expression within the Entente itself, the League of Nations (should it be formalized) will merely play the role of a Holy Alliance of the capitalists for the suppression of the workers' revolution. Propagandizing for the "League of Nations" is the best way to confuse the revolutionary consciousness of the working class. It replaces the slogan of an International of revolutionary workers' republics with the slogan of an international alliance of ostensible democracies, supposedly to be achieved through a coalition between the proletariat and the bourgeois classes.

The "League of Nations" is a misleading slogan that the social traitors in the service of international capital use to split the forces of the proletariat and advance the imperialist counterrevolution.

In every country of the world, the revolutionary proletariat must resolutely combat the Wilsonian concept of the "League of Nations" and protest entry into this league of plunder, exploitation, and imperialist counterrevolution.

Foreign and domestic policy in the defeated countries

During the first period of the revolution the military destruction and internal collapse of Austrian and German imperialism led to rule by bourgeois social-opportunist regimes in the central European states. Disguising their actions with talk of democracy and socialism, the German social traitors are protecting and reinstituting the economic rule and political dictatorship of the bourgeoisie. The aim of their foreign policy is to restore German imperialism by demanding the return of the colonies and admission of Germany into the rapacious League of Nations.

As the bands of White Guards grow stronger in Germany and as disintegration progresses in the Entente camp, the great-power ambitions of the bourgeoisie and social traitors also increase. At the same time, the bourgeois social-opportunist government also undermines international proletarian solidarity and divides the German workers from their brothers in other countries by carrying out counterrevolutionary tasks for the Entente and, as a particular favor to it, by whipping up the German workers against the Russian workers' revolution. The policy of the bourgeoisie and the social opportunists in Austria and Hungary is a milder version of the policy of the bourgeois-opportunist bloc in Germany.

The vassal states of the Entente

The goal of Entente policy in the vassal states and in the republics it recently created (Czechoslovakia, Yugoslavia, and also Poland, Finland, and so on) is to organize centers for a national counterrevolutionary movement based on the ruling classes and social nationalists. This movement is meant to target the defeated states, maintain a balance of power among the newly created states, subordinate them to the Entente, retard revolutionary movements within the new "national" republics, and, lastly, furnish the White Guards needed for the struggle against the international revolution and the Russian revolution in particular.

As for Belgium, Portugal, Greece, and other small countries allied with the Entente, their policies are wholly determined by those of the larger robbers, to whom they are completely subjugated and whose assistance they solicit in acquiring petty annexations and war reparations.

The neutral states

The neutral states end up as the less-favored vassals of Entente imperialism, against whom the Entente applies a milder version of the same methods it uses against the vanquished countries. The more favored neutral states make a variety of demands on the Entente's opponents: thus, Denmark claims Flensburg, and Switzerland proposes internationalizing the Rhine. At the same time, they follow the Entente's counterrevolutionary orders by expelling Russian ambassadors, recruiting White Guards in Scandinavian countries, and in other ways. Still others are in danger of being dismembered (the plan to annex the Dutch province of Limburg to Belgium and to internationalize the mouth of the Scheldt).

The Entente and Soviet Russia

The predatory, inhuman, and reactionary character of Entente imperialism stands out most sharply in its policy toward Soviet Russia. From the beginning of the November [1917] revolution the Entente powers took the side of the Russian counterrevolutionary parties and governments. With the help of the bourgeois counterrevolutionaries, they have annexed Siberia, the Urals, the coasts of European Russia, the Caucasus, and part of Turkestan. They are stealing timber, petroleum, manganese, and other raw materials from these annexed territories. With the help of mercenary Czechoslovak bands they stole the gold reserves of the Russian empire. Directed by the British diplomat Lockhart, British and French spies organized the bombing of bridges and destruction of the railways and tried to cut off food supplies. The Entente supplied money, weapons, and military aid to the reactionary generals Denikin, Kolchak, and Krasnov, who have hanged and shot thousands of workers and peasants in Rostov, Yuzovka [Donetsk], Novorossisk, Omsk, and elsewhere.

Through Clemenceau's and Pichon's speeches, the Entente has openly proclaimed the principle of "economic encirclement," in other words, starving out and destroying the revolutionary workers' and peasants' republic. They have also promised "technical assistance" to the bands of Denikin, Kolchak, and Krasnov.

The Entente has repeatedly rejected the Soviet republic's peace offers. On January 23, 1919, when the more moderate current was temporarily predominant among the Entente powers, they proposed that all Russian governments send representatives to the Princes Islands. Undoubtedly, this proposal was also intended as a provocation against the Soviet government. On February 4 the Entente received a positive response from the Soviet government expressing its readiness to go so far as to accede to annexations, reparations, and other concessions in order to free the Russian workers and peasants from the war the Entente was forcing on them. Nevertheless, this peace offer by Soviet Russia as well was left unanswered by the Entente.

This confirms that the annexationist and reactionary currents in the ranks of the Entente imperialists are firmly in control. They threaten the socialist republic with more annexations and counterrevolutionary attacks.

The Entente's "peace policy" toward Russia conclusively reveals to the proletariat of the world the essence of Entente imperialism and of imperialism in general. It also proves that the imperialist governments are incapable of concluding either a "just" or a "just and lasting" peace, and it proves that finance capital is unable to restore the ravaged national economies. If finance capital continues to rule, the result will be either the complete destruction of civilization or else intensified exploitation, enslavement, political reaction, rearmament, and ultimately, new wars of destruction.

REPORT ON THE INTERNATIONAL SITUATION AND THE POLICY OF THE ENTENTE (EXCERPT)

OBOLENSKY: The immediate task of the proletariat is active defense against the violent, reactionary, and predatory imperialist offensive.[7] A very essential, basic role in this struggle falls to the proletariat in the Entente countries, the heartland of triumphant imperialist reaction. It is particularly vital for the Communist organizations there to break fully with the illusions about Wilsonism that are very widespread in those countries. These illusions impede the development of the proletarian struggle against imperialist reaction. The break with these illusions must also be a break with the agents of imperialism in the Socialist ranks: the social traitors who cultivate these illusions in the working class.

The specific task of the German revolutionary proletariat in international politics today is to resist the Scheidemann government's subservience to reaction and its efforts to revive imperialism. The German bourgeois-compromiser regime is taking advantage of the recent and continued strengthening of the White Guard bands and of the increasingly open breakdown of the Entente alliance to step up its attempts to restore an imperialist foreign policy. This is also expressed in the German government's request for the return of its colonies and its desire to be admitted to the League of Nations when peace is concluded, which is an expression of German imperialism's thirst for great-power status.

The proletariat of Germany, in its struggle against the Scheidemann government, must call for a complete break with these great-power tendencies. In particular, it must demand rejection of that gang of bandits, the League of Nations; repudiation of the colonies; an end to all reactionary concessions and servitude to the Entente; reorientation of foreign policy to one encompassing defense of the workers' revolution against the onslaught of imperialism and rapprochement with the revolutionary proletariat of other countries. The best means of building solidarity is to develop the revolution in Germany.

The revolutionary proletariat in the Entente's vassal states has the special task of exposing the national chauvinism propagated by the Entente to counter workers' revolution. It must struggle for international proletarian solidarity.

The proletariat in the neutral countries must fight with all means to keep these countries from being used as agents for the Allies' robbery.

The proletariat's worldwide revolutionary struggle is the best base of support for the countries where revolution is victorious or moving towards victory. Above all, it is the mainstay of the workers and peasants in Russia, whose immediate task is to carry the internal revolutionary struggle through to the end, that is, to overcome the counterrevolution inside Russia and then throw all available forces into the building of the new social order, whose growing strength will be an example inspiring the proletariat everywhere to win power.

PLATTEN: Comrades, we must cut the session short. No translation is available from Russian to German. We have no choice but to propose ending the session at this point and assigning the resolutions commission to review in detail Comrade Obolensky's theses on the policy of the Entente. The commission will also report on any amendments that are proposed. These may now be submitted to the commission in writing.

Tomorrow we still have to cover the White Terror, the manifesto, election of the bureau, and organization. The bureau proposes beginning tomorrow's session at 11:00 a.m.; it must end by 3:00 p.m. An intense and concentrated effort will be required, because a public rally is scheduled for the afternoon in the Bolshoi Theater. Do I take it that everyone agrees? So, it is agreed that we will reconvene at eleven in the morning. Please arrive on time; Comrade Lenin has just noted that we will begin at 11:00 a.m. whether the comrades are all present or not.

FIFTH DAY OF SESSIONS

MARCH 6, 1919

8. The manifesto of the Communist International

LENIN *(opens the session at 11:30 a.m.):* Comrade Chicherin will speak for the Credentials Commission.

CHICHERIN: The Credentials Commission has reviewed the question of Comrade Guilbeaux's mandate. Comrade Guilbeaux is a permanent representative of the Zimmerwald Left tendency of France; that is to say, he represents the supporters of Loriot in the Zimmerwald association. The French Zimmerwald Left did not see the Zimmerwald conference as something provisional but as the beginning of the Third International. In view of that, his mandate is valid for this conference as well.

He has been in constant contact with France and, through his wife, corresponded with Loriot just recently. He is a representative of Loriot's tendency in the fullest sense of the word. Therefore, the Credentials Commission felt we could grant him full voting rights as the representative of the French Zimmerwald Left. Since that is the only tendency that can represent the revolutionary forces of the proletariat of France, the Credentials Commission also believes we can give him the full number of votes reserved for France, that is, five votes.

If the body agrees to this, I will ask the comrades with the list to update it to that effect. Thus there are now nineteen countries represented here instead of eighteen, and thirty-three delegates have full voting rights instead of thirty-two.

I would also like to ask comrades to correct a small inaccuracy under number thirty-three: the Chinese workers' organization. It should not say "Chinese Workers League" but rather "Chinese Socialist Workers Party." For Korea, it should read, "Korean Workers League." The names of the delegates from the Chinese organization are comrades Liu Shaozhou and Zhang Yongkui. For the Korean Workers League the list should read Comrade Kain.

In addition, we have accepted Comrade Balabanoff as the representative of the Zimmerwald commission with a consultative vote. That means there are eighteen delegates present with consultative vote.

LENIN: We will now proceed to point eight on the agenda, the manifesto. It has been moved that the manifesto be read.

PLATTEN: Comrades, I would like to propose that we ask Comrade Trotsky to read the manifesto. He is its author, and it will certainly make a good impression if he reads it himself.

(Trotsky reads the manifesto.)

MANIFESTO OF THE COMMUNIST INTERNATIONAL TO THE PROLETARIAT OF THE ENTIRE WORLD

Seventy-two years have passed since the Communist Party proclaimed its program to the world in a manifesto written by Karl Marx and Frederick Engels, the proletarian revolution's greatest educators.[1] No sooner had communism entered the arena of struggle than it was beset by the vicious baiting, lies, hatred, and persecution of the possessing classes, who correctly sensed that it was their mortal enemy. During these seven decades, communism has developed along a difficult path: stormy upsurges as well as periods of decline; successes, but also grave defeats. Yet fundamentally, it followed the path indicated by the *Manifesto of the Communist Party*. The epoch of the final, decisive conflict arrived later than the apostles of social revolution hoped and expected. But it has arrived. We Communists, the representatives of the revolutionary proletariat of the different countries of Europe, America, and Asia who have gathered in Soviet Moscow, consider ourselves the heirs and executors of the cause whose program was proclaimed seventy-two years ago. Our task is to generalize the revolutionary experience of the working class, cleanse the movement of the corroding influence of opportunism and social patriotism, and rally the forces of all truly revolutionary parties of the world proletariat. Thus we will facilitate and hasten the victory of the communist revolution in the entire world.

Now that Europe lies covered with rubble and smoking ruins, the most villainous arsonists are busily seeking someone to blame for the war. Behind them stand their professors, parliamentarians, journalists, social patriots, and the bourgeoisie's other political pimps.

Over the course of many years, socialism predicted the inevitability of imperialist war and recognized that its cause lies in the insatiable greed of the possessing classes of both major camps and also of all capitalist countries in general. At the Basel congress, two years before the war broke out, the responsible Socialist leaders in every country denounced imperialism as the cause of the impending war. They threatened to inflict socialist revolution upon the bourgeoisie as proletarian retribution for the crimes of militarism.

Today, after the experience of the last five years, after history has exposed both Germany's insatiable appetites and the no less criminal acts of the Entente states, the Socialist statesmen of the Entente join their governments in unmasking again and yet again the overthrown German kaiser. On top of that, the German social patriots, who in August 1914 proclaimed the Hohenzollerns' diplomatic White Book as the peoples' holy gospel,[2] now obsequiously join the Entente Socialists in laying the primary blame on the overthrown German monarchy—which they once served so slavishly.[3] Thus they hope to obscure their own guilt and ingratiate themselves with the victors. But fast-moving events and diplomatic revelations show that the ruling classes of France, Britain, Italy, and the United States have equaled the measureless depravity of the fallen dynasties of the Romanovs, Hohenzollerns, and Hapsburgs and their respective capitalist cliques.

British diplomacy stood by with enigmatically lowered visor until the very moment war broke out. The government of the City avoided any unambiguous statement of its intention to go to war on the side of the Entente lest it frighten the Berlin government away from the war.[4] In London they wanted war. They therefore contrived to induce Berlin and Vienna to hope for Britain's neutrality at the same time that Paris and Petrograd were definitely counting on its involvement.

The war, prepared by the course of development over decades, was unleashed by the direct and deliberate provocation of Great Britain. The British government planned to provide Russia and France just enough support so that they would exhaust themselves while crippling Germany, the mortal enemy. But the power of the German military machine proved too formidable, and Britain was forced to undertake not merely a token intervention into the war but a real one. The role of smug spectator, which by long tradition belonged to Great Britain, passed to the United States.

The British blockade one-sidedly restricted the ability of the American stock exchange to speculate in European blood. But the government in Washington was all the more easily reconciled to this violation of "international law" since the American bourgeoisie was compensated through fat profits from the Entente countries.

Germany's overwhelming military superiority, however, persuaded Washington to shed its feigned neutrality. The United States took over the role in Europe that Britain had played in earlier continental wars and wanted to play in the last one: it used one side to weaken the other and intervened militarily only to the extent necessary to secure for itself all benefits of the situation. By the standards of American gambling, Wilson's wager was not large, but it was the last one down, and that assured him the jackpot.

For humanity, the war translated the contradictions of the capitalist system into the brutal torments of hunger, cold, epidemics, and moral brutalization. It also settled once and for all the academic debate in the socialist movement over the theory of pauperization and the gradual transition from capitalism to socialism.[5] Statisticians and pedants who advocate the theory that capitalism's contradictions were being resolved labored for decades dredging up real or imaginary facts from the four corners of the earth testifying to the rising living standards of various layers and sectors of the working class. It came to be assumed that the theory of pauperization had been buried under the contemptuous jeers of bourgeois academic eunuchs and social-opportunist hacks. Today pauperization stands before us—not just social pauperization but the full, shocking reality of physiological and biological pauperization.

The catastrophe of imperialist war swept clean away all conquests of the trade union and parliamentary struggles—and this war was just as much a product of the inner tendencies of capitalism as were the economic deals and parliamentary compromises that it buried in blood and muck.

Finance capital, which hurled humanity into the abyss of war, itself suffered catastrophic transformations as the war proceeded. The dependence of paper money upon the material basis of production was completely disrupted. Progressively losing its significance as a means and regulator of capitalist commodity circulation, paper money was transformed into a means of requisition, robbery, and military-economic violence in general. The utter debasement of paper money reflects the generalized mortal crisis of capitalist commodity exchange.

In the decades prior to the war, the system of trusts and monopolies displaced free competition as the regulator of production and distribution in the main sectors of the economy. In the course of the war, the role of regulator was shown to have been wrested away from the cartels and placed directly in the hands of the militarized state. The distribution of raw materials; the exploitation of Baku or Romanian petroleum, Donets coal, or Ukrainian grain; the fate of German locomotives, railway cars, and automobiles; supplying starving Europe with bread and meat—all of these basic questions of world economic life are regulated neither by free competition nor by alliances of national or international trusts and cartels, but by direct application of military force seeking to perpetuate itself. Just as completely subordinating the state to the rule of finance capital led the human race to the imperialist slaughtering block, finance capital in turn, in the course of this mass slaughter, completely militarized not only the state but also even itself. It is no longer able to carry out its essential economic functions by any means other than blood and iron.

Before the World War, the opportunists urged the workers to be moderate for the sake of a gradual transition to socialism. During the war they demanded class submission for the sake of "civil peace" and defense of the fatherland. Now they are demanding self-sacrifice from the proletariat once again, this time in order to overcome the dreadful consequences of the war. Were the working masses to heed their preaching, capitalist development would celebrate its restoration on the bones of several generations in new and still more concentrated and ghastly forms and bring the prospect of a new and inevitable world war. Fortunately for humanity, that is no longer possible.

The control of economic life by the state, against which capitalist liberalism railed so loudly, has become a fact. There is no returning: not to free competition, nor even to rule by trusts, syndicates, and other economic monstrosities. The only question is, what will be the vehicle of state-controlled production in the future: the imperialist state or the state of the victorious proletariat?

In other words, shall all of toiling humanity be the serfs of a victorious world clique, which uses the name of the League of Nations and the aid of an "international" army and an "international" navy to plunder and strangle the proletariat here, toss it a crumb there, but enchain it everywhere for the sole purpose of perpetuating its own rule? Or will the working class of Europe and other advanced countries of the world take the broken and destroyed national economies into their own hands in order to guarantee their reconstruction on a socialist basis?

The present epoch of crises can be shortened only by the measures of proletarian dictatorship, which neither looks back to the past nor respects hereditary privileges and private property rights. It proceeds instead from the need to rescue the starving masses and mobilizes all means and resources to that end; it introduces the duty of all to work and establishes a regime of labor discipline in order, in the course of a few years, not only to heal the gaping wounds caused by the war, but also to raise humanity to new and undreamed-of heights.

The national state, which gave a mighty impulse to capitalist development, has become a fetter on further development of the productive forces. That made the position of the small states, scattered among the great powers of Europe and across the rest of the world, that much more precarious. These small states originated at various times, as fragments of larger ones, as small change in payment for various services rendered, or as strategic buffers. They have their own dynasties, ruling gangs, imperialist pretensions, and diplomatic intrigues. Before the war, their illusory independence rested on the same foundation as did the European balance of power: the continuous conflict between the two imperialist camps. The war upset this balance. By giving Germany an overwhelming initial advantage, the war forced the smaller nations to seek their salvation and deliverance in the generosity of German militarism. After Germany was beaten, the bourgeoisies of the small countries together with their patriotic "Socialists" turned to the victorious imperialist Allies and began to search among the hypocritical points of Wilson's program for assurances of their continued independent existence.

At the same time, the number of small states has increased. New national entities emerged from the possessions of the Austro-Hungarian monarchy and from fragments of the tsarist empire. Hardly had they been established when they went for each others' throats over national boundaries. The imperialist Allies, meanwhile, organize combinations among the petty states new and old, to keep them tied down in mutual hatred and generalized impotence.

While oppressing and violating the smaller and weaker peoples and dooming them to hunger and abasement, the Entente imperialists—just like the imperialists of the Central Powers not long ago—never cease talking about the right of nations to self-determination. That right, however, has been ground into the dust both in Europe and throughout the rest of the world.

Only the proletarian revolution can guarantee the small nationalities the possibility of a free existence. It liberates the productive forces of all countries from the narrowness of the national state, unites nations in close economic cooperation through an overall economic plan, and gives even the smallest and weakest nation the opportunity to develop its culture freely and independently, without detriment to the unified and centralized economy of Europe and the entire world.

The last war, which was not least of all a war over colonies, was also a war fought with the help of the colonies. The colonial peoples were drawn into the European war as never before. Indians, blacks, Arabs, and Malagasy fought on the European continent. For what? For the right to remain slaves of Britain and France. Never has capitalist rule shown itself more shamelessly. Never has the problem of colonial slavery been posed more sharply than it is today.

That is why there are open rebellions and revolutionary ferment in all the colonies. In Europe itself, the bloody street fighting in Ireland served as a reminder that the latter is still an oppressed nation and sees itself as such. During the war, troops from the bourgeois republic [France] had to put down more than one uprising of the colonial slaves in Madagascar, Annam [Vietnam], and other countries. Nor did the revolutionary movement let up for a single day in India. Recently it led to Asia's greatest workers' strike, which the British government responded to by sending armored cars into action in Bombay.[6]

The colonial question in its full scope has thus been posed, not only at the green table of the diplomats' congress in Paris, but also in the colonies themselves. At best, Wilson's program aims at no more than changing the label on colonial slavery. The liberation of the colonies is possible only together with the liberation of the working class in the imperialist centers. The workers and peasants, not only of Annam, Algeria, and Bengal, but also of Persia and Armenia, will gain the possibility of an independent existence only when the workers of Britain and France have toppled Lloyd George and Clemenceau and taken state power into their own hands. Already today, the struggle in the more developed colonies is waged not merely under the banner of national liberation but immediately acquires a clearly defined social character. Capitalist Europe dragged the underdeveloped parts of the world into the capitalist maelstrom by force; socialist Europe will come to the aid of the liberated colonies with its technology, organization, and intellectual influence in order to facilitate the transition to a planned and organized socialist economy.

Colonial slaves of Africa and Asia: the hour of proletarian dictatorship in Europe will also be the hour of your liberation![7]

The entire bourgeois world accuses the Communists of destroying freedom and political democracy. That is not true. Once in power, the proletariat does no more than reveal the complete impossibility of applying bourgeois-democratic methods. It then creates the conditions and forms of the new and higher workers' democracy. The entire course of capitalist development undermined political democracy, especially in the final, imperialist epoch, not only by splitting nations into two irreconcilable classes, but also by condemning the numerous petty-bourgeois and semiproletarian layers, as well as the lower layers of the proletariat, to permanent economic debilitation and political impotence.

In countries where historical development provided the opportunity, the working class took advantage of conditions of political democracy to organize the fight against capital. That will continue to happen in those countries where the conditions for a workers' revolution have not yet matured. But capitalism retards the historical development of the broad middle layers both in the countryside and in the cities, and they remain whole epochs behind. Peasants in Baden and Bavaria who cannot see beyond the village church steeple; small French winegrowers, ruined by big capitalists who adulterate their wine; small farmers in America, who are fleeced and cheated by bankers and politicians: all these social layers, forced out of the mainstream of development by capitalism, are called upon by the democratic regimes, on paper, to participate in government. But in reality, the financial oligarchy decides all important questions that affect the people's destiny behind the back of parliamentary democracy. That was true on the war question, and that is now happening on the question of peace.

Whenever the financial oligarchy finds it useful to provide cover for its acts of violence with parliamentary votes, the bourgeois state, to achieve the necessary goal, has at its disposal all the methods inherited from previous centuries of class rule, now multiplied by the miracles of capitalist technology: lies, demagogy, baiting, slander, bribery, and terror.

To demand of the proletariat that it meekly follow the dictates of bourgeois democracy while engaged in its final life and death battle with capitalism is like asking someone fighting for their life and limb against bandits to observe the artificial, restrictive rules of French wrestling, which the enemy establishes but does not follow.

In this kingdom of destruction, where not only the means of production and transportation but also democratic institutions lie in bloody ruins, the proletariat must create its own instrument in order above all to weld the working class together and ensure it the opportunity of revolutionary intervention into humanity's future development. That instrument is the workers' councils. The old parties and the old trade unions, personified by their leaders, have proven that they cannot understand, let alone carry out, the tasks posed by the new epoch. The proletariat created a new kind of instrument that encompasses the entire working class, regardless of trade or level of political development. It is a flexible instrument that can constantly renew and extend itself, draw one new layer after another into its orbit, and open its doors to the layers of workers in the city and the village closest to the proletariat. This irreplaceable organization of working-class self-rule, of its struggle, and of its future conquest of state power has been tested by the experience of several countries and stands as the proletariat's greatest conquest and most powerful weapon in our time.

In every country where the masses' thinking has awakened, workers', soldiers', and peasants' councils will continue to be built. The main task facing class-conscious, honest workers in every country today is to consolidate the councils, increase their authority, and counterpose them to the bourgeois state apparatus. Through the councils, the working class can save itself from the decomposition caused in its ranks by the hellish sufferings of war, famine, the violence of the possessing classes, and the betrayals of their former leaders. Through the councils, the working class will take power most surely and easily in all countries where it uses them to rally the majority of the working people. Through the councils, the working class, having taken power, will govern all aspects of economic and cultural life, as it is already doing in Russia.

The breakdown of the imperialist state, whether tsarist or the most democratic, goes hand in hand with the breakdown of the imperialist military system. The multimillioned armies mobilized by imperialism could be sustained only as long as the proletariat remained obediently under the yoke of the bourgeoisie. The disintegration of national unity inevitably entails the disintegration of the army. That is what happened first in Russia, then in Austria-Hungary and Germany, and must be anticipated in other imperialist states. The uprising of the peasant against the big landowner, of worker against capitalist, and of both against monarchical or "democratic" bureaucracies leads unavoidably to the uprising of the soldier against the commander and further, to a sharp split between the proletarian and bourgeois forces in the army. The imperialist war, which pitted nation against nation, became transformed and is becoming transformed into civil war, which pits class against class.

The clamour of the bourgeois world against civil war and Red Terror is the most outrageous hypocrisy the history of political struggles has yet produced. There would be no civil war if the cliques of exploiters, who brought humanity to the brink of ruin, had not resisted every forward step of the working masses, instigating conspiracies and murders and calling in armed assistance from outside, in order to preserve or restore their predatory privileges.

Civil war is forced upon the working class by its archenemies. The working class must answer blow for blow if it does not want to renounce itself and its own future, which is also the future of all humanity. The Communist parties never artificially provoke civil war. If it becomes an iron necessity, they strive to shorten its duration as much as possible, limit the number of its victims, and above all, assure victory to the proletariat. From this flows the need to disarm the bourgeoisie in time, arm the workers, and form a communist army to defend proletarian power and the integrity of its socialist structure. Such is the Red Army of Soviet Russia, which originated to protect the gains of the working class against every attack from within and without. The councils' army is inseparable from the councils' state.

Conscious of the world-historic character of their tasks, advanced workers have striven for an international association since their first steps to organize the socialist movement. The cornerstone was laid in 1864 in London with the founding of the First International. The Franco-Prussian War, out of which Hohenzollern Germany emerged, cut the ground from under the First International while at the same time giving impetus to the development of national workers' parties.[8] Already in 1889, these parties came together at the Paris congress and created the organization of the Second International. But in that period, the center of gravity of the workers' movement remained entirely on national soil, within the framework of the national state, based on national industry, and working within national parliamentarism. Decades of organizational and reform work created a generation of leaders who in their majority verbally acknowledged the program of social revolution, but renounced it in reality and became mired in reformism and in adaptation to the bourgeois state. The opportunist character of the Second International's leading parties was completely exposed and caused the greatest debacle in world history at the moment when the course of events called for revolutionary methods of struggle by the workers' parties. If the war of 1870 dealt a blow to the First International by revealing that the power of united masses did not yet stand behind its revolutionary socialist program, so too the war of 1914 killed the Second International by revealing that above the solidly welded masses stood parties that had become servile organs of the bourgeois state.

This does not apply only to the social patriots, who today have openly gone over to the camp of the bourgeoisie and who have become its trusted and preferred agents and the reliable executioners of the working class. It also applies to the amorphous, unstable Socialist center, which is now busy trying to revive the Second International, that is, to revive the narrow-mindedness, opportunism, and revolutionary helplessness of its leading elite. Groups such as the Independent Social Democratic Party of Germany, the current Socialist Party majority in

France, the Menshevik group in Russia, the Independent Labour Party in Britain, and others are actually trying to take the place occupied before the war by the old, official parties of the Second International. As before, they are coming forward with ideas of compromise and unity and thus are doing everything possible to paralyze the proletariat's energy, prolong the crisis, and thereby intensify Europe's suffering. The struggle against the Socialist center is a necessary precondition for a successful struggle against imperialism.

Rejecting the vacillation, lies, and rottenness of the outlived official Socialist parties, we Communists, united in the Third International, consider ourselves the direct continuators of the heroic endeavors and martyrdom of a long succession of revolutionary generations, from Babeuf to Karl Liebknecht and Rosa Luxemburg.

If the First International foresaw the road that lay ahead and indicated its direction; if the Second International assembled and organized millions of proletarians; then the Third International is the International of open mass action, the International of revolutionary realization, the International of the deed.

Socialist criticism has sufficiently denounced the bourgeois world order. The task of the international Communist Party is to overthrow this system and construct in its place the socialist order.

We call upon working men and women of all countries to unite behind the communist banner, under which the first great victories have already been won.

Workers of the world: in struggle against imperialist barbarism, against monarchy, against the privileged classes, against the bourgeois state and bourgeois property, and against all forms and kinds of social and national oppression—unite!

Under the banner of workers' councils and the revolutionary struggle for power and the dictatorship of the proletariat, under the banner of the Third International—workers of the world, unite!

(The manifesto was signed in Moscow on March 6 by the following delegates:)

Max Albert, Germany; N. Lenin, Russia;
K. Gruber, German Austria; E. Rudnyánszky, Hungary;
Otto Grimlund, Sweden; Fritz Platten, Switzerland;
B. Reinstein, United States of North America;
C. Rakovsky, Balkan federation;
J. Unszlicht (Jurovsky), Poland; Yrjö Sirola, Finland;
Skrypnik, Ukraine; K. Gailis, Latvia;
Hans Pögelman, Estonia; Haikuni, Armenia;
G. Klinger, German Volga Colonists;
Yalymov, Eastern Peoples of Russia;
Henri Guilbeaux, Zimmerwald Left of France.

Banner: “Free in my Caspian homeland.” Bolshevik poster shows Asian woman turning her back on the veil, religious hierarchy, and other defenders of past oppression.

The congress in session; Leon Trotsky speaking.

9. The White Terror

PLATTEN: All resolutions will be voted on later. Now is the point on "White Terror." The resolution was submitted by the Finnish comrades. Comrade Sirola has the floor.

REPORT ON THE WHITE TERROR

SIROLA:[1] Comrades, the "civilized" world is seized by a very symptomatic state of excitement. Under the banner of "civilization" and "humanism" the eunuchs of capitalism—with their Social Democratic lackeys by no means lagging behind them—are trying to inveigle the peoples of the world into a crusade against international Bolshevism and especially against the Soviet power in Russia. To this end they point to the civil war, the Red Terror, and so on.

The hypocritical scoundrels! They can strain every muscle, they can turn themselves inside out, trying to mislead the people, but they will not be able to deceive the proletariat any longer. Every day it sees things more and more clearly. On the basis of its own experience, the working class knows that if capitalism came into the world "covered from head to toe with blood and filth,"[2] then it has been getting bloodier every year, right up to our own times. There is no need for me to describe to the comrades present here all the manifestations of the murderous capitalist system. That systematic mass slaughter, the World War, should have opened the eyes of the international proletariat to the fact that there can be only one relationship between this system and the working class—a struggle to the death. Unfortunately, that understanding has not sufficiently matured. Even after the war, the workers of the great powers show a tendency to vacillation. The bloodletting of the great slaughter has produced an irresistible craving for peace.

But capitalism is seeing to it that there will be no peace under its rule and that the true character of its system is not concealed. And one of the means of conducting this practical education is *White Terror.*

In itself, the method is far from new. In ancient times, after Spartacus, leader of the rebel slaves, had fallen in battle, the surviving slaves were crucified by the thousands along the Appian Way for the amusement of the tyrants intoxicated with their victory. Since that time an unbroken chain of violence, great and small, has stretched from century to century. Thus have the parasites and exploiters celebrated the suppression of their slaves' uprisings—right up to the days of June 1848 in Paris, to the execution of the heroic Communards by machine guns, to the tsarist punitive expeditions in 1906 and after.[3]

However, contemporary White Terror also has new traits—above all its universal prevalence. That fully corresponds to the imperialist stage of capitalism. The entire population of the world is divided into those who rule with the aid of White Terror, and those who are subjected to it. That may sound strange, but it is true.

Is there any country where the ruling class is not guilty of White Terror? Take the governments of the Central Powers and their hangers-on. They have been convicted for their crimes and the verdict has been pronounced. The same goes for their accomplices, the Scheidemanns, forever disgraced in the eyes of the working class. And the ruling cabals of the Western powers? Look around you! What is happening in Murmansk, in Arkhangel'sk, in the Urals, in the Caucasus, in Crimea, in the Ukraine, in Romania, Bulgaria, Hungary, Germany, Ireland, India? The capitalist class is frightened to death. Everywhere it is on the rampage, trying to prop up this predatory and murderous system.

The workers of the Entente countries must draw conclusions from all that is happening there. Reactionary forces are gathering strength there, thanks to the toleration of the working class. The workers must understand that in the final analysis those forces will turn against them. The black soldiers that their rulers are preparing to send to the Ukraine can also be used against the working class in London. If today Russian and British officers are killing members of workers' councils in other countries, then it is possible that tomorrow they will be killing members of workers' councils in Britain. If they are now persecuting and hanging striking workers in the Ukraine, then the strikers of the countries of the Entente cannot escape persecution. But then again, they are already being persecuted and have been persecuted for a long time. From London's Bloody Sunday to the savage treatment of striking workers and those refusing military service; from the "anarchist" trial in America to the violence against strikers, whose fitting continuation is found in the lynching of members of the IWW and other "subversives" and pronouncing twenty-year sentences against them—all this bears sufficiently eloquent witness.[4]

The Finnish proletariat could tell the workers of these "free" and "democratic" countries quite a lot about these matters. In Finland, even the tsarist Cossacks and the German "Huns" did not conduct such bloodbaths as were carried out by the "cultured" bourgeois and the "free" landowner. With machine-gun fire they swept away the best and noblest representatives of the working class. They shot women from the Red detachments without trial or investigation, forcing them to dig their own graves beforehand, even though they had carried out only first-aid duties. And the intelligentsia—the "freedom-loving" intelligentsia, so "devoted to culture"—sang hymns of praise to this terror.

These bourgeois and farmers of Finland and their intelligentsia are not some species of wild beast, however tempting such a supposition may be to us. Not at all. The *bourgeoisie of the whole world* will rage as fiercely as the Finnish bourgeoisie has raged in the last year or so, when they are faced with the need to defend their filthy and blood-soaked system. The murder of the Spartacists and their leaders, our highly esteemed comrades Karl Liebknecht and Rosa Luxemburg, is inscribed with letters of flame in the hearts of conscious workers. I am convinced that in the souls of the German workers burns hatred for the murderers—the White Guard thugs and Scheidemanns—and that they, just like the workers of Finland, hold sacred the word *vengeance*, revolutionary class vengeance.

There is no doubt that this vengeance will and must be realized under the sign of the Red Terror. How can it be otherwise? The armed assassins who are cold-bloodedly murdering our brothers and sisters—I will limit myself to the names of Volodarsky and Uritsky—the criminals who are aiming their weapons at the most gallant and noble hearts and clearest heads of humanity—such people and their accomplices must be shot down like mad dogs.

The workers of Russia, like the workers of Finland, Germany, and other countries, have shown a naive and even lackadaisical gentleness toward these people. In the future this must not be. Every healthy-minded person will understand that I am not advocating bloodbaths and pogroms. The healthy instincts of the working class would not allow them. But these bloodthirsty dogs must understand that they will be dealt with in the same way that they deal with others.

Comrades! I had intended to present together with my speech some statistical material concerning White Terror. I must forego this due to lack of time. But it is to be hoped that one of the first propaganda tasks of the Third International will be to publish several fiery protests against the bloodthirsty capitalist system, especially against the White Terror. The material I have collected can be used at that time. I am moving adoption of the resolution worked out by the commission on this question.

(*Sirola reads the resolution.*)

RESOLUTION ON THE WHITE TERROR

From its inception the capitalist system has been a system of robbery and mass murder.[5] It produced the horrors of the primitive accumulation of capital; it produced colonialism, which along with the Bible, brandy, and syphilis brought the ruthless extermination of entire tribes and peoples. Capitalism brought misery, starvation, exhaustion, and the premature deaths of countless millions of exploited proletarians; bloody suppression of the working class whenever it rose up against its exploiters; and finally, the gigantic, monstrous butchery that transformed world production into the production of human cadavers. That is the picture presented by the capitalist order.

The ruling classes, who murdered over ten million people on the battlefields and crippled many more, also instituted the rule of bloody dictatorship within their own countries from the very first day of the war. The tsarist government of Russia shot and hanged workers, organized pogroms against the Jews, and destroyed every living thing in the country. The Austrian monarchy drowned in blood the uprising of the Ukrainian and Czech workers and peasants. The British bourgeoisie slaughtered the best representatives of the Irish people. German imperialism rampaged within its own borders, and the revolutionary sailors were the first casualties of that beast. In France, Russian soldiers who refused to defend the profits of French bankers were shot down.[6] In the United States, the bourgeoisie lynched internationalists, sentenced hundreds of the proletariat's best people to twenty years in prison, and shot down striking workers.

As the imperialist war began to turn into civil war, the ruling classes, the worst criminals human history has ever known, faced the imminent downfall of their bloody regime. Their bestiality then knew no bounds.

In its struggle to preserve the capitalist order, the bourgeoisie resorts to the most unheard-of methods, which make all medieval horrors, the inquisition, and colonial plunder pale by comparison.

The bourgeois class, standing at the edge of its own grave, is now physically exterminating the proletariat, the most important productive force in human society.

The bourgeoisie's White Terror completely reveals its naked hatefulness.

The Russian generals, the living incarnation of the tsarist regime, massacred masses of workers and continue to do so today with direct or indirect support from the social traitors. During the reign of the Socialist Revolutionaries and Mensheviks in Russia, thousands of workers and peasants filled the prisons, and the generals wiped out entire regiments for insubordination. Now Krasnov and Denikin, who enjoy the benevolent support of the Entente powers, have murdered and hanged many thousands of workers and shot "every tenth one." They have even let the victims' bodies hang from the gallows for three days to terrorize the survivors. In the Urals and on the Volga, bands of Czechoslovak White Guards cut off the legs and hands of prisoners, drowned them in the Volga, or buried them alive. In Siberia the generals murdered thousands of Communists and exterminated countless workers and peasants.

The bourgeoisie and the social traitors in Germany and Austria abundantly demonstrated their cannibalistic nature in the Ukraine where they used portable iron gallows to hang the workers and peasants they had robbed, Communists, and their own citizens—our Austrian and German comrades.

In Finland, that land of bourgeois democracy, they helped the Finnish bourgeoisie send to the firing squad thirteen to fourteen thousand proletarians. Over fifteen thousand were tortured to death in the prisons.

In Helsingfors [Helsinki] they drove women and children before them as shields against machine-gun fire. With their support, the Finnish White Guards and their Swedish accomplices carried out bloody orgies against the defeated Finnish proletariat. In Tammerfors [Tampere], women and children were sentenced to death and forced to dig their own graves. In Vyborg, thousands of Russian men, women, and children were butchered.

Within their own borders, the reactionary frenzy of the German bourgeoisie and Social Democrats reached its highest level with the bloody suppression of the Communist workers' uprising, the bestial murder of Karl Liebknecht and Rosa Luxemburg, and the murder and annihilation of the Spartacus workers. The bourgeoisie marches under the banner of mass and individual White Terror.

It is the same in other countries. In democratic Switzerland, everything is prepared for the execution of the workers should they dare to violate capitalist law. In America, the favorite symbols of democracy and freedom are the penitentiary, lynching, and the electric chair.

In Hungary and Britain, Bohemia and Poland, everywhere it is the same. The bourgeois assassins will stop at no atrocity. To defend their rule they incite chauvinism and organize frightful pogroms against the Jews, which far exceed those organized by the tsarist police. Examples of this are offered by bourgeois democracy headed in the Ukraine by the Menshevik Petlyura, or in Poland by the social patriot Pilsudski, and others. And the murder of Russian Red Cross workers by reactionary "Socialist" Polish mobs is but a drop in the ocean of crimes and horrors committed by bourgeois cannibalism in its death agony.[7]

The "League of Nations," which according to its creators' pronouncement is supposed to bring peace, proceeds with its vicious war against the world proletariat. To save their rule, the Entente powers are using black troops to pave the way for unbelievably brutal terror.

The First Congress of the Communist International calls down a curse on the capitalist murderers and their Social Democratic accomplices, and calls upon the workers of all countries to bring all of their strength to bear to abolish this system of murder and robbery by overthrowing the power of the capitalist regime.

LENIN: We propose that all rise in honor of the victims of the White Terror.

(All rise. Lenin thanks them.)

10. Election of the bureau and other business

LENIN: Comrade Platten has the floor as reporter for the resolutions commission.

PLATTEN: Comrades, after all reports had been received, the resolutions commission decided to move that all resolutions be approved by the congress today. Since a great many points need to be resolved, we must request that discussion be avoided, if possible. Let me assure you that the commission met late into the night to study as many proposals as possible and to incorporate them insofar as was possible. Content and form were thoroughly reviewed as well.

We come now to the platform. It reads as follows:

PLATFORM OF THE COMMUNIST INTERNATIONAL

The contradictions of the world capitalist system, formerly hidden deep within it, have erupted with colossal force in a gigantic explosion: the great imperialist World War.[1]

Capitalism sought to overcome *its own anarchy* by organizing production. Mighty capitalist associations formed, such as syndicates, cartels, and trusts, replacing the numerous, competing entrepreneurs. Bank capital merged with industrial capital. The finance capitalist oligarchy came to dominate all of economic life; it used its organization, based on this power, to achieve exclusive supremacy. Monopoly took the place of free competition. Capitalists in association replaced the *individual* capitalist; organization replaced insane anarchy.

However, the more that capitalist organization replaces anarchy within each country, the more acute become the contradictions, competition, and anarchy in the world economy. The struggle among the largest, best-organized predator nations led with iron necessity to the monstrous imperialist World War. Greed for profits drove world capital to fight over new markets, new spheres for capital investment, new sources of raw materials, and the cheap labor power of colonial slaves. Once the imperialist states had divided up the whole world among themselves and transformed the many millions of African, Asian, Australian, and American workers and farmers into beasts of burden, sooner or later a violent collision was bound to occur, revealing the true, anarchic nature of capital. Thus originated the greatest crime of all, the predatory World War.

Capitalism also tried to overcome its contradictory *social structure*. Bourgeois society is a class society. In the largest "civilized" nations, capital wanted to conceal its social contradictions. It bribed its wage slaves at the expense of the plundered colonial peoples, thereby forging common interests between exploiter and exploited with respect to the oppressed colonies—the yellow, black, and red colonial peoples—and shackling the European and American working class to the imperialist "fatherland."

But continuous bribery, the very technique that made the working class patriotic and enslaved it psychologically, was transformed by the war into its opposite. Physical annihilation and utter enslavement of the proletariat; enormous hardship, suffering, and degradation; worldwide famine—these were the final payoff for the "civil peace." This "peace" was shattered. *The imperialist war was turned into a civil war.*

A new epoch is born: The epoch of capitalism's decay, its internal disintegration; the *epoch of the proletarian, communist revolution.*

The imperialist system is collapsing. Turmoil in the colonies and in the newly independent small nations; proletarian revolts and victorious proletarian revolutions in some countries; disintegration of the imperialist armies; utter incapacity of the ruling classes to guide the destinies of nations any further—that is the true picture of conditions around the world today.

With all civilization in ruins, humanity itself faces the danger of complete destruction. Only one force can save it, and that is the proletariat. The old capitalist "order" no longer exists; it can no longer endure. The end result of the capitalist mode of production is chaos, which only the largest productive class, the working class, can overcome. This class must establish a real order, the communist order. It must break the domination of capital, make wars impossible, destroy all national borders, transform the whole world into a community that produces for itself, and make the brotherhood and liberation of the peoples a reality.

Against this, world capital is arming itself for the final battle. Using the "League of Nations" and pacifist phrase-mongering to conceal its intentions, it is making a last attempt to paste the crumbling pieces of the capitalist system back together and rally its forces against the ever-growing proletarian revolution.

The proletariat must answer this outrageous new conspiracy of the capitalist class by conquering political power, directing that power against the class enemy, and wielding it as a lever of economic transformation. The final victory of the world proletariat will mean the beginning of the real history of liberated humanity.

1. The conquest of political power

The conquest of political power by the proletariat means destroying the political power of the bourgeoisie. The bourgeoisie's mightiest instrument of power is the bourgeois state apparatus with its capitalist army led by officers of the bourgeoisie and landed aristocracy, its police and security forces, its judges and jailers, preachers, government bureaucrats, and so forth. The conquest of political power does not mean merely a change of personnel in the ministries. Instead, it means destroying the enemy's state apparatus; seizing real power; disarming the bourgeoisie, the counterrevolutionary officers, and the White Guards. It means arming the proletariat, the revolutionary soldiers, and the workers' Red Guard; removing all bourgeois judges and organizing proletarian justice; abolishing the rule of reactionary government officials; and creating new organs of proletarian administration. The key to victory for the proletariat lies in organizing its power and disorganizing that of the enemy; it entails smashing the bourgeois state apparatus while constructing a proletarian one. Only after the proletariat has achieved victory and broken the resistance of the bourgeoisie can it make its former enemies useful to the new order, placing them under its control and gradually drawing them into the work of communist construction.

2. Democracy and dictatorship

The proletarian state is an apparatus of repression like every other, but it is wielded against the enemies of the working class. Its purpose is to break and eliminate the resistance of the exploiters, who use every means in a desperate struggle to drown the revolution in blood. The dictatorship of the proletariat, which openly gives the working class the favored position in society, is at the same time a provisional institution. As the bourgeoisie's resistance is broken, and it is expropriated and gradually transformed into a part of the work force, the proletarian dictatorship wanes, the state withers away, and with it, social classes themselves.

So-called democracy, that is, bourgeois democracy, is nothing but a veiled dictatorship of the bourgeoisie. The highly touted general "will of the people" is no more real than national unity. In reality, classes confront each other with antagonistic, irreconcilable wills. But since the bourgeoisie is a small minority, it needs this fiction, this illusion of a national "will of the people," these high-sounding words, to consolidate its rule over the working class and impose its own class will on the proletariat. By contrast the proletariat, the overwhelming majority of the population, openly wields the class power of its mass organizations, its councils, in order to abolish the privileges of the bourgeoisie and to safeguard the transition to a classless, communist society.

Bourgeois democracy puts the primary emphasis on purely formal declarations of rights and freedoms, which are beyond the reach of working people, the proletarians and semiproletarians, who lack the material resources to exercise them. Meanwhile, the bourgeoisie uses its material resources, through its press and organizations, to deceive and betray the people. In contrast, the council system, the new type of state power, assigns the highest priority to enabling the proletariat to exercise its rights and freedom. The power of the councils gives the best palaces, buildings, printing plants, paper stocks, and so forth to the people for their newspapers, meetings, and organizations. Only thus does real *proletarian* democracy even become possible.

Bourgeois democracy, with its parliamentary system, only pretends to give the masses a voice in running the government. In reality the masses and their organizations are completely excluded from real power or participation in state administration. Under the council system the mass organizations govern, and through them the masses themselves, since the councils involve a constantly increasing number of workers in administering the state. Only in this way is the entire working population gradually integrated into actually governing. Therefore the council system rests on the mass organizations of the proletariat: the councils themselves, the revolutionary trade unions, the cooperatives, and so on.

Bourgeois democracy and the parliamentary system widen the gulf between the masses and the state by separating legislative and executive power and by means of parliamentary elections without recall. Under the council system on the other hand, right of recall, the unification of legislative and executive powers, and the character of the councils as working bodies all serve to connect the masses with the administrative organs of government. This bond is further strengthened by the organization of elections in the council system on the basis of production units, not artificial geographic districts.

Thus, the council system puts into practice true proletarian democracy, democracy by and for the proletariat and against the bourgeoisie. This system favors the industrial proletariat as the best organized, most politically mature, and leading class, under whose hegemony the semiproletarians and small farmers in the countryside will make gradual progress. The industrial proletariat must utilize its temporary advantages to tear the poorer petty-bourgeois masses in the countryside away from the influence of the large peasants and the bourgeoisie and to organize and educate them as fellow workers in the construction of communism.

3. Expropriation of the capitalists and the socialization of production

The breakdown of capitalist order and work discipline makes it impossible to return to production on the old basis under the existing relationship of class forces. Even when they are successful, workers' struggles for higher wages fail to bring the desired improvements in the standard of living, as soaring prices on all basic necessities wipe out every gain. The workers' living conditions can be raised only when the proletariat itself, and not the bourgeoisie, controls production. The powerful struggles for higher wages by workers in every country, through their elemental driving force and tendency to become generalized, clearly express the desperate situation workers face. These battles make it impossible for capitalist production to continue. The resistance of the bourgeoisie prolongs the old society's death agony and threatens to destroy economic life completely. In order to break this resistance and to expand the productive forces of the economy as rapidly as possible, the proletarian dictatorship must expropriate the big bourgeoisie and landed aristocracy and transform the means of production and distribution into collective property of the proletarian state.

Communism is now being born amid the rubble of capitalism; history leaves humanity no other way out. The utopian slogan of reconstructing the capitalist economy, advanced by the opportunists as a way to put off socialization, only prolongs the process of disintegration and creates the danger of complete collapse. Communist revolution, on the other hand, is the best and the only means by which society can preserve its most important productive force, the proletariat, and thereby save itself.

The proletarian dictatorship most definitely will not divide up the means of production and distribution; on the contrary, its purpose is to subordinate production to a centralized plan.

The first steps toward socializing the whole economy include: socialization of the system of big banks, which now direct production; takeover by the proletarian state power of all of the agencies for economic control by the capitalist state; seizure of all municipal enterprises; socialization of branches of production dominated by cartels and trusts, as well as those where seizure is practical because capital has been concentrated and centralized; nationalization of agricultural estates and their transformation into socially operated agricultural enterprises.

As far as the small enterprises are concerned, the proletariat must gradually combine them, depending on their size.

It must be made very clear here that small property owners will not be expropriated under any circumstances, nor will proprietors who do not exploit wage labor be subject to any coercive measures. This layer will gradually be drawn into socialist organization by example and experience, which will show it the advantages of the new system.

This system will free the small farmers and the urban petty bourgeoisie from the economic yoke of usury capital and the landed aristocracy, and from the burden of taxation (in particular by canceling all government debts).

The proletarian dictatorship will be able to accomplish its economic task only to the degree that the proletariat can establish centralized agencies to administer production and introduce workers' management. To that end it will have to use the mass organizations that are most closely linked to the production process.

In the sphere of distribution, the proletarian dictatorship must replace the market with the equitable distribution of products. To accomplish this the following measures are in order: socialization of wholesale firms; takeover by the proletariat of all distribution agencies of the bourgeois state and the municipalities; supervision of the large consumer cooperatives, which will continue to play a major economic role during the transitional period; and gradual centralization of all these institutions and their transformation into a single system distributing goods in a rational manner.

In the sphere of distribution as in that of production, all qualified technicians and specialists should be utilized, provided their political resistance has been broken and they are capable of serving the new system of production rather than capital.

The proletariat will not oppress them; for the first time it will give them the opportunity to develop their creative abilities to the utmost. Capitalism created a division between manual and intellectual labor; the proletarian dictatorship, by contrast, will foster their cooperation and so unite science and labor.

Along with the expropriation of the factories, mines, estates, and so on, the proletariat must also do away with exploitation of the population by capitalist landlords. It must place the large buildings in the hands of the local workers' councils and resettle workers in the bourgeoisie's houses, and so forth.

During this time of great upheaval, the council power will have to steadily centralize the entire administrative apparatus, while also involving ever broader layers of the working population in direct participation in government.

4. The road to victory

The revolutionary epoch requires the proletariat to use methods of struggle that bring all of its strength to bear. That means mass action and its logical consequence, direct confrontations with the bourgeois state machinery in open battle. All other methods, such as revolutionary utilization of bourgeois parliament, must be subordinated to this goal.

In order for this struggle to be successful, it will not be enough to split with the outright lackeys of capital and the hangmen of the communist revolution, the role played by the right-wing Social Democrats. It is also necessary to break with the center (the Kautskyites), who abandon the proletariat in its hour of greatest need and flirt with its sworn enemies.

On the other hand, a bloc is needed with the forces in the revolutionary workers' movement who, although not previously part of the Socialist party, now for the most part support the proletarian dictatorship in the form of council power. Certain forces in the syndicalist movement are an example of this.

The revolutionary movement's growth in all countries; the danger of its being strangled by the league of capitalist states; the attempts of social-traitor parties to unify their forces by founding the Yellow "International" in

Bern, the better to serve Wilson's League of Nations; and moreover, the absolute necessity of coordinating proletarian actions: all these considerations make it essential to establish a truly revolutionary and proletarian Communist International.

The International, which puts the interests of the international revolution ahead of so-called national interests, will make mutual aid among the proletariat of different countries a reality. Without economic and other forms of mutual assistance, the proletariat cannot organize the new society. By the same token, in contrast to the Yellow social-patriotic International, international proletarian communism will support exploited colonial peoples in their struggles against imperialism in order to hasten the ultimate downfall of the world imperialist system.

At the beginning of the World War, the capitalist criminals claimed that they were only defending the common fatherland. But the bloody deeds of German imperialism in Russia, the Ukraine, and Finland soon showed its actual predatory nature. Now the Entente countries are being exposed, even before the backward layers of the population, as international bandits and murderers of the proletariat. In concert with the German bourgeoisie and social patriots, and mouthing hypocritical rhetoric about peace, they are strangling the proletarian revolution in Europe with their war machines and with brutalized, barbaric colonial troops. The White Terror of the bourgeois cannibals defies description. The working class's victims are without number. It has lost its best: Liebknecht and Luxemburg.

The proletariat must defend itself against this terror no matter what the cost. The Communist International summons the whole world proletariat to this final battle. Weapon against weapon! Power against power!

Down with capital's imperialist conspiracy!

Long live the international republic of proletarian councils!

PLATTEN: Under the "Other Business" point we have received a resolution from Comrade Reinstein,[2] which the congress found it necessary to reject. But Comrade Reinstein claims he was told that he could introduce it under the "Other Business" point. The commission feels it would be in order to refer it to the bureau.[3] It is very possible that the resolution could be very significant for some countries, but we believe that the bureau is quite capable of attending to the matter.

In addition, Comrade Rutgers has submitted a motion. It is a resolution based on articles published earlier in the press in which the Japanese Socialist Party expresses its opposition to sending Japanese troops to Russia.

(*Rutgers reads the following resolution.*)

MESSAGE FROM THE JAPANESE SOCIALISTS

To our Russian comrades:[4]

Since the very beginning of the Russian revolution we have followed your fearless activities with enthusiasm and deep admiration. Your work has had a great influence on our people's consciousness.

Today, *we are indignant that our government has sent troops into Siberia* under whatever pretext. This undoubtedly serves as an impediment to the free development of your revolution. We deeply regret that we are too weak to counter the peril with which you are threatened by our imperialist government. We are quite unable to do anything because the government is persecuting us with severity.

However, you may rest assured that *the red flag of revolution will wave over all of Japan in the not too distant future.*

Along with this letter, we are sending you a copy of the resolution approved at our May 1, 1917, rally.

With revolutionary greetings,

the Executive Committee of the Socialist Groups in Tokyo and Yokohama

RESOLUTION OF THE JAPANESE SOCIALISTS

We, the socialists of Japan, assembled in Tokyo May 1, 1917, express our deepest sympathy for the Russian revolution, which we follow with admiration.

We recognize that the Russian revolution is both a political revolution of the bourgeoisie against medieval absolutism and a revolution of the proletariat against modern-day capitalism.

Transforming the Russian revolution into a world revolution is not a matter for only the Russian socialists; it is the responsibility of socialists of the entire world.

The capitalist system has already reached its highest stage of development in all countries, and we have entered the epoch of fully developed capitalist imperialism.

In order not to be deceived by the ideologists of imperialism, socialists of all countries must steadfastly defend the positions of the International, and all the forces of the international proletariat must be directed against our common enemy, international capitalism. Only thus will the proletariat be able to fulfill its historic mission.

Socialists of Russia and of all other countries must do everything in their power to put an end to the war and assist the proletariat of the warring countries to turn their weapons, today aimed at brothers on the other side of the trenches, against the ruling classes of their own countries.

We have faith in the courage of the Russian socialists and of our comrades around the world. We are firmly convinced that the revolutionary spirit will spread and permeate all countries.

The Executive Committee of the Socialist Group in Tokyo

PLATTEN: The bureau moves that this resolution be approved. That will encourage the Japanese comrades to rededicate themselves to revolutionary work despite their difficult situation.

Next is a resolution by Comrade Kollontai on the necessity of winning proletarian women to the Communist Party. I will read it.

RESOLUTION ON THE NEED TO DRAW WOMEN WORKERS INTO THE STRUGGLE FOR SOCIALISM

The congress of the Communist International holds that the successful achievement of all the tasks it has set itself, as well as the final victory of the world proletariat and the complete abolition of the capitalist system, can be assured only through the common, united struggle of working-class men and women.[5]

There has been a tremendous increase in the use of women's labor in all branches of the economy. Women's work produces no less than half the world's wealth. Proletarian women play an important, widely recognized role in constructing a new, communist society, especially in making the transition to the communist household, reforming family life, and developing socialist public education of children in order to provide the council republics with able-bodied citizens imbued with the spirit of solidarity. All these considerations make it the urgent task of every party that belongs to the Communist International to work forcefully and energetically to win proletarian women to their ranks. They must use every means to educate women workers about the new form of society and the ethics of communist social and family life.

The dictatorship of the proletariat can be won and maintained only with the energetic and active participation of working-class women.

PLATTEN: The bureau moves that this resolution be approved. We thoroughly agree with the line of thinking expressed in it.

In addition, I must mention that a document has been submitted to this commission by Comrade Sadoul with the intention that it be referred to the bureau as a statement by the French delegation. Since the comrades are not acquainted with the text, I assume that the Presiding Committee would like Comrade Sadoul to read it to the congress.

LENIN: Comrade Sadoul has the floor. Ten copies of the German text are available, which the secretary will distribute.

(*Sadoul reads the memorandum.*)

TO THE WORKERS OF ALL COUNTRIES [STATEMENT OF THE FRENCH DELEGATION]

The first congress of the Third International, which convened in the Kremlin on March 5, 1919, expresses its gratitude and admiration to the Russian proletariat and to its leading party, the Bolshevik Communist Party.

The mighty revolution was carried out to return socialist doctrine, too long corrupted by the opportunists, to its Marxist origins. For nearly a year and a half, a superhuman effort has been exerted to replace the old, bourgeois order with a new, communist society, encompassing both moral and intellectual culture and also material needs, whether collective or individual, political, economic, or social. The revolution has consistently aided the workers of all countries against their militaristic and oppressive governments. These achievements deserve the universal, enthusiastic approval of the toiling classes of all countries.

Enormous success has already been achieved in constructing a society based on work and equality: all large-scale industry has become a collective enterprise administered overall by the supreme economic council and locally by workers' committees. A labor code has been enacted implementing a series of reforms that go beyond the Social Democratic party's old minimum program. The courts, universities, hospitals, palaces, in short all institutions of public life have in practice already passed over to the people's hands. In several other spheres the liberation of the proletariat has not only begun, it has been accomplished.

The revolution extends its liberating and regulating effects to the countryside as well. It is not enough to give land to the peasants and rescue them from the spiritual and material yoke of village money lenders. Those reforms were already carried out in November 1917 and March 1918. Now cultivation of the liberated land and its organization on a communist basis is in full swing, both in the village communities and on all large state farms. In each, the state is applying the latest advances in agronomy and is providing a fruitful example of model cultivation. These reforms all aim to increase labor productivity and thereby promote the people's welfare.

However, it is not the fault of the Soviet system and Bolshevism if this goal has not yet been reached, nor if the population in the Russian cities suffers from hunger and growing shortages of finished products. On the contrary, it was the Soviet system and Bolshevism alone that decisively ended the anarchy and chaos caused by Kerensky and bourgeois democracy, and enabled the country as far as possible to maintain the existing level of economic life.

Responsibility for the crisis falls solely on the internal and external enemies of council power; their sabotage, conspiracies, and military interventions have forced Russia to expend a large part of its forces, energy, and resources to create a new army.

Despite their deep yearning for peace, the entire Russian people had the courage to understand and accept this necessity. The great success the Soviet government has had in carrying out this tremendous task is well known. One can level accusations at Bolshevism, but the best way to find out whether or not the Bolsheviks are to blame would be for the Entente powers to stop forcing the Soviet state to defend itself militarily.

To do this, they must not only stop sending armed forces into Russia and withdraw from its ports, they must also end all internal interference and stop supporting counterrevolutionary bands with money, arms, and advisers. Without outside backing from the Entente, these forces would rapidly break up on their own.

The Red Army soldiers could then return to their families, thereby making immediately available the best workers, the most devoted organizers, and the most capable engineers. Their contribution to peacetime production would quickly yield considerable results.

But it must be remembered that Russian industry is young and has never been able to do without help from abroad. The Entente is paralyzing economic reorganization by forbidding specialists from other countries, who were in fact managing Russian industry, from returning to Russia. It is impeding the construction and maintenance of factories and the shipment of raw materials and fuel. It is destroying industry and creating unemployment by blocking all imports of machinery, rail cars, and locomotives into Russia. Inadequate means of transportation make it impossible to supply the cities with food. The harvests themselves are in danger because the peasants can no longer obtain indispensable agricultural machinery and implements, all of which came from abroad.

Time and again the council republic has officially requested continued assistance from industry and specialists in other countries. It has declared its willingness to pay dearly for these services, which are essential to the development of Russia's economic life. However, the Entente did not even bother to respond to these proposals. Instead, using threats and violence, it has imposed a harsh blockade on Russia and even on the Central Powers and neutral countries.

The toiling masses of all countries must demand that their governments genuinely halt all direct and indirect intervention against Soviet Russia. In order to give form to this demand, the congress of the Third International proposes to all peoples the following program of action.

Honor, independence, and the basic interests of the world proletariat demand immediate action, using all available means, including revolutionary means if necessary, to carry out the following program:

1. Stop interference by the Entente in the internal affairs of Soviet Russia.

2. Immediately withdraw all European and Asian Allied troops presently in Russia.

3. End all direct or indirect intervention, whether in the form of provocations, material or moral support to the Russian counterrevolutionaries, or support to reactionary countries on Russia's borders.

4. Annul the treaties that have already been signed that promote intervention by the Entente itself, by Russian counterrevolutionaries, or by neighbors of the Russian state. Immediately withdraw to their country of origin the diplomatic and military missions sent by the Entente governments to northern and southern Russia, Romania, Poland, Finland, and the Czech territories in order to provoke war with the council republic.

5. Recognize the council government, which, after eighteen months' existence, is more stable and popular than ever.

6. Resume diplomatic relations, which also means sending official socialist representatives to Russia and recognizing Russian representatives to other countries.

7. Admit delegates of the Soviet government to the Paris peace conference as representatives, the sole representatives, of the Russian people. A European peace, discussed and concluded without Russia, would be very unstable at best. It would be malicious and absurd to admit the puppets of the artificially created regional governments as representatives of all or part of Russia, even only as part of the delegation, and not admit the Bolsheviks. These regimes exist only thanks to the support of the Entente and have scarcely any separate ambitions or interests.

8. End the economic blockade. Continuing it will quickly result in famine and industrial ruin in Russia.

9. Resume trade relations and conclude commercial treaties.

10. Send several hundred, or better yet, several thousand technicians to Russia: engineers, supervisors, and reliable workers, especially metalworkers. They would be of invaluable assistance to the young socialist republic in industry, especially in carrying out the most important tasks: repairing the railways and rolling stock and organizing transportation.

LENIN: Does anyone wish to have the French or German text read aloud? No one does. Comrade Guilbeaux has the floor.

HENRI GUILBEAUX *(translated by Kollontai):* When I was last in contact with the Russian comrades, as they were leaving Switzerland, I told them, "The next time we meet will be in Russia." That has actually happened. Now I am present at a great event here, the founding of the Third, Communist International, the true International. The failing of the Second International was its bourgeois and opportunist character. In 1914, the opportunists went over to the bourgeois parties and formed an alliance with them. Now, at the Bern conference, the murderers of Karl Liebknecht and Rosa Luxemburg shook hands with Thomas, who as a supporter of the war was the murderer of so many hundreds of thousands of soldiers. But all those people are now outside of the International that has just been formed. The greatest danger for the new International is wavering elements such as Kautsky and Longuet. While they stand up for Lenin and Trotsky and call themselves friends of the new movement, at the same time they are playing Wilson's game. Loriot, who represented France at the Bern conference, stated in his speech that the Zimmerwald movement is now dead, and that there are really only two camps left in the world: the bourgeoisie on one side and the Communists on the other. On behalf of the French Zimmerwald participants, I tell you that I share the view that the Zimmerwald movement is dead and now hail the new International, the International that is alive and viable and will register more victories in the future.

LENIN: Comrade Platten will speak for the resolutions commission.

PLATTEN: Next is the resolution on the Bern conference.[6] It has been read aloud by Comrade Zinoviev and reviewed by the commission, and there was no reason to make any changes. The commission recommends that the resolution be approved.

LENIN: Is anyone opposed? There is no opposition. (*The resolution is adopted.*)

PLATTEN: Regarding the point "Theses on the International Situation": after a thorough discussion, the commission decided to recommend deleting the final section of this document, which outlines the international proletariat's tasks.[7] It should be deleted because enough has been said on the proletariat's political tasks under all other agenda points; repeating them would be superfluous. The commission recommends that the final section be deleted.

LENIN: Are there any objections? Does anyone wish to be recognized? That is not the case, so the motion carries.

PLATTEN: Next we come to the manifesto by Comrade Trotsky. You have heard it. It was considered in great detail at a long evening session, and it is plain that the bureau must immediately see to it that it receives the widest possible distribution. We recommend that it be approved.

LENIN: Does anyone wish to speak on this question? No one does.

PLATTEN: The commission decided further that when this manifesto is published it should be signed. At the end of the manifesto, the organization should be shown next to the names of the respective delegates who participated in the congress. This motion was made by delegates from abroad, the only ones who could have objected on grounds of secrecy. Thus, all voting delegates to the congress who are present will sign it.

Regarding the resolution on White Terror: you heard it read by Comrade Sirola today. The commission approved this resolution with no changes.

LENIN: Does anyone wish to speak on this point? As there are no speakers, we will now proceed to the organization question.

PLATTEN: The commission spent an exceedingly long time discussing the organization question. The question is, what form will permit us to move as rapidly as possible to a firmly established organization. The commission said earlier that there should be two leading bodies, an executive committee and a bureau. Now, after discussing the executive committee question, the commission decided that body should include representatives from countries belonging to our organization. It should be headquartered in Moscow, with the understanding that the bureau and executive committee are authorized to change their location, should that become necessary. As delegates to this congress, we must first return to our countries, give reports, and win agreement to carry out these resolutions—that is, elect delegates to the executive committee in Moscow.

It will be some time before the delegates arrive here, and that raises the question: Who is to take responsibility for the necessary work in the interim? We have come up with a solution, which we have put in writing and now present to you on behalf of the commission. The text is short; the final form of the statutes will be proposed at a later date. The text reads:

RESOLUTION ON ORGANIZING THE INTERNATIONAL

In order that work may begin without delay, the congress elects the necessary bodies at this time, in the understanding that the final form of the Communist International's constitution will be proposed by the bureau at the next congress and determined there.[8]

Leadership of the Communist International shall be entrusted to an executive committee, consisting of one representative from each of the Communist parties of the most important countries. The following parties should immediately send representatives to the first executive committee: Russia, Germany, German Austria, Hungary, Balkan federation, Switzerland, Scandinavia.

Parties joining the Communist International before the second congress of the Communist International convenes shall be entitled to one seat on the executive committee.

Until such time as representatives from abroad arrive, the comrades in whose country the executive committee is based shall perform its functions.

The executive committee shall elect a bureau of five persons.

LENIN: Does anyone wish to speak? No one does. The motion carries.

That concludes our work.

CLOSING REMARKS

LENIN: That we have been able to gather despite all the persecution and all the difficulties created by the police, that we have been able without any serious differences and in a brief space of time to reach important decisions on all the vitally urgent questions of the contemporary revolutionary epoch, we owe to the fact that the proletarian masses of the whole world, by their action, have brought up these questions in practice and begun to tackle them.[9]

All we have had to do here has been to record the gains already won by the people in the process of their revolutionary struggle.

Not only in the eastern European but also in the western European countries, not only in the vanquished but also in the victor countries, for example in Britain, the movement in favor of soviets is spreading farther and farther, and this movement is, most assuredly, a movement pursuing the aim of establishing the new, proletarian democracy. It is the most significant step towards the dictatorship of the proletariat, towards the complete victory of communism.

No matter how the bourgeoisie of the whole world rage, how much they deport or jail or even kill Spartacists and Bolsheviks—all this will no longer help. It will only serve to enlighten the masses, help rid them of the old bourgeois-democratic prejudices, and steel them in struggle. The victory of the proletarian revolution on a world scale is assured. The founding of an international Soviet republic is on the way. (*Loud applause*)

Opposite page: southern Russia, the Ukraine, and the Caucasus, showing pre-1918 borders of Germany, Austria-Hungary, and Romania.

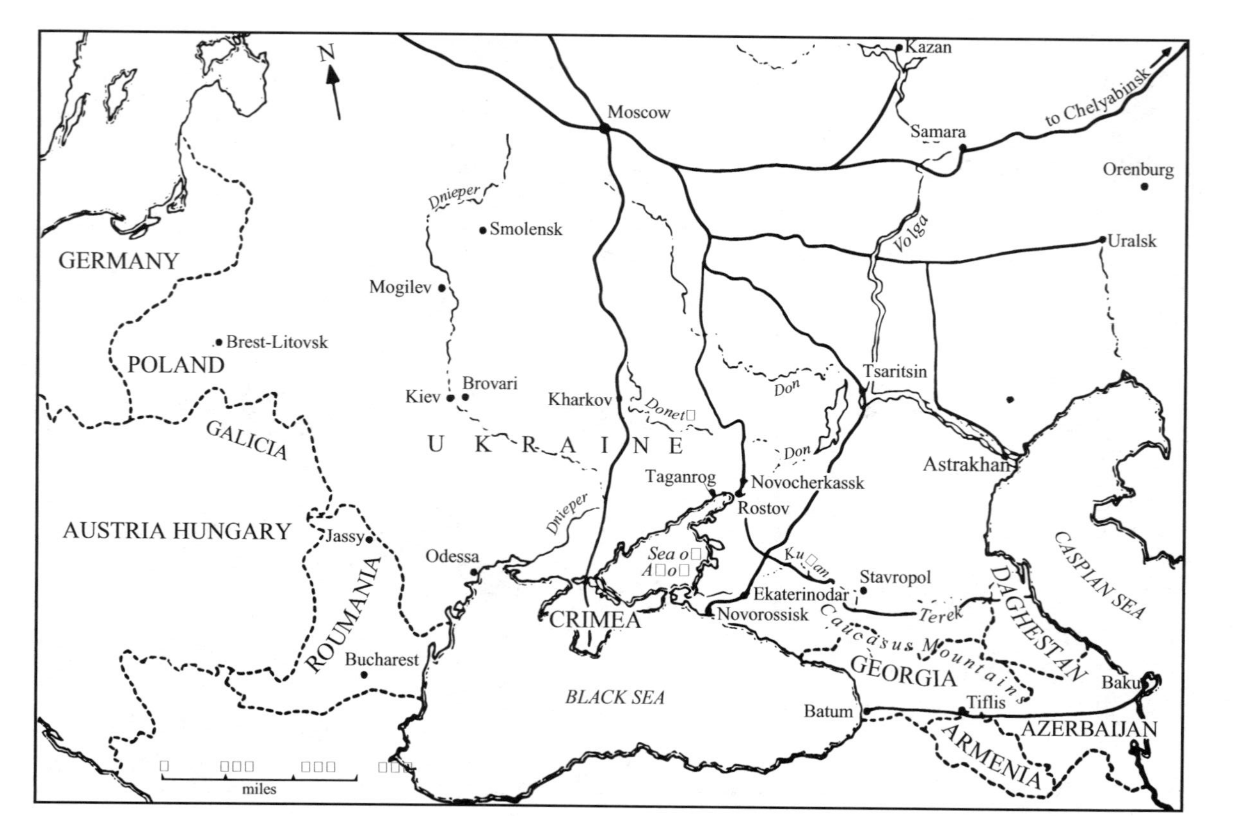

N
GERMANY
POLAND
Brest-Litovsk
GALICIA
AUSTRIA HUNGARY
ROUMANIA
Jassy
Bucharest
Dnieper
Smolensk
Mogilev
Kiev
Brovari
Kharkov
U K R A I N E
Odessa
CRIMEA
BLACK SEA
Moscow
Kazan
Samara
to Chelyabinsk
Orenburg
Uralsk
Volga
Tsaritsin
Don
Don
Astrakhan
Taganrog
Novocherkassk
Rostov
Stavropol
Ekaterinodar
Novorossisk
Terek
Caucasus Mountains
CASPIAN SEA
DAGHESTAN
GEORGIA
Batum
Tiflis
Baku
AZERBAIJAN
ARMENIA
miles

Above: Egyptian peasants demonstrate in Cairo during March 1919 anti-British uprising; below: British police attack during Indian anti-colonial upsurge March–April 1919.

11. Written reports to the congress

MINUTES OF THE CREDENTIALS COMMISSION

Session of March 2, 1919

A list of participants drawn up by a preliminary meeting of conference members was adopted and the proportion of their votes determined.[1]

On the credentials of Comrade Reinstein (Socialist Labor Party of America): his written credentials were seized in Tornio.[2] He is a standing member of its international bureau. Moreover, the provision was made that should a new, left International be formed, he will be the representative to the new organization. Comrade Rutgers has confirmed Comrade Reinstein's report to be correct; Comrade Sirola confirms that Comrade Reinstein participated in the Stockholm conference of Zimmerwald supporters in June 1917 as a representative of the Socialist Labor Party.[3] His credentials are declared valid.

Comrade Rutgers does not have credentials from the American Socialist Propaganda League for this conference; therefore, he is granted a consultative vote.

As a founding member of the Social Democratic Party of Holland and as its former regular correspondent in America, Comrade Rutgers can have an additional consultative vote as its representative.

As for the Japanese Socialist Group: Comrade Rutgers has delivered a resolution from them saluting Soviet Russia (*Pravda,* September 27, 1918); but he was in Japan only in transit for six weeks. The Japanese Socialist Group will therefore be removed from the list.

The credentials of Comrade Klinger (the German colonists' region) are recognized; Chairman Ebenholz's signature has confirmed their validity, and they are accepted.

The credentials of the Russian Communist Party are recognized.

The German Communist Party: Comrade Albert could not carry written credentials with him. Comrade Leviné (from Rosta),[4] who was to confirm Albert's credentials as a delegate, was arrested en route. Comrade Platten confirms that Comrade Albert was delegated to the conference. He learned this from the Communist Party Central Committee in Berlin. The credentials are declared valid.

The Swiss Social Democratic Party: the party has declared itself firmly in favor of the Third International.[5] Comrade Platten, who can easily testify to that for his party, was not able to carry written credentials. His credentials are recognized.

Lithuania-Belorussia: a telegram from Joffe reads, "Unification of the two parties. Credentials go to Gedris." Accepted.

Finland: credentials for five delegates delivered by the Central Committee. Accepted.

Poland: credentials for Unszlicht—by telegram from Joffe. Accepted.

Latvia: a telegram written in code by Stuchka with credentials for Gailis. Accepted.

Estonia: Pögelman's credentials. Accepted.

Norway: the authority of Grusenberg is transferred to Comrade Stang. Accepted.

Credentials have been received from the Central Bureau of the Eastern Peoples for the representatives from the sections of the Bashkirs, the Kirghiz, the Tatars, and the Caucasus Mountain Peoples. We grant one decisive vote to these delegates taken as a single group. Further, we grant each delegate a consultative vote.

Armenia: Comrade Haikuni's credentials are accepted.

Hungary: Comrade Rudnyánszky. Accepted.

We grant consultative votes to the Czech, Bulgarian, Yugoslav, and French groups and to the Swiss Communists.

Session of March 3, 1919

The Balkan revolutionary federation: Comrade Rakovsky, who serves as its secretary, represented the federation at the Stockholm Zimmerwald conference and is its delegate on the Zimmerwald commission. The Bulgarian Tesnyaki and the Romanian Communist Party fully and unconditionally share his views. Accepted.

We recognize two delegates from the Ukraine, one from the Left Social Democracy in Sweden, two from German Austria, and Comrade Unszlicht from Poland. Their credentials are attached.

Session of March 4, 1919

We grant Comrade Balabanoff a consultative vote as a representative of the Zimmerwald commission.

The Korean Workers League: we grant Comrade Kain a consultative vote.

Session of March 5, 1919

The Chinese Socialist Workers Party: we grant comrades Liu Shaozhou and Zhang Yongkui a consultative vote.

Session of March 6, 1919

Comrade Guilbeaux is a permanent representative of the Zimmerwald Left current in France within the Zimmerwald movement, considered by this tendency to be a starting point for the Third International. He has remained in continuous contact with them (and through his wife, he had contact with Loriot not long ago). Therefore, his credentials are recognized for this conference. He receives the five votes for France.

Max Albert, Yrjö Sirola,
E. Rudnyánszky, G. Chicherin

Report on Armenia

by Gurgen Haikuni

Comrades, the Armenian Communist Party is honored and pleased that today, when our party celebrates its anniversary,[6,7] it is taking part in the international congress of Communist parties that is preparing to launch the Third, Communist International. The October proletarian revolution opened a new era in human history, an era when imperialist wars were transformed into a civil war that leads inevitably to the victory of the proletariat over the bourgeoisie and to the establishment of a communist order in the entire world.

The October proletarian revolution, the enemy of all oppression and coercion, has advanced many emancipatory slogans, among them that of the real, unadulterated self-determination of peoples, including the self-determination of Armenia.[8]

For the first time the peoples of Armenia were able to breathe freely and to freely build their own future. At the same time, however, an enormous danger arose that the bourgeois-nationalist parties, having utilized the slogan of self-determination, would work even more intensively to unleash nationalist passions and, under the guise of self-determination, turn the country into the theater of new national wars. To their policy of national exclusiveness we must counterpose the class unity of the toiling Armenian peoples. We must transform the national war into a civil war to liberate the exploited and oppressed classes from the yoke of their exploiters and oppressors. The Armenian Communists faced the crucial task of correctly determining their line of march and organizing themselves according to the principles of revolutionary Marxism so as to give the toiling masses a weapon in their struggle for genuine self-determination.

In November 1917 a group of native Armenian members of the RSDLP (Bolsheviks) took the initiative of posing the question of organizing a workers' party that would be able to draw to it the proletarian and semiproletarian layers of the Armenian peoples against the bourgeois-chauvinist parties. After a number of meetings, it was decided to send one of the comrades to the Bolshevik Central Committee in Petersburg to carry out negotiations for organizing a party of Armenian Bolsheviks.

The Bolshevik Central Committee gave its agreement at the end of January 1918, and the Organizing Committee set about further work. On March 4, 1918, the party's

Central Committee issued its first manifesto to the people of Armenia in the name of the *Armenian Communist Party.*

The Armenian Communist Party emerged in the arena of political struggle under the difficult conditions of the Dashnak-Menshevik-bey reaction.[9] The bourgeois-nationalist parties went so far in their criminal policy of national isolation as to create a "national republic." In their chauvinist madness the ruling parties shed the last vestige of shame. For them the main enemy was Bolshevism and its standard bearer, the Russian proletariat. In the struggle with Bolshevism, the Transcaucasian "democracy" of Dashnaks, Mensheviks, and beys was ready to unite with anyone. Messrs. Zhordania, Gegechkori, and Tsereteli found worthy brothers-in-arms in the persons of the Northern Caucasian counterrevolutionaries Filimonov, Polovtsev, Karaulov, and other such ringleaders of the Transcaucasian counterrevolution.

A mighty force in the developing revolutionary movement was the Russian army of the Caucasus. The revolutionized Russian soldiers, armed to the teeth, did not let the "Transcaucasian democracy" rest on its laurels. The latter had to get rid of the "anarcho-Bolshevik plague" and drive the Russian army beyond the borders of Transcaucasia. And so, by order of the Menshevik Zhordania, an unheard-of crime took place: they treacherously began the disarmament of the Russian army, shedding the blood of thousands of soldiers.[10] When the Bolshevik Party protested, the reaction only became more intense. Raids and arrests were carried out against "mutinous troops" and "anarcho-Bolsheviks." The prisons were crammed full of them. The best comrades landed in jail. The workers' press was stifled. To commemorate the February 10 opening of the Transcaucasian parliament, the repressions and persecutions against the revolution were crowned with a horrible execution at the workers' rally in the Alexander Gardens of Tiflis [Tbilisi].[11]

Conditions were particularly intolerable in the provinces with a mixed Armenian and Tatar population. The petty-bourgeois Armenian Dashnaks, on the one hand, and the Musavat, the party of the Tatar landlords, on the other, openly propagandized for national slaughter. Armenians butchered Tatars, and Tatars Armenians. Deceiving the popular masses, subjecting entire villages to fire and sword, the Dashnaks, who had sold themselves to the Armenian bourgeoisie, and the Musavatists, representatives of the Tatar beys, continued to sit side by side in the same government with surprising shamelessness, the whole time weaving plots against one another and pushing the worker and peasant masses of the two fraternal peoples to terrible mutual destruction. The internal counterrevolutionary work of these parties was rounded out by their foreign policy. A literal sellout began, a haggling with the Turkish feudalists, a policy that could only disgust and repel any democrat with the least bit of honesty.[12]

Although calling themselves socialists, the Mensheviks conducted old-style secret diplomacy, haunting the diplomats' corridors and weighing each of the two warring imperialist groups in order to take the side of the stronger.

Even as the Musavat shamelessly expressed its delight with the Turkish offensive and, growing ever bolder, talked as if it were master of the situation, Chkhenkeli and his friends rushed headlong to the Turkish pashas in Trebizond [Trabzon] aiming to appease them with the sale of Batum [Batumi]. They hoped that afterwards, without any pangs of conscience, they could lay all the blame on the Bolsheviks.

But what of Gegechkori and Tsereteli? What an unprecedented comedy these gentlemen played out! In order to deceive the masses, they came down on Chkhenkeli in party meetings with all the power of their eloquence, declaring that the betrayal was a personal action by Chkhenkeli.[13] The government was still oriented to the Russian democracy, they said, and had no other orientation whatsoever. The interests of the Georgian princes demanded staging before the masses a comedy of supposed discord in order to consummate the conspiracy against the Georgian proletariat and peasantry quickly. It is no surprise that the Menshevik cavaliers, Gegechkori, Chkhenkeli, and Tsereteli, fulfilled the roles allocated among them with great success.

But whatever were the pathetic Armenian chauvinists up to? The same sellout policy, but more cynical and undistinguished. Look who reappears among the diplomats: yesterday's singer of eulogies to the tsar, the "socialist" Dashnak, Khatisov [Khatisian], who conducts negotiations with the Turkish pashas in the name of "the toiling Armenian masses." At the same time that the invading Turkish gangs lay waste whole districts, one wing of the Dashnaks pretends to make every effort to defend the front, while in Trebizond and Batum, Khatisov and Kachaznuni spend weeks on end flattering the German-Turkish imperialists.[14] It should not seem strange that the front treacherously fell apart at the bidding of the imperialists; city after city surrendered, and the nationalist army, internally demoralized, deserted the front by the thousands, fleeing panic-stricken before the enemy's small forces.

And once again, for the thousandth time, out of the mouths of the social traitors was heard a curse on Bolshevism, which, they say, had infiltrated the army and demoralized its ranks.

They were obliged to justify these ignominious defeats before the masses. They had to find someone to blame.

As always in similar cases they ran the gamut of insults against that awful enemy, Bolshevism, which gives no rest to the gentlemen social patriots—the Mensheviks and Dashnaks. What alarmed the Menshevik-Dashnaks and Musavatists even more was the supremacy in Baku of Soviet power, proletarian power, which tied its fate to that of the Russian proletariat.[15]

Like the red flag before the bull, Baku drove the Menshevik-Musavatist bulls into a rage. A new betrayal of the revolution was being carried out, a new conspiracy, this time against the heroic Baku proletariat.

Chkhenkeli, Gegechkori, Zhordania, and Company, in close alliance with the Tatar beys, organized a secret attack on Baku and, to that end, armed the Tatars with millions of cartridges, machine guns, and cannon balls from the Tiflis arsenal.[16]

The lackeys of imperialism were ready reverently to do the bidding of the German kaiser and the Turkish sultan. Georgian detachments with armored trains were linked up with the Tatar bands and carried out the secret attack on Baku at a time when the workers and peasants knew nothing about this, and when the Baku proletariat, after having smashed the counterrevolutionary forces in civil war, was occupied with the consolidation of Soviet power.

In these political conditions, when the members of the routed Bolshevik organizations were forced to shift to underground work, when even a word of criticism subjected one to cruel persecution, in these difficult conditions the Armenian Communist Party appeared in the arena of struggle. From the very first days of its existence, it conducted an independent and courageous struggle against the Mensheviks and Dashnaks.

On March 4 our party began publishing its official organ *Karmir orer* [Red days], which appeared with a manifesto.

With a multitude of facts it showed the worker-peasant masses the treacherous policy of the Menshevik-Dashnak chauvinists, unfurled the program of communism before the toilers, and explained the meaning of the coming world socialist revolution.

The servants of imperialism, the Mensheviks and Dashnaks, opened up a savage campaign against us in their newspapers. Victimizations and persecutions rained down on our comrades in Tiflis and the provinces. Our newspaper was closed, the print shop padlocked, and our headquarters seized. Yet all this did not weaken us, but strengthened us even more.

The circulation of our official organ, *Karmir orer,* initially 250 to 300 copies, rose to between 3,000 and 3,500 copies in Tiflis alone, something unprecedented by Armenian standards. It competed successfully with the Dashnaks' official organ. On every street, groups of Armenian soldiers and workers were reading and distributing our newspaper. Delegations of peasants and workers came for our newspaper from Aleksandropol [Leninakan], Shulavery [Shaumyani], and other places, because the Menshevik-Dashnak bandits had destroyed every copy that fell into their hands. Peasants disseminated *Karmir orer* from village to village and were delighted with its audacious revolutionary spirit. Hundreds of copies of *Karmir orer* penetrated the nationalist regiments that arrived from Odessa, Crimea, and southern Russia. At first distributed secretly and free of charge, it was later circulated openly and for money. This revolutionized the soldiers' thoughts and feelings and educated them in the lucid ideals of communism.

In the space of one month our central publication attracted to itself the worker, soldier, and peasant masses and became their beloved and steadfast comrade. They considered *Karmir orer* their own.

An abundance of soldiers' and workers' correspondence filled the pages of *Karmir orer*. In the evenings the editorial office was surrounded by masses of soldiers impatiently awaiting the paper's appearance. And it is not surprising that under these circumstances the newspaper sold out to the last copy. The Communist organ awakened unprecedented animation and interest.

With the success of the newspaper, our lectures, gatherings, and mass meetings became even more crowded and lively.

In a short time the number of party members in Tiflis alone reached several hundred. The number in the armed flying squad reached three hundred. The many thousands of sympathizers grouped around the party should also be mentioned.

Already by April the Armenian military units in Tiflis were linked to the Armenian Communist Party. Our comrades penetrated these units and lived among the soldiers, and as a result their propaganda and agitation for Communist ideas produced brilliant results. Thanks to the energy of our comrades, the Dashnak officers' school was completely linked with us. At any moment we could get machine guns, grenades, and rifles. The reserve artillery units in Avlabar and Artachali sent us their representatives. The motor vehicles at the disposal of the Mensheviks were to pass over to our side in the event of an insurrection.

In many districts of Tiflis the militiamen awaited our instructions. And especially significant for the development and strengthening of the party was the fact that the 4,000 armed Armenians from Turkey deployed near the arsenal organized a mass meeting at the initiative of our party. The meeting was addressed by members of our party alone, and a resolution proposed by the Armenian Communist Party was adopted with the slogans: "Down with the Seym [assembly]! Long live the proletariat! Long live the Armenian Communist Party! Long live the Third International!" All the measures taken by the Dashnaks and Mensheviks, even the provocations and the mobilizations of armored cars, had no influence whatsoever, and the rally continued to its conclusion, surrounded by armed detachments sympathetic to the Armenian Communist Party. The enthusiasm knew no bounds. Members of the Armenian Communist Party, armed with grenades and rifles, repeatedly organized demonstrations in front of the buildings of the national councils. An entire regiment in Aleksandropol dispatched its representatives to establish ties with our party. Comrade I., the chairman of the soviet of workers' and soldiers' deputies in Akhaltsikhe, informed us that it was possible to seize power there. The Lori comrades announced explicitly that in the event of an insurrection in Tiflis, the revolutionary peasants would come down from the hills by the thousands to help if necessary.

A connection was also established with Yerevan.

There was an ongoing liaison with Kermen, the Bolshevik organization of Ossetia. Peasant uprisings flared up in a number of Georgian districts.

In this tense atmosphere, the population of Tiflis waited from one hour to the next for power to pass into the hands of the Bolsheviks.[17] It seemed that the capital of Transcaucasia must surely be taken by the proletariat in the course of a single night. At that moment when our protracted efforts had produced the most favorable climate, due to a number of unexpected circumstances, not the least of which, we must admit, was the indecisiveness of some leading comrades, our forces began to disintegrate and scatter. The masses displayed greater revolutionary energy than their leaders.

Sensing and seeing the danger that threatened, the Mensheviks surrounded Tiflis with their troops. Field artillery and machine guns were placed on the surrounding heights. An armored train was moved to the railway station.

With every passing day the detachments of Turkish imperialism advanced closer to the center of the revolutionary movement—to Tiflis.

Thus because of a number of internal and external factors, the revolutionary movement temporarily suffered defeat in Transcaucasia and Armenia. Red Baku stood alone in its struggle. The disarming of revolutionary units began along with the persecution of the active comrades, many of whom were forced to go into hiding or to emigrate to Northern Caucasia. Inspired by their successes, the Mensheviks and Dashnaks instituted a White Terror against the Communists. As a result many comrades were imprisoned and many were shot.

Though forced underground, however, our comrades have continued revolutionary work in secret to this day, issuing illegal leaflets. They are deeply convinced that the hour of Anglo-American imperialism's inevitable collapse is not far off and that Soviet Russia will serve as a mighty buttress for the toiling peoples of Armenia in their uprising to take power.

Regarding the Armenian Communist Party's activity, reference must be made to the members of our organization dispatched by the party's Central Committee for the struggle against the counterrevolution to establish Soviet power in the city of Sukhumi. The counterrevolutionary Armenian bourgeois-nationalist organizations in Northern Caucasia were liquidated through the efforts of party members.

The Dashnak party lost every scrap of authority and was driven out of the ranks of the toiling masses.

Members of the Armenian Communist Party who had emigrated to Northern Caucasia entered the Soviet institutions and took posts of responsibility for consolidating the toilers' power. A regiment named after Comrade Lenin was organized in Northern Caucasia with members of the Armenian Communist Party at its head. The party's Central Committee resumed publication of its central organ, *Karmir orer,* in Pyatigorsk. It called on those who had come there from Armenia to join the Red Army, struggle against the counterrevolutionary bands, and strengthen Soviet power in Northern Caucasia for further offensives on the borders of Transcaucasia and onward into Armenia. The goal of these actions is to drive out the Anglo-American imperialists and to establish workers' and peasants' rule in Armenia.

In Sukhumi, now ruled by the Mensheviks, hundreds of exiles from Armenia have taken refuge in the hills and organized partisan detachments. Arms in hand they await the approach of the Red troops of the Soviet Republic.

We know that the bourgeois republics of Armenia and Georgia were not even successfully established before they showed signs of breakdown.

The Dashnaks and Mensheviks, only yesterday "friends," are today going to war against each other, spilling the blood of the two fraternal peoples. But the patience of the toiling masses has its limits. Dispersed by the violence of the foreign invasion, they may today be powerless and silent. But tomorrow they will close ranks and succeed, with the strong, fraternal support of the world proletariat, in destroying the power of the despicable hirelings of Anglo-American imperialism.

In "republican Armenia" all is not tranquil. The Armenian Dashnaks are shooting the Armenian Mensheviks. But that is not all. The Dashnaks have begun to terrorize even their own milieu; they are executing their party comrades, former government ministers. With the breakdown of the bourgeois and petty-bourgeois Dashnak party, the party of Armenian big business moves to the fore. Under the command of British military authorities, the British protégé and merchant Boghos Nubar-Pasha and the tobacco manufacturer Enfiadjian rule today over the people of Armenia, with the blessing of the head of the Armenian priests, called the catholicos, and accompanied by the foul groveling of the Dashnak leaders before their new masters.

But British gold can buy only a small number of adventurers, who have already sold themselves repeatedly to imperialism. We are firmly convinced that the peoples of Armenia will rally around our party at the very first opportunity, under the slogan of insurrection against imperialist oppression.

Hailing the international congress of Communist parties, the Armenian Communist Party, in the name of the Armenian peoples, considers it its duty to declare before the whole world:

"The Republic of Armenia" is an unprecedented mockery of the Armenian worker-peasant masses.

"Independent Armenia," as defined by the Armenian bourgeoisie and priests, is a shameless mockery of the worker and peasant masses of Armenia.

The government of Armenia is the government of the Armenian robbers, extortionists, and butchers, who have found employment with Anglo-American imperialism.

The Armenian Communist Party proclaims its resolute protest against any imperialist aggression and intervention into the destiny of the long-suffering peoples of Armenia. The party is conducting a resolute struggle against Anglo-American violence towards the peoples of Armenia.

We state categorically that the Armenian delegations that haunt the corridors of the Entente countries do not express the aspirations of the laboring masses of Armenia and carry no mandate from them.

The "Armenian Socialists" who participated in the Bern conference of the Yellow International do not express the opinions of the toiling masses of Armenia. They belong to the ranks of those turncoats and traitors whose hands are steeped in the blood of the workers and peasants. The Armenian Socialists who were seated in Bern are the hirelings of Anglo-American imperialism.

The Armenian Communist Party, the sole spokesperson for the interests of the toiling masses of the Armenian peoples, scorns the Armenian "Socialists" from the Yellow International, hails the congress of the international communist proletariat, and proclaims: Down with imperialism! Long live civil war! Long live the Third, Communist International!

Delegate and member of the
Central Committee of the
Armenian Communist Party,
G. Haikuni[18]

Report on Austria

by Karl Petin

The first congress of the Communist Party of German Austria took place February 9 in Vienna. Representatives assembled from all parts of the country, as well as from the Czechoslovak and Hungarian Communist parties.[19]

From the reports given there it was clear that the party in Vienna is supported by district workers' groups and also by a section of the Viennese garrison (the People's

Militia), which has formed a council of soldiers' deputies.[20] The strongest of the organizations in the provinces is in Styria, where the Social Democratic Party has tried from the beginning to stifle the Communist movement by suspending the right to assembly. We now have a whole organizational network there. In Salzburg the party has had strong support among the poor people of the mountains.

A food crisis in Upper Austria at the end of January caused big disturbances—for three days all commercial establishments and restaurants were closed. In Linz the council of workers' and soldiers' deputies is presently under the influence of Communists, and tactical considerations alone prevent the council from taking power. In the industrial region of Ternitz in the suburbs of Vienna, the broad masses of workers held significant leadership during the January 1918 general strike, and the official party tried in vain to win them over to its side.

Previously the peasantry in German Austria, influenced by the clergy, was nationalist in outlook, and completely supported the reactionary parties. However, a revolutionary movement is beginning among farm laborers and poor peasants. German prisoners of war returning from Russia are the foremost carriers of revolutionary ideas and are spreading the notion among the poor that large-scale landed property should be abolished.[21] In some provinces of German Austria, attempts were made to expropriate the landed estates, but these were quickly put down by the government.

The Social Democratic Party has naturally aimed its hatred at the Communist movement. Our comrades were mercilessly thrown out of the factories, and the fear of being left without a job keeps many workers from joining our party.

The party publishes a newspaper in Vienna called *Die soziale Revolution* [Social revolution], which comes out three times a week. In addition, we produce the weekly publications *Der rote Soldat* [Red soldier], *Das revolutionäre Proletariat* [Revolutionary proletariat], *Die kommunistische Jugend* [Communist youth], and a popular theoretical newspaper *Kommunist* [Communist].

A Social Democratic commissioner heads up the police force. It victimizes our press as much as possible, confiscates our newspapers, prevents us from selling them on the street, and says openly that the right of free press does not exist for us.

Our party congress discussed the elections to the National Assembly and decided by majority vote not to participate in them. The congress also dealt with the founding of the Third International, a subject that has been discussed in the party press.

I can assure you that the Communists in German Austria are convinced of the necessity to create a Third International. Furthermore they anticipate its formation by the Moscow international conference.

Report on East Galicia

by Moshe Freylikh

In 1889 the workers' movement in Galicia, under the influence of the International Socialist Congress held that year, took on an organized character.[22] This led to the formation of a Social Democratic party, which embarked at once on a course of revolutionary propaganda. In the following year May Day began to be celebrated as an international workers' holiday in major centers of the Galician working class, and subsequently their economic and political movements had a socialist character. However, there were no major, deep-going actions in the decade following the founding of the Second International. The Brünn [Brno] congress, which adopted the well-known Austrian program for nationalities, led to the creation in Galicia of three national parties:[23] the PPSD (Polish Social Democratic Party), the USDP (Ukrainian Social Democratic Party), and the ZPSD (Jewish Social Democratic Party).[24]

The PSD was organized first. Headed by Ignacy Daszynski, Dr. Herman Diamand, and Dr. Herman Lieberman, it was by far the strongest party of the urban proletariat and it was to remain so until the fall of the Hapsburg monarchy. The USDP was next to organize, but it was to remain weak in comparison with the PPSD, its influence being most evenly divided between town and country. Beginning in 1906 a serious separatist movement arose among the Jewish workers who had joined the PPSD; a result, on the one hand, of anti-Semitism and, on the other, of a logically consistent attempt to duplicate the example of the other parties, which had been organized by nationality. In addition, the Austrian constitution did not consider the Jews to be an autonomous nation. And since the PPSD, pointing to this fact, refused to recognize the autonomy of the organized Jewish proletariat, many of its prominent figures left this party and gradually won over the bulk of the Jewish proletariat who had at first been frightened of a split in the party.[25] In this way, the ZPSD was constituted as an independent party and recognized as such by the Second International.

At the end of the last century the country's Socialist parties were functioning legally, advocating that workers undertake a revolutionary struggle for various socialist demands, for example, the right of universal suffrage, the eight-hour day, old-age pensions, and so forth.

The demand for universal suffrage was always to the fore, which—the party leaders insisted—would enable the proletariat to realize the minimum program by parliamentary means and thus lay the basis for putting the maximum program into practice.

In 1899 a fifth curia was added to the voting system,[26] allowing workers and peasants the chance to penetrate the Austrian parliament. Access to the Galician provincial assembly, however, was now even more tightly restricted. Daszynski was sent from Galicia in the elections to the Vienna parliament, where he joined a fraction made up of ten Austrian Social Democratic deputies.

In 1904 the first large-scale strikes occurred in Galicia. The bricklayers of Lvov [Lviv] and the workers of the Borislav [Boryslav] oil region played a leading role in them. Beginning in 1905 a powerful movement aimed at reforming the Austrian parliamentary election laws swept the whole country. In support of this movement the Social Democracy pulled out all possible stops and proclaimed a one-day general strike for November 25 of that year, which was a uniformly resounding success across all of Austria.[27] In Galicia, as in Austria as a whole, there were times when the workers' brave and courageous actions proved the masses capable of heroic deeds, when their leaders could convince them that they were joining battle for a genuinely revolutionary cause.

The first elections on the basis of equal, secret, direct, and universal suffrage took place in 1907. While they were a great success for the leaders, for the proletariat they were a bitter disappointment. Of the eighty-nine Social Democratic deputies elected to parliament, thanks to the staunch self-sacrifice of workers in Austria, there were six from Galicia—four from the PPSD and two from the USDP. Note that all six were from East Galicia, because in West

Galicia all the candidates of the PPSD, which was led by Daszynski, had lost. And this was in spite of the fact that West Galicia is in reality a Polish state and the nationalism of the local Social Democrats rivaled that of the other Polish parties. In East Galicia the following were elected: Lvov—Dr. Diamand and Hudec; Przemysl—Dr. Lieberman; Stry [Stri]—Moraczewski, all from the PPSD. In the rural regions: Drogobych [Drohobych]-Borislav-Turka—Vityk; Ternopol [Ternopil]-Zbarazh—Ostapchuk, both from the USDP. For the most part, the PPSD won in the cities because the Jewish proletariat decided in a spirit of socialist solidarity not to run their own candidates and cast all their votes for the PPSD. During the election campaign all candidates advocated the most relentless struggle against the government and the bourgeois parties. However, all this lasted only up to the moment they stepped over the threshold of parliament, whereupon their shameful compromises quickly earned them the nickname "his Royal-Imperial Majesty's Social Democrats."

The proletariat felt tremendous disappointment, and after the mass enthusiasm that prevailed during and even somewhat after the elections, they sobered up completely, finally lapsing into indifference. It's true that in the next elections in 1911 practically the very same persons won again, but these elections were not accompanied by the revolutionary upsurge evident in 1907. The good Social Democratic showing can best be explained by new features of the political situation at the time that led the petty-bourgeois masses to become camp followers of the Social Democrats, correctly recognizing them as defenders of their interests.

In general, the entire seven years of parliamentary activity preceding the World War passed without any kind of brilliance or success, and the largest by far of the fractions in the Austrian parliament, which called itself Social Democratic, hardly played a role in the historical development of the proletariat. Then thanks to their traitorous conduct during four and a half long years of war, the waters of shame and deception rose so high that the broad masses, alarmed by this flood, awakened to the true ideals of the proletariat. Moreover, the collapse of the imperialist bastions in Central Europe revealed the Social Democratic leaders who had fled into the chauvinist camp all the more clearly to the working masses as the traitors that they were.

On November 1, 1918, a new era began in former Austria-Hungary. Galicia, the largest of the territories of the Austrian crown, became an important factor. And there, as in all of Austria, the discord among the nationalities, following the collapse of the monarchy, led to war between the Polish gentry and the bourgeoisie on one side and the Ruthenian [West Ukrainian] nationalities on the other. The PPSD leaders took the side of the Polish imperialists while the USDP leaders backed the Ukrainians, and both, wielding the usual patriotic slogans, dispatched their mercenaries into a new slaughter.

Actually, the broad masses of workers, exhausted by four and a half years of war, had rejoiced when it was over and abandoned their guns. Unfortunately no revolutionary party was present that could explain to the masses the catastrophic results that would threaten them after such an action and could prevent the outcome that the bourgeoisie of both camps would end up armed—and the proletariat disarmed. Only for that reason was it possible to split the country into two hostile camps, with mercenary regimes lording over both. The Ruthenian nationalist parties in East Galicia, aided by regular soldiers and a nondescript volunteer rabble from the collapsed Austrian army, succeeded in organizing a certain fighting force and seizing the country. But in the very first week of their rule they had to concede the two most important cities in the country to the Poles—Lvov and Przemysl.[28] The most visible leaders of Ruthenian national politics, who were stranded in these cities, were arrested by the Poles. For their part, the Ukrainian authorities resorted to similar measures in relation to Polish political figures residing in East Galicia.

Cut off from the main metropolitan centers and deprived of an administrative apparatus of any kind, the new masters of [East] Galicia wandered like nomads across their country, settling first in Ternopol, then in Stanislav [Ivano-Frankovsk], where they eked out a miserable existence. The government, called the National Secretariat, and the parliamentary body, the National Rada, proved to be completely incompetent legislators. The new state, accustomed to the old Austrian dictates and decrees, was led into a situation where each town had its own laws, or more precisely, its own lawlessness. Its sole accomplishment was the introduction of an intensified state of siege that banned travel without a permit and imposed a seven o'clock curfew. Besides the ordinary and at times quite insurmountable difficulties in the distribution of travel permits, the greatest abuses occurred and the worst bribery flourished under the guise of taking donations for the benefit of the Red Cross. But even the owner of a travel permit is in no way guaranteed personal immunity: often at the very next station a guard simply declares a document, even though obtained through all the formalities, to be invalid, so that he can get another bribe. The evils of this system are compounded by the fact that corruption comes from above, from the government leaders who intentionally create conditions that encourage it.

It is impossible to enumerate the facts that illustrate the political immorality of the current rulers, but I must mention one incident, since it touches on the main basis of the economy of our country—the Drogobych-Borislav oil fields. A gang of crooks from the local Rada set up a special oil commissariat with Vityk, the social patriot, in charge. He usurped the exclusive right to command the huge supply of crude oil, refined kerosene, paraffin, and candles, and gave away all the country's riches to speculators exclusively in return for bribes. For example, they sold a load of kerosene worth 40,000 crowns in Drogobych for no less than a half million in Ternopol. Moreover, all this takes place openly, in broad daylight, right in front of the government! This pitiful state of things had some positive, as well as negative, consequences for the proletariat. The proletariat became convinced that it could no longer remain indifferent to political matters and began to stir once more.

Party activity picked up everywhere. Although the activists in the Social Democracy were new, everyone felt the necessity for a fundamental revision of the program, and especially of party policy. Proceeding from the former divisions, parties began to form anew according to nationality. Powerful as it was before, the PPSD was persecuted by the Ruthenian authorities and could not grow to its former size, especially since the economically better-off layer of the working class sympathized with the bourgeois government in Poland. The once weak USDP was almost completely dissolved in the prevailing nationalism, and only the ZPSD developed energetic, organized activity that reached the whole country.

Soviets of workers' deputies were formed and they achieved a certain influence over the government. Steps were taken to unite the two sister parties. In December of last year this met with some success, since we were able to establish a center and start publishing a weekly newspaper, "Red Flag." At the same time the party executive committee held an election for a narrower committee that was to be entrusted with all the necessary underground work. This small, five-person committee delegated a comrade to Budapest who held discussions in early January with representatives of the Central Committee there. He set up the necessary connections and journeyed to Russia to establish relations with the leaders of the Soviet government. Upon this delegate's return from Budapest, a party conference was convened for January 18 and 19. Many delegates from almost every area of the country attended. This two-day meeting was almost exclusively concerned with questions of a programmatic and tactical nature.

A standing committee was chosen to carry out a thorough discussion and work out specific resolutions. Two currents in sharp, mutual conflict emerged in this commission. One stood for an outright proletarian dictatorship in the form of workers' and peasants' soviets, and therefore for a total rejection of parliamentarism; the other took the side of bourgeois parliamentarism, which in the opinion of this current's leaders would be an effective means for the workers to reach the same ends, only at a more measured tempo. Of course, no agreement could be made with such differences, and each group submitted its own separate resolution. But since the right wing held the majority in the commission, we, remaining in the minority, submitted our resolution to the plenum of the committee, where we held the majority, to the utter consternation of our opponents.

The Communist faction, by the way, had put forward a motion to declare the meeting closed, since it was concerned with questions of party policy. This action sparked absurd rumors and led to the dispatch of government troops to the city. The troops surrounded the house where our group was meeting, and the officers, soldiers, and policemen burst into the meeting hall just as the resolutions were being put to a vote. Taking advantage of the ensuing confusion, the Menshevik who was chairing called for a second vote. Since some delegates obviously did not know which resolution was being voted upon first, the final tally gave the moderate resolution a two-vote majority. But even that resolution says that the workers' and peasants' soviets are to be regarded as but the embryos for seizing all power in the country in the future.[29]

The conference elected a Central Committee, which includes this reporter, and the committee endorsed underground work.

In general, we are still going through an organizational period aimed at forming a single Communist party divided into three national sections—Polish, Ukrainian, and Jewish.[30] These three sections should be united by common party leadership committees and by a common executive committee embracing the whole country. In addition, the latter committee has set the task of integrating the existing soviets of worker-deputies now based on nationality and of scheduling new general elections for them as soon as possible. On assignment from this committee, this reporter traveled around the country and noted lively activity for communism under way everywhere.

The old Social Democratic leaders are no longer respected. Everywhere people long to drive out the barbarians arms in hand and proclaim a Soviet Republic of East Galicia, occupying the area from the San River to the Zbruch River. The political structure and ethnographic composition of the country make unity with Poland impossible. And it is exactly the same with the Ruthenians, an almost exclusively rural population, who have no right to claim a ruling position over an urban population consisting of Jews and Poles. A Soviet government would drive such nationalistic elements from the face of the earth.[31]

In closing, I would like to announce on behalf of the Communist Party of East Galicia our entry into the Third International. We unconditionally approve of and consider ourselves bound by all decisions and resolutions made at the March 2–6, 1919, Moscow congress. We are hopeful that we will be a useful member of the new proletarian family. It is not necessary to make a separate announcement about our leaving the Second International since we have already expressed our contempt for the gravediggers of the proletariat at the Bern conference. As regards our party's representation on the executive committee, I would like to request that this reporter be considered the temporary representative, until such time as our Central Committee is in the position to appoint a permanent one.

TASKS OF THE PROLETARIAN REVOLUTION IN FINLAND

The January 1919 Petrograd conference of the Finnish Communist Party, which included representatives from Finland, adopted the following theses on the immediate tasks of the socialist revolution in Finland:[32]

1. In order to end the exploitation of one person by another, the power of the exploiting class must be smashed.

Therefore, the fighting strength of the bourgeoisie must be obliterated, and the property-owning class must be disarmed.

A Red Army of the proletariat must be organized that will guarantee victory in the revolutionary struggle to the working class and protect the gains of the revolution so that the exploiters cannot seize power again.

2. The proletariat must take into its own hands the state power as a whole.

The whole apparatus of bourgeois class power must be destroyed and replaced by an organization of full proletarian rule. The bourgeois bureaucracy must give way to the self-government of the proletariat; the bourgeois parliament and bourgeois governmental bodies must give way to governmental organs chosen by the proletarian masses; the proletariat must directly take part in administrative activity and in creating a socialist system. Instead of a bourgeois democracy that guarantees freedom to the proletariat's oppressors, a free, organized democracy of the proletariat must be established.

This organization of proletarian power must be the socialist Soviet republic of all the workers, Red Army soldiers, and the toiling, oppressed population of the countryside.

3. Through its organization of power, the proletariat must force the class exploiters to submit absolutely to revolutionary discipline and to comply with the obligation of all to work. The private property of the rich must be immediately expropriated, and private ownership over the means of production must be brought to an end.

4. The capitalist industrial enterprise and other manufacturing establishments, which have enabled the capitalists to appropriate without working the fruits of the proletariat's labor, must be transformed into manufacturing institutions of the socialist labor commune.

The management of each large productive enterprise must be put in the hands of work associations of all workers or of the labor commune, with the participation of representatives of the Soviet government's central organs. This kind of management must be organized on the principles of centralization and economic planning.

5. In no way will we allow the transfer of land from the toilers who have worked it into the hands of speculators and exploiters, however that transfer might take place: whether in the guise of a sale, mortgage, or any other transaction. Land belonging to idle loafers who do not work it themselves and get rich through the labor of others must be taken away from these owners, declared the common property of the entire people, and handed over to the toilers who actually work it.

Agricultural workers must join together in work associations that take on the economic direction of the large estates. For that kind of economy, the Soviet government must take the initiative in organizing a central management body to take care of ensuring them the necessary agricultural machines and experienced leaders.

6. In order to smash the rule of capital definitively, the Soviet government must immediately take all banks into its hands.

7. Commercial institutions including their stocks must be expropriated, and the distribution of products must be organized by society itself.

8. Buildings and apartments of rich citizens, with all their furniture, must be expropriated without delay to meet the needs of the working population.

9. The workers' soviets must be both the legislative and the executive organs of the revolution. They must be elected so that their composition really answers the will of the toiling layers of the population. The right to vote must belong to the workers, the soldiers of the Red Army, and the village proletariat; the exploiters and the enemies of the working class must be deprived of the right to vote.

10. A general congress of all the workers' soviets in the country, convening as often as the need arises, is the su-

preme power in all the country's affairs. It chooses the executive committee of the Soviet republic, which has the right to appoint and dismiss the people's commissars.

11. Voters must have the right to recall at any time representatives elected by them who for some reason have lost their trust.

12. The Finnish Socialist Soviet Republic must unite with proletarian Soviet republics of other countries. All Soviet republics must form one common worldwide union.

REPORT OF THE FRENCH COMMUNIST GROUP

The French Communist Group salutes the revolutionary Russian people and expresses the grateful admiration of the conscious elements of the French working class for their organized and heroic efforts and labors that resulted in the creation of the socialist state.[33]

The group salutes in particular the workers' and peasants' Red Army, which is conducting the struggle forced upon it by the rapacious imperialism of the Entente governments and victoriously resisting it.

The group declares its solidarity with the vanguard of the socialist revolution, that is, with the Bolshevik Communist Party, and agrees with the content of paragraphs 1 to 19 of its program, published on February 25, 26, and 27, 1919.[34]

With regard to the concrete political, economic, and social goals of this program, the group agrees with them to the extent that they apply to the prevailing revolutionary situation in France.

With regard to seizing power, the group intends to convince the French people of the urgent necessity of replacing the current bourgeois-democratic form of government with the Soviet form.

In its propaganda, the group emphasizes that bourgeois democracy is totally unable to solve the urgent problems of the day and thereby exposes the inevitable bankruptcy of bourgeois democracy in France, as in other countries.

The following facts characterize this bankruptcy in the real political world:

Despite formal equality based on universal suffrage, the bourgeoisie preserves all the class privileges that ensure its rule. In reality, it possesses all the means that go into making up its political power: the instruments of production, accumulated capital, experience at wielding power, and the social position it has already attained. It also has all the means that enable it to keep working people hypnotized, the armed forces that repress the people, the schools and the press to lull them to sleep. Thus, the ballot is of value only to the bourgeois voter. For the proletariat, it is nothing but a deception. During the last fifty years, the right to vote in France has been merely lies and trickery, corruption, open and secret.

Thus, in both politics and economics the bourgeoisie remains the absolute master.

This sham equality has given the working and peasant classes only illusory benefits.

But bourgeois democracy, which rests on the principle of freedom and equality for all citizens, is destroying itself, since it actually counts on the subjugation and obedience of the overwhelming majority of the people. It is a hypocritical lie. In reality, it cannot be otherwise in a class society, for the theoretical freedom and equality between those who hold the power and the weak exist only to harm the weak and benefit the rulers.

Moreover, the development of capitalist domination leads ever increasingly to ensuring that one class, representing a minority, rules over the majority of the toiling people, that the means of production are concentrated and centralized, and in this manner an industrial and financial oligarchy becomes dominant.

The deceived working class wrongly thinks that with the right to vote it holds a share in the national sovereignty. The bourgeoisie also considers itself sovereign, whereas the country's entire economic and political life rests solely in the hands of a few kings of high finance and heavy industry. Their secret plans and selfish ambitions drag the country into colonial adventures. They almost set off a European war over Morocco,[35] and their competition with their German rivals contributed to the 1914 war.

They did everything to prolong the conflict and called the Paris conference in order to conclude a peace corresponding to their own interests, scorning the will of the people.

By this dual process, so-called bourgeois democracy is transformed through its unavoidable degeneration into a regime in which real power inevitably falls into the hands of the oligarchy. French bourgeois democracy, which previously was the hidden dictatorship of a class, is now a dictatorship by a group of individuals.

If the goal of the Socialist Party is to replace class privileges with true political and social equality, it must first abandon the idol of universal suffrage, forcibly annihilate the current rulers' domination, and turn power over exclusively to the proletariat.

The bourgeois parliamentary system in France has supplied proof through its self-destruction that the time for that revolution has come.

The 1914 war showed that bourgeois democracy, dominated by the capitalist oligarchy, must necessarily renounce its own principles. The bourgeoisie, which thought that it held power, did not want this war, just like the proletariat. However, the endless maneuvers of this financial and industrial oligarchy led imperceptibly to war. And the French people, having declared themselves the defenders of law and freedom, were unexpectedly implicated in imperialism's prolonging this worldwide carnage, which was undertaken and provoked solely by the interests of large manufacturers who demanded the Saar and Briey valleys and the total annihilation of the German competitors.[36]

The French people, compelled in this way by the direct consequences of the bourgeois dictatorship to continue the absurd struggle against the German people, would never have found a way out of that conflict without the German revolution.

The thought of being the first to give way frightened both nations. Each feared being the victim of the other's nationalist passions; both were embittered and misused by the selfish aims of their leaders. Only the German revolution brought peace. "French democracy," however, whose mechanism is enslaved by imperialist capital, is compelled by the very logic of its doctrine to sow the seeds of a new conflict. It annexes Alsace-Lorraine without first consulting the population and thus renounces its first ideal. It demands the German population of the left bank of the Rhine. It goes so far as to incite hatred in the very heart of Germany by violent occupations. It seeks territories in Asia.

It realizes the future danger of this hatred, but finds only an absurd remedy: to crush its rival by demanding even greater reparations, hoping thereby to destroy German industry forever. Thus, not only is it laying the basis for a new war of revenge directed against itself, but it also generates conflicts with its allies of yesterday, which have now become its competitors.

Inevitably degenerate, bourgeois democracy shows itself to be a mortal enemy of the Russian revolution. As such, it supports and concocts counterrevolutionary conspiracies and hurls against Soviet power all the forces of the Entente, without, however, the "democratic" form of the Entente institutions giving the working class and peasantry a chance to act effectively against this imperialist and reactionary policy.

And this could not be otherwise. The French parliamentary constitution, in granting deputies total power for the duration of their term, uncontrollable and unimpeachable, gives the "sovereign people" no true sovereignty.

The war broke out and was prolonged for fifty months. An armistice was concluded and the diplomats are conducting peace negotiations without giving the masses of people any opportunity whatsoever to express, by universal suffrage, their views on the horrible World War and collapse that exacted nearly two million victims and devastated the country.

These bogus representatives possess an independence from the exercise of universal suffrage that permitted a domination to be forcibly prolonged, a domination that is destined by the system's own logic to be an illusion. In fact, it is tied to adopting in parliament measures dictated by the heads of the industrial trusts who answer to no one.

On the economic and social levels, the war led to the concentration of capitalist industry, condemning to death a significant portion of small industry on the one hand and, on the other, rapidly increasing the exploitation of the working class. The combination of exploitation of the working class and of the state as buyer produced unprecedented profits for the arms suppliers.

Rights that the proletariat had won through hard struggle over fifty years were taken away from it because of the increasing influence of the ruling class, promoted by the government.

Freedom of speech, of assembly, and of the press were abolished, as were most of the laws safeguarding labor and regulating sanitary conditions in the workplace, the workday, and working conditions for women and children. Militarization of the factories deepened the subjugation of the working class and led to abolition of the right to strike in defense industries—a result of state control of various branches of production throughout industry.

In short, the bankruptcy of bourgeois democracy is upon us—bankruptcy on the international level, bankruptcy on the political level, and bankruptcy on the social level.

Through the development of its own internal logic, democratic institutions have consolidated the dictatorship of a bourgeois oligarchy, thereby embittering class rivalries and preparing the workers' uprising.

French bourgeois democracy—that is, the financial and industrial oligarchy who unleashed the war and exhausted the country financially and economically—is now embarking upon imperialist conquests to make up for its losses, thereby heading toward a sharp conflict of interests with its former allies. It thought up the League of Nations with these allies, who were also victims of its plans. This league, however, will more be an instrument of a few privileged nations with which to fight against other nations and will have nothing to do with harmony and understanding. This crowning of the pseudodemocratic society, which in the future is supposed to eliminate the consequences of internal failures and problems, only reveals more clearly its decay.

The rival oligarchies, who would have liked to have come to an agreement in Paris to avert the inevitable but deadly competition, are, against their own wishes, preparing new wars, pregnant with yet more wars. Moreover, in their search for exploitable markets, they are dividing among themselves control of the small nations, which they deceitfully claim to wish to liberate. Finally, they are compelled, with help from the mercenaries of the league they control, to extend in all countries the subjugation of the toiling classes, to which they owe their existence.

The threefold nature of the path chosen by the heads of the bourgeois democracies to prevent the catastrophe threatening them leads inevitably to a world war among the rival dominant nations and to the national uprising of the exploited small nations and the subjugated proletariat.

This triple, final, and inevitable failure of the last measures to save the bourgeois democracies is the ultimate stage still separating them from the world social revolution.

France, like all other countries, is moving relentlessly into the era of the proletarian dictatorship, together with this League of Nations, which represents the failure of all of bourgeois democracy's attempts to prolong its existence. Only the dictatorship of the proletariat, free of all obstacles and prejudices, can accomplish the new tasks.

The task of the French Communist Group is to prepare the French working class to become conscious of this process and to take power.

(Adopted unanimously by the French Communist Group at its meeting of March 1, 1919.)

HUNGARIAN COMMUNIST PARTY STATEMENT

MOSCOW, APRIL 10, 1919

The Communist Party of Hungary named us as delegates to the first congress of the Third International.[37] We regret that communication difficulties and the fighting between detachments of the Ukrainian Soviet Republic and the hordes of the Ukrainian "National Republic" meant that we could not arrive in time for the congress sessions. We would have been happy and greatly honored to have been able to take part in this historic world event—the founding of the Third International.

On behalf of the Hungarian Communist Party, we approve all the statements and positions of Comrade Rudnyánszky who replaced us in representing our party at the congress.

L. Rudash
G. Kohn

Report for the Communist Organizations of the Peoples of the East

by Gaziz Yalymov

I speak on behalf of the Muslim Communist organizations, renamed a few days ago the Central Bureau of the Communist Organizations of the Peoples of the East.[38] This organization unites Communist workers of the non-Russian nationalities of Turkestan, Bashkiria, the Volga Tatars, Kirghizia, the Caucasian Mountain Peoples, and Communist groups of emigrés from Turkey, Persia [Iran], Azerbaijan, Bukhara, and Georgia. To reflect this national diversity, the central bureau organized sections: Tatar, Bashkir, Kirghiz, Mountain Peoples, Turkestan, Azerbaijan, and others.

If you do not count the Azerbaijanis, Georgians, Persians, Turks, and Bukharians, there are no less than 30 million non-Russians in the remaining regions of the central bureau's territory. Today the central bureau unites at least 10,000 organized Muslim workers and peasants in these regions. I will not even mention the tremendous moral influence of the central bureau among the Muslim working masses nor the sympathy for communism of Muslims in the Red Army, who number more than 50,000 men, fighting side by side with the Russian Red Army men on the eastern and southern fronts against Krasnov, Denikin, Kolchak, and Dutov. The numbers of workers organized by the central bureau is comparatively small because, first, the peoples of the East were only recently freed from servitude and are culturally backward. Second, the territory of these peoples—from the Caucasus to Kazan and from Ufa to Tashkent—is a theater of military operations, liberated arms in hand from the imperialist predators and their White Guard agents. All this makes systematic socialist work much more difficult.

I will not discuss the atrocities of the Georgian White Guards and their allies, the Georgian Mensheviks led by Tsereteli, who twice fired on workers' meetings in Tiflis in January 1918, devastated the Georgian Communist organization, and clapped its leaders in jail. What the traitors, the Scheidemanns and Eberts, have done in Germany, the Menshevik party has been doing for some time in Georgia. I also leave aside the atrocities of the Turkestan Right Socialist Revolutionaries and Mensheviks, who, serving as butchers for British imperialism, shot our experienced comrades, Dzhaparidze, Shaumyan, Korganov, and Petrov.[39] I will not discuss the outrages by the Right Socialist Revolutionary and Menshevik parties and by the members of the Constituent Assembly: the shooting of workers and peasants by the hundreds; our Muslim comrades whose eyes were gouged out. All this is fact, known to all, repeatedly made public in print.

Despite these incredible conditions, the central bureau has not lost heart and has continued its socialist work hand in hand with the Russian Communist Party. To describe the central bureau's work, I must mention that the leading forces of the eastern Communists, who united in the central bureau last December, succeeded in publishing in the ten months from January to November 1918 more than four million copies of newspapers, pamphlets, and leaflets in Tatar, Turkish, and Kirghiz. From last December, when these forces came together in the central bureau, until this January—that is, in *two* months—the central bureau succeeded in publishing, in Moscow alone, more than two million copies of newspapers, pamphlets, and leaflets in Arabic, Turkish, Persian, Tatar, Azerbaijani, Tadzhik, Uzbek, Kirghiz, and Kalmuk. At present the central bureau and its local organizations publish fifteen newspapers as well as the central organ *Eshche* [*Worker*] (in Tatar) and *Yeni Dünya* [*New world*] (in Turkish).

I do not doubt that given the Russian Communist Party's moral and ideological support for the central bureau, the cause of communism will flourish in the East, and the oppressed peoples of the East will rally around Soviet Russia in their struggle against imperialism. I will not elaborate on how important the awakening of the East is for the expanding workers' revolution in the West. The East represents the underbelly of world imperialism, its source of supply. If the East arises and stretches out a hand to the socialist West, imperialism will be surrounded, and then the hour of triumph for world socialism will have sounded. That is precisely why the central bureau poses as its basic task the awakening of the peoples of the East.

That is why I say: Long live the revolutionary union of the oppressed peoples of the East with the socialist workers of Russia and Europe!

Report on Poland

by Józef Unszlicht

MOSCOW, MARCH 4, 1919

The outbreak of the World War could not cause any confusion, hesitations, or deviations within the ranks of the SDKPiL [Social Democracy of the Kingdom of Poland and Lithuania], our old party, which had been proved through many years of struggle and to which all nationalism and opportunism was alien.[40] Our party was the only one in Poland that, right from the beginning of the war, raised the slogan: Down with the imperialist war, long live the civil war. Despite the extremely difficult conditions of illegal work under the regimes of both Nicholas and Wilhelm,[41] the party took this slogan into the streets of the industrial cities, where the masses of working people adopted it. But the revolution in Poland was not yet able to break out. The flower of the Polish proletariat had been forcibly transported to Germany for compulsory labor; masses of people were also removed to Germany. The industrial centers that had been blooming were stifled as well. Only here and there were a few tens of thousands of workers left, out of 100,000. In these difficult and arduous political and economic conditions, we carried out ongoing work.

News of the revolution in Russia, the Russia with which we had always marched forward together, brought a colossal rise in revolutionary aspirations. Demonstration followed demonstration. The proletariat responded to each provocation by the Beseler government by pouring into the streets.[42] Economic strikes were transformed into political battles. Illegal citywide councils of workers' delegates were created. Red Guards were organized. Our party carried out energetic agitation toward this end and called on the proletariat to take power in their own hands. That had already been accomplished in the Dabrowa basin.[43]

Neither the social patriots nor the petty-bourgeois nationalist National Workers Union were in any position to fight the creation of the workers' councils, the authority and popularity of which were increasing daily, not only among the urban but also the rural proletariat. So they started up their own councils. In Warsaw, three councils existed for a time.[44] But under the pressure of the working masses new elections took place, involving all the workers. And so we now have general councils in Warsaw and Lodz, for example. We do not yet have a majority in all the councils, because, as we have already indicated, the number of factory workers is small. But our fraction's presentation of a clearly outlined and resolute program of struggle is winning for us an ever growing number of supporters among undecided and wavering elements in these councils.

By the beginning of November of last year, councils existed in all the big cities, such as Warsaw, Lodz, Dabrowa, Radom, Czestochowa, and Lublin, and even in smaller ones, Plock, Zyrardów, and others.

With the news of the revolution in Germany, the occupation collapsed. For the first time Polish workers took to the streets behind our party's banner. Huge demonstrations took place. Sent out against them, the German army refused to disperse the revolutionary workers.

Meanwhile, the Polish bourgeoisie and petty-bourgeoisie launched a wave of brutal chauvinist pogroms. The bourgeoisie, unable to foresee what course the revolution in Germany would follow, was in no rush to take power in its own hands.

Thanks to this, the Polish Socialist Party–Revolutionary Faction [PSP-RF] found itself at the helm of power, as the heir of Beseler's Regency Council.[45] From the very beginning, its rule was marked by pogromistic orgies by nationalistic elements who went unpunished. On November 10 bands of hooligans destroyed the press and editorial offices of the Communist newspaper *Naszy Trybune* [Our tribune]. At the same time, police arrested members of our party, beat them, and tortured them with the most barbaric methods.

The government of Józef Pilsudski has not only let all these crimes go unpunished but has overlooked attacks on demonstrating workers who support him. Drawn mainly from the intelligentsia, the legions shoot down unarmed workers without mercy.

The prisons are filled with Communists, and our comrades returning to Poland from Russia are being treacherously shot at the border. That happened to a Red Cross mission headed by Comrade Wesolowski, a founder of our party, as well as to Comrade Fabierkiewicz and others.

The two-month period (from mid-November to mid-January this year) of the social-patriotic government was a period of feverish organization by the bourgeoisie, nurtured and supported by the social traitors.

The Pilsudski government did not actually hold power. That rested in the hands of the different military commanders, who acted as they chose and totally ignored the central government.

The government of Pilsudski and Wasilewski was certainly aware that its days were numbered. The only solution would have been to appeal to the working masses for support. But to appeal to the working masses to come out against the bourgeoisie would have brought not only victory over the bourgeoisie, but also the downfall of the petty-bourgeois government and the passing of power into the hands of the proletariat. The experience of Russia, of Kerensky's fate, was too well known to the social patriots.[46]

They preferred to disappear from the face of political life, preserving their alliance with the bourgeoisie, rather than allow the proletariat itself to come to power.

And so the government of the Polish social traitors capitulated, handing its authority over to the National Democracy, this party of national shame, of what may well be the world's most disgraceful bourgeoisie, which yesterday was always a prop of the tsarist government and today, of international capital.

New outrages against the Polish proletariat have now begun. The editorial board of our newspaper was crushed and the most effective comrades were arrested. While the government of Pilsudski and Wasilewski tolerated pogroms against the Jews, such pogroms are now being initiated and carried out officially by the bourgeois government itself. The pogromistic orgies are taking ever more savage and unbridled forms.

Despite these outrages, our efforts have brought fruitful results. Of necessity, the central focus of our work has moved to the countryside. Communist ideas are rapidly finding a warm hearing among the poor peasantry. Our party organizations are proliferating. A countrywide wave of strikes by agricultural workers has practically everywhere acquired a class-struggle character, in which the strikers are aiming for improved economic conditions or for the seizure of the estates. This movement is free of disorderly factors, such as the burning of property, pillaging of stocks, and the like. Recently this movement has spread to the southern part of the country, bordering on the Ukraine. Our peasant newspaper, *Gromada* [The village], is being snatched up. Newspapers are coming out in Warsaw, Lodz,

Dabrowa, and Lublin. For the Jewish workers there is *Rote Fahne* [Red flag].[47] Our strongest organization is in the largest industrial center, in the Dabrowa Basin, where more that 50,000 workers were employed before the big industrial stagnation at the end of the [German] occupation.

The first Council of Workers' Delegates was created there, and it took power immediately after the occupation. In late December, the social-patriotic government then still in power participated in the crushing of this council. Artillery was used to disarm the Red Guards. But the disarming led to the occupation of buildings previously held by the Red Guards. And even today it cannot be said that the authority of the Dabrowa Basin council has been totally eliminated.

The raids to disarm the Red Guards will be fruitless. Our ranks are growing. The Communist fraction is becoming ever stronger within the councils of delegates. The councils in Dabrowa and Lodz are publishing their own newspapers. Agitation in the army is embracing ever broader circles. The bourgeois press is crying out in alarm. The peasant is raising deeply felt demands and taking over the estates of his age-old oppressors. The soldier who is with the people is adopting the ideas of communism. Multitudes of workers are returning from Germany. They are marching back to Poland with banners proclaiming the dictatorship of the proletariat. Feelings of fraternity with Soviet Russia are growing. Last year, our party adopted a resolution calling for the closest ties between the Polish proletariat and Soviet Russia.

Changing our party's name was not as urgent a matter for us as in Russia, since we were the only Social Democratic party. The entire leadership of the PSP-Left, which had previously gone with the Mensheviks, came over to our position, having learned from the experience of the Russian revolution's development and having been hardened by the pressure of the workers. It accepted not only our program but also communist tactics. There was no reason for the existence of two similar parties. In December last year the SDKPiL merged with the PSP-Left to form the Communist Workers Party of Poland, publishing *Sztandar Socjalizmu* [Socialist banner] as its central organ.

The growing revolutionary movement, with the ever stronger involvement of the proletariat in the ranks of a single Communist party, is engendering greater fears among both the social patriots and the bourgeoisie itself.

The working masses, coming under the influence of the Communists, are collaborating with them wherever they appear. For example, in a number of cities, not only workers of the PSP-Revolutionary Faction but also the "people's militia" organized by the social patriots are taking part, together with the Communists, in the disarming of the military. In Radom, during a battle between the workers and the army, the militia fought on the side of the workers.

The Revolutionary Faction, having withdrawn from the National Democracy government, continues to collaborate with it.

Not only the current government but also the PSP-Faction are calling on the people to come out against Soviet Russia, which threatens the Polish bourgeoisie. Their common wish and aim is a Poland from sea to sea. To the east their claims extend as far as Smolensk.

British, French, and American capital, giving its blessing to their designs, is encouraging the creation of a Polish army, lavishly supplying it with money, food, ammunition, and uniforms. That is because today, for international capital, which is suffering defeats on all fronts of the Russian revolution, the Polish front is the ultimate gamble, the last resort.

Believing in the support of the Russian proletariat, we Polish Communists state most emphatically that this front too will be broken by the Soviet Red Army. For our part, we will prepare ourselves for the final battle. Already Communist detachments are disarming the government's army in a whole number of localities in different parts of the country. The councils of workers' delegates and the peasant poor are seizing power in their hardy hands. The revolutionary wave is sweeping over the entire country. The Polish people will not be blind tools in the hands of an international gang of capitalist bandits.

When the armed detachments of the proletariat of Lithuania and Belorussia stand at the Polish border, that will be for us the signal for a general armed uprising to overthrow the government of the capitalist clique, to sweep away the domestic bourgeoisie, and to proclaim the dictatorship of the proletariat.

Unszlicht (Jurowski)

ADDRESS OF THE SERBIAN SOCIAL DEMOCRATIC PARTY TO THE BUREAU OF THE THIRD, COMMUNIST INTERNATIONAL

Dear comrades,

The Serbian Social Democratic Party was very glad to learn that the First Congress of the Communist International is meeting in February in Moscow.[48] We greatly regret that we learned of this too late to be able to send our delegates to the congress. However, our party is pleased to be able to send you cordial and sincere greetings and to wish you success in organizing the Communist International.

Comrades, you already know how our party conducted itself both during the Balkan War and during the World War.[49] We remained completely faithful to the doctrine of our great teachers Marx and Engels. We have always treated the betrayers of socialism with disgust and disdain. Even in the most critical hour our party did not for one moment forget its internationalist duty. Even when our bourgeoisie celebrated the victory over the Turks and the Bulgarians, even during the great defeat when our population and the army had to retreat over the high mountains of Albania,[50] even when our people suffered under the yoke of the barbarian occupation, we recognized that the only obligation we had to our bourgeoisie was to wage an irreconcilable war against it. In Serbia, "civil peace" never received citizenship papers. We recognized only one war, the war between labor and capital. *When the social patriots just recently invited us to send delegates to Bern, our party answered with a refusal, because we did not want to have anything to do with traitors to socialism.*

Nearly six years of war brought our ranks into tremendous disarray. Our best comrades perished in the trenches, doing forced labor, and in internment camps. Many died in prisoner of war camps. Many were victims of epidemics. Almost half of our party workers are missing. But regardless of these great sacrifices, the spirit of our ranks has not sunk one bit. Conscious that Europe has entered an epoch of social revolution, we have taken great steps, after a three-year break, to rebuild our party's activity.

Broad layers of the masses are rallying around our party. After long and painful experiments, they are convinced that our party alone is capable of defending the interests of the working masses and the "rural poor." This is the only explanation for our party's tremendous success in the last three months.

Incredibly high prices, the shortage of food and clothing, unscrupulous speculation, and the suspension of rail service all give rise to more and more dissatisfaction among the broad masses. The situation has not improved at all with our national unification. Our Yugoslavian bourgeoisie has proved incapable of completing the national revolution.

Among the resolutions adopted by the conference of Croatian and Slavonian Social Democratic parties, which took place January 25–26 in Zagreb, was the following: "The conference salutes Soviet Russia, the social revolution in Germany and Austria-Hungary, and the revolutionary movement in other countries."[51] This congress revealed how strong the Communist current is among the Yugoslav proletariat.

In eight weeks a Yugoslav Social Democratic congress will be convened in order to organize a single Yugoslav workers' party. There is no doubt that the Communist current will carry the day. *The Serbian Social Democratic Party and the Social Democratic Party of Bosnia-Herzegovina stand on a communist platform.* Workers of Croatia and Slavonia are confident, as are we, that *the path to socialism leads through the dictatorship of the proletariat* and that the form of this dictatorship is *Soviet power.*

Comrades, we are convinced that the First Congress of the Communist International will fashion an instrument of militant struggle that meets the common needs of world revolution.

Therefore we again convey our heartfelt and sincere fraternal greetings.

Long live the new Communist International!

The Serbian Social
Democratic Workers Party
D. Lapčević
F. Filipović

Report on Serbia

by Iliya Milkić

Comrades, in my report on the workers' movement in Serbia I will briefly explain the position of the Serbian proletariat.[52] In his report today on the Balkan situation and the positions of the Socialist parties there, Comrade Rakovsky noted with regret that during the war the Serbian Socialist Party abandoned its revolutionary internationalist position and went over to a nationalist platform. This impels me to take time at today's session so that you comrades attending this historic conference will not go away with an undeservedly unfavorable opinion of the Serbian proletariat. Furthermore, I feel compelled to make this explanation because for eighteen years, that is, since the establishment of our party, I have been active in the Serbian workers' movement and have held all the significant posts that a proletarian party can assign to its members.

It is not true that the Serbian Socialist Party gave up its previous revolutionary position. The opinions expressed by Comrades Kaclerović and Popović do not represent the views of either our party or our working class. It is enough to remind you of how these two comrades came to Stockholm.

In the fall of 1915 Serbia was overrun by Austria and Bulgaria. Not only members of the party but the members of the Central Committee were scattered across Europe, Asia, and Africa in countries under the control of neutral and belligerent governments. Our party as an organized entity ceased to exist. Since then, and until the party was restored and the comrades returned, no one could have a real mandate to speak in its name. The simple reason was that there was no authoritative body that could issue such a mandate.

Comrades Kaclerović and Popović were sent to Stockholm by two members of the Central Committee who were then located in Belgrade. However, it is important to point out that since then these two Central Committee members have declared their dissatisfaction and disagreement with the position taken by Comrades Kaclerović and Popović in Stockholm.

As proof that this is not merely my personal opinion, I am pleased to be able to quote a witness whom you may well trust more readily than me. Comrades Trotsky and Rakovsky give him a most favorable recommendation. That witness is Comrade Dragiša Lapčević.

Writing to me from Belgrade on April 22, 1917, he gives the following opinion about the International, our party, and the position of Comrades Kaclerović and Popović: "It gives me satisfaction that you confirm my long-standing opinion that these gentlemen (Socialists) in Europe are worse than the bourgeoisie."

In his note of November 5, 1917, Comrade Lapčević writes, "I am not going to any conference, simply because our party organization does not exist. We have no organization that could carry out a decision, determine a course of action, control the work of the delegates, and to which the latter could report on their activities."

In his letter of May 12, 1918, he writes, "It was a big mistake for Kaclerović and Popović to go to Stockholm. Since our party has not had the chance to express its own opinion, it would have been a lot better for the party as such and for its organization in the interior if they had not gone to Stockholm, expressed their opinion there, and taken on themselves such responsibilities."[53]

Finally on July 7, 1918, he writes, "I think I will not go to Stockholm for both a principled and a practical reason. The principled reason is that I do not wish to have dealings with parties that have lost their significance and their reason for existence as Socialist parties. I desire not to fight for peace but rather to wage an internationalist struggle against the war."

Further, "Kaclerović and Popović were delegated by Timotić and Janović. But the latter comrades have themselves demonstratively protested against the opinion laid out by the so-called delegates."

I could provide even more letters written not only by Comrade Lapčević but by other influential members of the Serbian workers' party. However I do not find this necessary. It will be enough to remind you of two recent developments that demonstrate that the Serbian Socialist party really did not betray its honorable revolutionary position:

1. The Serbian Socialist party has not only rejected entering into the formation of the new government of Yugoslavia, but it has criticized the Croatian Socialist Party, which delegated one of its members for the new parliament.[54] In this regard, our party has declared that a Socialist in a bourgeois ministry is no different than a capitalist minister and that the party can only denounce him and struggle against him.

2. Our party did not take part in the Bern conference, which is very significant.

Taking all these facts into consideration, I can assure you that the Serbian proletariat is neither opportunist nor nationalist and that it will be a truly revolutionary and internationalist movement, as it has been to this day. It will march together with the international revolutionary proletariat. Soon it will form its own soviets and socialist republic and in this way will join in the great communist international republic of soviets. On this basis I think I am justified in stating here that the Serbian proletariat adheres with enthusiasm to the proletarian Third International.

Report on Sweden

by Otto Grimlund

The Swedish party of Left Socialists arose almost two years ago with the active assistance of all the organizations of young workers.[55] It was born in reaction to the ever-increasing deviation from the principles of socialism by the old Social Democratic Party led by Branting. I must add that the old party was totally terrorized by its Executive Committee and by many local party leaders, who used nothing less than repression against minority viewpoints and mercilessly suppressed all opposition, that is, any principled defense of party program or party policy.

The new party immediately joined the organization that during the war had united around it all the revolutionary nuclei and minority groups loyal to the International, that is, the Zimmerwald committee. The Swedish party has always belonged to its left wing.[56] The party has always adhered to a clearly expressed revolutionary viewpoint, conducting a consistent and relentless struggle in its newspapers and brochures against the social patriots in general and their Swedish counterparts in particular. Party agitation was directed mainly at stirring workers into class struggle, into revolutionary action. We should note that this agitation was not without results. The party's membership is growing each month, and it already includes close to two hundred branches. The entire young workers' organization backs its revolutionary platform. Many trade union organizations that up to now were social patriotic and reactionary in character are starting to come over to us.

At its beginning the party had only one newspaper, which came out three times a week. Today, however, the central party publication *Politiken* [Politics] is an eight-page daily and is widely distributed among workers. In the same period we founded no less than twelve newspapers in the provinces. Three of these are dailies, while the rest are published three times a week. The youth organization publishes its own widely distributed newspaper *Stormklockan* [Storm bell].

After the Russian October revolution, the propaganda and organizational activity of the party was put to a severe test. Recognizing fully from the start its duty as a class party, it proclaimed its solidarity with the Russian revolution. All our newspapers, in particular the central organ *Politiken,* wage a sharp battle every day against the false and slanderous campaign carried out consciously and systematically by counterrevolutionary publications in Stockholm and Helsingfors. The most servile paper fighting against the Russian revolution is Branting's *Social-Demokraten* [Social democrat]. Accordingly we considered it our duty to stress to workers the sharp difference between us and the social patriots. The practical work of our Russian comrades provided us with an illustration of our theoretical positions. Many examples also let us clearly demonstrate to workers how close the views of the Swedish social patriots were to those of the Russian Mensheviks and the German Scheidemanns. In spite of its youth and small size, our party did everything possible to impress the revolutionary point of view upon the masses and win their support. Likewise the tragic end of the Finnish revolution gave us a reason to develop strong agitation against the bourgeoisie and the social patriots.

Our party strove for the necessary revolutionary unity by linking up with left proletarian organizations such as the syndicalists and the antiparliamentary young socialists, and also the Workers' and Soldiers' Association, which aims to unite workers and soldiers in solidarity.[57]

Together with these groups the party has advanced slogans, issued proclamations, carried out agitational activities, and implemented some necessary preparatory organizational work.

However, there are some elements in the party whose views do not fully coincide with the party's line. These forces came over to us because there were no satisfying activities in the old party, but they do not hold firmly set points of view. We see this in statements by their leader Lindhagen opposing the dictatorship of the proletariat and revolutionary force. They, on the contrary, advocate "humanism" and "pacifism." Every member of the party understands that the coming party congress must put a definitive end to such bourgeois dreams.

The Executive Committee of our party was happy to receive the invitation to participate in the founding of the Third International, which represents the logical development of the Zimmerwald movement. It goes without saying that the party shares the main positions expressed in the invitation. Only with respect to some specific practical proposals did the members of the party Executive Committee take a "wait and see" position. I was instructed to vote for the founding of the Third International. We can join it officially only after the upcoming party congress.

LETTER OF RAOUL VERFEUIL

BERN, FEBRUARY 10, 1919

The Socialist internationalists of France resolved to participate in the Bern conference in order to condemn chauvinist fanaticism and defend the principles of class struggle adopted by the Amsterdam congress.[58,59] We also hoped that the conference would declare its solidarity with the Russian workers' revolution, which is now threatened by the imperialism of the Entente, just as it was earlier threatened by German imperialism.

The absence of the Russian, Italian, Swiss, Romanian, and Serbian comrades prevented us from attaining this goal. We were able only to avert an official condemnation of the Soviet government. Although this is a gain only in the negative sense, I nonetheless consider it to be very significant. If the comrades who did not wish or were not able to come to Bern attend the next international congress, we will achieve a genuine victory. I ask them to do so.

The International ought to adopt the tactic that we applied in our French section: the rule of the "majority" must be overthrown and its leadership of the International ended. In this way we will restore to it the viability and the revolutionary character that it lacks.

With all my heart I greet the Russian proletariat in its struggle for final liberation and express the warmest wishes for its victory, which will simultaneously be the victory of the working class of all countries.

R. Verfeuil

Above: Madrid workers demonstrate on May Day, 1919; below: anti-imperialist demonstration in Shanghai June 1919.

APPENDIX

The Bolsheviks evaluate the congress

[On the final day of the congress, March 6, the founding of the Communist International was announced in Moscow's papers. And a special meeting was held that evening in the Bolshoi Theater to celebrate the event. This chapter contains evaluations of the congress by several leading Bolsheviks, together with British journalist Arthur Ransome's description of the March 6 rally.]

Won and recorded

by V.I. Lenin

MARCH 5, 1919

The only firm gain in a revolution is that which has been won by the mass of the proletariat.[1] The only gain worth recording is that which has really been firmly won.

The founding of the Third, Communist International in Moscow on March 2, 1919, was a record of what has been gained not only by the Russian workers, but also by the German, Austrian, Hungarian, Finnish, Swiss—in a word, by the workers of the world.

Precisely because of this the founding of the Third, Communist International really is firm.

Only four months ago it was impossible to say that Soviet government, the soviet form of state, was an international achievement. There was something in it, and moreover something essential, which belonged to all capitalist countries as well as to Russia. But until it had been put to the test, it was still impossible to say what changes, of what depth and importance, the development of the world revolution would bring.

The German revolution has provided this test. An advanced capitalist country, coming after one of the most backward, has demonstrated to the whole world in a matter of a hundred-odd days not only the same principal revolutionary forces and principal direction of the revolution, but also the same principal form of the new, proletarian democracy—the soviets.

At the same time in Britain, a victor country, the richest in colonies, the longest-serving model of "social peace," or so it was reputed, the oldest capitalist country, we can see an extensive, irrepressible, intense, and powerful growth of soviets and of new soviet forms of mass proletarian struggle—the shop stewards committees.

In America, the strongest and youngest capitalist country, the workers have tremendous sympathy with the soviets.

The ice has been broken.

The soviets have triumphed throughout the world.

They have triumphed first and foremost because they have won the workers' sympathy. That is the main thing. No savagery by the imperialist bourgeoisie, no persecution or murder of Bolsheviks can deprive the people of this gain. The more the "democratic" bourgeoisie rages, the firmer the grip these gains will take on the hearts of the workers, on their moods, on their minds, and the more they will inspire their heroic struggle.

The ice has been broken.

That is why the work of the International Conference of Communists in Moscow, which founded the Third International, has proceeded so easily, so smoothly, with such calm and firm resolution.

We have recorded what has already been won. We have written down what has already taken a firm grip on the people's minds. Everyone knew, and what is more, everyone saw, felt, sensed, each from his own country's experience, that a new proletarian movement was in full swing. Everyone realized that this unprecedentedly strong and deep-going movement cannot be confined to any of the old frameworks or held in check by the past masters at petty politics, neither by the world-schooled, world-skilled Lloyd Georges and Wilsons of British and American "democratic" capitalism nor by the Hendersons, Renaudels, Brantings, and all the other case-hardened heroes of social chauvinism.

The new movement is heading toward the dictatorship of the proletariat, making headway despite all the vacillation, despite desperate reverses, despite the unparalleled and incredible "Russian" chaos (if one judges superficially as an onlooker). It is heading for *Soviet government* with the torrential might of millions and tens of millions of workers sweeping everything from their path.

This is what we have recorded. We have embodied in our resolutions, theses, reports, and speeches what has already been won.

Marxism, illuminated by the bright light of the new, universally rich experience of the revolutionary workers, has helped us to understand the inevitability of the present development. It will help the workers of the whole world, who are fighting to overthrow capitalist wage slavery, more clearly to appreciate the aims of their struggle, to march more firmly along the path already outlined, more confidently and firmly to achieve victory and to consolidate it.

The founding of the Third, Communist International heralds the international republic of soviets, the international victory of communism.

Great days

by Leon Trotsky

The tsars and the priests—ancient rulers of the Moscow Kremlin—never, we must assume, had a premonition that within its gray walls would one day gather the representatives of the most revolutionary section of modern humanity.[2] Yet this did occur. Today, in one of the halls of the Courts of Justice, where weary ghosts of criminal statutes from tsarist codices still wander, the delegates of the Third International now sit in session. Assuredly, the mole of history did not excavate poorly beneath the Kremlin walls.[3]

This material setting of the Communist congress is only an external expression and confirmation of the enormous changes that have occurred in the last ten or twelve years in the entire world situation.

In the era not only of the First International but also of the Second, tsarist Russia was the chief bulwark of world reaction. At the international Socialist congresses the Russian revolution was represented by emigrés upon whom the majority of the opportunist leaders of European socialism looked down with ironic condescension. These parliamentarist and trade unionist functionaries were filled with an unshakable conviction that it was the lot of semi-Asiatic Russia to suffer the evils of revolution, while Europe remained assured of a gradual, painless, tranquil evolution from capitalism to socialism.

But in August 1914 the accumulated contradictions of imperialism ripped to shreds the "peaceful" exterior of capitalism with its parliamentarism, with its legislated "freedoms," and its legalized prostitution, political and otherwise. From the heights of civilization humanity was cast into an abyss of horrifying barbarism and brutal savagery.

Despite the fact that Marxist theory had foreseen and foretold the bloody catastrophe, the social-reformist parties were caught unawares. Perspectives of peaceful development turned into smoke and rubble. The opportunist leaders could find themselves no other task than to summon the working masses to the defense of the bourgeois national state. On August 4, 1914, the Second International ignobly perished.

From that moment all genuine revolutionists, heirs to the spirit of Marx, set as their task the creation of a new International—the International of irreconcilable revolutionary struggle against capitalist society. The war unleashed by imperialism knocked the entire capitalist world out of equilibrium. All questions were revealed as questions of the revolution. The social-patriotic patch-sewers brought into play all their skill in order to preserve a semblance of former hopes, old deceits, and old organizations.[4] In vain. War—not for the first time in history—turned out to be the mother of revolution. The imperialist war became the mother of the proletarian revolution.

To the Russian working class and its battle-tempered Communist Party belongs the honor of making the beginning. By its October revolution the Russian proletariat not only swung open the Kremlin doors for the representatives of the international proletariat but also laid the cornerstone for the edifice of the Third International.

The revolutions in Germany, Austria, Hungary, the tempestuous sweep of the soviet movement and of civil war, sealed by the martyrdom of Karl Liebknecht, Rosa Luxemburg, and many thousands of nameless heroes, have demonstrated that Europe has no roads different from Russia. Unity in methods of struggle for socialism, disclosed in action, guaranteed ideologically the creation of the Communist International and at the same time made it impossible to postpone the convocation of the Communist congress.

Today this congress convenes within the Kremlin walls. We are witnesses to and participants in one of the greatest events of world history.

The working class of the whole world has seized from its enemies the most impregnable fortress—the former tsarist empire. With this stronghold as its base, it is uniting its forces for the final and decisive battle.

What a joy it is to live and to fight in such times!

Paris—Bern—Moscow

by Gregory Zinoviev

The *bourgeoisie* is founding an "International" in Paris.[5] That part of the bourgeoisie that has for the moment escaped the onslaught of the workers' revolution is rushing in haste and agitation to build an "International" to dam up communism's surging torrent, which threatens at any moment to wash away the last strongholds of capitalist rule.

The "bacillus" of internationalism is in the air. It cannot be stopped with bayonets. They must adopt a protective disguise. They must deceive, announcing, "We ourselves thirst for international unity. We also zealously desire an end to wars. To guarantee you a lasting peace we are creating the 'League of Nations.'"

After the epidemic of chauvinism, which shook entire nations during the four-and-a-half-year war, the peoples openly yearned for a simple, reasonable word about friendship and solidarity of workers of different countries. Just as the earth after a long and torrid drought thirsts for rain, so the worn-out peoples, weary from longing, thirst for international unity.

Such a situation cannot be endured forever. During the four and a half years of inhuman war, people developed a disdain for death. Life was cheapened. For four and a half years death ruled on all sides, and in this way it lost its terror.[6] . . . cannot hold back the socialist revolution.

The bourgeoisie had to deceive the people once again. Just as the monstrous lie about "defending the fatherland" helped the world bourgeoisie get their grip on the workers at the beginning of the war, another such immense deception, the League of Nations, is surfacing today.

Under the guise of this League of Nations, the imperialist robbers are organizing a bandit gang to perpetuate their division of the world, better exploit the conquered countries, and, above all, stifle the unrelenting, inevitable communist revolution in Europe and in the whole world.

Such is present-day *Paris*.

In Bern a *Yellow* International of social traitors is being founded.

During the war the Social Democrats were given the mission of convincing the workers that by killing and maiming each other they were "defending the fatherland." Now the property owners are setting a new task for the Social Democrats:

"Convince the workers that the war should be settled by *our* (bourgeois) methods, and not by communist methods.

"Convince the proletariat that they are the ones who must bear the costs for the destruction of workers in one country by workers in another. Convince them that it is in the workers' own interests to take on their shoulders all the burdens of the war, all the taxes and war debts.

"Convince the workers that it is in their own interests to leave power in the sacred hands of those divinely chosen governments that brought happiness to the people by succeeding, in the course of only one war, lasting but four and a half years, in reducing the population throughout Europe to such an impressive extent.

"Convince the workers that their main task is to preserve the old army and the power of those officer-aristocrats, who with such distinction executed rebellious proletarians.

"Convince the workers that the most abominable villains in this best of all possible worlds were Rosa Luxemburg and Karl Liebknecht, who therefore, in the interests of brotherhood among the peoples of the world, had to be hacked to pieces.

"Convince the workers of western and central Europe that their only enemies are the Russian workers and peasants who had the audacity to propose handing over the factories and mills to the workers, handing over the land to the laboring peasants, and handing over the banks—to the people as a whole!"

The orders have been given. The social traitors have assiduously undertaken to carry them out. It is true that during the war years the German social traitors hurled accusations at the French social compromisers and vice versa. But now—what's the point? "We're the same kind of people," they say, "let's try to get along. We knew all the time that we were brothers, twins. We always advocated a mutual amnesty." Now that the war is ending, the masters are making up with each other, and so too, now, the lackeys from both sides must shake hands.

Such is present-day *Bern*.

In Moscow on March 4, 1919, the Third International was formed—a Communist International. A great and unforgettable day! Working people of all countries will always look back on it with gratitude. And the oppressors and exploiters, when they think of this day, will always gnash their teeth—right up to the moment we cleanse our planet of the bourgeois scum.

The workers of all countries paid dearly for their failure on August 4, 1914, to rise up against the bourgeoisie. That imperialist war cost *us,* the workers of all countries, ten million lives. A savage lesson! But not in vain.

Now—finally—we have united not only on a common ideological platform but in a framework of one international proletarian organization. Worker-communists of all countries have joined hands in unity.

In the Kremlin, behind the walls where the tsars used to live, the foundations of the International Soviet Republic of Labor have been laid. We Russian Communists could never have dreamed of anything more gratifying.

The call to battle has been sounded. It will not end until labor attains victory over capital.

The Yellow banners raised in Paris and Bern will soon be lowered. The proletariat of Paris and Bern will help us tear them down from the mansions of kings and bankers.

But the red banner, which is being raised by workers of all countries in Moscow, will triumph as surely as day follows night.

Long live the Communist International!

The Communist International and the colonies

by Nikolai Bukharin

The great proletarian liberation movement is at the same time a movement liberating all of humanity.[7]

Up to now the so-called civilized world has been based on the merciless plunder of the colonial peoples. It is there, in the colonies, that all the filth and dirt, all the barbarism and contempt of capitalist relations finds its full expression. There you find the most repulsive decay and also the most active agent generating it: capitalism. Ancient Greek democracy sprang from the bones of *slaves*—mercilessly exploited, deprived of their rights, turned into objects. In the same way contemporary bourgeois democracy, just like the capitalist monarchies, blossomed with splendid flowers on soil watered by the sweat and blood of a hundred million Indians, Chinese, Africans, East Indians, and countless other colonial peoples large and small, beneath the iron heel of the bankers who rule Europe and America.

Furthermore, it was not only the American, European, and Japanese bourgeoisies, but even to some extent the proletariat of these countries who benefited from this, for crumbs fell to them from the master's table. The proletariat looked down on the "barbarian people" and thought them worthy only of being fertilizer for European civilization.

Imperialism's war tore the benevolent mask off the *real* barbarian—the capitalist regimes of the most "advanced" and most "civilized" countries. Up to now the European and American working class had obediently followed their bourgeoisie, receiving as a reward hunger, destruction and unprecedented enslavement. Now they are rising up everywhere and marching with firm and confident steps toward their dictatorship.

But though imperialist rule saps the strength of the enslaved peoples, the colonial countries are beginning to stir. For decades, for whole centuries, they have groaned under the yoke of these "civilized" bandits, who benefit from the toleration of the proletariat in the civilized countries. Now that the proletariat has seen that its enemies are at home, it *welcomes* the uprisings of the colonial peoples. The rebellion of the colonies *hastens the collapse of imperialism*. The movement in the colonies, therefore, although it may not be socialist at all, has joined the broad stream of the great liberation struggle that is shaking up the entire immense structure of world capitalism.

The Second International was shaped by the bygone epoch of "peace" on the continent and frenzied robbery in the colonies. It failed to pose the problem with the sharpness that is indispensable here. And its pathetic remains, the Bern Yellow "International," gave its blessing to the transfer of colonies to the thieves in the "League of Nations" so that the fate of hundreds of millions of people may be decided by the bankers of New York, London, and Paris.

Our International, the Communist International, born in the storm of civil war, firmly supports the oppressed in their liberation struggle. It is no accident that at the first congress of our Communist International for the first time we heard a speech in the *Chinese language*. This is a profound historical symbol, a symbol of unity among revolutionary proletarian forces under capitalism with the efforts of colonial peoples who are liberating themselves. Under their blows the hateful capitalist system will be shattered into many pieces.

Working Women's Day and the Third International

by Alexandra Kollontai

In the 1860s when the first workers' International began its great work of fighting for the emancipation of labor, women's labor played only a secondary role in the economy.[8] There was still no talk of a socialist movement of women workers. Even in the trade unions, women were an insignificant minority.

Therefore the First International's statements for recognition of equal rights for women were abstract in character. The struggle for women's emancipation had not yet become an urgent necessity for the working class.

The Second International took a more defined position on the question of women's rights. However, the policy of peaceful parliamentary action that tainted the Second International throughout its whole existence led the Social Democratic parties to regard the working women's movement chiefly as a struggle for political rights. The greater the role that women began to play in the national economy and the faster the growth of the number of women working independently, the more acutely did Social Democrats face the question of how to utilize this fresh, untouched layer of the population as voters. As early as the 1890s, the question of extending voting rights to women proletarians was incorporated into the programs of a large number of Social Democratic parties. And at the 1907 Stuttgart congress the international Social Democracy adopted a resolution on the need to fight for voting rights for women.[9]

Working Women's Day was established in Copenhagen as a day of agitation for women's suffrage.[10]

The Second International went no further than this demand for the formal equalization of women's rights with those of men. It set aside women's social liberation and liberation from domestic life until after the complete achievement of the socialist order.

The great Russian proletarian revolution solved the problem of political rights for women with one stroke. Working women and peasant women have now become full-fledged citizens of Soviet Russia. The goal of Working Women's Day has been fulfilled.

Yet it is now, in the heat of sharp battle with the old, obsolete bourgeois world, that life presents the international proletariat with many new, mature, and urgent challenges in the fight for women's emancipation.

Women workers and peasant women enjoy the right to vote on a par with men. Nevertheless, despite this formal recognition, this right is nothing more than a means, a weapon for the fight against the conditions of life, the relics of capitalism, that oppress women.

Women workers and peasant women are still very much domestic slaves, still chained to the bourgeois family, still objects of shameful commerce as unwilling prostitutes.

Among the large number of extremely important tasks facing the Third International is the task of women's thoroughgoing emancipation. Today this question is no longer merely abstract and theoretical. Real life calls for action. Over the last half century women's labor acquired enormous weight in production. The further planned development of the national economy and its productive capacity has become inconceivable without the assistance of women's labor power. To use this power expediently in the communist economy, women must be relieved of their burdens and spared unnecessary, unproductive, and wasteful labor in housework and child rearing. Building the new society demands that the living, fresh energy of women must be directed toward constructing life on new principles.

Instead of doing unproductive housework, women can play an enormous role in organizing the new economic order; instead of educating the family, women can contribute greatly to strengthening and developing the beginnings of socialist public education. The new, Third, Communist International needs only to set itself the task of utilizing the female proletariat, of developing the entire breadth of its initiative in order to draw the women workers into the cause of struggling for and building a new way of life and developing a new ethic, a new relationship between the sexes.

Therefore, "Working Women's Day" this year is not only a celebration of the outstanding achievement by working-class women—their acquisition of full equality in civil rights—but a day to project new tasks for the cause of the social and economic emancipation of women through the efforts of the Third, Communist International.

Comrades from the Third International must not forget that without the active participation of working women the dictatorship of the proletariat cannot be stable and complete.

A celebration at the Bolshoi

by Arthur Ransome

I got to the theater at about five, and had difficulty in getting in, though I had a special ticket as a correspondent.

There were queues outside all the doors.[11] The Moscow Soviet was there, the executive committee, representatives of the trade unions and factory committees, etc.

The huge theater and the platform were crammed, people standing in the aisles and even packed close together in the wings of the stage. Kamenev opened the meeting by a solemn announcement of the founding of the Third International in the Kremlin. There was a roar of applause from the audience, which rose and sang the "Internationale" in a way that I have never heard it sung since the all-Russian assembly when the news came of the strikes in Germany during the Brest negotiations. Kamenev then spoke of those who had died on the way, mentioning Liebknecht and Rosa Luxemburg, and the whole theater stood again while the orchestra played, "You Fell as Victims."

Then Lenin spoke. If I had ever thought that Lenin was losing his personal popularity, I got my answer now. It was a long time before he could speak at all, everybody standing and drowning his attempts to speak with roar after roar of applause. It was an extraordinary, overwhelming scene, tier after tier crammed with workmen, the parterre filled, the whole platform and the wings. A knot of workwomen were close to me, and they almost fought to see him, and shouted as if each one were determined that he should hear her in particular. He spoke as usual, in the simplest way, emphasizing the fact that the revolutionary struggle everywhere was forced to use the soviet forms. "We declare our solidarity with the aims of the Sovietists," he read from an Italian paper, and added, "and that was when they did not know what our aims were, and before we had an established program ourselves."

Albrecht [Eberlein] made a very long reasoned speech for Spartacus, which was translated by Trotsky. Guilbeaux, seemingly a mere child, spoke of the socialist movement in France. Steklov was translating him when I left. . . . When I got outside the theater, I found at each door a disappointed crowd that had been unable to get in.

[The following is a newspaper report of Lenin's address to the meeting.]

Founding the Communist International

by V.I. Lenin

(*Stormy ovation*) Comrades, at the First Congress of the Communist International we did not succeed in getting representatives from all countries where this organization has most faithful friends and where there are workers whose sympathies are entirely with us.[12] Allow me, therefore, to begin with a short quotation which will show you that in reality we have more friends than we can see, than we know, and than we were able to assemble here, in Moscow, despite all persecution, despite the entire, seemingly omnipotent union of the bourgeoisie of the whole world. This persecution has gone to such lengths as to attempt to surround us with a sort of Great Wall of China and to deport Bolsheviks in dozens from the freest republics of the world. They seem to be scared stiff that ten or a dozen Bolsheviks will infect the whole world. But we, of course, know that this fear is ridiculous—because they have already infected the whole world, because the Russian workers' struggle has already convinced working people everywhere that the destiny of the world revolution is being decided here, in Russia.

Comrades, I have here a copy of *L'Humanité,* a French newspaper whose policy corresponds more to that of our Mensheviks or Right Socialist Revolutionaries. During the war, this paper was utterly ruthless in its attacks on those who supported our viewpoint. Today it is defending those who during the war went along with their own bourgeoisie. This very newspaper reports in its issue of January 13, 1919, that a mammoth meeting (as the newspaper itself admits) took place in Paris of active party and trade union members of the Seine Federation, i.e., the district nearest to Paris, the center of the proletarian movement, the center of all political life in France. The first speaker was Bracke, a Socialist who throughout the war took the same line as our Mensheviks and right-wing defense advocates. He was meek and mild now. Not a word about a single burning issue! He ended by saying that he was against his government's interference in the struggle of the proletariat of other countries. His words were drowned in applause. The next speaker was a supporter of his, a certain Pierre Laval. He spoke of demobilization, the burning issue in France today—a country which has probably borne greater sacrifices than any other country in this criminal war. And this country now sees that demobilization is being dragged out, held up, that there is no desire to carry it through, that preparations are being made for a new war that will obviously demand new sacrifices from the French workers for the sake of settling how much more of the spoils the French or British capitalists will get. The newspaper goes on to say that the crowd listened to the speaker, Pierre Laval, but when he started running down Bolshevism, the protests and excitement stopped the meeting. After that, Citizen Pierre Renaudel was refused a hearing, and the meeting ended with a brief statement by Citizen Péricat. He is one of the few people in the French labor movement who in the main is in agreement with us. And so the newspaper has to admit that the speaker who began to attack the Bolsheviks was immediately pulled up.

Comrades, we have not been able to get even one delegate here directly from France, and only one Frenchman, Comrade Guilbeaux, arrived here, and he with great difficulty. (*Enthusiastic applause*) He will speak here today. He spent months in the prisons of that free republic, Switzerland, being accused of having contact with Lenin and preparing a revolution in Switzerland. He was escorted through Germany by gendarmes and officers, for fear, evidently, that he might drop a match that would set Germany on fire. But Germany is ablaze without this match. In France, too, as we can see, there are sympathizers with the Bolshevik movement. The French people are probably among the most experienced, most politically conscious, most active and responsive. They will not allow a speaker at a public meeting to strike a false note: he is stopped. Considering the French temperament, he was lucky not to have been dragged down from the rostrum! Therefore, when a newspaper hostile to us admits what took place at this big meeting, we can safely say that the French proletariat is on our side.

I am going to read another short quotation, from an Italian newspaper. The attempts to isolate us from the rest of the world are so great that we very rarely receive Socialist newspapers from abroad. It is a rare thing to receive a copy of the Italian newspaper *Avanti!,* the organ of the Italian Socialist Party, a party which participated in Zimmerwald, fought against the war, and has now resolved not to attend the Yellow congress in Bern, the congress of the old International, which was to be attended by people who had helped their governments to prolong this criminal war. To this day, *Avanti!* is under strict censorship. But in this issue, which arrived here by chance, I read an item on party life in a small locality called Cavriago (probably a remote spot because it cannot be located on the map). It appears that the workers there adopted a resolution supporting their newspaper for its uncompromising stand and declared their approval of the German Spartacists. Then follow the words *"Sovietisti russi"* which, even though they are in Italian, can be understood all over the world. They sent greetings to the Russian *"Sovietisti"* and expressed the wish that the program of the Russian and German revolutionaries should be adopted throughout the world and serve to carry the fight against the bourgeoisie and military domination to a conclusion. When you read a resolution like that, adopted in some Italian Poshekhonye,[13] you have every right to say to yourself that the Italian people are on our side, the Italian people understand what the Russian *"Sovietisti"* are, what the program of the Russian *"Sovietisti"* and the German Spartacists is. Yet at that time we had no such program! We had no common program with the German Spartacists, but the Italian workers rejected all they had seen in their bourgeois press, which, bribed as it is by the millionaires and multimillionaires, spreads slander about us in millions of copies. It failed to deceive the Italian workers, who grasped what the Spartacists and the *"Sovietisti"* were and declared that they sympathized with their program, at a time when this program did not exist. That is why we found our task so easy at this congress. All we had to do was to record as a program what had already been implanted in the minds and hearts of the workers, even those cast away in some remote spot and cut off from us by police and military cordons. That is why we have been able to reach concerted decisions on all the main issues with such ease and complete unanimity. And we are fully convinced that these decisions will meet with a powerful response among workers elsewhere.

The soviet movement, comrades, is the form which has been won in Russia, which is now spreading throughout the world, and the very name of which gives the workers a complete program. I hope that we, having had the good fortune to develop the soviet form to victory, will not become swelled-headed about it.

We know very well that the reason we were the first to take part in a soviet proletarian revolution was not because we were as well or better prepared than other workers, but because we were worse prepared. This is why we were faced with the most savage and decrepit enemy, and it is this that accounted for the outward scale of the revolution. But we also know that the soviets exist here to this day, that they are grappling with gigantic difficulties which originate from an inadequate cultural level and from the burden that has weighed down on us for more than a year, on us who stand alone at our posts, at a time when we are surrounded on all sides by enemies, and when, as you know perfectly well, harrowing ordeals, the hardships of famine, and terrible suffering have befallen us.

Those who directly or indirectly side with the bourgeoisie often try to appeal to the workers and provoke indignation among them by pointing to the severe sufferings of the workers today. And we tell them: yes, these sufferings are severe and we do not conceal them from you. We tell the workers that, and they know it well from their own experience. You can see we are fighting to win socialism not only for ourselves, to ensure that not only our children shall recollect capitalists and landowners only as prehistoric monsters; we are fighting to ensure that the workers of the whole world triumph together with us.

And this First Congress of the Communist International, which has made the point that throughout the world the soviets are winning the sympathy of the workers, shows us that the victory of the world communist revolution is assured. (*Applause*) The bourgeoisie will continue to vent its fury in a number of countries; the bourgeoisie there is just beginning to prepare the destruction of the best people, the best representatives of socialism, as is evident from the brutal murder of Rosa Luxemburg and Karl Liebknecht by the White Guards. These sacrifices are inevitable. We seek no agreement with the bourgeoisie, we are marching to the final and decisive battle against them. But we know that after the ordeal, agony, and distress of the war, when the people throughout the world are fighting for demobilization, when they feel they have been betrayed, and appreciate how incredibly heavy the burden of taxation is that has been placed upon them by the capitalists, who killed tens of millions of people to decide who would receive more of the profits—we know that these brigands' rule is at an end!

Now that the meaning of the word "soviet" is understood by everybody, the victory of the communist revolution is assured. The comrades present in this hall saw the founding of the first Soviet republic; now they see the founding of the Third, Communist International (*Applause*), and they will all see the founding of the World Federative Republic of Soviets. (*Applause*)

The Third, Communist International

by V.I. Lenin

In March of this year of 1919, an international congress of Communists was held in Moscow.[14] This congress founded the Third, Communist International, an association of the workers of the whole world who are striving to establish Soviet power in all countries.

The First International, founded by Marx, existed from 1864 to 1872. The defeat of the heroic workers of Paris—of the celebrated Paris Commune—marked the end of this International. It is unforgettable, it will remain forever in the history of the workers' struggle for their emancipation. It laid the foundation of that edifice of the world socialist republic which it is now our good fortune to be building.

The Second International existed from 1889 to 1914, up to the war. This was the period of the most calm and peaceful development of capitalism, a period without great revolutions. During this period the working-class movement gained strength and matured in a number of countries. But the workers' leaders in most of the parties had become accustomed to peaceful conditions and had lost the ability to wage a revolutionary struggle. When, in 1914, there began the war that drenched the earth with blood for four years, the war between the capitalists over the division of profits, the war for supremacy over small and weak nations, these leaders deserted to the side of their respective governments. They betrayed the workers, they helped to prolong the slaughter, they became enemies of socialism, they went over to the side of the capitalists.

The masses of workers turned their backs on these traitors to socialism. All over the world there was a turn toward the revolutionary struggle. The war proved that capitalism was doomed. A new system is coming to take its place. The old word *socialism* had been desecrated by the traitors to socialism.

Today, the workers who have remained loyal to the cause of throwing off the yoke of capital call themselves

"Communists." All over the world the association of Communists is growing. In a number of countries Soviet power has already triumphed. Soon we shall see the victory of communism throughout the world; we shall see the foundation of the World Federative Republic of Soviets.

Notes

Introduction

1. The revolution that triumphed on October 25, 1917, by the Julian (old style) calendar used in prerevolutionary Russia, has become universally known as the October revolution. By the more modern Gregorian calendar used in the other imperialist countries and much of the colonial world, the victory occurred on November 7. The Gregorian calendar was introduced in Soviet Russia on February 14, 1918. All dates in this book are given by the Gregorian calendar. For events in countries where the Julian calendar was then in use, the Julian date is given in parentheses.
2. V.I. Lenin, *Collected Works* (hereinafter *CW*)(Moscow: Progress Publishers, 1974), vol. 29, pp. 306, 307. Lenin's article is printed as a prologue to the present volume.
3. Documents on this collapse can be found in John Riddell, ed., *Lenin's Struggle for a Revolutionary International: Documents 1907–16, the Preparatory Years* (New York: Pathfinder Press, 1984, 1986), pp. 183–223 [2019 printing], a volume of *The Communist International in Lenin's Time.*
4. For the text of these statements, see Riddell, *Lenin's Struggle,* pp. 58–62, 77–80, 124–26, 153–56.
5. Lenin, "The Tasks of Revolutionary Social-Democracy in the European War," in *CW,* vol. 21, pp. 16, 17.
6. Lenin, "The War and Russian Social-Democracy," in *CW,* vol. 21, pp. 33, 34.
7. For excerpts from the Zimmerwald conference proceedings and the documents of the conference see Riddell, *Lenin's Struggle,* pp. 421–91.
8. Riddell, *Lenin's Struggle,* pp. 454–57.
9. See Riddell, *Lenin's Struggle,* pp. 353–71 and 575–608.

10. See Lenin, "The Tasks of the Proletariat in Our Revolution," in *CW,* vol. 24, pp. 84–88.
11. When the Communist International was founded, workers in Europe often referred to representative councils elected by workers, soldiers, and peasants as *soviets,* the Russian word for *council.* They also used the word in their own language for *council,* particularly in countries such as Germany where such formations were widespread.

    In the German-language text from which the congress proceedings in this volume have been translated, both the German word *Rat* and the Russian word *soviet* are used. The translation has preserved the different usages in the German text through the use of both the words *council* (for *Rat*) and *soviet.*
12. The Bern conference is discussed in chapter 6 of this volume. Portions of the debate on Bolshevism at the Bern conference are printed in John Riddell, ed., *The German Revolution and the Debate on Soviet Power: Documents 1918–19, Preparing the Founding Congress* (New York: Pathfinder Press, 1986), pp. 544–70 [2018 printing], a volume of *The Communist International in Lenin's Time.*
13. The text of this appeal and other statements preparatory to the March 1919 congress are printed in Riddell, *German Revolution,* pp. 584–621.
14. Lenin, *CW,* vol. 42, pp. 119–20.
15. Ruth Stoljarowa, "Zur Entstehungsgeschichte des Aufrufs 'Zum 1. Kongress der Kommunistischen Internationale' vom Januar 1919," *Zeitschrift für Geschichtswissenschaft,* no. 11 (1968), pp. 1387–88.
16. Lenin, "The Terms of Admission into the Communist International," in *CW,* vol. 31, p. 206.
17. See Lenin, "Letter to Workers of Europe and America," in *CW,* vol. 28, pp. 429–36. This letter is reprinted in Riddell, *German Revolution,* pp. 27–32 and 600–603.
18. Hugo Eberlein, "Souvenirs sur la fondation de l'Internationale Communiste," *La Correspondance internationale,* vol. 4, no. 15 (February 27, 1924), p. 154.

In another account, written in 1929, Eberlein quoted Luxemburg as saying that the new International should be founded only when there were "revolutionary mass movements sweeping over almost all the countries of Europe" and many Communist parties had arisen. Luxemburg envisaged a short postponement, Eberlein stated, favoring a congress date between April and June. Eberlein, "The Foundation of the Comintern and the Spartakusbund," *The Communist International,* vol. 6, nos. 9–10 (1929), pp. 436–37. Both accounts by Eberlein are printed in Riddell, *German Revolution,* pp. 603–6.

Another party leader of that time, Heinrich Brandler, recalled in 1948, almost thirty years after Luxemburg's death, that she said that the International, if founded prematurely, "will be a Russian *Krämerei* [shop] with which we shall be unable to cope. We shall perish with it." Isaac Deutscher, "Dialogue with Heinrich Brandler," in *Marxism, Wars and Revolutions: Essays from Four Decades* (London: Verso, 1984), p. 134.

19. Since an early stage of the war, Luxemburg had declared the old International "a heap of rubble," destroyed by its chauvinist majority leadership, and repeatedly called for a new International launched on a revolutionary class-struggle basis. For her articles expressing this view, see Riddell, *Lenin's Struggle,* pp. 290–304, 618–22, 767–68.

20. Many of Luxemburg's criticisms of the Bolsheviks in mid-1918 are set forth in her draft article, "The Russian Revolution," printed in Mary-Alice Waters, ed., *Rosa Luxemburg Speaks* (New York: Pathfinder Press, 1970), pp. 524–68 [2017 printing].

For the evolution of Luxemburg's thinking in the last months of her life, see Riddell, *German Revolution,* pp. 428–30.

Some comments by Lenin on Luxemburg's positions after 1914 and on the German revolutionary movement of these years can be found in "The Junius Pamphlet," in *CW,* vol. 22, pp. 305–19 (reprinted in Riddell, *Lenin's Struggle,* pp. 647–63); his 1921 "A Letter to the German Communists" in *CW,* vol. 32, pp. 512–13; and his 1922 "Notes of a Publicist" in *CW,* vol. 33, pp. 210–11 (the last two items are reprinted in Riddell, *German Revolution,* pp. 394–96).

A criticism by Bolshevik leader Karl Radek of Luxemburg's policies in the January 1919 Berlin uprising is printed in Riddell, *German Revolution,* pp. 378–88.

Two later assessments by Trotsky can be found in *Writings of Leon Trotsky (1932)* (New York: Pathfinder Press, 1973), pp. 172–86 [2019 printing] and *Writings of Leon Trotsky (1935–36)* (New York: Pathfinder Press, 1970, 1977), pp. 34–38 [2017 printing].

21. Documents related to the January fighting in Berlin can be found in Riddell, *German Revolution,* pp. 330–96.

22. Riddell, *German Revolution,* pp. 594–600.

23. The list of organizations invited to the congress was as follows:

"(1) The Spartacus League (Germany); (2) the Communist Party (Bolsheviks) (Russia); (3) the Communist Party of German Austria; (4) the Communist Party of Hungary; (5) the Communist Party of Poland; (6) the Communist Party of Finland; (7) the Communist Party of Estonia; (8) the Communist Party of Latvia; (9) the Communist Party of Lithuania; (10) the Communist Party of Belorussia; (11) the Communist Party of the Ukraine; (12) the revolutionary forces of the Czech Social Democracy; (13) the Bulgarian Social Democratic Party (Tesnyaki); (14) the Romanian Social Democratic Party; (15) the left wing of the Serbian Social Democratic Party; (16) the Swedish Left Social Democracy; (17) the Norwegian Social Democratic Party [Norwegian Labor Party]; (18) the *Klassekampen* [Class Struggle] group in Denmark; (19) the Dutch Communist Party; (20) the revolutionary forces in the Belgian Workers Party; (21) and (22) the groups and organizations within the French socialist and syndicalist movement in basic solidarity with Loriot; (23) the left Swiss Social Democracy; (24) the Italian Socialist Party; (25) the left forces in the Spanish Socialist Party; (26) left forces in the Portuguese Socialist Party; (27) the left forces in the British Socialist Party (in particular, representatives of the Mac-

Lean current); (28) the Socialist Labour Party (Britain); (29) the Industrial Workers of the World (Britain); (30) the Industrial Workers (Britain); (31) revolutionary forces in the shop stewards' movement (Britain); (32) revolutionary forces in Irish workers' organizations; (33) Socialist Labor Party (America); (34) left forces of the American Socialist Party (especially the current represented by Debs and that represented by the Socialist Propaganda League); (35) Industrial Workers of the World (America); (36) Industrial Workers of the World (Australia); (37) Workers International Industrial Union (America); (38) Socialist groups in Tokyo and Yokohama (represented by Comrade Katayama); (39) the Socialist Youth International (represented by Comrade Münzenberg)." *Pervyy kongress Kominterna mart* 1919 *g.* (Moscow: Partiynoye izdatel'stvo, 1933; Milan: Feltrinelli, 1967) (hereinafter *Pervyy kongress* [1933]), p. 255.

24. See Riddell, *Lenin's Struggle,* pp. 35–57.
25. Lenin, *CW,* vol. 19, p. 100. This article and two others by Lenin on this topic are printed in Riddell, *Lenin's Struggle,* pp. 169–75.
26. Bukharin's article is printed in the appendix to this volume.
27. Boris Nicolaevsky, "Le récit du 'camarade Thomas,'" in Jacques Freymond, ed., *Contributions à l'histoire du Comintern* (Geneva: Librairie Droz, 1965), p. 8.
28. Paulo Spriano, *Storia del Partito comunista italiano* (Turin: Giulio Einaudi, 1982), vol. 1, p. 22.
29. Tom Bell, *The British Communist Party: A Short History* (London: Lawrence and Wishart, 1937), p. 50.
30. *Vos'moi s"ezd RKP(B). Protokoly* (Moscow: Gosizdat., 1959), p. 135. The Central Committee statement referred to here was delivered by Zinoviev during the opening session of the congress (see chapter 1).
31. The nine delegates who came to the congress from abroad were Henri Guilbeaux (France), Karl Steinhardt and Karl Petin (German Austria), Eberlein (Germany), Rutgers (the Nether-

lands and the United States), Stang (Norway), Otto Grimlund (Sweden), and Fritz Platten and Leonie Kascher (Switzerland).

32. Eberlein, "Souvenirs sur la fondation," p. 155.

33. Lenin's November 1915 letter to the Socialist Propaganda League took up several points on which the U.S. organization had been influenced by the ultraleft positions of the Dutch revolutionaries. See Lenin, "Letter to the Secretary of the Socialist Propaganda League," in *CW,* vol. 21, pp. 423–28, also printed in Riddell, *Lenin's Struggle,* pp. 516–19.

34. Writing on the foundation of the Comintern, historians James W. Hulse, Branko Lazitch, and Milorad M. Drachkovitch stated that Platten could not have represented Swiss Communists since he had been resident in Russia since 1917. Hulse, *The Forming of the Communist International* (Stanford: Stanford University Press, 1964), p. 18; Lazitch and Drachkovitch, *Lenin and the Comintern* (Stanford: Hoover Institution Press, 1972), pp. 67–69.

    This is incorrect. Platten had returned to Switzerland by August 1918, and he played a leading role in the mass struggles there that autumn. See Leonhard Haas, "Lenin an Platten: Ein Briefwechsel aus dem Jahr 1918," *Schweizerische Zeitschrift für Geschichte,* vol. 18, no. 1 (1968), pp. 75–76, and Fritz N. Platten, "Mein Vater, Fritz Platten, ein Leben für die russische Revolution," *Turicum: Vierteljahresschrift für Kultur Wissenschaft und Wirtschaft* (September–November 1972), pp. 19–20.

35. While in Switzerland, Guilbeaux accepted funds from a German citizen to finance his internationalist newspaper *Demain.* This action was sharply criticized by Angelica Balabanoff and some other antiwar Social Democrats as providing ammunition for French chauvinist propaganda. Lenin found Guilbeaux's explanation convincing, however, and in 1918 he wrote the Soviet ambassador in Switzerland in Guilbeaux's defense. See Lenin, *CW,* vol. 44, pp. 153, 158.

    In November 1918 Guilbeaux was expelled from Switzerland on the grounds of his collaboration with the Soviet embassy there. In February 1919 a French military court sentenced him in absentia to death for high treason.

When Guilbeaux arrived in Moscow, Jacques Sadoul, leader of the French Communist Group in Russia, objected to his being seated as a delegate representing French revolutionaries. Sadoul raised with Lenin the charges against Guilbeaux's actions in Switzerland, but without success.

36. Rudas and Mézáros succeeded in reaching Moscow after the congress ended and submitted a statement, which is printed below in chapter 11.

37. See Angelica Balabanoff, *My Life as a Rebel* (New York: Harper & Brothers, 1938), pp. 216–17.

38. The four former prisoners were Jaroslav Handlir, Gustav Klinger, Petin, and Rudnyánszky.

39. See J.D. White, "The Revolution in Lithuania 1918–19," *Soviet Studies,* vol. 23, no. 2 (October 1971), pp. 186–200.

For the pre-1914 debate on national self-determination see Luxemburg's 1908–9 essay, "The National Question and Autonomy," in Horace B. Davis, ed., *The National Question* (New York: Monthly Review Press, 1976), pp. 101–287, and Lenin's reply, "The Right of Nations to Self-Determination," in *CW,* vol. 20, pp. 393–454.

Several articles from the discussion in 1916 are printed in Riddell, *Lenin's Struggle,* pp. 526–73. See also Luxemburg's 1918 draft, "The Russian Revolution," in Waters, *Rosa Luxemburg Speaks,* pp. 524–68.

For Luxemburg's position in 1918 on the agrarian question in the Russian and German revolutions, see Riddell, *German Revolution,* pp. 314–21.

40. See, for example, Lazitch and Drachkovitch, *Lenin and the Comintern,* p. 72.

41. See Wolfgang Leonhard, *Völker hört die Signale: Die Gründerjahre des Weltkommunismus* 1919–1924 (Munich: Wilhelm Goldmann Verlag, 1981), pp. 13, 63.

Communists in the Volga German republic were organized not as a separate party but under the Central

Bureau of German Sections of the Russian Communist Party. See Rasma Karklins, "La révolution mondiale et les allemands d'Union soviétique," *Cahiers du monde russe et soviétique,* vol. 16, nos. 3–4 (July–Dec. 1975), pp. 425–443.

42. Such denunciations are still heard today. Alexander Solzhenitsyn wrote in 1974, "Did not the revolution throughout its early years have some of the characteristics of a foreign invasion? . . . When the organs of the Cheka teemed with Latvians, Poles, Jews, Hungarians, Chinese?" Quoted in Marc Jansen, "International Class Solidarity or Foreign Intervention?" *International Review of Social History,* vol. 31, part 1 (1986), p. 75.

43. V.M. Ustinov, "Kitayskiye kommunisticheskiye organizatsii v Sovetskoy Rossii," *Voprosy historii KPSS,* no. 4 (1961), pp. 107–15.

44. N.I. Skrypnik was driven to suicide in 1933; Bukharin, N. Osinsky, and Zinoviev were condemned and executed during the great frame-up trials of 1936 and 1938; Rakovsky was condemned at the 1938 trial and died in prison in 1941; Trotsky was murdered in 1940.

45. Jacques Sadoul, "La Fondation de la Troisième internationale," *La Correspondance internationale,* vol. 4, no. 17 (March 12, 1924), p. 180.

46. "Rozhdeniye Tret'ego internatsionala," in *Pravda,* March 7, 1919.

47. Sadoul, "La Fondation de la Troisième internationale," p. 180.

48. Arthur Ransome, *Russia in* 1919 (New York: B.W. Huebsch, 1919), pp. 215 and 217.

49. Lenin, *CW,* vol. 29, p. 307.

50. *The Communist International,* no. 1 (May 1919), p. 23.

51. Lenin, "Speech at a Meeting of the Moscow Soviet in Celebration of the First Anniversary of the Third International, March 6, 1920," in *CW,* vol. 30, p. 417.

52. See chapter 10 of this volume.

53. The errors in this pamphlet's first edition drew from Lenin a letter to the State Publishing House demanding "measures to guarantee that such an outrage is not repeated."

The pamphlet, Lenin commented, "is a horrible piece of work. A slovenly mess. No table of contents. Some idiot or sloven, evidently an illiterate, has lumped together, as though he were drunk, all the 'material', little articles, speeches, and printed them *out of sequence*.

"No preface, no minutes, no exact text of the decisions, no separation of decisions from speeches, articles, notes, nothing at all! An unheard-of disgrace!

"A great historic event has been disgraced by such a pamphlet." Lenin, letter to V.V. Vorovsky of October 24, 1919, in *CW,* vol. 35, p. 427.

54. *Manifest, Richtlinien, Beschlüsse des ersten Kongresses. Aufrufe und offene Schreiben des Exekutivkomitees bis zum Zweiten Kongress* (Hamburg: Verlag der Kommunistischen Internationale, 1920; Milan: Feltrinelli, 1967).

55. *Der I. Kongress der Kommunistischen Internationale: Protokoll der Verhandlungen in Moskau vom 2. bis* 19. *März* 1919 (Hamburg: Verlag der Kommunistischen Internationale, 1921; Milan: Feltrinelli, 1967).

56. *Pervyy kongress Kommunisticheskogo internatsionala* (Petrograd: Izdatel'stvo Kommunisticheskogo internatsionala, 1921).

57. Pierre Broué, *Les Congrès de l'Internationale communiste: Le Premier congrès—2–6 mars 1919* (Paris: Études et documentation internationales, 1974).

Primer congreso de la Internacional Comunista (Mexico: Editorial Grijalbo, 1975).

Pero Damjanović, et al., eds., *Prvi kongres Komunističke internacionale,* volume 1 of *Komunistička internacionala: Stenogrami i dokumenti kongresa* (Gornji Milanovac: Kulturni centar, 1981).

58. See, for example, Lazitch and Drachkovitch, *Lenin and the Comintern,* p. 75.

59. Eberlein's 1929 reminiscence stated, "The printed report fails to give my personal statement that I fully agreed with

the conference, and that, had I a free hand, I should have voted for the immediate establishment of the Communist International. Lenin's arguments had convinced me. The difference between my opinion and my mandate was expressed by the fact that I did not vote against the resolution, but withheld my vote." Eberlein, "Foundation of the Comintern," p. 438.

60. Riddell, *German Revolution,* pp. 550–52.

Prologue

1. Lenin, *CW,* vol. 29, pp. 305–13.
2. See Frederick Engels, letter to Karl Marx, October 7, 1858, in Marx and Engels, *Collected Works,* (New York: International Publishers, 1983), vol. 40, p. 344.
3. In February 1848 a workers' uprising in Paris overturned the restored monarchy in France and won reestablishment of a republic. Four months later, the anti–working class measures of the new bourgeois-led government provoked first mass protests and then armed resistance, which was brutally suppressed.

   The year 1871 saw the establishment of the first attempt at a workers' government, the Paris Commune. It lasted seventy-two days before being crushed by the bourgeois-led counterrevolution.
4. Marx, letter to Engels, April 16, 1856, in Marx and Engels, *Collected Works,* vol. 40, p. 41.
5. See for example Lenin, "The Revolutionary-Democratic Dictatorship of the Proletariat and the Peasantry," in *CW,* vol. 8, pp. 293–303.
6. The 1905 revolution in Russia began in January when tsarist troops fired on a peaceful demonstration in St. Petersburg (Leningrad). It led to general strikes, the formation of the first soviets, widespread peasant rebellion, and mutinies in the army. The revolution culminated in an insurrection in Moscow in December, which was bloodily suppressed, although unrest continued well into 1906. Although the tsar was forced to create a parliamen-

tary structure, the State Duma, tsarist autocracy and the privileges of the landed aristocracy survived essentially intact.

Minutes of the March 1 preliminary meeting

1. *Pervyy kongress* (1933), p. 256. This meeting was attended by Eberlein, Lenin, Klinger, Yrjö Sirola, Boris Reinstein, Zinoviev, and perhaps others.
2. In fact, when Rutgers arrived, the congress granted him only a consultative vote, because he did not carry written credentials from his organization.

List of congress delegates

1. This list is taken from the 1933 Russian edition of the congress proceedings, pp. 250–51, which in two cases allocates voting rights differently from the 1921 German edition. The names of organizations are given as they appear in the Russian text. Delegates' names or initials have been provided by the editor where missing.

   Included here are all delegates who participated in any part of the congress. Many of these arrived late, while others left early.
2. The 1921 German edition of the congress proceedings lists Platten as representing the Swiss party as a whole, as do the minutes of the congress Credentials Commission, printed below in the appendix. In the 1921 and 1933 Russian editions of the congress proceedings, however, he is listed as representing only the left opposition in the Swiss party, and that is how he introduces himself in his report on Switzerland, printed in chapter 2.
3. In the 1921 German edition of the congress proceedings and in the minutes of the Credentials Commission, Guilbeaux is given five votes. The 1921 and 1933 Russian editions of the congress proceedings give him only one vote, but provide no explanation for this discrepancy with the German-language proceedings.

Chapter 1: The congress opens

1. Lenin, *CW,* vol. 28, pp. 455–56.
2. During 1919 counterrevolutionary White Guard armies launched offensives into Soviet-held territory from the Don River region in the south, from Siberia, and from the Baltic region. These forces were supported and supplied by interventionist armies of the Entente powers that occupied wide stretches of Soviet territory near the White Sea in the north, on the Black Sea in the south, in the Caucasus, and in Siberia. The British navy conducted operations along the Baltic coast, while counterrevolutionary German forces combated Soviet troops in the Baltics. During 1919 the interventionist armies embraced several hundred thousand troops from about a dozen countries.

   In Germany, the January uprising in Berlin marked the beginning of several months of sharp fighting between government troops and militant workers.

   In Hungary, a revolutionary government based on workers' councils was established only two weeks after the international Communist congress in Moscow adjourned.
3. See Lenin's report and theses, "Bourgeois Democracy and the Dictatorship of the Proletariat," printed below in chapter 4.

   The soviets of workers', peasants', and Red Army soldiers' deputies in Russia in 1919 were made up of delegates chosen by assemblies of workers, soldiers, and peasants in their workplaces, military units, or villages. Neighborhood, municipal, or regional soviets were the authoritative local government bodies and chose delegates to the All-Russian Soviet congress. This congress elected the Soviet government and acted on matters of state policy.

   The soviets included representatives of different political parties who abided by the Soviet constitution and did not participate in or abet counterrevolutionary activity, as well as delegates belonging to no party. From 1918, the large majority of delegates elected to the All-Russian Soviet congress were Bolsheviks.

4. In Britain during World War I, the trade union leadership used the weight of the union apparatus to support the war effort and to oppose workers' efforts to defend their class interests. The shop stewards' movement began with the strike of munitions workers in the Clyde Valley in February 1915, which was opposed by the official union leaderships. Shop stewards elected by local union organizations and other stewards elected by workers meeting outside the union structures united to establish a regional coordinating committee. This body took permanent form as the Clyde Workers' Committee. Subsequently, stewards' committees were set up across Britain composed of representatives of all workers in a factory, regardless of formal union affiliation, while Workers' Committees were formed to unite representatives of stewards' bodies in a particular area.

   The struggles led by these bodies, initially focused on workers' rights on the job, broadened to include opposition to the drafting of workers into the army and other questions. Revolutionary socialists came to play a significant role in their leadership.

   The shop stewards' movement in Britain is discussed in Fineberg's report, printed in chapter 2.

5. The reference is to the Birmingham shop stewards committee.

6. The fourth member of the Presiding Committee was the permanent secretary, Klinger. The Presiding Committee was usually referred to by congress participants as the bureau.

7. Zinoviev later reported to the Russian Communist Party's eighth congress that Balabanoff and Vorovsky had acted as secretaries at the international gathering. Klinger, however, did form part of the congress presidium.

Chapter 2: National reports

1. On October 27, 1918, sailors of the German North Sea fleet mutinied against the High Command's plans to send

them on a final, hopeless assault on the British Navy. The revolution spread across Germany during the following days, ousting the imperial authorities with little resistance. Workers' and soldiers' councils were formed, and the revolution was welcomed by most of the rural population.

On November 9 the kaiser was forced to abdicate. The kaiser's prime minister, Prince Max von Baden, appointed Friedrich Ebert, a leader of the Social Democratic Party of Germany (SPD), to organize a new cabinet. Ebert pulled together a coalition government consisting of himself, Philipp Scheidemann, and Otto Landsberg for the SPD and Hugo Haase, Wilhelm Dittmann, and Emil Barth for the centrist-led "Independents"—the Independent Social Democratic Party of Germany (USPD).

In this book the initials *SPD,* derived from the party's name in German, always refer to the Social Democratic Party of Germany. Other social democratic parties are often referred to by the initials *SDP.*

2. "Majority Socialists" and "majority party" refer to the SPD. During the war the majority leadership of the SPD, headed by Ebert and Scheidemann, openly supported the imperial government's war effort and called for a halt to workers' struggles. Early in 1917, this majority leadership expelled the minority that opposed its war policies. The expelled forces, which included both centrists and revolutionaries, founded the USPD in April 1917.
3. See Riddell, *German Revolution,* pp. 84–85.
4. The Executive Committee of the Berlin Workers' and Soldiers' Councils acted as the provisional executive body for the councils across Germany, pending a national congress of the councils. The executive committee was acknowledged by the Ebert government and all working-class political parties as the formal source of governmental authority. In practice, however, Ebert's cabinet bypassed the executive committee and the councils, ruling through the ministries and state apparatus inherited from the imperial regime.
5. While the armistice of November 11 recognized the government of the newly born German republic, the Allied

powers maintained the blockade that kept the German population near starvation. The SPD-led German government itself secretly encouraged the Allied powers to state that food shipments would be made only "if public order is maintained." See Riddell, *German Revolution,* pp. 112–14.

6. The SPD-led government's course of protecting and restabilizing capitalism in Germany ran up against a rising wave of workers' struggles. To put down these workers, the government relied increasingly on the army High Command inherited from the kaiser and on the Freikorps, volunteer military detachments organized by right-wing officers to fight against "Bolshevism" on the eastern frontier and internally.

   On January 4, 1919, the SPD regime in Prussia dismissed the popular head of Berlin's police force, a member of the USPD's left wing. Berlin workers mobilized to defend him, and many armed themselves. On January 5, the Revolutionary Committee coordinating these protests decided to try to overthrow the SPD government. Little was done to carry out that goal, however, and the next day the centrists leading the committee opened negotiations with the government, hoping to resolve the crisis peacefully.

   On January 8 the government launched the Freikorps against the revolutionary workers' detachments. Armed resistance was crushed in three days, and the triumphant Freikorps instituted a reign of terror against militant workers. The official tally was 156 dead; in reality the toll was much higher. Among the dead were Liebknecht and Luxemburg.

   Documents on the January 1919 Berlin uprising are printed in Riddell, *German Revolution,* pp. 330–96.

   In subsequent weeks the Freikorps were sent into action several times to crush centers of strength of the councils and of workers' militancy across Germany. National Assembly elections were held on January 19, 1919. The SPD received 37.9 percent of the vote and the USPD 7.6 percent; the German Communist Party abstained from the elections. The bourgeois parties won a majority; two of them then joined the SPD in forming a coalition government.

7. Haase and Georg Ledebour led the eighteen SPD parliamentary deputies who joined Liebknecht in December 1914 in voting against war credits. Liebknecht had voted alone against war credits a year earlier. The Haase-Ledebour current became the nucleus of the USPD.

8. The date given here is incorrect. It was on December 29, 1918, that a national conference of the Spartacus League voted to break from the USPD and found a revolutionary party. The founding convention was then held December 30, 1918–January 1, 1919. For selected proceedings of the congress, see Riddell, *German Revolution,* pp. 224–90 and 320–25.

9. The order to fire on the demonstrators did not come directly from the Ebert-Scheidemann government, but rather from right-wing officers attempting a counterrevolutionary coup. They were foiled by a mobilization of Berlin workers and of the People's Naval Division, a detachment of revolutionary sailors stationed in that city.

   Although the Ebert-Scheidemann government insisted it had no part in the coup, one of the top conspirators from the army High Command later testified that he had consulted with Ebert on the coup in advance. Also, one detachment involved in the coup attempt had marched on the Reich chancellery and proclaimed Ebert "president." Moreover, following the coup, the government insisted that the arrested conspirators be released.

   Among those wounded on December 6 was the head of the Red Soldiers' League, Willi Budich, a leader of the Spartacus League. Eberlein was mistaken to say that these revolutionary soldiers belonged to the German Communist Party, which was not founded until several weeks later.

10. The Socialist Republic of Brunswick, headed by the Spartacist August Merges, was one of the most radical of the regimes established in Germany's federal states by the November revolution.

11. On December 21, 1918, members of the People's Naval Division participated in a demonstration called by the Red Soldiers' League. The government then demanded

that 80 percent of the division's troops be discharged and that it evacuate its headquarters. When the sailors refused, the government organized a military assault against them. German workers' outrage against this action forced the USPD members of the cabinet to resign on December 29.

12. The German trade union movement was dominated by unions aligned with the SPD. Smaller Catholic and liberal union federations were scorned by militant workers as "scab" or "Yellow" unions.

 With the outbreak of war in 1914, the pro-SPD union leadership took an open stand for collaboration with the government and the employers and enforced this policy throughout the union movement. As workers began to fight back, they improvised new coordinating bodies: shop stewards' committees, factory councils, and citywide workers' committees.

 After the kaiser's overthrow, however, the pro-SPD union leaders moved quickly to regain their authority, taking credit for many gains made possible by the workers' victory of November 9, such as the eight-hour day. The unions recruited new members in large numbers, while the factory councils began to lose momentum. In the first year after the November 9 revolution, union membership rose from 1.7 million to 5.5 million.

 Most German Communists initially rejected working in the reformist-led trade unions. It was not until October 1919 that a congress of the young German Communist Party recognized the need to fight within the SPD-led unions for a revolutionary course. See Riddell, *German Revolution,* pp. 262–72.

13. The Red Guards were volunteer detachments of revolutionary workers, usually organized on a factory basis, that formed spontaneously in Petrograd after the fall of the tsar. Although these formations were integrated into the Red Army early in 1918, the term *Red Guards* was still sometimes used to designate the pro-Soviet armed forces in the civil war.

14. On January 5, 1919, (not January 19) revolutionary Berlin workers occupied the building of *Vorwärts,* the SPD's daily newspaper, publishing it for several days as the "Organ of the Revolutionary Workers of Greater Berlin."

    The antagonism of radical Berlin workers toward *Vorwärts* dated back two years. Prior to October 1916, it had been a voice of the antiwar opposition in the SPD. That month the government seized the *Vorwärts* premises and turned the paper over to the SPD's pro-war majority leadership. Revolutionary workers held this action to be outright theft and saw the paper as rightfully theirs.

15. For a fuller account of the murders of Liebknecht and Luxemburg, see J.P. Nettl, *Rosa Luxemburg* (London: Oxford University Press, 1966), vol. 2, pp. 772–78. See also Riddell, *German Revolution,* pp. 685–86.

16. Radek had been sent to Germany in December 1918 as a representative of the Russian Communist Party and the Russian soviets. He was arrested February 12, 1919, and held in jail in solitary confinement. Five months later, he gained improved quarters and the right to receive visitors. He was released in January 1920.

    For Radek's own colorful account of his arrest and of what he called his "political salon" in a Berlin jail, see Radek, "November," *Soviet Studies,* vol. 3, no. 4, April 1952, pp. 418–28.

17. When the terms of the Brest-Litovsk treaty were voted in the German Reichstag on March 22, 1918, SPD deputies abstained, explaining that although the treaty had deficiencies, it did bring peace in the east. The Progressives and the Center party, who became the SPD's coalition parties in 1919, voted in favor of the treaty.

    By its terms, Germany occupied territories containing one third of the population, 73 percent of coal production, and 89 percent of the iron ore production of the former tsarist empire. Independent Soviet governments in the Ukraine, Belorussia, Latvia, and Estonia were overthrown by the German military, which also tipped the balance in the Finnish civil war.

18. The reference is to the Grütli Association (see glossary).
19. Robert Grimm visited Russia in the spring of 1917 in his capacity as chairman of the Zimmerwald International Socialist Committee. Right-wing forces in Russia attacked him as a German agent seeking a separate peace between Germany and Russia. While in Russia, Grimm contacted a Swiss government minister and asked for information on the war aims of the great powers. He received a reply outlining the diplomatic stance of the German government, which was intercepted and published by the Russian provisional government. It then deported Grimm as a tool of German diplomacy. The ensuing scandal forced Grimm to resign from his post in the Zimmerwald movement.
20. In February 1918 a coordinating body of Swiss working-class organizations, the Olten Action Committee, was formed. Headed by Robert Grimm, it included representatives of the Social Democratic Party (SDP), the unions, and the party's parliamentary fraction and press. In July a general workers' congress was held, composed of union and party representatives. It gave the Olten committee a mandate for action, including general strike if necessary, to achieve democratic political rights, a forty-eight-hour workweek, social insurance, and better food supplies for the population.
21. In early November 1918, the Swiss government responded to the spread of revolution through central Europe and to a planned celebration in Zurich of the anniversary of the Russian revolution (November 7) by sending troops to occupy the city. The Olten committee then called a one-day protest strike across the country, which was successfully carried out November 9 in more than fifteen cities. When government troops fired on workers' rallies in Zurich, the Olten committee called an extended national general strike.

    The strike began November 11 and was very effective, embracing 300,000 to 400,000 workers. Troops were sent against the workers and there was fighting in several cities. Although the strikers were prepared to continue the struggle, the Olten committee called for the strike to end on

November 15. The SDP left wing denounced this action as capitulation and betrayal, and militant workers continued the strike briefly in Zurich and some other centers.

22. The reference is to the small ultraleft Communist group represented at the congress by Kascher. Led by Jakob Herzog, this current founded the newspaper *Die Forderung* in the autumn of 1917 and organized a Communist Party of Switzerland in October 1918.

23. The Swiss SDP held an extraordinary congress on December 21, 1918, in Bern. It elected as party chairman Gustav Müller, a leading right-winger who had defied the party's decision that parliamentary deputies refuse to vote for military appropriations. Another extraordinary party congress, convened February 2, 1919, removed Müller from the chairman's post.

24. During July and August 1917, the Russian Provisional Government, headed by Alexander Kerensky, severely repressed the revolutionary workers' movement.

25. The second All-Russian Congress of Trade Unions, held January 16–25, 1919, emphasized the unions' vital functions in helping to reconstruct the war-shattered economy and organize and monitor industrial production. S.A. Lozovsky spoke at the congress for a minority advocating what they termed "trade union independence." For Lenin's speech for the majority position, see Lenin, "Report at the Second All-Russia Trade Union Congress," in *CW,* vol. 28, pp. 412–28. He stressed that the task of the trade unions above all was "to teach vast numbers of working people how to run the state and industry."

    Lenin's most thorough presentation of the Communist position on this question can be found in his speeches during the "trade union controversy" in 1921 and in his theses, "The Role and Functions of the Trade Unions Under the New Economic Policy," in *CW,* vol. 33, pp. 184–96.

26. The Soviet constitution of 1918 gave voting rights to all residents who earned their living by productive and socially useful labor or by housekeeping for this group, as

well as to Red Army soldiers and the incapacitated of these groups. It denied voting rights to those whose income was derived from employing hired labor for profits, from interest on capital, or from rent, as well as to private merchants, clergy, former members of the tsarist police, secret service, and ruling dynasty, and certain criminals.

"The disenfranchisement of the bourgeoisie is not a necessary and indispensable feature of the dictatorship of the proletariat," Lenin commented in "The Proletarian Revolution and the Renegade Kautsky." Their exclusion *"emerged* of itself in the course of the struggle. . . . Even when the Mensheviks . . . still ruled the Soviets, the bourgeoisie cut themselves off from the Soviets of their own accord, boycotted them . . . and intrigued against them." Lenin, *CW,* vol. 28, pp. 271–72.

"Depriving the exploiters of the franchise is a *purely Russian* question," Lenin stated, which had to be assessed in the light of the experience of this revolution. "For theory," on the other hand, the relevant question was "whether democracy can be *preserved for the rich, for the exploiters* in the historical period of the overthrow of the exploiters and the replacement of their state by the state of the exploited." Lenin, *CW,* vol. 28, p. 255.

27. In January 1918 the German government made demands on the Soviet republic at the Brest-Litovsk peace negotiations for the annexation or occupation of vast territories. One current in the Bolshevik Central Committee, led by Bukharin, favored rejecting this ultimatum and waging "revolutionary war" against German imperialism. Another current, led by Trotsky, proposed declaring the war at an end but refusing to sign the treaty with its onerous terms. Trotsky held that this course would best assist the revolutionary movement in Germany and the other warring imperialist powers.

A third current supported Lenin's view that there was no alternative but to accept the German ultimatum and sign the proposed "incredibly harsh, rapacious and humiliating peace." Lenin, "Resolution on Ratification of the Brest Treaty," in *CW,* vol. 27, p. 200.

In view of the disintegration of the peasant-based army and the extreme war weariness of the population, Lenin argued, an attempt to continue the war would isolate the Soviet regime and tear apart the worker-peasant alliance on which rested the Soviet state and its capacity for self-defense. A breathing space was required, in his view, to prepare for the impending civil war and imperialist onslaught and so improve the chances of the Soviet republic for survival—which was essential for the further advance of world revolution.

On January 24 (11) the Central Committee voted to adopt Trotsky's position. The Soviet delegation concluded the Brest-Litovsk negotiations on February 10 (January 28), declaring the war was at an end but rejecting the proposed treaty.

When the German army launched a general offensive eight days later, this convinced another layer of the Soviet Communist leadership of the correctness of Lenin's position. On February 18 the Central Committee voted by a narrow majority, which included Trotsky, to accept the terms demanded by the German government and sign the treaty.

28. Albert Thomas, Arthur Henderson, and other progovernment leaders of Social Democratic parties went to Russia in the spring and summer of 1917 on a mission from their governments to persuade the Russian Provisional Government and socialists in Russia to continue the war.

29. The "Dreyfus affair" of 1917 was the witch-hunt against the Bolsheviks mounted after the "July days" crisis by the parties supporting the Provisional Government. The campaign was orchestrated around charges that the Bolshevik leaders were German agents. Lenin and Zinoviev were forced to go into hiding, and Trotsky was imprisoned.

The original Dreyfus affair took place in France, where Alfred Dreyfus, a general staff officer of Jewish origin, was tried in 1894 on trumped-up charges of high treason and espionage for Germany. His trial and conviction were the pretext for a right-wing campaign, which had strong anti-Semitic overtones, against French republican institutions and democratic liberties. A campaign in his defense by democrats and socialists met intransigent opposition from reactionary circles but ultimately won his release and reinstatement into the army.

30. In speaking of a "capitulation" by the Right Socialist Revolutionaries, Zinoviev may have been referring to their failure to organize a defense of the Constituent Assembly when it was dissolved by the Soviet government on January 19 (6), 1918. Within a few months, however, this party was actively engaged in armed revolt against the Soviet republic.

31. The Paris Commune of 1871 represented the first attempt to establish a revolutionary government of the toilers. The working people of Paris held and administered the city from March 18 until May 28, when their resistance was crushed by the forces of the French bourgeoisie working in league with the German army. More than 17,000 working people of Paris were massacred in the ensuing terror.

32. In December 1918 the British government under Prime Minister David Lloyd George, aware of the unpopularity among the British people of the Allied powers' war against Soviet Russia and faced with mutinies in the army, raised with its allies strong doubts about prolonging the war of intervention in Russia. Rumor of these hesitations caused an outcry in British ruling circles and the right-wing press.

    On February 11 Lloyd George, addressing the British House of Commons on Russian policy, said that "everybody agrees that you cannot intervene . . . [since nothing] short of a big expeditionary force . . . would be of any use. . . . Has anyone calculated the cost?" Arno J. Mayer, *Politics and Diplomacy of Peacemaking* (New York: Alfred A. Knopf, 1967), p. 444.

33. Until 1917 Finland formed part of the Russian Empire. Twice in 1917 the Finnish SDP, poised to take power, had pulled back. After the October revolution, the Soviet government recognized Finland's right to self-determination. An independent Finnish republic under a bourgeois government was established in December 1917. The Finnish bourgeoisie organized White Guards and prepared an as-

sault aimed at disarming the revolutionary workers' Red Guards and repressing the workers' movement. The working class responded on January 27 (14), 1918, with an uprising in Helsinki that established a revolutionary government controlling the major cities and towns.

The bourgeois government took refuge in the north and launched a civil war. It appealed to imperial Germany for assistance, and on April 3 German troops landed in force.

Although the Soviet republic was formally barred under the Brest-Litovsk treaty from involvement in the Finnish struggle, it nevertheless supplied the Finnish revolutionary government with arms, ammunition, and some instructors. See Lenin, *CW,* vol. 27, p. 105.

Yet when the German army landed in Finland, the Soviet government could not escape the very unfavorable relationship of forces that had been registered in the terms of the Brest-Litovsk treaty; it was unable to intervene to halt the march of German and White forces on Helsinki.

34. During the Finnish revolution and civil war the Finnish Communists continued to work in the Social Democratic Party, which also contained opportunist currents. After the civil war, the Finnish Communists concluded that remaining in a united party with these forces had been an error.

35. These theses are printed in chapter 11.

36. The "German adventure" was the effort of the right-wing Finnish government in 1918 to forge an alliance with German imperialism. To curry favor with German ruling circles, the Finnish senate went so far in October 1918 as to elect a German prince as the king of Finland. But German imperialism collapsed the following month, and the German prince never ascended a Finnish throne.

37. The first workers' councils appeared in Christiania (Oslo) in December 1917. They quickly spread throughout the country, encompassing 60,000 workers by February 1918. The first national congress of the councils took place March

24, 1918. The hostility of the Norwegian Labor Party contributed to the decline of the councils, and they dissolved by the end of 1918.

38. The conference adopted a resolution proposing a course of mass action and approving use of the general strike. The left wing, led by Martin Tranmael, took a majority of seats on the party Central Executive Committee and the editorship of its main newspaper.

39. The Laborers Union organized unskilled workers. At the time it was the largest union in the Norwegian Labor Federation (Landsorganisationen) and was a stronghold of the radical left wing.

40. At the Socialist Party's St. Louis convention in April 1917, a resolution was adopted by a large majority opposing U.S. entry into the war, affirming working-class internationalism, and calling for renewed class struggle for socialism in wartime. The resolution was sponsored by Morris Hillquit, Charles Ruthenberg, and Algernon Lee. Two months later, an overwhelming majority of the members confirmed this position in a party referendum.

Following the convention, the centrist forces led by Hillquit carried out quite a different policy, which combined appeals for a negotiated peace with maneuvers toward a pro-war line. See Farrell Dobbs, *Revolutionary Continuity: The Early Years 1848–1917* (New York: Pathfinder Press, 1980), pp. 185–93 [2019 printing].

41. In January 1919 U.S. president Woodrow Wilson, adopting Lloyd George's proposal to discuss peace terms with the Bolsheviks, called for a conference on the Turkish island of Prinkipo [Büyük Ada] in the Princes Islands [Kizil Adalar] aimed at ending the war in Russia.

At this time U.S. soldiers, fresh from the European battlefields, were pouring back into the labor market, and a wave of radicalism was sweeping the country. A strike wave of unprecedented scope developed, and in February 1919, a general strike broke out in Seattle. Opposition mounted against U.S. intervention in Russia. A few weeks after the Comintern's founding congress, a company of U.S. soldiers in Arkhangel'sk refused orders to advance to the front, touching off fears of a general mutiny. In October 1919, Seattle longshoremen made international headlines when they discovered and refused to load munitions intended for White armies in Siberia.

42. The Communist Party of Hungary was launched November 4, 1918, in Moscow by members of the Hungarian section of the Russian CP, recruited from the half-million Hungarian prisoners of war in Russia. During November 1918 some 200 of these Hungarian Communists returned to Hungary. The party was refounded in Budapest on November 24 by these repatriated Communists together with local revolutionists.

    Among those who rallied to the new party were the Revolutionary Socialists. This current, formed in the spring of 1917 by left-wing SDP members, syndicalists, and anarchists, had played a key role in launching the January 1918 strikes in Hungary.

    By January 1919 the Hungarian CP claimed 10,000 members.

43. Reports of an impending attack by progovernment troops prompted revolutionary Hungarian workers and soldiers on the night of October 31, 1918, to occupy the government buildings and strategic points in Budapest. Hoping to save the Hapsburg monarchy, Archduke Joseph, the regent of Hungary, called on Count Mihály Károlyi, a liberal aristocrat, to form a new government. Károlyi's government was made up of right-wing Social Democratic and bourgeois politicians. Increasing popular pressure forced Hungary's National Council on November 16 to end the monarchy and proclaim Hungary a republic.

44. In mid-November 1917, in response to news of the Soviet government's decree on peace, demonstrations and protests were held in Zurich for peace and against war production. Police fired on an action on November 17, killing three demonstrators.

    The SDP took no part in these protests. The November 17 action was called by the *Forderung* group, which had originated in the SDP's youth movement but which frequently called actions on its own.

45. Zurich bank workers went on strike at the end of September 1918 for union recognition and wage increases. The Zurich Workers' Union, a municipal council of delegates from workers' organizations led by Platten and the SDP left wing, organized a broad sympathy strike. Under this pressure, even the city government felt compelled to speak up for the bank workers. The bank owners gave way, and the strike ended in victory.

46. Leon Trotsky, *Pyat' let Kominterna* (Moscow: Gosizdat., 1924), vol. 1, pp. 14–17. This text differs from the 1921 editions of the congress proceedings only through minor stylistic changes.

    Related articles by Trotsky on the founding of the Communist International are printed in *The First Five Years of the Communist International* (New York: Pathfinder Press, 1945, 1972), volume 1.

47. Following the treaty of Brest-Litovsk, the Red Army rapidly gained strength, repulsing the first major White Guard offensive in the summer of 1918. The outbreak of revolution in Central Europe that fall forced Germany and Austria-Hungary to withdraw their armies from most occupied Soviet territory. The Allied powers then stepped up their anti-Soviet intervention. By the March congress, however, this invasion was rapidly losing momentum, and within a few months Allied armies were in full retreat.

    In March 1919, French soldiers began refusing to fight, and in April the French Black Sea fleet mutinied. All French forces withdrew from the Black Sea coast by early May.

    Beginning in January 1919 a number of mutinies broke out among the British forces in Russia. Faced with unrest in its colonies and at home, the British government began its withdrawal in the summer of 1919 and pulled out its last troops a year later.

    In Italy and the United States, workers blocked the dispatch of military cargo to the interventionist and White Guard armies. Both governments were soon compelled to withdraw from Russia. Japanese detachments in Vladivostok, the last of the interventionist armies, withdrew in 1922.

48. In the summer of 1918, Right Socialist Revolutionaries carried out a coup in Samara (Kuibyshev), where many right-wing members of the former Constituent Assembly had assembled. A government was organized in the name of these deputies under the protection of Czech anti-Soviet forces. In November 1918, White Guard officers dispersed this government. Among the fugitives, the more radical Socialist Revolutionaries sought refuge in Soviet territory.

49. The left-wing forces around the newspaper *De Tribune* were expelled from the Dutch Social Democratic Workers Party in 1909. They founded the Social Democratic Party, a revolutionary grouping with a few hundred members, which formed the Communist Party of the Netherlands in November 1918.

50. A high point of mass action by the German Social Democratic Party was the demonstration for equal voting rights of 150,000 in Berlin on March 6, 1910, which was organized successfully despite a police ban. Other large actions against the war danger were held on several occasions before August 1914.

51. The Joint Cooperative Workers' Associations (Samenwerkende Arbeidersverenigingen) campaigned for immediate demobilization of the Dutch army and, in view of the severe food shortages among Dutch workers, for an end to the export of food. This work reached its high point in 1916, when the committee organized a "Protest Congress Against the War," gathered 77,500 signatures on a petition, and held a series of demonstrations culminating in a June 21 rally of 25,000 in Amsterdam.

52. The beginning of the German revolution led to a brief but sweeping working-class upsurge in the Netherlands that became known as the "Red Week." Soldiers' councils arose and mass workers' strikes took place.

    Under the impact of these events, the opportunist Social Democratic Workers Party's main leader, Pieter Troelstra, told a Rotterdam rally that proletarian revolution was necessary. Troelstra's statement, however, was disavowed by his party and by union leaders, and he soon dropped his revolutionary tone. Congresses of the party and trade unions November 16–17 presented a program for limited reforms and succeeded in keeping the lid on the movement.

53. The Dutch colonial empire then included the islands that make up present-day Indonesia as well as Suriname and several islands in the Caribbean.

54. Trotsky's "Order of the Day Number 83 to the Red Army and Navy," which conveyed these greetings, is printed in Trotsky, *First Five Years,* vol. 1, pp. 51–52 [2019 printing].

55. The minutes of the Credentials Commission are printed in chapter 11.

56. The reference is to the provisional list of delegates drawn up by the preliminary meeting on March 1.

57. Rakovsky was mistaken; the former Romanian Social Democratic Party had taken the name "Socialist" late in 1918. It was not until 1921 that it formally took the name Communist and voted to join the Communist International.

58. On December 13, 1918, 50,000 workers demonstrated in Bucharest for a republic and for socialism. Troops were ordered to fire on them, and hundreds were killed. In the spring of 1919 a strike wave began that spread to several industries and lasted into the summer, involving a total of 150,000 workers.

59. When war broke out in August 1914, the Serbian Social Democratic Party was, aside from the two wings of Russian Social Democracy, the only Social Democratic party in a warring country whose parliamentary deputies voted against war credits. The Serbian party joined the Zimmerwald movement, and its representative at the Kienthal conference of 1916, Triša Kaclerović, voted there with the Zimmerwald Left. The following year Kaclerović and another Serbian socialist leader, Dušan Popović, went to

Stockholm, where an international conference had been called under right-wing Social Democratic auspices.

The conference did not materialize. Kaclerović and Popović, however, wrote two memoranda for the committee that had tried to organize it. The first described conditions in Serbia under occupation by the Central Powers, and the second proposed peace terms that included several of the demands of Serbian nationalism that had been taken up by the Allied powers.

Serbian revolutionaries condemned these actions as playing into the hands of the Allied powers and representing a break with internationalism.

60. Milkić's remarks were not included in any edition of the congress minutes. However, a written version of his report in reply to Rakovsky was printed in the fourth issue of *The Communist International* in 1919 and included as an appendix to the 1933 edition of the congress proceedings. This version is printed below in chapter 11.

61. Two weeks after the October 1917 revolution, the Rada, a parliamentary council hostile to the soviets' assuming power, proclaimed the Ukrainian People's Republic. The Soviet government in Petrograd recognized this action. But the Rada soon began collaborating with counterrevolutionary White Guard armies. A Bolshevik-led all-Ukrainian congress of soviets, meeting in Kharkov December 24 (11), proclaimed the Ukraine a Soviet republic. The Rada, which had resisted peasant demands for land, was unable to rally support, and its armed forces quickly disintegrated. Soviet forces occupied Kiev, the Ukrainian capital, on February 8 (January 26), 1918.

The Rada then appealed for help to the German government. The German army swept across the Ukraine, ousting from power first the Ukrainian Soviet government and then the Rada itself and installing as its puppet ruler the former tsarist general P.P. Skoropadsky. He proclaimed himself monarch with the old Cossack title of hetman. Following the November 1918 revolution in Germany, the German military withdrew and Skoropadsky's rule collapsed. Forces from the Rada, led by S.V. Petlyura and V.K. Vinnichenko, established the Directory, a new anti-Soviet government propped up by interventionist Allied troops. Pro-Soviet forces launched an offensive and reoccupied Kiev on February 5, 1919.

At the time of the Comintern congress most of the Ukraine was once more under the rule of the Ukrainian soviets, while Petlyura's forces fought on in the west, and France and French-sponsored White Guard armies occupied territories along the Black Sea coast.

Counterrevolutionary armies were to sweep across the Ukraine twice more in the course of the civil war: Kiev was occupied by the White army of A.I. Denikin in August 1919 and by the Polish government's army in May 1920. Armed resistance to Soviet rule ended in 1921.

62. The Red Army in the Ukraine was a component part of the Red Army as a whole, which defended all the Soviet republics.

63. At the sixth congress of the Ukrainian Social Democratic Labor Party, held January 10–12, 1919, a left wing broke away and established the Ukrainian Social Democrats (Independents). Although the Independents declared for Soviet rule in an independent Ukraine, they held that the Bolshevik-led Ukrainian governments of 1918 and 1919 linked themselves too closely to the Russian Soviet regime, followed a policy of Russification, refused to establish Ukrainian as the national language, and were ethnically too Russian in composition.

64. Vinnichenko broke with the Directory in early 1919. In 1920 he linked up with the Ukrainian Social Democrats (Independents) and joined the Ukrainian Soviet government for a brief period. Petlyura's forces retreated westward and continued their war against the Soviet government in 1919, conducting ruthless massacres of the Jewish population. Petlyura took part in the unsuccessful Polish invasion of the Ukraine in 1920.

65. The Galician National Democrats were a current in the western Ukraine, also called East Galicia. A report on East Galicia is printed in chapter 11.

66. The experience in 1918 of Skoropadsky's regime, when Ukrainian "independence" proved to be only a mask for its pillage by the German occupation forces, largely discredited the demand for an independent state among the Ukrainian masses. In the months following the congress, however, nationalist feeling in the Ukraine rebounded, and it influenced the later course of the civil war in the Ukraine.

In October 1919, Denikin's White Guards were routed by the Red Army, and Soviet rule was established in the Ukraine for the third time. On November 29, 1919, the Central Committee (CC) of the Russian Communist Party (RCP) adopted a resolution on Soviet rule in the Ukraine that codified many lessons of the revolution there regarding the Ukrainian nationalist movement. The resolution reaffirmed the Ukraine's right of self-determination and recognized the independence of the Ukrainian Soviet Socialist Republic. With regard to Ukrainian nationalism, the resolution stated:

"In view of the fact that Ukrainian culture (language, school, etc.) has been suppressed for centuries by Russian tsarism and the exploiting classes, the C.C., R.C.P. makes it incumbent upon all Party members to use every means to help remove all barriers in the way of the free development of the Ukrainian language and culture. Since the many centuries of oppression have given rise to nationalist tendencies among the backward sections of the population, R.C.P. members must exercise the greatest caution in respect of those tendencies and must oppose them with words of comradely explanation concerning the identity of interests of the working people of the Ukraine and Russia.

"R.C.P. members on Ukrainian territory must put into practice the right of the working people to study in the Ukrainian language and to speak their native language in all Soviet institutions; they must in every way counteract attempts at Russification that push the Ukrainian language into the background and must convert that language into an instrument for the communist education of the working people. Steps must be taken immediately to ensure that in all Soviet institutions there are sufficient Ukrainian-speaking employees and that in future all employees are able to speak Ukrainian." Lenin, "Draft Resolution of the C.C., R.C.P.(B.) on Soviet Rule in the Ukraine," *CW,* vol. 30, pp. 163–64.

The resolution was discussed and adopted the following week by the party's eighth all-Russian conference.

The following month, Lenin explained the Bolsheviks' views on Ukrainian independence more fully in his "Letter to the Workers and Peasants of the Ukraine Apropos of the Victories over Denikin," in *CW,* vol. 30, pp. 291–97.

Another article by Lenin that month explained the thinking behind the Bolsheviks' stand. "To ignore the importance of the national question in the Ukraine—a sin of which Great Russians are often guilty . . .—is a great and dangerous mistake," he wrote. "As internationalists it is our duty, first, to combat very vigorously the survivals (sometimes unconscious) of Great-Russian imperialism and chauvinism among 'Russian' Communists; and secondly, it is our duty, precisely on the national question, which is a relatively minor one (for an internationalist the question of state frontiers is a secondary, if not a tenth-rate, question), to make concessions.

"We must not be in the least surprised or frightened," he continued, "even by the prospect of the Ukrainian workers and peasants trying out different systems, and in the course of, say, several years, testing by practice union with the R.S.F.S.R. [Russian Soviet Federated Socialist Republic], or seceding from the latter and forming an independent Ukrainian S.S.R. [Soviet Socialist Republic]." Lenin, "The Constituent Assembly Elections and the Dictatorship of the Proletariat," in *CW,* vol. 30, pp. 270–71.

67. The translation of this report has been edited on the basis of a comparison with the French text of Sadoul's remarks published in *L'Internationale Communiste,* no. 3 (1919), col. 397–404.

The written report of the French Communist Group, of which Sadoul was a member, is printed in chapter 11.

68. This paragraph, which is contained in the 1921 German- and Russian-language editions of the congress proceedings, is omitted from the Russian-language edition of 1933. Other favorable references to Trotsky in Sadoul's report are also omitted from the 1933 edition.

69. The tsarist regime recruited the Czechoslovak divisions from among Czech and Slovak prisoners in Russia, promising them the liberation of their homeland through victory over Austria-Hungary and Germany. After the October 1917 revolution, the Czechoslovak leadership of these divisions asked the Soviet government to send their units to western Europe to fight there alongside the Allied powers.

The Czechoslovak troops, numbering about 40,000, were sent eastward across Siberia toward Vladivostok, from where they were to proceed by ship to Europe. In May 1918, while these divisions were strung out along the railroad line in western Siberia, they rebelled against the Soviet authorities. The Allied powers were complicit in the revolt and gave it their support.

In June, a British expeditionary force of about 3,000, which had occupied Murmansk on the Barents Sea, advanced three hundred miles inland, disarming Red detachments sent to reassert Soviet control.

70. The Red Army was founded as an international rather than a specifically Russian force and fought to defend not only the Soviet government in Russia but also other Soviet regimes established in neighboring countries.

71. The majority Socialists of the French SP, led by Pierre Renaudel, favored France's waging all-out war to victory and opposed any contacts with Socialist parties on the other side of the battle line.

The *minoritaires,* the minority wing led by Jean Longuet, also supported national defense and voted for war credits. However, they advocated that France seek a compromise peace and hoped to reestablish contact with the Social Democratic parties in Germany and its allies in order to reach agreement on peace terms and urge them on the warring powers.

The revolutionary left wing in the French SP and the trade unions was organized in the Committee for Resumption of International Relations, which became the Committee for the Third International in May 1919.

72. At this October 6–19, 1918, conference, the Longuet current obtained a majority and took over the party leadership.

73. Sadoul was referring to the German November revolution of 1918.

74. Raoul Verfeuil's letter to the congress is printed in chapter 11 of the present work. Fernand Loriot's declaration to the Bern conference is printed in Riddell, *German Revolution,* pp. 550–52.

75. About ten million workdays were lost in strikes in Britain in 1911 and nearly forty million in 1912. The "Liverpool massacre" of August 1911, in which the army and police attacked a rally of rail workers, injuring several hundred, sparked a general strike of rail workers. A nationwide miners' strike in 1912 grew to encompass one million strikers and brought to a halt much of British industry, which was dependent on coal. The strikers succeeded in obtaining a minimum wage law. See Lenin, "The British Labour Movement in 1912," in *CW,* vol. 18, pp. 467–68.

76. The first large wartime strike in Britain was that of the Scottish workers in the Clyde Valley in February and March 1915. Work stoppages spread across the country; 448,000 workers participated in strikes in 1915. The government responded in July 1915 and January 1916 with laws virtually banning strikes in essential war industries, and these came to cover 80 percent of all workers. In 1916, the year when the German army resumed the offensive in the west and the British army was defeated on the Somme, the number of strikers fell somewhat—to 276,000 workers. In 1917, however, when the U.S. entered the war, there were 872,000 participants in strike action, and in 1918, 1,116,000.

77. "Civil peace" translates the German term *Burgfrieden,* used after August 1914 for the majority Social Democratic and trade union leaderships' policy of support for the government in prosecuting the war effort and opposition to workers' struggles during the war to defend their interests.

78. In the wake of the 1917 strikes, the British government appointed a committee of employers and union leaders, chaired by J.H. Whitley, then deputy speaker of the House of Commons, to make proposals on how to secure better labor relations. Their chief recommendation was for joint boards of management and unions in each industry, which were to discuss not only wages and working conditions but questions of company management and efficiency.

79. The Leeds conference was called on the initiative of the British Socialist Party and the Independent Labour Party. It was attended by 1,150 delegates representing five million organized workers and reflecting a broad spectrum of opportunist and revolutionary viewpoints.

80. More than 100,000 metalworkers in the Clyde valley went on strike in January 1919 for the forty-hour week. Their action, not sanctioned by their unions, was led by shop stewards' and factory committees. The government sent in the army to occupy Glasgow, and the strike was crushed. A similar struggle in Belfast at that time was also defeated. Britain's coal miners were also threatening strike action.

    During 1919 as a whole the number of days lost in strikes in Britain jumped to more than 36 million, from 5 million in 1918. Most often, the workers won part or all of their demands. More than six million workers won a shorter workday, and a similar number won pay raises.

81. In January 1919 British soldiers mutinied and demonstrated in Folkestone, Dover, Pas de Calais, Shoreham, Shortlands, Luton, Glasgow, and Belfast, demanding immediate demobilization. Soldiers organized a demonstration in London, and on January 7 about 1,500 marched to the prime minister's residence on Downing Street.

In many cases soldiers mutinied when given orders to leave England for service abroad. So strong was their opposition to service in Russia that the British chief of staff informed the government on January 10 that British forces there could not be reinforced.

82. In the December 1918 British parliamentary elections, seventy-three members were elected from Sinn Fein, the revolutionary nationalist party of Ireland. Refusing to take their seats in the House of Commons, the Sinn Fein deputies constituted themselves as the Dáil, the Irish parliament, and declared Irish independence. In response, the British army tightened its grip on Ireland and heightened repression. A few months after the Comintern congress, in the summer of 1919, the Irish Republican Army launched the armed struggle against British rule. This led in 1921 to British withdrawal from the twenty-six southern counties and recognition of the Irish Free State, while the six northern counties remained under British rule.

83. The Irish Easter Rebellion of 1916 was the first major outbreak of revolt by the oppressed and exploited in Europe during the World War. An independent Irish republic was proclaimed, and more than a thousand Irish patriots held out for five days in Dublin against the British army, hoping to inspire a national uprising for Irish freedom. The revolt was crushed, and James Connolly, a revolutionary socialist and a central leader of the Republican uprising, was executed by the British, along with fourteen other Irish leaders.

84. Capitalizing on Britain's victory in the war, the Conservative-Liberal coalition led by Lloyd George swept the elections in December 1918, winning 501 seats to Labour's 57.

Chapter 3: Platform

1. Grimlund's report is printed in chapter 11.

2. The last gathering of the Second International before its collapse in 1914 was the emergency congress held in Ba-

sel, Switzerland, in November 1912 to respond to the Balkan Wars crisis. Its manifesto is printed in Riddell, *Lenin's Struggle,* pp. 153–56.

3. During the war, the belligerent imperialist powers of Europe instituted far-reaching state control of their economies to assure supplies of essential war goods and regulate consumption. This process went furthest in Germany, where the government took control of distribution of most foods, set their prices, and imposed rationing. A degree of economic planning was introduced, which included government seizure of needed supplies. In addition, labor was militarized, and all males between the ages of seventeen and sixty were liable to compulsory labor in the war industries. This system worked in conjunction with the black market and corporate profiteering to impoverish working people and enrich the capitalists.

   When the war ended, the capitalist governments moved to eliminate most of these wartime controls.

4. See section 2, paragraph 1 of the platform, which is printed in chapter 10.

   The following are some of the passages where Karl Marx and Frederick Engels discuss the "withering away" of the state during the transition to communist society:

   Marx, "The Poverty of Philosophy," in Marx and Engels, *Collected Works,* vol. 6, p. 212;

   Marx and Engels, "Manifesto of the Communist Party," in Marx and Engels, *Collected Works,* vol. 6, pp. 505–6;

   Engels, letter to Theodor Cuno, January 24, 1872, in Marx and Engels, *Selected Correspondence* (Moscow: Progress Publishers, 1975), p. 257;

   Engels, letter to August Bebel, March 18–28, 1875, in Marx and Engels, *Selected Correspondence,* pp. 275–76;

   Engels, *Anti-Dühring* (Moscow: Progress Publishers, 1977), pp. 340–41;

   Engels, letter to Philip Van Patten, April 8, 1883, in Marx, *On the First International* (New York: McGraw Hill, 1973), p. 582;

Engels, "The Origin of the Family, Private Property and the State," in Marx and Engels, *Selected Works* (hereinafter *SW*) (Moscow: Progress Publishers, 1977), vol. 3, p. 330.

5. The following are a few of the passages where Marx and Engels discuss the destruction of the bourgeois state apparatus:

   Marx, "First Outline of 'The Civil War in France,'" in Marx and Engels, *On the Paris Commune* (Moscow: Progress Publishers, 1971), pp. 151–52;

   Marx, "The Civil War in France," in Marx and Engels, *SW,* vol. 2, p. 217–23;

   Engels's introduction to the 1891 edition of "The Civil War in France," in Marx and Engels, *SW,* vol. 2, pp. 187–89.

6. Following the entry of the United States government into World War I, the U.S. Congress adopted the Espionage Act. Purportedly directed against German spies, this law severely restricted democratic rights, prohibiting the utterance of "any disloyal, profane, scurrilous, or abusive language about the form of government of the United States," its constitution, or its armed forces. The law was utilized for raids on headquarters of the Socialist Party and the IWW, for widespread arrests of antiwar activists, and to deny second-class mailing rights to newspapers containing antiwar opinions.

7. "What the Spartacus League Wants," originally published in December 1918 and accepted as the initial program of the German Communist Party formed that month, is printed in Riddell, *German Revolution,* pp. 174–85.

8. The draft of the platform discussed by Rutgers is not found in the congress proceedings. The final, edited text is printed below in chapter 10. The edited version of the passage cited by Rutgers can be found in section 3 of the platform, paragraph 7.

9. See section 4, paragraph 5 of the platform.

10. See section 4, paragraph 6 of the platform. Later in the discussion, Platten reported that the editing commission was proposing a change in this passage along the lines of Rutgers's proposal.

11. See section 4, paragraph 6 of the platform.

Mutinies by soldiers in the imperialist armies of Europe between 1917 and 1919 and soldiers' involvement in revolutionary uprisings led the imperialist governments to form plans to use non-European troops from the colonies against workers' struggles and the Soviet republic. The imperialists calculated that troops from Asia and Africa, unacquainted with European languages and less directly influenced by the European class struggle, would be less sympathetic to workers in Europe than were the mass conscript armies of European workers and peasants.

More than 100,000 African troops had fought in Europe during the war, and some 20,000–30,000 troops recruited in the colonies were stationed permanently in France when it ended. A large proportion of French interventionist armies along the Black Sea coast and in Vladivostok were made up of troops from Algeria, Senegal, and Indochina. In the workers' movement in several European countries, fear of this new ruling-class threat was sometimes combined with racism promoted by the ruling classes against the colonial peoples.

Leading Bolsheviks attacked this new move by the imperialist powers to exploit the colonial peoples and set them against workers and peasants in Europe. The Bolsheviks had long been the party most strongly identified with the demand for immediate independence of colonial peoples and with resolute defense of their struggles. See Riddell, *Lenin's Struggle,* pp. 168–75.

The platform adopted by the Moscow congress offered full support to colonial struggles against imperialism. Despite Rutgers's suggestion, however, the words "brutalized, barbaric colonial troops" were not removed from the resolution's final text.

Even as the Moscow congress took place, African troops in the French interventionist army showed they felt no commitment to their colonial oppressors' war against the Soviet republic. An Algerian unit refused to embark from Romania for Sevastopol in Crimea, and the Algerian and Senegalese soldiers already in Sevastopol, a majority of the French army forces there, were a center of discontent. French generals complained that troops from the colonies could not stand the weather, that they lacked discipline, and that their units needed more French sergeants to maintain control.

Despite this experience, the French army continued to station colonial troops in France and occupied Germany. This issue was addressed in 1921 by the "Theses on Tactics" adopted at the third Comintern congress as follows: "The presence of black troops in France and in the occupied territories gives the French Communist Party special responsibilities. It provides the French Party with the opportunity of approaching these colonial slaves and explaining to them that they are serving their own oppressors and exploiters, of rallying them to fight against the colonial regime and establishing links with the peoples of the French colonies." Alan Adler, ed., *Theses, Resolutions and Manifestos of the First Four Congresses of the Third International* (London: Pluto Press, 1983), p. 295. (Documents of this congress will appear in a new translation in a forthcoming volume of *The Communist International in Lenin's Time*.)

The Communist Youth in France worked actively among these troops, publishing an Arabic-language newspaper for this purpose. When African troops were used in the French government's occupation of the German Ruhr district in 1923–24, the Communists campaigned to alert them to the danger that they would be used to repress German workers. A young Algerian Communist, Mahmoud Ben Lekhal, was jailed for five years for his leading role in this work. On at least one occasion, an Algerian contingent refused an order to fire on a demonstration of German unemployed workers.

Subsequently, the French and other imperialist governments shelved plans to use colonial troops to repress workers' struggles in Europe.

12. See section 3, paragraph 1 of the platform.
13. See section 2, paragraph 4 of the platform.
14. The International Working Men's Association, the First International, was founded September 28, 1864, at a meet-

ing in St. Martin's Hall in London. Marx wrote to Engels that the meeting hall was "packed to *suffocation.*" Marx and Engels, *Selected Correspondence,* p. 137.

Present at the meeting were representatives of diverse political currents that then influenced the workers' movement in the different countries of Europe: central leaders of the British trade union movement; some veteran leaders of Chartism, the first mass working-class movement of Britain; John Weston, a leader of the Owenite utopian socialist movement; Proudhonists (a French petty-bourgeois socialist current); representatives of the French petty-bourgeois democratic left; representatives of Italian bourgeois-democratic revolutionist Giuseppe Mazzini; Polish emigré revolutionists; as well as leaders of the German Communist Workers' Educational Association in London, in which Marx was then a leading participant.

15. Kuusinen was mistaken: Wilhelm Liebknecht was not present at the St. Martin's Hall meeting; moreover, it was not organized on a delegated basis. Liebknecht had returned in 1862 from London to Germany where he helped organize the First International in 1865–66.

16. Steinhardt had just arrived in Moscow after a grueling trip across eastern Europe and had gone directly from the railway station to the congress.

"We were listening to a boring speech," related Thomas, "when the door banged open and, preceded by an attendant, a man in Austrian uniform entered. His beard unkempt, his soldiers' greatcoat in tatters (one whole side was torn), he went right up to the presiding committee. 'I am the delegate of the Austrian Communists.' He immediately pulled out a knife with which he proceeded to cut open his coat and extract his credentials." "Récit de 'Thomas,'" in Freymond, *Contributions,* p. 10.

"When I reached the podium," Steinhardt recalled, "I dumped my bag on the floor and handed the invitation to Comrade Lenin. Lenin rose, stepped up to me and, standing on his tiptoes, placed both his hands on my shoulders and in Russian fashion kissed both my cheeks, which were bristling with stubble. . . . 'Comrade delegate, you will speak at once,' he said." Steinhardt, "Der österreichische Antrag," in *Lenin und die Internationale: Erinnerungen von Zeitgenossen* (Berlin [GDR]: Dietz Verlag, 1983), p. 70.

Referring in 1924 to Steinhardt and his traveling companion, Petin, Zinoviev wrote, "Two of them practically rode the whole way on the buffers of trains, pretending to be prisoners of war. They brought with them a whiff of the powder and smoke of the great combats which at that time were taking place in many countries. And they were entirely on our side, on the side of those who thought it necessary to proclaim the Communist International at that very Congress." Zinoviev, "Five Years: The Constituent Congress of the Communist International," *International Press Correspondence,* no. 21, 1924.

17. The January 1918 upsurge in Austria-Hungary, while sparked by a sharp reduction in the meager food rations, also expressed workers' desire for an immediate peace and their suspicion of the government's conduct in the Brest-Litovsk peace negotiations. The strike movement began January 14 in the industrial city of Wiener Neustadt and grew to include nearly 250,000 workers in the region around Vienna. Leadership of the strike initially fell to the more radical leaders of the workers' movement. Nevertheless, the Social Democratic party (SDP) convinced the Vienna workers' council to halt the strike on January 20, just as the Hungarian workers were going out. Only two days later a mutiny broke out in the navy; half the navy was in insurgents' hands for three days in early February.
18. The "party of social traitors" was the Austrian SDP, most of whose leaders had backed the imperial government since 1914 in the prosecution of the war.
19. On January 17, in an effort to undercut the radical demands raised by the workers' councils, the SDP leaders presented four demands to the government: first, that it "give calming reassurances that . . . it would not permit any territorial demands to cause the collapse of the Brest-Litovsk peace negotiations" and that it keep workers' leaders informed

on the negotiations; second, that it "fundamentally reorganize the food supply system"; third, that it move to introduce universal, equal, and direct suffrage for municipal representatives; and fourth, that it "end the militarization of the factories." Hans Hautmann, *Die verlorene Räterepublik* (Vienna: Europa Verlag, 1971), pp. 53–54.

20. Soon after the war began, a Left Radical current began to form in Austria, first of all in the SDP youth organization. This group distributed the Zimmerwald Manifesto and material from the German Spartacists; it also had ties with the radical leadership of the Socialist Youth International in Switzerland. A Left Radical Action Committee was formed in the winter of 1915–16 and sent a delegate (who arrived late) to the Kienthal conference in April 1916. The Left Radicals played a significant role in the January 1918 strikes, after which most of their leaders were imprisoned. Although hampered by severe repression, they continued their activity after the strike. Many Left Radicals joined the Communist Party of German Austria between December 1918 and February 1919.

21. Soldiers' revolts erupted in the Austro-Hungarian army in October 1918, and the army on the Italian front crumbled during the last week of that month. Austria-Hungary disintegrated as its non-German nationalities declared their independence. On October 30, a massive demonstration of workers and soldiers assembled in front of the parliament building in Vienna, demanding proclamation of a republic. Workers' and soldiers' councils were formed. The alarmed parliament established a provisional government of German Austria headed by the right-wing Social Democrat Karl Renner. Under mounting popular pressure, this government proclaimed the Austrian republic on November 12.

22. The "triumvirate" refers to the State Directorate formed on December 19, 1918. The three co-presidents of this body represented each of German Austria's three major political formations: Johann Nepomuk Hauser for the Christian Social Party, Franz Dinghofer for the German National Party, and Karl Seitz for the Social Democratic Party.

23. In the spring of 1918 the Left Radicals began discussions with the Friedländer group, composed of opposition intellectuals around Elfriede and Paul Friedländer and Steinhardt, which sought to found a Communist party. The Left Radicals opposed this. They wanted to broaden the layer of radical leadership in the working class and did not want to leave the SDP. A secret conference met in Vienna in early June 1918 with 150 participants from all the socialist opposition groups, including radical shop stewards, Left Radicals, Friedländer supporters, left Poale Zion members, and a few anarcho-syndicalists. It reached no agreement on founding a new party. Another strike wave broke out in June, and the ensuing repression disrupted the ongoing discussions aimed at working out a common program and launching a Communist party.

24. The first issue of *Weckruf* was prepared by the Friedländer group for distribution on May Day 1918, but was confiscated by the police on April 26. The paper did not reappear until November.

25. The gunfire wounded three people, and twenty-four were injured in the ensuing panic, two of whom later died. It was Steinhardt who had read before the parliament building the declaration of the Communist Party of German Austria calling for a workers' and peasants' government.

    Later that day, Steinhardt and Elfriede and Paul Friedläder took part in a brief occupation of the offices of the bourgeois newspaper *Neue freie Presse* (New free press). Before being forced out, they published a special issue in which they stated that the "social republic" had been proclaimed that afternoon. Bourgeois parties and Social Democrats claimed these incidents showed the CP to be "putschist," and the government jailed Steinhardt and Elfriede Friedländer.

26. The "Russian friends" were members of the Vienna Bolshevik Group, a group of Russians living in Vienna that had joined the Austrian CP.

27. When founded on November 3, 1918, the Austrian CP was no more than an underground circle of about fifteen people, principally from the Friedländer and Vienna Bol-

shevik groups. However, the new party grew significantly between early December 1918 and February 1919, uniting with much broader forces from the Left Radicals and the Federation of Revolutionary Socialists (International) and recruiting many returning Austrian prisoners of war. When the first regular party congress was held on February 9, 1919, it had 3,000 members.

28. An international conference of reformist-led trade unions was held in Bern, Switzerland, in February 1919 simultaneously with the Bern conference of Social Democratic parties. A subsequent congress in Amsterdam in July 1919,attended by delegates from unions with a combined membership of 17,740,000 in thirteen European countries and the United States, formed the International Federation of Trade Unions, taking the name of the prewar federation that had collapsed in 1914. It was generally known as the Amsterdam International.

29. The "resolutions commission" appears to have been another name for the Presiding Committee or "bureau," which often invited to its meetings delegates responsible for drafting different resolutions.

30. See section 4, paragraph 6 of the platform.

31. No position was adopted at the first congress on the trade union question.

    At the time of the congress most of the Communist currents outside Russia opposed work inside the reformist-led trade unions, and in subsequent years the proposal of fighting to transform these unions was the subject of much debate in the Comintern.

    The trade union question was taken up by Lenin in his 1920 pamphlet, "'Left-Wing' Communism—an Infantile Disorder." Lenin, *CW,* vol. 31, pp. 46–56. The second Comintern congress, held in 1920, called on Communists to "join the unions in order to develop them into bodies consciously struggling for the overthrow of capitalism and the creation of Communism." See "The Trade Union Movement, Factory Committees and the Third International," in Adler, *Theses, Resolutions and Manifestos,* pp. 106–113.

Chapter 4: Dictatorship of the proletariat

1. Lenin, *CW,* vol. 28, pp. 457–68.
2. See, for example, Engels's 1891 introduction to "The Civil War in France," which states, "In reality, however, the state is nothing but a machine for the oppression of one class by another, and indeed in the democratic republic no less than in the monarchy." Marx and Engels, *SW,* vol. 2, p. 189.
3. Marx, "The Civil War in France," in Marx and Engels, *SW,* vol. 2, p. 221. Marx's words are mistranslated in that edition as "misrepresent." Lenin's translation, "represent and suppress," is accurate.
4. Lenin, *CW,* vol. 28, pp. 468–74.
5. Lenin is probably referring to the resolution, "On Changing the Name of the Party and the Party Programme," adopted at the seventh congress of the Russian Communist Party in March 1918.

   This resolution reads, in part:

   "The Congress resolves to change the Programme of our party after reworking the theoretical part or supplementing it by characterizing imperialism and the opening of the era of socialist revolution.

   "Therefore the change in the political part of our Programme must consist in the most exact and detailed reference possible to the new type of state, the Soviet republic, as a form of dictatorship of the proletariat and as a continuation of the gains of the international workers' movement that were begun by the Paris Commune. The Programme must indicate that our party will not refrain from using even bourgeois parliamentarianism if the course of the struggle forces us backward for a time to that historic stage which our revolution has now surpassed. But in any case, the party will fight for the Soviet republic as the superior democratic type of state and as a form of the dictatorship of the proletariat, the overturning of the yoke of the exploiters and the suppression of their resistance." Richard Gregor, ed., *The Early Soviet Period:* 1917–1929, vol. 2 of Robert H. McNeal, ed., *Resolutions and Decisions of the*

Communist Party of the Soviet Union (Toronto: University of Toronto Press, 1974), p. 49.

6. The relevant portions of Kautsky's pamphlet are printed in Riddell, *German Revolution,* pp. 417–26. The full text is found in Karl Kautsky, *The Dictatorship of the Proletariat* (Ann Arbor, Michigan: University of Michigan Press, 1964).

7. This resolution, entitled "On Securing Party Unity," was published in the January 6, 1919, issue of *Gazeta Pechatnikov,* newspaper of the Typographical Workers Union.

8. In early 1919 the Hungarian government resorted to force to try to block the mounting pressure from land-hungry peasants and militant workers. On February 21, the police destroyed the CP's presses and arrested its leaders. But massive protest strikes and unrest continued to spread across the country. By the time of the Communist congress in Moscow, Hungary was in a situation of revolutionary crisis.

   In Switzerland, on the other hand, mass struggles declined after the November 1918 general strike.

9. This general position is expressed in Rosa Luxemburg's "The Beginning," published in *Rote Fahne,* November 18, 1918. A translation is printed in Riddell, *German Revolution,* pp. 124–27.

10. The Bolsheviks' "Decree on Land" of November 8 (October 26), 1917, nationalized the land and turned it over to the peasant soviets and land committees to satisfy the land hunger of the poor peasants and agricultural laborers. See Lenin, *CW,* vol. 26, pp. 258–61.

11. The text of Lenin's resolution, which follows, appears not to have been taken up by the congress; it is not found in the 1921 editions of the minutes. It was printed in *Pravda* on March 11, 1919, in the May 1919 issue of the journal *Communist International,* and in *Manifest, Richtlinien, Beschlüsse* in 1920.

12. Lenin, *CW,* vol. 28, p. 475.

13. Platten was referring to the motion to constitute the Communist International, printed in chapter 5.

Chapter 5: Decision to found the International

1. The invitation to the congress is printed in Riddell, *German Revolution,* pp. 594–600.
2. Longuet had written the Russian Communist Party inviting it to send delegates to the Bern conference. See Platten's report in chapter 6.
3. Eberlein was mistaken here. See Grimlund's remarks in this chapter.
4. There was no Greek delegate at the congress. Besides Rakovsky, the two Balkan delegates present were Stojan Djorov, a Bulgarian, and Milkić, a Serb.
5. Zinoviev told a Russian CP congress on March 20, 1919, that the arrival of Grimlund, Steinhardt, and Rakovsky and the course of the congress itself had influenced the views of both Eberlein and the Bolshevik delegation. "To the degree that delegates began to arrive and to read the reports," he stated, "the German Communists became markedly more flexible on this question, and it became more and more clear to us that not to proclaim the Third International now would signify committing a betrayal of the working class and making a horrendous error. The question was put to the congress." *Vos'moi s"ezd,* p. 135.

   Writing in the March 7 *Pravda,* V.V. Vorovsky emphasized in particular the impact of Steinhardt's report on German Austria. This was "a rare and memorable moment" in the congress, he stated, which "deeply etched itself into the hearts and minds of those present." Describing Steinhardt's "tall, maladroit figure, that of a typical worker, with high boots, threadbare clothes and unkempt beard," Vorovsky said he represented "the image of the proletariat itself, at work and in struggle, thinking and suffering. . . . It was impossible to listen without deep emotion to the simple tale of this Austrian comrade."

   Five years later, Zinoviev emphasized that the Austrian delegates' speeches, in particular, "influenced the conduct even of the representatives of the German Communist Party." *International Press Correspondence,* no. 21 (1924), p. 187.

Steinhardt's arrival was particularly significant because he brought a proposal of his party's congress to launch the International. "When I arrived I gave the conference Presiding Committee the decision of our party congress," he related.

According to Steinhardt, Lenin played the central role in discussions leading to the presentation of such a motion to the congress. Lenin reported to him, Steinhardt stated, that such a proposal had been shelved at the first day's session. "Lenin told me that he intended to move at the beginning of the morning session that the Austrian motion be discussed," Steinhardt added, "with the motivation . . . that an important delegation had not been able to get to the conference in time." A resolution was then drawn up, Steinhardt recalled, bearing the signatures of himself, Lenin, Grimlund, and Rakovsky. Steinhardt, "Österreichische Antrag," in *Lenin und die Internationale,* pp. 72–73.

Several other accounts, including those by Sadoul, Body, and Pascal, also emphasize Lenin's leading role in preparatory discussions.

Zinoviev stated in 1924 that the Russian delegation cosigned the resolution. In fact, Rakovsky was the only Russian CP member formally to sponsor it, and he did so as a delegate of the Balkan Socialist federation.

By contrast, the accounts of two other participants, written after they had broken with communism, portray the decision to launch the International as sudden, ill-prepared, and contrived.

Thomas (Y.S. Reich) stated that when Steinhardt finished his report, "Someone at the Presiding Committee table whispered, 'Shout "Long live the congress of the Communist International."' The Austrian did so immediately." Then Balabanoff proposed dissolution of the Zimmerwald committee. At that moment, Thomas continued, Lenin or Zinoviev rose to move constitution of the Communist International. "Forewarned, a portion of the delegates immediately began cheering. All the delegates stood, raised their hands, and sang the *Internationale*. Caught up in the mood, Eberlein too raised his hand. The chair used this to state that the proposal was adopted unanimously." "Recit de 'Thomas,'" in Freymond, *Contributions,* p. 10.

Balabanoff, for her part, recounted that the conference concluded without any decision to launch the International. But it was then reconvened, she stated, to hear the report of Steinhardt, whom she described not as coming from Austria but as an Austrian prisoner of war in Russia. The launching of the new International was then proposed and adopted despite the objections of herself and Eberlein, both of whom abstained on the vote. Balabanoff termed this procedure "a fraud that probably has no precedent in the history of relations among men with a minimum of morality." Balabanoff, "Lénine et la création du Cominterne," in Freymond, *Contributions,* pp. 32–33.

These two accounts are factually at odds with each other and with all other records of the congress.

6. At the 1916 Kienthal conference of the Zimmerwald International Socialist Committee, the Zimmerwald Left joined with delegates of Spartacus (Internationale Group) and other revolutionary currents to oppose any moves aimed at reviving the pre-1914 Socialist International and its leadership bodies. The theses of these delegates called for a new International, "born of the revolutionary class struggle." These theses were an amended version of a resolution of an Internationale Group conference. See Riddell, *Lenin's Struggle,* pp. 767–69.

7. The third Zimmerwald conference was held in Stockholm, September 5–12, 1917. On November 8, 1917, the Zimmerwald International Socialist Committee and the Bolshevik Party's representatives abroad issued a joint appeal to workers of all countries to rally in support of the newly formed Soviet government in Russia. Their statement is printed in O.H. Gankin and H.H. Fisher, *The Bolsheviks and the World War* (Stanford: Stanford University Press, 1976), pp. 691–92.

8. Balabanoff had been expelled from Switzerland in November 1918 and denied the right to reenter Sweden, where

the office of the Zimmerwald committee was then located.

Writing in 1938, Balabanoff stated that her remarks to the congress constituted a refusal to comply with the request that she turn over the archives. "Some of the Bolsheviks were annoyed by this display of 'legalistic' squeamishness on my part," she added. Balabanoff, *My Life as a Rebel,* p. 215.

Balabanoff's name is not found among those signing the Declaration on Zimmerwald printed at the end of this chapter.

9. The Swedish Left Social Democrats did in fact affiliate to the Communist International in June 1919; they assumed the name "Communist" only in 1921.

10. The stenographic record of Unszlicht's comments was lost and turned up only fifty years later in an archive in Moscow. The Russian text was first published in 1969 in the Polish journal *Z pola walki,* vol. 12, no. 2 (1969), pp. 126–27, from which this translation is taken.

    A report by Unszlicht on Poland is printed in chapter 11.

11. At the 1915 Zimmerwald Conference, Ledebour and Rakovsky were both members of the commission that drafted the conference's manifesto. Ledebour vetoed inclusion within it of a call on deputies of Social Democratic parties to vote against war credits. In the plenary session he justified this stand by saying merely that such a call was superfluous. Two other delegates from his current, however, offered the explanation that German law barred Reichstag deputies (like Ledebour) from making any commitment to outsiders on how they intended to vote within the Reichstag. See Riddell, *Lenin's Struggle,* pp. 467, 478–79.

12. The Allied powers' conference in Paris was then preparing the formation of the League of Nations.

    The Holy Alliance was an agreement in 1815 between the rulers of Russia, Prussia, and Austria to act together to defend "Christian principles," that is, to protect the established order and block revolutionary change. Later signed by other continental European states, the agreement was a symbol of reaction in the decades following the fall of Napoleon.

13. The Bern conference established a commission to investigate conditions in the Soviet republic. The commission was to consist of Longuet or Paul Faure from France, Kautsky or Rudolf Hilferding from Germany, Friedrich Adler or Otto Bauer from Austria, and Ramsay MacDonald of Britain. The Soviet government signaled its willingness for them to come, but the Allied governments denied them passports, and the trip was never made.
14. Fineberg represented British Communists resident in Russia.
15. The German delegate cast five votes under the weighted voting system adopted when the congress opened.
16. Balabanoff, who had a consultative vote, wrote in 1938 that she had refused to vote "on the ground that I had no mandate from Zimmerwald to do so." Balabanoff, *My Life as a Rebel,* p. 216.
17. *Manifest, Richtlinien, Beschlüsse,* p. 72.
18. *Manifest, Richtlinien, Beschlüsse,* p. 73.
19. The reference is probably to Balabanoff's speech on founding the International, printed in this chapter.

Chapter 6: The Bern conference

1. The bureau referred to here was the International Socialist Bureau, the executive body of the Second International. When war was declared in 1914, the bureau ceased functioning, and its members on opposite sides of the battle line broke off relations. All attempts during the war to revive it failed.
2. At the 1907 Stuttgart congress of the Second International, a left wing led by Lenin and Luxemburg secured adoption of a resolution committing the International's parties, if war should break out, "to strive with all their power to utilize the economic and political crisis created by the war to rouse the masses and thereby hasten the downfall of capitalist class rule."

   The congress also rejected a proposal to place the International in support of a "socialist colonial policy," adopting a resolution opposing any support to colonialism. For the text of these resolutions and excerpts from the Stuttgart congress debates see Riddell, *Lenin's Struggle*, pp. 35–80.

3. The extraordinary congress of the Swiss party, held on February 2, one day before the Bern conference began, voted not to participate in it.

4. The Soviet embassy had been expelled from Switzerland in November 1918.

5. Characteristic of this position was Verfeuil's letter to the Moscow congress, printed below in chapter 11.

6. "Betritos" probably refers to George Petridis of Greece; "Marnus" refers to Valeriu Marcu of Romania.

   Also present at the meeting organized by the Swiss Zimmerwaldists were Martin Tranmael and a number of Swiss Socialists including Robert Grimm and Charles Naine.

7. The bureau referred to here was the committee organizing the Bern conference established by a meeting of Social Democratic and labor organizations of the Allied powers; its original members were Arthur Henderson, Albert Thomas, and Émile Vandervelde. It worked in collaboration with Camille Huysmans, the former secretary of the International Socialist Bureau, who supposedly represented continuity with the prewar International.

8. The "territorial question" was posed by the demands of the victorious Allied powers and newly formed states to annex territory from their vanquished foes. The most prominent case was France's demand for the return of Alsace-Lorraine, which had been annexed by Germany at the conclusion of the Franco-Prussian War in 1871.

9. Different resolutions hostile to the Soviet republic and to Bolshevism were presented to the Bern conference by the influential right-wing Social Democratic leaders Renaudel (France), Hjalmar Branting (Sweden), and Otto Wels (Germany–SPD). They then joined with Ramsay MacDonald (Britain) and Kurt Eisner (Germany–USPD) to present a joint resolution expressing their anti-Soviet stand

in more cautious terms. Adler led an opposition current that considered such an anti-Bolshevik stand likely to discredit the conference in the eyes of European workers and undermine its efforts to unite all Social Democratic currents in a common International. The conference held a debate on Bolshevism, but no resolution was adopted. For excerpts from this debate see Riddell, *German Revolution,* pp. 544–70.

10. In December 1918 the Italian party executive committee adopted a resolution rejecting the demand then current in Italy for a constituent assembly and calling for "establishment of the socialist republic and the dictatorship of the proletariat." Luigi Cortesi, *Il socialismo italiano tra riforme e rivoluzione* (Bari: Editori Laterza, 1969), p. 694.

    Although the leadership failed to set the party on a course toward that goal, its decision widened the breach between the Italian party and the Social Democratic leaders then working to build a reformist International. Only two weeks after the Comintern was launched, the Italian SP voted to affiliate to it.

11. Albert Thomas, Marcel Sembat, and Jules Guesde, right-wing leaders of the French SP, became ministers in the French capitalist government during the course of the war.

12. "Syndicalists" refers to the left wing of the French trade union federation, the General Confederation of Labor (CGT). Although syndicalist leaders had been influential in the CGT before the war, by 1914 it was dominated by a reformist current that took a chauvinist stand during the war. A left opposition developed, led in 1919 by Pierre Monatte and Raymond Péricat. Although still strongly influenced by syndicalism, this current rallied to the Third International and formed a separate union federation in 1921.

13. The conferences referred to were those of the British Labour Party, a federated organization made up of affiliated trade unions, parties, and other groups. Before 1914, some affiliated parties, such as the Independent Labour Party and the British Socialist Party, elected their own delegates to Second International congresses. When these two organiza-

tions radicalized under the impact of the war and the Russian revolution, the Labour Party's right-wing leadership secured the election of all such delegates by Labour Party conferences, where it could count on a secure majority.

14. The proceedings of the Bern conference have now been published in Gerhard A. Ritter, ed., *Die II. Internationale* 1918/1919: *Protokolle, Memoranden, Berichte und Korrespondenzen* (Berlin [West]: Verlag J.H.W. Dietz Nachf., 1980), vol. 1, pp. 179–570.
15. *Die Resolutionen der Internationalen Arbeiter-und Sozialistenkonferenz in Bern* (3.–10. Februar 1919) (Basel: A.C. Jünger, [1919]), p. 6.
16. Ibid. This was actually the resolution's sixth point.
17. For example, see Kautsky's speech on colonialism to the 1907 Stuttgart congress of the Second International, in Riddell, *Lenin's Struggle,* pp. 45–47.
18. These sentences were incorporated into the Bern conference resolution on the League of Nations. See *Resolutionen,* p. 4.
19. The term "Brusilov offensive" usually refers to the successful Russian offensive of June–August 1916, commanded by General A.A. Brusilov. In this case, however, Troelstra was speaking of the offensive launched under Brusilov's command by the Provisional Government in late June–early July 1917 in a desperate effort to restore discipline in the army and rally popular support for continuing the war. The offensive, sharply opposed by the Bolsheviks, encountered massive opposition and defiance among Russian soldiers and quickly collapsed.

    The Stockholm conference was called in April 1917 by right-wing Social Democrats in the Netherlands, soon joined by their counterparts in Scandinavia, the Mensheviks in Russia, and the majority of the executive committee of the Petrograd Soviet. Its declared goal was to unite Social Democratic parties of both warring coalitions around commonly agreed terms for a compromise peace, which could then be urged on the belligerent powers.

The Bolsheviks and the Zimmerwald Left opposed this plan as a vehicle for maneuvers by the imperialist powers, particularly those led by Germany, the weaker side in the war and the most interested in a compromise peace. Moreover, they maintained that such joint gatherings with the chauvinist Social Democratic leaders obstructed the cause of workers' unity.

In the end, the key Allied governments blocked attendance by delegates from their countries, and the conference was never held.

20. The quotation is from a summary of Kautsky's speech in the *Neue zürcher Zeitung*. For the stenographic record of these remarks, see Riddell, *German Revolution,* pp. 566–67.
21. The delegation was composed of the executive committee established by the Bern conference (Branting, Henderson, and Huysmans), supplemented by Longuet, MacDonald, Renaudel, and George Stuart-Bunning.
22. See Carl Grünberg, "Die Internationale und der Weltkrieg, Materialien," in *Archiv für die Geschichte des Sozialismus und der Arbeiterbewegung,* vol. 6 (1916), pp. 373–541, and vol. 7 (1917), pp. 99–248. A selection of documents from this collection is published in Riddell, *Lenin's Struggle,* pp. 193–219.
23. The August 4, 1914, SPD Reichstag declaration backing the German government in the war was printed the following day in the party's central organ, *Vorwärts*. During the next two years, however, *Vorwärts* voiced opposition to the progovernment course of the Ebert-Scheidemann party leadership.

    When the Italian government entered the war in May 1915, on the other hand, the Italian Socialist Party's parliamentary deputies voted against war credits. The party leadership and its central organ, *Avanti!,* attempted to steer a middle course between national defense and revolutionary struggle, adopting the slogan, "Neither support nor sabotage." The Italian party played an important role in initiating the September 1915 Zimmerwald conference and leading the Zimmerwald movement.

24. Karl Kautsky, "Internationalism and the War," in Riddell, *Lenin's Struggle,* pp. 237–38.

25. Such an "amnesty" signified that Social Democratic leaders in both of the warring camps would forgive their counterparts on the other side of the battle lines for having supported the "enemy" side and promoted its war effort.

26. *Manifest, Richtlinien, Beschlüsse,* pp. 45–52.

27. Riddell, *Lenin's Struggle,* pp. 154–55.

28. In this sentence, where *Manifest, Richtlinien, Beschlüsse* reads "of the Second International," the 1921 German-language edition of the congress proceedings reads "of the Second International's main parties."

29. The Bolsheviks' analysis of the labor bureaucracy and other "petty bourgeois 'camp followers'" is explained more fully in Lenin, "Imperialism and the Split in Socialism," in *CW,* vol. 23, pp. 105–20; and Zinoviev, "The Social Roots of Opportunism," *New International,* No. 2 (1983), pp. 165–232. [2008 printing]. Excerpts of both can be found in Riddell, *Lenin's Struggle,* pp. 705–48.

30. See the September 1914 statement of the Bolshevik Party, "The War and Russian Social Democracy," in Lenin, *CW,* vol. 21, pp. 25–34. Liebknecht's parallel slogan, "Civil war, not 'civil peace,'" was included in the September 1915 founding statement of the Zimmerwald Left. See Riddell, *Lenin's Struggle,* pp. 456–57.

31. The International Women's Bureau, affiliated to the Second International, was formed by the first International Socialist Women's Conference held in Stuttgart in 1907; Clara Zetkin was its secretary. At the 1910 Copenhagen congress of the Second International, Zetkin secured adoption of March 8 as International Women's Day. An underground conference of socialist women held in Switzerland in 1915 was the first international gathering of internationalist oppositionists in the Social Democratic parties. Its manifesto was widely circulated, and Zetkin was jailed for distributing it. See Riddell, *Lenin's Struggle,* pp. 423–26. Zetkin supported the formation of the Com-

munist International, and in 1920 she became its international secretary of socialist women.

32. In this sentence, where *Manifest, Richtlinien, Beschlüsse* reads "broad masses of the people," the 1921 German-language edition of the congress proceedings reads "broad masses of the proletariat."

33. *Pervyy kongress* (1933), pp. 242–43. The Chinese delegate's report is not found in the 1921 editions of the congress proceedings. It was printed in *Pravda* on March 6, 1919.

34. The Open Door policy, announced by the United States in 1899, claimed to provide the major imperialist powers with equal access to trade with China, while preserving it as a formally independent territorial and administrative entity. This policy promised to give the U.S. capitalists, handicapped by their late start in acquiring colonial possessions, access to the exploitation of China equal to that of the longer-established European colonial empires.

    China was thus spared formal partition, but the imperialist powers carved out wide "spheres of influence" within its territory, imposed unequal treaties limiting the sovereignty of its government, and intervened militarily as required to safeguard this exploitative system from challenge.

35. When the Manchu or Qing dynasty was overthrown in 1912, Sun Yat-sen, the main leader of the Kuomintang, the party of the revolutionary national bourgeoisie, was proclaimed provisional president of the newly established Chinese republic. Later that year he was pressured into resigning in favor of Yuan Shikai, the most powerful of the Manchu military leaders, who was backed by the Western powers as well as by Chinese landlords, monarchists, and bureaucrats from the old regime. Yuan imposed a military dictatorship obedient to the imperialist powers.

    In 1915 Yuan moved to crown himself emperor. That provoked a wave of revolts that were close to victory when Yuan died the following year. General Zhang Xun's unsuccessful attempt to restore the monarchy followed in 1917. That same year a republican government opposed to the Beijing regime was established in Guangzhou (Canton) under Sun Yat-sen's leadership, but in 1918 Sun was ousted by right-wing military chieftains in the south. Nevertheless, the social and political crisis in China continued to grow.

Early in 1919 it became clear that despite the lofty declarations on self-determination by U.S. President Woodrow Wilson and other Allied leaders, the Paris conference had no intention of ending China's domination by the imperialist powers. Shortly after the first Comintern congress, on May 4, 1919, a student demonstration took place in Beijing protesting the decisions of the Paris conference and the servility of the Chinese government. This action initiated the nationalist revolutionary upsurge of the 1920s.

36. The address "To All Working Muslims of Russia and the East," signed by Lenin and Stalin, was published in *Izvestia,* no. 232, November 22, 1917.

Chicherin wrote to Sun Yat-sen on August 1, 1918, in reply to greetings sent to the Soviet republic by the Chinese Assembly and by Sun as head of the republican regime in Guangzhou. Chicherin attacked the Beijing regime as "the creature of the foreign bankers" and affirmed that the Russian and Chinese revolutions had common aims, namely, "the establishment of universal peace following from the universal brotherhood of the labouring classes." Jane Degras, *Soviet Documents on Foreign Policy* (London: Oxford University Press, 1951), vol. 1, pp. 92–93.

37. *Pervyy kongress* (1933), pp. 244–46. Subhi's report was published in the March 6, 1919, issue of *Izvestia* as a speech delivered to the congress, but his report was not included in the 1921 editions of the congress proceedings. The date on which Subhi spoke, March 5, is given by *Prvi kongres Komunističke internacionale,* p. 269; no information is available as to when in the session the report was delivered.

38. In 1915 the government of the Turkish Ottoman Empire decided to deport the empire's entire Armenian population of 1.75 million from Asia Minor to Syria and Mesopotamia, on the pretext that their loyalty was in question. The de-

portations were conducted with a brutality that bordered on genocide. About a third of the deported Armenian population perished in the course of this operation.

39. The Ottoman Empire, allied with Germany in the World War, sought to justify its expansion into Russian-held territory by calling for unity of all Turkic peoples. These included the Azerbaijanis of the Caucasus and northern Persia, the Tatars of Kazan and elsewhere in Russia, and several peoples east of the Caspian Sea in Turkestan. Following the treaty of Brest-Litovsk, Turkish armies pressed north and by September 1918 occupied much of Transcaucasia.

40. After the Ottoman Empire surrendered in October 1918, it was dismembered by the Allied powers. They seized its southern territories, inhabited chiefly by Arabs; assigned much of Asia Minor to other states; removed the straits between the Black Sea and the Mediterranean from Turkish control; occupied its capital, Constantinople; and took control of government finances.

    In the months following the Moscow congress, a Turkish nationalist resistance movement developed under the leadership of Mustafa Kemal (Atatürk). This movement waged a successful three-year war for national independence and abolished the Ottoman Sultanate.

41. In the years before his death in 1914, French SP leader Jean Jaurès spoke out in defense of colonial peoples. He met Mustafa Subhi several times.

Chapter 7: The international situation

1. The draft of the theses on the international situation presented at this point by Osinsky did not differ significantly from the resolution's final text. The edited text is therefore printed here in place of Osinsky's report. This report, omitted from the 1921 editions of the proceedings, can be found in *Pervyy kongress* (1933), pp. 149–59.

2. *Manifest, Richtlinien, Beschlüsse,* pp. 53–64.

3. The words "destroyed intermediate social layers" are not found in the text of the resolution in *Manifest, Richtlinien,*

Beschlüsse. They are taken from the 1933 Russian-language edition of the congress proceedings.

4. The 1918 Treaty of Bucharest ended the war between the Central Powers and Romania.
5. The eight-hour day had been won in Germany as one of the immediate fruits of the November 1918 revolution.
6. The reference is to the Fourteen Points, proclaimed by U.S. President Woodrow Wilson on January 8, 1918, in response to peace proposals of the Soviet government. The democratic pretensions of the Fourteen Points were largely disregarded by the Paris conference and repeatedly violated in the resulting Treaty of Versailles.
7. *Pervyy kongress* (1933), pp. 158–59. The following paragraphs formed the concluding section of Osinsky's draft of the resolution. They were omitted from the final text of the resolution because their topic, the International's tasks, was considered to have been adequately covered in other resolutions.

Chapter 8: Manifesto

1. *Manifest, Richtlinien, Beschlüsse,* pp. 3–18.
2. The White Book was a memorandum and a collection of documents published by the German government shortly after the outbreak of fighting in 1914 in an attempt to prove that Germany was fighting a war of national defense. See *Vorläufige Denkschrift und Aktenstücke zum Kriegsausbruch,* (Berlin, 1914).
3. The manifesto refers here to an incident at the Bern conference mentioned by Zinoviev in his report, printed in chapter 6. A dispute between German and French delegates over responsibility for the war was smoothed over by a compromise in which SPD delegates declared that in November 1918 German workers had overthrown the "old system" responsible for the war. The conference as a whole then hailed the German statement and referred the question of ultimate responsibility for the war to some subsequent gathering.
4. The City is the financial district of London.

5. Between 1896 and 1899 Eduard Bernstein, a prominent German Social Democrat, published views fundamentally revising the positions of Marxism. See Bernstein, *Evolutionary Socialism* (New York: Huebsch, 1909).

   Bernstein took issue with the revolutionary strategy of Marxism and with its analysis of the increasing contradictions of capitalist society, arguing that these contradictions could be resolved gradually without revolution. His positions set off a debate in the SPD and the International. The defense of Marx's positions was led by Luxemburg, Kautsky, and Georgiy Plekhanov. Bernstein's "revisionist" theories were rejected by congress resolutions of the SPD in 1903 and the Second International in 1904. Yet revisionism continued to gain influence among party and trade union leaders in the Second International and was openly embraced by the Social Democratic parties after World War I and the Russian revolution.

6. Opposition to French rule in its colony of Madagascar led during the war to the rapid growth of a nationalist secret society, the Vy Vato Sakelika. It was outlawed by French authorities and suppressed.

   In May 1916 the French rulers of Vietnam suppressed a rebellion led by the Vietnamese emperor Duy Tan.

   The nationalist movement in India grew rapidly during the war, leading to massive strikes in 1918. In Bombay 125,000 textile workers were on strike during December 1918 and January 1919. In early 1919 a mass protest movement developed against repressive legislation. The sharpening conflict was to lead in April 1919 to the massacre of Amritsar, where troops under British command fired without warning on unarmed demonstrators, killing several hundred.

7. As the liberation movement in the colonies unfolded in the years immediately following the 1919 Moscow congress, the leadership of the Comintern and the Russian Communist Party placed greater emphasis on this movement's weight in the world revolution and its importance in the politics of the imperialist countries themselves.

Thus on November 22, 1919, Lenin told a congress of the Communist Organizations of the Peoples of the East, "The socialist revolution will not be solely, or chiefly, a struggle of the revolutionary proletarians in each country against their bourgeoisie–no, it will be a struggle of all the imperialist-oppressed colonies and countries, of all dependent countries, against international imperialism. . . . The civil war of the working people against the imperialists and exploiters in all the advanced countries is beginning to be combined with national wars against international imperialism." Lenin, *CW,* vol. 30, p. 159.

In a report on July 5, 1921, at the third Comintern congress, Lenin noted that among the opportunist-led parties, "the movement in the colonial countries is still regarded as an insignificant national and totally peaceful movement. But this is not so. It has undergone great change since the beginning of the twentieth century: millions and hundreds of millions, in fact the overwhelming majority of the population of the globe, are now coming forward as independent, active and revolutionary factors. . . . The movement of the majority of the population of the globe, initially directed towards national liberation, will turn against capitalism and imperialism and will, perhaps, play a much more revolutionary part than we expect." Lenin, "Report on Tactics of the R.C.P.," in *CW,* vol. 32, pp. 481–82.

Weighing the lessons of the world class struggle since the Russian revolution, Lenin wrote in 1923, "In the last analysis, the outcome of the struggle will be determined by the fact that Russia, India, China, etc., account for the overwhelming majority of the population of the globe. And during the past few years it is this majority that has been drawn into the struggle for emancipation with extraordinary rapidity, so that in this respect there cannot be the slightest doubt what the final outcome of the world struggle will be. In this sense, the complete victory of socialism is fully and absolutely assured." Lenin, "Better Fewer, but Better," in *CW,* vol. 33, p. 500.

8. The Franco-Prussian War of 1870–71 resulted in the defeat of France, the creation of a French bourgeois republic, and

the unification of Germany under Prussian domination. With German troops on the outskirts of Paris, a revolutionary government, the Commune, was established in the city on March 26. The French bourgeoisie, acting in collaboration with the German army, succeeded in crushing the Paris workers nine weeks later on May 28. The defeat of the Paris Commune was a severe setback for the workers' movement across Europe.

Chapter 9: The White Terror

1. *Pervyy kongress* (1933), pp. 162–64. Sirola's report was published in the Finnish newspaper *Vapaus* (Freedom) on September 24, 1919, but was not included in the 1921 editions of the congress proceedings.
2. Sirola is paraphrasing Marx's statement that capital comes into the world "dripping from head to toe, from every pore, with blood and dirt." Marx, *Capital,* vol. 1, chap. 31, p. 926.
3. After the defeat of the Paris Commune in 1871, an estimated 17,000 of its supporters (Communards) were executed. The punitive expeditions of the tsarist army were sent into the countryside after the revolutionary upsurge of 1905 to repress the insurgent peasant movement.
4. London's Bloody Sunday took place on November 13, 1887, when troops fired on a demonstration against unemployment in Trafalgar Square.

   The "anarchist" trial probably refers to the Haymarket frame-up. At a Chicago labor rally in 1886 a bomb exploded in police ranks. Eight labor leaders were arrested for murder and tried on the basis of their anarchist political beliefs. Although no evidence connected them with the bombing, all were convicted, and four were eventually hanged.

   Under the Espionage Act adopted in the United States in 1917, William "Big Bill" Haywood and ninety-four other IWW leaders were arrested in a bid to destroy the IWW. They were tried in 1918 on charges of impeding the war effort, and the chief defendants, including Haywood, were sentenced to twenty years' imprisonment. Meanwhile, hundreds of militant workers were arrested under "criminal syndicalism" laws. Vigilantes in several cities attacked IWW-organized workers, and on August 1, 1917, IWW organizer Frank Little was lynched by a Montana mob. In 1918 socialist leader Eugene V. Debs was sentenced to ten years in prison for delivering an antiwar speech in Canton, Ohio.

5. *Manifest, Richtlinien, Beschlüsse,* pp. 65–68.
6. In 1916 about 40,000 Russian soldiers were sent to France to fight on the western front, where they were assigned to some of the bloodiest fighting. After the February 1917 revolution, the Russian soldiers set up soviets of soldiers' deputies. Beginning in May, many of these soldiers refused to fight and demanded to be sent home. The French government, encouraged by the Russian Provisional Government, put down this rebellion in a pitched battle, killing at least 1,000. Many of the Russian soldiers were exiled to forced labor in France's African colonies. The Bolshevik government negotiated their release in exchange for captured French interventionist troops.
7. In December 1918 a Russian Red Cross mission arrived in Poland to negotiate matters concerning prisoners of war and refugees. The mission was immediately arrested and ordered to leave Poland. While the mission was under Polish police escort back to the Soviet frontier, four of its five members were assassinated. The head of the Polish government was then Józef Pilsudski, long a leader of the right-wing faction of the Polish Socialist Party.

Chapter 10: Election of the bureau

1. *Manifest, Richtlinien, Beschlüsse,* pp. 19–29. The platform was drafted by Bukharin and Eberlein.
2. Reinstein's motion on the trade union question, presented by Platten before the vote on the platform, is printed in chapter 4 of this volume.
3. The term *bureau* is used in this chapter to refer both to the Presiding Committee of the congress itself and to a body

elected to lead the International after the congress. In this case, it is the post-congress leadership that is meant.

4. *Pervyy kongress* (1933), pp. 165–66. This message is not found in the 1921 editions of the congress proceedings.
5. *Manifest, Richtlinien, Beschlüsse,* pp. 68–69.
6. The resolution is printed in chapter 6.
7. This final section of the draft resolution was presented by Osinsky in his report; it is printed in chapter 7.
8. *Manifest, Richtlinien, Beschlüsse,* p. 71.
9. Lenin, *CW,* vol. 28, pp. 476–77.

Chapter 11: Written reports

1. This chapter contains written materials submitted by congress delegates or, in some cases, by delegates who arrived only after the congress was over. Many of these items were published in the months following the congress. Although not included in the 1921 editions of the congress proceedings, these documents were printed in the 1933 Russian-language edition, except for the report on Poland, first published in 1969.
2. Tornio is a town in Finland on the Swedish border.
3. Although Reinstein arrived in Stockholm in June, the meeting of Zimmerwald supporters there did not take place until July 3.
4. Rosta was the Soviet news agency.
5. The Credentials Commission was mistaken here. Although the Swiss party congress of February 1919 expressed solidarity with Soviet Russia and refused to attend the Bern conference, it did not declare for the Third International. See Platten's report, chapter 2.
6. *Pervyy kongress* (1933), pp. 235–41. Haikuni's report was first published in *Pravda,* March 11, 1919. Another version of the report was published in Armenian. See *Hayastani Komunistakan kusaktsutian nerkayatsutsichi zekutsume errord Komunistakan Internatsionalin* (Moscow, 1919).

7. The Armenian Communist Party was founded by Armenian intellectuals from Turkish Armenia in Tiflis (Tbilisi), the capital of Georgia, in early 1918.

8. Until World War I, Armenia, an agricultural country with an overwhelmingly Christian population, was divided into an eastern region ruled by Russia and a western part ruled by Ottoman Turkey. When the Armenians in Turkey were deported and massacred in 1915, large numbers of them took refuge on the Russian side of the frontier.

The Armenians under Russian rule lived in Transcaucasia together with Georgians (mostly Christian), Azerbaijanis (at that time often termed "Tatars," overwhelmingly Muslim in religion), and other smaller nationalities. The Soviet government quickly recognized the right of these oppressed nationalities to national self-determination.

Support for the Soviet government in Russia was concentrated in Baku, the region's one major industrial city. In Tiflis, on the other hand, the Menshevik party was dominant. There, the Transcaucasian Commissariat, an autonomous government hostile to the Soviet republic, was established. It was a coalition of three petty-bourgeois, anti-Bolshevik parties, each dominant in one of the three major nationalities: the Dashnaktsutiun (Armenian Revolutionary Federation–Dashnaks) among the Armenians, the Musavat Party in Azerbaijan, and the Mensheviks in Georgia.

A Transcaucasian parliament, the Seym, convened in Tiflis in February 1918; in April it declared Transcaucasian independence from Russia. This government was quickly broken apart, however, by the impact of intervention by three competing great powers. In February 1918 the Turkish army launched an offensive to conquer Russian-held Armenia and annex Azerbaijan, which is Turkic in population. Germany moved to take control of Georgia as a stepping stone to domination of Transcaucasia and expansion toward Persia and India. The British army, based in northern Persia, sought to block these moves through its own advance into Transcaucasia. The Soviet government in Russia, for its part, was largely cut off from the Transcaucasus by the German army's advance through the Ukraine and the outbreak of White revolts on the Don River.

The Mensheviks sought to counter the Turkish advance by proclaiming a separate Georgian republic on May 26 and by inviting the German army to send troops into Tiflis. In response, the Musavatists and Dashnaks declared separate republics of Azerbaijan and Armenia respectively.

The Menshevik government set out to establish Georgian predominance in Tiflis, where Armenians were the largest national group. Several government measures attacked Armenians in business, city administration, and the civil service. A brief border war between Georgia and Armenia broke out in December 1918.

National antagonism between Armenian and Turkic peoples in Transcaucasia was fueled by the invasion by armies of the Turkish government, which promised liberation to the Azerbaijanis, while awakening fears among Armenians that they would share the fate of their compatriots under Ottoman rule during the war. Mutual suspicion flared into open battles.

In Baku, the main center of Bolshevik influence in Transcaucasia, events took a different course. For several months following the October revolution, the Baku Soviet, led by the Bolsheviks, contended with several bourgeois councils for political authority. Supported by local Dashnaks, the soviet opposed the Transcaucasian regime in Tiflis and its declaration of Caucasian independence. In April 1918, the Baku Soviet, after putting down a rising by anti-Soviet Azerbaijani forces, assumed full power over the city and surrounding region. Recognizing the authority of the central Soviet government, it nationalized the banks and the oil industry and took other measures in the interests of working people.

9. The beys were the feudal officials and landholders in Azerbaijan. When Soviet power was established in Baku, the beys threw their support behind the Musavat Party.

10. By late 1917 the Bolsheviks had won substantial support in the Russian army of the Caucasus. With the armistice

of December 1917, soldiers began to demobilize spontaneously. They set off for home, trying to take their arms with them. But the counterrevolutionary forces in the region forcibly disarmed and robbed the returning units. Often the soldiers resisted. There were several pitched battles, followed by massacres, including one at Shamkhor in January 1918, where about 1,000 Russian soldiers were killed.

11. A Bolshevik-led workers' meeting in Tiflis was dispersed by gunfire on February 23.

12. The Menshevik-led Transcaucasian regime had signed an armistice with Ottoman Turkey in December 1917. Peace negotiations began at Batum (Batumi) in May 1918. Meanwhile, the Turkish army continued its advance into Transcaucasia. When the Musavat Party opposed offering any resistance to the Turkish forces, the Transcaucasian government fell apart into its three national components. On June 4 the now-independent Georgian regime signed a peace treaty with Turkey.

13. Turkish annexation of Batum had been among the terms of the Brest-Litovsk treaty forced on the Soviet government of Russia in March 1918. When the treaty was debated at an all-Russian soviet congress in March, Menshevik delegates, led by Martov, denounced the treaty for accepting annexation of Russian territories and called strongly for its rejection. Yet only three months later, the Menshevik government of Georgia had to sign its own separate peace with the Central Powers, one that also agreed to the annexation of Batum.

14. When the Turkish army advanced into Russian-occupied Armenia in April 1918, it rapidly scored major gains. The Turkish forces came within twenty-five miles of eastern Armenia's chief city, Yerevan. Faced with this threat and with the resulting collapse of the Transcaucasian government, the Dashnak leadership in Tiflis declared Armenian independence (May 28), signed a peace treaty with Turkey (June 4), and moved to Yerevan to organize a national government. Meanwhile a Turkish army continued its advance toward Baku.

15. When the Baku Soviet assumed power in April 1918, the Musavatists organized a rival government in Elisavetpol (Kirovabad) and blockaded Baku, cutting off food supplies.

In July 1918 the Turkish army drew up to Baku. Defense of the starving city was crippled by its isolation from the Red Army in Russia and its lack of support among the Azerbaijani peasantry and much of the urban Azerbaijani proletariat.

The Dashnaks, who had strong influence among the Armenian soldiers making up most of the pro-Soviet armed forces, began agitating to invite British troops, stationed in northern Persia, to come to Baku. The Right Socialist Revolutionaries also raised this demand, which they held to be the only means of saving the city from the Turkish army. Despite Bolshevik opposition, this proposal won a narrow majority in the Baku Soviet on July 25. This brought about the fall of the Soviet government. Twenty-six Bolshevik leaders left the city and were captured; later they were executed with the active complicity of the British army.

The subsequent arrival of a British military detachment in Baku did not prevent its fall to the Turkish army on September 14.

16. Although there were rumors in 1918 that the Georgian government would join the Turkish and Musavatist forces attacking Baku, this did not take place. There is no record that the Tiflis government gave arms to the forces marching against Baku or that Georgian troops participated in an attack on Baku. The Georgian regime, however, permitted Turkish troops to cross Georgian territory during their march on Baku.

17. Mass actions occurred in Tiflis when the Armenian city of Kars fell on April 25 to Turkish assault. Armenians in Tiflis poured into the streets to protest the Transcaucasian government's failure to organize an effective defense of the city. Haikuni's report of Bolshevik strength, however, is probably exaggerated. According to other accounts, the Menshevik government of Georgia remained in firm control of Tiflis in the spring of 1918.

18. Late in 1919 the British government was forced to withdraw its forces from all of Transcaucasia except Batum. This enabled the workers' movement in Transcaucasia to renew the struggle for Soviet power, and in April 1920 a Communist-led rising in Baku established Soviet power in Azerbaijan. In October of that year a renewed Turkish offensive into Armenia led to the collapse of the Dashnak government; the Armenian Socialist Republic was established in November. The overthrow of the Georgian Menshevik regime and the establishment of a workers' and peasants' government there followed in February 1921. The three Transcaucasian Soviet republics established links to Soviet Russia through treaties of military and economic alliance.

By 1921, the imperialist powers had been forced to abandon their war of intervention against the Soviet republics and were under pressure to open normal trade and diplomatic relations with them. The routed White Guards were driven from Soviet soil. In April, Lenin wrote to Communists of the three Transcaucasian republics and two Soviet republics of the Northern Caucasus region, suggesting how, under these conditions, their course could differ from the course followed by the Bolsheviks in Soviet Russia.

Unlike the Russian soviets after the October revolution, Lenin explained, the soviets in the Caucasus did not stand alone, benefiting as they did from the political and military assistance of the Russian Soviet republic. Furthermore, they no longer faced civil war or imperialist intervention. "The Caucasian Republics have an even more pronounced peasant character than Russia," Lenin continued, and in addition, they were "in a position to start trading and 'living together' with the capitalist West sooner and with greater ease."

The Russian soviets "fought to make the first breach in the wall of world capitalism," Lenin continued; "We have maintained our positions in a fierce and superhuman war." The Caucasian Communists, however, "have no need to force a breach. You must take advantage of the favourable international situation in 1921, and learn to build the new with greater caution and more method." Lenin stressed that they needed to seek trade with capitalist countries and economic agreements with capitalist concerns in order to develop local economic resources.

"You will need to practice more moderation and caution, and show more readiness to make concessions to the petty bourgeoisie, the intelligentsia, and particularly the peasantry. . . . You must make immediate efforts to improve the condition of the peasants and start on extensive electrification and irrigation projects," Lenin stated. Emphasizing the importance of concentrating resources on aiding the peasantry to develop agriculture, he stressed that "what you need most is irrigation, for more than anything else it will revive the area and regenerate it, bury the past and make the transition to socialism more certain."

"Do not copy our tactics," Lenin advised the Caucasian Communists, "but analyse the reasons for their peculiar features, the conditions that gave rise to them, and their results; go beyond the letter, and apply the spirit, the essence and the lessons of the 1917–21 experience." Lenin, "To the Comrades Communists of Azerbaijan, Georgia, Armenia, Daghestan, and the Mountaineer Republic," in *CW*, vol. 32, pp. 316–18.

19. *Pervyy kongress* (1933), pp. 222–23. Petin's report was first printed in *Izvestia* on March 6, 1919.

20. The People's Militia was formed November 4, 1918, by the Austrian SDP, partly in order to bring under its control the Red Guard initiated three days earlier by revolutionary forces. A radical unit within the militia broke away on December 10, setting up an independent unit pledged to build the Third International. A "Revolutionary Soldiers' Committee" was formed to link this unit with revolutionaries scattered throughout the militia.

21. Between December 1918 and March 1919 some 200,000 German-Austrian prisoners of war returned from Russia.

22. *Pervyy kongress* (1933), pp. 231–35. Freylikh's report was published in 1919 in the fourth issue of *The Communist International* among the "reports of the delegates" to the

congress. However, Freylikh was not listed among delegates in the first congress minutes. He probably arrived after the conference concluded.

23. Until 1918 Galicia was a province in the Austrian portion of the Austro-Hungarian Empire. It was inhabited by three peoples: Poles (a majority in the west); Ukrainians (a majority in the east); and Jews (concentrated in the cities, a minority in both sections). In Austria as a whole, ethnic Germans were barely more than a third of the population. Among the other peoples in Austria were Czechs, Slovenes, and Italians.

The 1889 program of the Austrian Social Democratic Workers Party stated that it was an international party that rejected nationalism and national struggles as diversionary maneuvers of the bourgeoisie. The Austrian SDP never recognized the distinction between oppressed and oppressor nations, which formed the heart of the Bolsheviks' program on nationalities and was central to the Comintern's resolutions on the colonial and national question. Thus the party failed to counter the national chauvinism fostered by the dominant German-Austrian bourgeoisie and to respond to the national aspirations of the oppressed peoples in the empire.

In 1897, as a concession to mounting nationalist pressure of the oppressed peoples, the party adopted a federal structure, with independent parties for each nationality, linked by a common Austria-wide executive body and parliamentary fraction.

The party's 1899 Brünn congress adopted a program on the national question, demanding Austria's transformation into a "democratic multinational state," to be divided into "autonomously administered regions corresponding to national boundaries." Implicitly, the existing boundaries of Austria-Hungary were accepted as the framework for such a reform.

In the years that followed, the German-Austrian party leadership shifted away from advocating such territorial autonomy toward a proposal for "cultural-national autonomy," which would give all members of a nationality, regardless of where they lived, democratic rights in determining the cultural policy for that nationality throughout the empire. This proposal envisaged not revolution but democratic reform of the monarchy and did not include the democratic right of oppressed nations to secede from the empire.

The divisions between the national parties rapidly deepened, extending into the trade union movement. In 1912 a German-Austrian party congress recognized that the multinational party no longer existed.

Lenin criticized the proposal for "cultural-national autonomy" on many occasions. See, for example, "Theses on the National Question," in *CW,* vol. 19, pp. 247–50; "'Cultural-National' Autonomy," in *CW,* vol. 19, pp. 503–7; and "Critical Remarks on the National Question," in *CW,* vol. 20, pp. 33–51.

24. Freylikh used the initials PPS, UPS, and ZPS.

25. In 1905 a portion of the Jewish membership of the Polish SDP split to form the Jewish SDP.

26. By the terms of Austria's restrictive voting franchise, each of the main social classes voted in a separate curia, that is, as a separate body of electors choosing its own deputies. The possessing classes had the most representation while the workers and poor peasants had virtually none.

    An electoral reform enacted in 1897 (not 1899) established a fifth curia, based on general male suffrage, through which the dispossessed could seek representation. Only 17 percent of legislative seats were allocated to the fifth curia, however, with the remainder going to the curiae of the privileged classes.

27. Demonstrations and mass strikes for universal suffrage swept Hungary in October 1905. When news arrived that the revolutionary upsurge in Russia had forced the tsar to concede certain political freedoms, the movement spread to the Austrian part of the empire. On November 28 hundreds of thousands demonstrated in major cities of the empire. In Galicia, farm workers and peasants played an active role.

This strike and protest movement extended into 1906. In January 1907 the emperor signed a new electoral law granting general male suffrage, subject to some significant restrictions, and unified elections to the imperial parliament.

28. On October 31, 1918, the Ukrainian deputies from East Galicia in the former Austrian parliament constituted the West Ukrainian People's Republic. Within a few days Polish armed detachments seized Lvov and Przemysl, unleashing a war between the newly formed Polish and West Ukrainian states.

29. When the conference, which was held in Stry, voted down the Communists' resolution, Freylikh's faction proclaimed itself the Communist Party of East Galicia and declared its adherence to the Third International.

Parallel to these events, other Communist groups had been formed independently in Drogobych, Ternopil, Stanislav, and elsewhere. The formation of the CP of East Galicia should be dated from a joint conference of these groups in Stanislav on February 8, 1919. Freylikh seems to have left East Galicia before that conference.

30. The Communist Party of East Galicia was formed through the fusion of three major currents. One of these was the left wing of the Jewish Social Democratic Party, whose January congress was described in Freylikh's report. Part of this current originated in the left wing of the Zionist labor organization Poale Zion. The other two components were the left wing of the Ukrainian Socialist Revolutionaries and the International Revolutionary Social Democracy, a group of about 500 revolutionary Ukrainian youth. Its newspaper was edited by Roman Rosdolsky, later a member in Poland of the communist opposition to Stalin's course led by Trotsky. Subsequently, the East Galician party was strengthened by forces from the Ukrainian and Polish CPs. See Janusz Radziejowski, *The Communist Party of Western Ukraine* (Edmonton: Canadian Institute of Ukrainian Studies, 1983), pp. 1–29.

31. In the summer of 1919, the Polish army, acting with the approval of the Allied powers, invaded and swiftly conquered East Galicia. The Ukrainian Galician Army retreated

eastward into formerly tsarist Ukrainian territories. After a brief alliance with Denikin's White Guard army, it took the name Red Ukrainian Galician Army and fought alongside the Red Army. It merged into the Red Army in April 1920.

During this period, an active guerrilla struggle developed in East Galicia in favor of incorporation into the Soviet Ukraine. In July 1920, during the Polish government's war against the Soviet republic, a Galician Soviet Republic was established in Ternopol under the leadership of the East Galician CP. After two months of Soviet rule, the region was reconquered by the Polish army and reincorporated into Poland. The East Galician CP, however, continued through the 1920s as a component of the Comintern, affiliated to the Polish CP. East Galicia was annexed to the Ukraine during World War II and is today part of the USSR.

32. *Pervyy kongress* (1933), pp. 257–58. This resolution of the Finnish party, submitted by Sirola as part of his report on Finland, was published in Petrograd in 1919 as part of a pamphlet by Kuusinen on the Finnish revolution.

33. *Die Kommunistische Internationale,* no. 1 (1919), pp. 9–13.

34. The Russian CP's draft program was published in installments in *Pravda,* February 25–27, 1919. The final text adopted by the Russian CP's eighth congress on March 22 is printed in Riddell, *German Revolution,* pp. 623–52. Paragraphs 1 to 19 of the draft program, the points endorsed by the French Communists, correspond to the general preamble of the final text.

35. In the Morocco crises of 1905 and 1911 France and Germany almost went to war over conflicting colonial ambitions in Morocco and elsewhere in Africa.

36. The Saar and Briey districts were major centers of the steel industry in Germany and France respectively.

37. *Pervyy kongress* (1933), p. 247. This statement was printed in the first issue of *Kommunisticheskiy internatsional,* published in May 1919.

38. *Pervyy kongress* (1933), pp. 241–42. Yalymov's report was first published in *Pravda,* March 12, 1919.

39. These were among the twenty-six executed leaders of the Baku Soviet government.
40. An abridged version of Unszlicht's report appeared in *Izvestia,* March 12, 1919. The report was omitted, however, from both the 1921 and the 1933 editions of the congress proceedings. The full text, in Polish, was first published in *Z pola walki,* vol. 12, no. 2 (46) (1969), pp. 129–33, from which this translation is taken.
41. Before World War I, most of Poland was ruled by Russian tsar Nicholas II. Smaller portions were ruled by Germany and Austria-Hungary. In 1915 the German army drove Russian forces out of Poland. German kaiser Wilhelm II henceforth ruled much of Russian Poland, while Austria-Hungary administered the southern portion of the conquered territory.
42. Hans Hartwig von Beseler was governor of German-held Poland from 1915 to 1918. He tried to set up a Polish government, the Regency Council, and army under German control.
43. A strike in October 1918 in the Dabrowa coal-mining district touched off a general strike that quickly led to revolution and the creation of a Polish state.

    At the beginning of November, the workers in the Dabrowa basin formed a council, which called on workers to take over the mines and factories, proclaimed a general strike, and established detachments of Red Guards. For several weeks the council's power overshadowed that of the official governmental organs in this region.

    More than 100 councils were formed across Poland, but only in Dabrowa did workers achieve a measure of power. As indicated later in Unszlicht's report, the Pilsudski government dispatched its army to Dabrowa in late December, disarmed the workers, and disbanded their councils.
44. A council of workers' delegates was formed in Warsaw on November 11, 1918, including supporters of the Social Democracy of Poland and Lithuania, the Polish Socialist Party–Left, and the Polish Socialist Party–Revolutionary Faction (PSP-RF). The PSP-RF quickly withdrew, convening a sepa-

rate assembly of workers' delegates on November 21. Elections to a unified Warsaw Council of Workers' Delegates took place December 12, and the new body convened on January 5, 1919. Efforts of the National Workers' Union to create a third council were unsuccessful.

45. The PSP-RF had backed Germany and the Central Powers during the war.

46. In August 1917 the provisional government of Russia headed by Kerensky faced a counterrevolutionary coup attempt led by Lavr Kornilov, head of the army. When Kerensky's government appealed for the support of the working class, the Bolsheviks led the workers' mobilization against the coup attempt. Kornilov was defeated and Kerensky retained office. But this remobilization of the working class laid the groundwork for the revolutionary overthrow of Kerensky three months later.

47. The principle Yiddish-language revolutionary newspaper was *Tsum kamf* (Struggle), published from 1918 first by the SDKPiL and then by the Polish CP.

48. *Pervyy kongress* (1933), pp. 246–47. The letter from the Serbian party, received in Moscow only after the end of the international congress, was first printed in *Kommunisticheskiy internatsional,* no. 1, (May 1, 1919).

49. A coalition of Serbia, Bulgaria, Greece, and Montenegro defeated Turkey in the First Balkan War of 1912–13. In the Second Balkan War of 1913, Bulgaria was defeated by a coalition of the other four states and Romania.

    Social Democratic parties in Serbia and the other warring states opposed "national defense" in these conflicts and voted in parliament against war credits, with the support of the Socialist International and its parties. For documents on this conflict, see Riddell, *Lenin's Struggle,* pp. 146–59.

50. In October 1915 the invading armies of Austria-Hungary, Germany, and Bulgaria defeated the Serbian army and forced it to undertake an arduous and costly retreat over the Albanian mountains to the Adriatic Sea. Serbia was occupied by the Central Powers for the remainder of the war.

51. The congress also called for unification of all Social Democratic parties in Yugoslavia and affiliation to the Third International.

52. *Pervyy kongress* (1933), pp. 230–31. This report by Milkić was published in the August 1919 issue of *The Communist International.* It is clearly an edited and expanded version of the remarks he made in reply to Rakovsky during the congress itself. See chapter 2.

53. This letter is published in *Prepiska srpskih socijalista u toku prvog svetskog rata* (Belgrade: Institut za savremenu istoriju, 1979).

54. Vitomir Korać (1877–1940), a pioneer of Croatian socialism, entered the capitalist government of the newly formed Yugoslav state in December 1918 as a representative of the Socialist Party of Croatia and Slavonia. The Serbian Social Democratic Party condemned this action.

55. *Pervyy kongress* (1933), pp. 228–29. A somewhat different version of Grimlund's report was published in *Pravda,* March 11, 1919.

56. At the Zimmerwald conference in September 1915, the Swedish and Norwegian socialist youth movement was represented by Zeth Höglund and Ture Nerman, who joined with other revolutionists there in founding the Zimmerwald Left.

57. The Workers' and Soldiers' Association was founded in April 1917 as an expression of a mass protest movement, later known as the "potato revolution," that swept Sweden that spring. This movement had begun when workers in Västervik, faced with acute food shortages, formed a committee to take charge of food distribution. Protests spread quickly across the country. Demands for adequate food supplies were linked to calls for universal suffrage and the release of political prisoners. Many soldiers declared their solidarity with this movement. The Workers' and Soldiers' Association was initiated by left-wing forces that had split from the Swedish Social Democratic Party and were shortly to form the Left Social Democratic Party.

58. *Pervyy kongress* (1933), pp. 258. Verfeuil's letter was read to the congress by Sadoul during his report on France. The letter was first published in *Die Kommunistische Internationale,* no. 1 (1919).

59. At the 1904 Amsterdam congress of the Second International, the French Social Democratic current led by Jules Guesde moved adoption of the resolution on revisionism passed the previous year by the SPD congress at Dresden.

"This congress," the resolution stated, "most decisively condemns the revisionist efforts to alter our existing policy–one which is based on the class struggle, has stood the test, and has been crowned with success–by substituting a policy of compromise with the existing order for that of the conquest of power through overcoming our enemies."

The resolution specifically barred Social Democratic parties from approving measures (such as budgetary appropriations) "that tend to maintain the ruling class in government," and reaffirmed that Social Democracy "cannot seek to share governmental power within bourgeois society." See *Internationaler Sozialisten-Kongress zu Amsterdam, 14. bis 20. August 1904,* p. 31, reprinted in *Kongress-Protokolle der Zweiten Internationale* (Glashütten im Taunus: Verlag Detlev Auvermann, 1975), vol. 1.

Victor Adler of Austria and Émile Vandervelde of Belgium proposed an amendment that would have removed explicit condemnation of the revisionist current, of revisionism, and of participation in bourgeois governments. After considerable discussion, this amendment was defeated by a 21–21 tie vote. (The delegation from each country received two votes.) The resolution was then adopted 25 votes to 5, with 12 abstentions.

Appendix

1. Lenin, *CW,* vol. 28, pp. 478–80. First printed in *Pravda,* March 6, 1919.

2. Translated from Trotsky, *Pyat' let Kominterna,* vol. 2, pp. 28–30, except as otherwise noted. First printed in *Pravda,* March 6, 1919.

3. Trotsky here recalled Marx's statement in 1852 that the French revolution, under the blows of Bonapartist reaction, was "still journeying through purgatory. It does its work methodically. . . . And when it has done . . . its preliminary work, Europe will leap from its seat and exultantly exclaim: Well grubbed, old mole!" Marx, "The Eighteenth Brumaire of Louis Bonaparte," in *Selected Works,* vol. 1, p. 476–77. The expression, "Well grubbed, old mole," is a reference to Shakespeare, *Hamlet,* act 1, scene 5.
4. The words "social-patriotic patch-sewers" are taken from the text in *Pravda,* March 6, 1919. The 1924 edition of this article in *Pyat' let Kominterna* reads at this point "revolutionary patch-sewers."
5. *Pravda,* March 6, 1919.
6. A line of type is missing at this point in the original text in *Pravda.*
7. *Pravda,* March 6, 1919.
8. *Pravda,* March 7, 1919. International Women's Day was the following day.
9. The Stuttgart congress resolution specified that campaigns by parties of the Second International to democratize the franchise should adopt the goal of universal suffrage for women as well as men. In countries where male suffrage had been largely achieved, it continued, the struggle for women's suffrage should be pursued with energy.

   The resolution, together with Clara Zetkin's speech introducing it, can be found in Philip S. Foner, ed., *Clara Zetkin, Selected Writings* (New York: International Publishers, 1984), pp. 98–107.
10. The Second International Women's Conference, held in Copenhagen in August 1910, adopted March 8 as Women's Day.
11. Ransome, *Russia in 1919,* pp. 220–22.
12. Lenin, *CW,* vol. 28, pp. 481–85. This article is a newspaper summary of Lenin's speech at the March 6 rally described above by Ransome. It was first printed in *Pravda,* March 7, 1919.

13. After nineteenth-century Russian writer M.Y. Saltykov-Shchedrin published his "Old Times in Poshekhonye," the name of this town became synonymous with provincial backwardness.
14. Lenin, *CW,* vol. 29, pp. 240–41. This is the text of a phonograph recording made by Lenin in late March.

Chronology

1914

August 4 – As imperialist governments of Europe launch World War, Social Democratic party deputies in Germany and France vote for war credits, sealing collapse of Second International.

November 1 – Bolshevik Central Committee calls for new proletarian International, freed from opportunism.

December – Liebknecht votes in German parliament against war credits; joins Luxemburg and others to launch revolutionary current.

1915

September 5–8 – Conference of antiwar Social Democrats in Zimmerwald, Switzerland; formation of Zimmerwald Left, precursor of Communist International.

1917

March 8 (February 23) – Russian revolution begins. General strike in Petrograd leads rapidly to formation of soviets and overthrow of tsar.

April 6 – U.S. enters World War I.

April 6–8 – Independent Social Democratic Party formed in Germany as result of split in SPD.

April – Food shortages in Sweden lead to mass protest movement.

May – Widespread mutiny in French army. Left Social Democratic Party of Sweden founded.

May–June – Strike wave sweeps France.

June – Leeds labor conference in Britain calls for solidarity with Russian revolution.

June–July – Russian soldiers' growing refusal to continue war contributes to failure of offensive launched by Provisional Government.

July – Sun Yat-sen becomes head of republican government in south China.

November 7 (October 25) – Bolshevik-led insurrection ousts Provisional Government in Russia and establishes workers' and peasants' government.

November 8 (October 26) – Congress of soviets in Russia adopts decrees on peace and on land.

November 20 (7) – Rada proclaims Ukrainian People's Republic.

December 15 (2) – Soviet government concludes armistice with Germany.

December 22 (9) – Beginning of Soviet peace negotiations with Central Powers at Brest-Litovsk.

December 24 (11) – Ukrainian Soviet Republic proclaimed.

1918

January 8 – U.S. President Wilson announces "Fourteen Points" to counter Soviet peace proposal.

January 14–20 – Mass political strikes in Austria-Hungary.

January 27 – Revolutionary workers' government established in Finland; White army launches Finnish civil war.

January 28–February 4 – Mass political strikes in Germany, encompassing more than 1 million workers in fifty cities.

February 10 – Bolshevik delegation at Brest-Litovsk declares war at an end but rejects German annexationist terms, quits peace negotiations.

February 18 – New German offensive against Soviet Russia begins.

March 3 – Brest-Litovsk peace treaty signed between German and Soviet governments.

March 4 – Leon Trotsky appointed to organize Red Army.

March 6–8 – Bolsheviks adopt name Russian Communist Party.

March 24 – National congress of Norwegian workers' councils.

March – Soviet Ukrainian government driven out of Ukraine by German army. Armenian Communist Party founded in Tiflis.

April 6 – Soviet assumes full power in Baku.

April 22 – Transcaucasian Federal Republic founded, declares independence from Russia.

April 29 – Fall of Vyborg marks defeat of Finnish revolution.

May 26 – Separate bourgeois republic proclaimed in Georgia; republics formed in Armenia and Azerbaijan two days later.

May – Czech divisions in Siberia revolt against Soviet republic, link up with Russian counterrevolutionaries.

June–September – Strike wave grows throughout Germany.

July 28 – Centrists win majority of French SP National Council.

July 31 – Fall of Baku Commune.

August 29 – Communist Party of Finland founded.

September 15–21 – Central Powers' front in Bulgaria collapses.

October – Polish miners spearhead general strike that leads to revolution and creation of Polish state.

October 27 – Austria-Hungary informs U.S. government of readiness to make separate peace. Mutinies begin in German fleet.

October 28 – Czechoslovakia declares independence from Austria-Hungary.

October 30 – Mass demonstrations, strikes sweep German Austria. Social Democrat Renner forms coalition government in Vienna.

October 31 – Workers' uprising in Hungary. Social Democrats join bourgeois-led coalition government in Budapest. Turkey surrenders to Allied powers. West Ukrainian People's Republic proclaimed in East Galicia.

November 3 – Austria-Hungary surrenders to Allied powers. Communist Party of German Austria founded.

November 4 – German revolution begins in Kiel, spreads to all major German cities in next five days. Hungarian Communist Party founded in Moscow.

November 9 – Revolution in Berlin. Kaiser ousted. SPD leader Ebert appointed imperial chancellor, forms joint cabinet with USPD.

early November – Mass strikes in Holland; workers' and soldiers' councils formed.

November 11 – Cease-fire between Germany and Allied powers.

November 11–14 – General strike in Switzerland; army attacks workers in several cities.

November 12 – Republic declared in Austria, deposing Hapsburg dynasty.

November 16 – Republic proclaimed in Hungary, abolishing monarchy. Communist Workers Party of Poland founded.

November 17 – Dutch *Tribune* group takes name Communist Party of the Netherlands.

November 24 – Hungarian CP refounded in Budapest.

December 13 – 50,000 workers demonstrate in Bucharest for republic and socialism; hundreds killed when fired on by troops.

December 27 or 28 – After meeting with German Spartacus envoy Fuchs, Lenin writes to Chicherin on calling international Communist congress.

December–January – Mass strikes in Bombay, India.

December 29–January 1 – Founding congress of Communist Party of Germany.

1919

January – Shop stewards lead strike of 100,000 in Glasgow; British soldiers mutiny in England and France.

January 3 – Red Army liberates Kharkov, and most of remainder of Ukraine by early February.

January 4 – SPD government of Prussia fires popular Berlin police chief Eichhorn, provoking January uprising.

January 15 – Luxemburg and Liebknecht murdered by SPD-instigated Freikorps.

January 18 – Victorious Allied powers open Paris conference to divide spoils of war.

January 19 – National Assembly elections in Germany result in bourgeois majority.

January 24 – Invitation to international Communist congress published in *Pravda*.

January – Mutinies break out among British intervention forces in Russia.

February 3–10 – International Socialist Conference held in Bern.

February 6–11 – General strike in Seattle, United States.

February 8 – Communist Party of East Galicia founded.

March – Mutiny in French army units in the Ukraine, spreads to fleet in April.

March 2–6 – Founding congress of Communist International held in Moscow.

March 3–12 – General strike and renewed fighting in Berlin.

March 5–9 – International Federation of Trade Unions congress held in Bern.

March 21 – Workers' and soldiers' soviets take power in Hungary.

April 13 – British troops massacre more than 300 protesters at Amritsar, India.

April 13–May 3 – German Communists lead workers' and soldiers' government in Bavaria.

April 20–25 – Yugoslav Socialist Workers Party founded.

May 4 – Student demonstration in Beijing protesting predatory decisions of Paris conference launches nationalist revolutionary upsurge in China.

Glossary

Adler, Friedrich (1879–1960) – son of Victor Adler; a secretary of Austrian SDP 1911–14; led opposition to party's collaboration with government during World War I; assassinated reactionary Austro-Hungarian Prime Minister Stürgkh as protest against war 1916; opposed foundation of Comintern; principal organizer and president of Two-and-a-Half International 1921–23; secretary of Socialist International 1923–39.

Adler, Victor (1852–1918) – organizer and leader of Austrian SDP and of European Social Democracy from 1880s until his death; chauvinist during World War I.

Albert, Max – see Eberlein.

Alexinsky, G.A. (1879–1971) – Bolshevik during 1905–7 revolution; with ultraleft *Vpered* group 1909–14; chauvinist during World War I; joined Plekhanov's group *Yedinstvo* (Unity) and organized smear campaign against Lenin and Bolsheviks 1917; opposed Soviet rule and emigrated.

Andriyevsky, Opanas (1878–1955) – a leader of Ukrainian Party of Socialist Independents, an extreme nationalist formation based on petty-bourgeois military circles; member of Directory from November 1918; emigrated to Czechoslovakia.

Armenian Communist Party – formed in Tiflis, Georgia, with fewer than 100 members by exiles from Turkish Armenia March 1918; goal was to work among exiles and in Turkish Armenia; driven out of Tiflis May 1918; worked among exiles in North Caucasus and Russia 1918–20; ceased activity 1920; most Armenian Communists organized in Caucasus regional committee of Russian CP 1918; Communists in the Republic of Armenia worked in Armenian component of Russian CP with 400 members 1919; founded CP of Armenia 1920; 3,000 members summer 1920; CP of Armenia headed Armenian Soviet republic from December 1920.

Babeuf, François Noel (1760–1797) – French revolutionary; prominent writer and organizer for utopian communist current; executed.

Baguirov, Mir Djafar (1896–1956) – joined Bolshevik Party 1917; Azerbaijani delegate to first Comintern congress and central bureau member of United Group of Eastern Peoples of Russia; headed Cheka (later GPU) of Azerbaijan 1921–31; first secretary of Azerbaijani Communist Party 1935; removed 1953 as Beria supporter; executed.

Balabanoff, Angelica (1878–1965) – born in Russia; joined Italian SP 1900; International Socialist Bureau member; attended Zimmerwald conference 1915; secretary of Zimmerwald International Socialist Committee in Bern and editor of its *Bulletin* 1917; joined Bolshevik Party 1917; secretary of Comintern 1919–20; left Russia 1922; broke with communism and rejoined Italian SP; lived in New York after 1936; returned to Italy after World War II and joined the more right-wing of the two Social Democratic parties.

Balkan Revolutionary Social Democratic Federation – founded July 1915 by Bulgarian (Tesnyaki), Greek, Romanian, and Serbian SDPs opposed to chauvinism and "civil peace"; favored founding new, revolutionary International; renamed Balkan Communist Federation 1920; Comintern coordinating body for Balkan parties until 1930s.

Barth, Emil (1879–1941) – German anarchist before 1910; later active in SPD and USPD; chairman of Revolutionary Shop Stewards February–November 1918; member of Ebert government November–December 1918; rejoined SPD 1921.

Bauer, Otto (Heinrich Weber) (1881–1938) – a leader of Austrian SDP and theoretician of Austro-Marxism; foreign minister of German Austria 1918–19; opposed Comintern and helped found centrist Two-and-a-Half International.

Bekentayev, Hussein – Tatar Communist; delegate to first Comintern congress.

Berzin, J.A. (1881–1941) – joined Latvian SDP 1902; emigrated 1908; represented Latvian party at Zimmerwald where he supported Zimmerwald Left; moved to Russia and elected to Bolshevik Central Committee 1917; Soviet ambassador to Switzerland until deported after general strike November 1918; active in Comintern and Soviet diplomatic service until recalled 1929; arrested during Stalin purges 1937.

Beseler, Hans Hartwig von (1850–1921) – German general; commanded troops that conquered Antwerp 1914; governor of Poland 1915–18; attempted to organize Polish government and army under German control.

Besteiro, Julián (1870–1940) – Spanish Social Democrat; delegate to the Bern conference 1919; chairman of Socialist Workers Party of Spain from 1925; president of parliament of Spanish republic 1931–36; jailed by Franco, died in prison.

Body, Marcel (1894–1984) – joined French SP 1914; joined French Communist Group in Moscow while part of French military mission in Moscow October 1918; worked with Comintern press 1920; Soviet foreign service in Norway 1921–25; refused to approve sanctions against Trotsky and Zinoviev 1927; expelled from CP 1928; thereafter sympathetic to revolutionary syndicalism; continued writing for left press into 1980s.

Bolsheviks – see Russian Communist Party.

Borodin, Mikhail (M.M. Grusenberg) (1884–1951) – joined Bolsheviks 1903; emigrated to U.S. 1907–18; Comintern envoy to U.S., Britain, and China 1920s; arrested in USSR 1949, died in prison camp.

Branting, Hjalmar (1860–1925) – longtime leader of Swedish Social Democrats and editor of *Social-Demokraten;* leader of Second International; chauvinist during World War I; a leading organizer and chairman of 1919 Bern conference; won Nobel Peace Prize 1921; Swedish prime minister 1921–23.

British Communist Group – small group of British Communists resident in Russia; affiliated to Federation of Foreign Groups of the Russian CP.

British Socialist Party – founded out of fusion of Social Democratic Federation and other groups 1911; antichauvinist during World War I; right-wing pro-war minority split off 1916; 10,000 members early 1919; joined Comintern 1919; majority fused with other groups to found British CP 1920.

Brouckère, Louis de (1870–1951) – leader and theoretician of Belgian Workers Party; main opponent of electoral bloc with Liberals before 1914; became chauvinist 1914 and subsequently entered Belgian government; president of Second International 1937–39.

Brusilov, A.A. (1853–1926) – tsarist general; commanded key breakthrough against Austria-Hungary 1916; supreme Russian commander May–July 1917; jailed briefly after October revolution; later joined Red Army, staff officer in Poland campaign 1920; retired 1924.

Bukharin, Nikolai (1888–1938) – joined Bolsheviks 1906; emigrated to western Europe 1911; helped edit *Kommunist* in Switzerland 1915 and *Novyy Mir* (New world) in New York 1916–17; returned to Russia 1917 and was leading member of Bolshevik Central Committee; led Left Communist faction of Bolshevik Party 1918; editor of *Pravda* 1919–29; one of main Bolshevik leaders of Comintern; head of Comintern 1926–29; headed right opposition and was expelled from Soviet CP 1929; later recanted and was readmitted; executed on Stalin's orders after third Moscow frame-up trial.

Bulgarian Communist Group – small group of Bulgarian Communists resident in Russia; affiliated to the Federation of Foreign Groups of the Russian CP. See also SDP of Bulgaria.

Bund (General Union of Jewish Workers of Lithuania, Poland, and Russia) – founded in Vilna 1897; affiliated to RSDLP 1898–1903 and from 1906; aligned with Mensheviks; chauvinist during World War I; backed Provisional Government after February 1917; majority joined Bolsheviks 1920; minority soon ceased activity; continued functioning in Poland into World War II.

Burian, Edmund (1878–1935) – joined Czech Social Democracy 1897; Czech CP executive committee member 1920–29; elected to Comintern executive committee at third congress; expelled as right oppositionist 1929; joined Social Democrats.

Cachin, Marcel (1869–1958) – joined French Workers Party led by Guesde 1891; member of French SP from 1905; chauvinist during World War I; supported SP's affiliation with Comintern 1920; leader of French CP until his death.

Central Bureau of Communist Organizations of the Peoples of the East – originated March 1918 as Socialist-Communist Muslim Party, uniting Communist groups among the primarily Islamic peoples in old tsarist empire; took name Russian Party of Muslim Communists (Bolsheviks) June 1918; affiliated to Russian CP and took name Central Bureau of Muslim Organizations of the Russian CP November 1918; expanded to represent Communists of all Asian minority peoples and took name Central Bureau of Communist Organizations of the Peoples of the East early 1919; represented at first Comintern congress.

Central Bureau of Eastern Peoples – see Central Bureau of Communist Organizations of the Peoples of the East.

Cheka (All-Russia Extraordinary Commission) – formed as security force and revolutionary tribunal in defense of

Soviet republic 1918; first headed by F. Dzerzhinsky; renamed GPU (State Political Administration) 1922.

Chicherin, Georgiy (1872–1936) – tsarist diplomat until 1904; supported 1905 revolution and joined RSDLP in exile; Menshevik before 1914; antichauvinist during World War I; returned to Russia January 1918 and joined Bolsheviks; People's Commissar of Foreign Affairs 1918–30; key organizer of first Comintern congress.

Chinese Socialist Workers Party – formed January 1919 by Chinese workers living in Russia who led the Union of Chinese Workers.

Chkhenkeli, A.I. (1874–1959) – Georgian Menshevik; Duma member during World War I; foreign minister for Menshevik government of Georgia 1918–21; emigrated 1921.

Clemenceau, Georges (1841–1929) – French prime minister, 1906–9, 1917–20; chief organizer of 1919 Paris conference and architect of Treaty of Versailles.

Communist Party (Bolsheviks) of the Ukraine – RSDLP in Ukraine before 1917 included few Bolsheviks; a national structure, RSDLP of the Bolsheviks in Ukraine, formed December 1917; held first congress with 4,000 members and took name CP of the Ukraine, a component of Russian CP, July 1918; underground during German occupation 1918; 23,000 members March 1919; 75,000 1920.

Communist Party of Belorussia – founded as component of Russian CP December 1918; led Belorussian Soviet republic from January 1919; 1,700 members November 1920; Lithuanian and Belorussian CPs functioned as united organization 1918–20.

Communist Party of East Galicia – formed by fusion of several local Communist groups February 1919; admitted to Comintern August 1919; participated in forming Communist Party of Galicia, which headed Galician Soviet Socialist Republic July–August 1920; affiliated to Polish CP 1920; split over Ukrainian national question 1921, reunited 1923; 1,500 members 1923; became

CP of West Ukraine 1923; leadership expelled from Comintern 1928.

Communist Party of Estonia – Estonian component of Bolshevik Party had 10,000 members late 1917; led Estonian Soviet government November 1917–February 1918; led Estonian Working People's Commune (Soviet republic) November 1918–January 1919; founded as independent party August 9–11, 1919; first congress November 1920 representing 700 members; underground until Estonia's incorporation into USSR 1940.

Communist Party of Finland – left wing won majority in Finnish SDP early 1918 and led unsuccessful revolution; forced into exile by White Terror; CP founded in Moscow August 29, 1918; helped found Comintern 1919; banned in Finland until after World War II.

Communist Party of German Austria – founded November 3, 1918, by a dozen representatives of Friedländer and Vienna Bolshevik groups; strengthened in following months by entry of Left Radicals, Federation of Revolutionary Socialists (International), and returning prisoners of war; 3,000 members at first congress February 1919; 40,000 members June 1919.

Communist Party of German Colonists in Russia – see German Sections of the Russian CP.

Communist Party of Germany – founded December 30, 1918, by Spartacus League with participation of International Communists of Germany; joined Comintern 1919; lost half its membership in 1919 split of ultraleft forces; 78,000 members going into fusion with USPD left wing 1920; 350,000 members after fusion.

Communist Party of Hungary – founded November 4, 1918, in Moscow by members of Hungarian section of Russian CP; reestablished in Budapest upon their arrival November 24; encompassed Revolutionary Socialist group in SDP and among shop stewards as well as other left forces; membership reportedly 10,000 January 1919; fused with SDP to form Socialist Party March 1919, which led Hungarian revolutionary government March–July 1919; SP then disintegrated; CP severely repressed, functioned in exile and isolated cells in Hungarian SDP 1919–25; 250 members in Hungary late 1921; reorganized September 1925.

Communist Party of Latvia – Social Democracy of the Latvian Territory affiliated to RSDLP 1904 and was allied with Bolsheviks; 1,000 members February 1917; led Latvian Soviet republic November 1917–February 1918 and again 1919; took name CP March 1919; 7,500 members 1919.

Communist Party of Lithuania – Lithuanian SDP founded 1896; fused with Polish SDP 1899; Lithuanian CP founded as component of Russian CP August 1918; first congress, representing 800 members, held underground October 1918; led Lithuanian Soviet republic December 1918–April 1919; Lithuanian and Belorussian CPs functioned as united organization 1918–20; underground 1919–40.

Communist Party of Romania – SDP founded 1893 but ceased to function about 1907; revived 1910; antichauvinist during World War I; participated in Zimmerwald; renamed SP November 1918; 24,000 members 1919; right wing split 1921 over call to join Comintern; majority took name CP, joined Comintern; underground 1924–44.

Communist Party of Sweden – see Left SDP of Sweden.

Communist Party of the Netherlands – SDP formed by expelled left-wing *Tribune* group of Social Democratic Workers Party 1909; antichauvinist and aligned with Zimmerwald Left during World War I; became CP November 17, 1918; 1,000 members late 1918; joined Comintern April 1919.

Communist Workers Party of Poland – Social Democracy of the Kingdom of Poland founded 1893; fused with Lithuanian SDP to form Social Democracy of the Kingdom of Poland and Lithuania (SDKPiL) 1899; affiliated to RSDLP 1906; split into two wings 1911; reunited 1916;

fused with Polish Socialist Party – Left to form Polish CP December 16, 1918; dissolved and most leaders murdered during Stalin purges 1938; reestablished 1942.

Connolly, James (1870–1916) – revolutionary Socialist leader of Irish labor and nationalist movements; founded Irish Socialist Republican Party 1896; founding member of Socialist Labour Party (Britain) 1903; organizer and secretary of Irish Transport and General Workers' Union; leader of Irish Easter Rebellion 1916; executed by British government.

Council of People's Commissars – government of Russian Soviet republic established after October 1917 revolution.

CP – Communist Party.

Croatian Socialist Party – see SDP of Croatia and Slavonia.

Czech Communist Group – Czech Communists resident in Russia affiliated to Federation of Foreign Groups of the Russian CP; revolutionary socialists in Czechoslovakia worked inside SDP early 1919; organized Marxist Left faction December 1919, which won leadership of party 1920; party took name CP 1921.

Dashnaktsutiun (Armenian Revolutionary Federation – Dashnaks) – nationalist petty-bourgeois party founded 1890; affiliated to Second International; supported Provisional Government after February 1917 revolution; headed anti-Soviet government of Armenia 1918–20; functioned in exile after Soviet power established in Armenia December 1920.

Daszynski, Ignacy (1866–1936) – headed Galician SDP 1892–1919; then a leader of unified Polish SP; headed SP parliamentary fraction 1920s; supported Pilsudski's coup d'etat 1926.

Däumig, Ernst (1866–1922) – an editor of *Vorwärts,* 1911–16; dismissed for opposing SPD war policy; leader of USPD and Revolutionary Shop Stewards 1918; became cochairman of USPD December 1919 and cochairman of German CP 1920; left CP 1921.

David, Eduard (1863–1930) – a leader of SPD revisionists and outspoken supporter of German imperialism; worked in imperial colonial ministry in Max von Baden government 1918; first president of National Assembly 1919; minister without portfolio 1919–20.

Debs, Eugene V. (1855–1926) – a founder and five-time presidential candidate for U.S. SP; spokesperson for party's left wing; helped found IWW; imprisoned for antiwar statements 1918–21; solidarized with Bolshevik revolution but remained in SP following 1919 split and establishment of U.S. CP.

Denikin, A.I. (1872–1947) – tsarist general; White Army commander in chief in southern Russia in civil war 1918–20; emigrated 1920 after defeat by Red Army.

Deutsch, Julius (1884–1968) – a leader of Austrian Social Democracy; organized Workers' Militia (Schutzbund), which he led until 1934; advisor to republic in Spanish civil war; active in Austrian SDP after World War II.

Diamand, Herman (1860–1931) – cofounder of Polish SDP in Austria; deputy to Austrian parliament 1907–18; member International Socialist Bureau for Poland from 1904; backed Austria in World War I; leader of Polish SP after 1918; deputy in Polish parliament 1919–30.

Directory – anti-Soviet government of Ukraine established after collapse of German-backed Skoropadsky government late 1918; led by Petlyura and Vinnichenko; supported by Allied powers; ousted by pro-Soviet forces early 1919.

Dittmann, Wilhelm (1874–1954) – SPD Reichstag deputy from 1912; joined centrist opposition 1915; USPD party secretary 1917–22; member of Ebert cabinet November–December 1918; USPD delegate to second Comintern congress 1920; opposed Twenty-one Conditions and unification with German CP; returned to SPD 1922.

Domes, Franz (1863–1930) – Austrian Social Democrat, secretary of metalworkers union 1898; parliamentary deputy 1911; influential union and governmental leader after 1918; member of Austrian Chamber of Workers and Employers 1920.

Dutov, A.I. (1864–1921) – tsarist colonel; general in Kolchak's White army 1918–19; defeated by Red Army; fled to China 1920; killed by own troops.

Dyorov, Stojan (1883–1950) – Bulgarian Social Democrat; joined RSDLP in Odessa 1908; joined Bolsheviks 1917; worked with Federation of Foreign Groups of Russian CP; represented Bulgarian Communists in Russia at first Comintern congress; returned to Bulgaria 1920 and left politics.

Dzerzhinskaya, Sof'ia Sigizmundovna (1882–1968) – Lithuanian Bolshevik from 1905; Social Democracy of the Kingdom of Poland and Lithuania Central Committee member; Soviet foreign service 1917–19; Soviet government and party posts 1918–46; Comintern executive committee 1937; retired 1946.

Dzhaparidze, Ilya (1880–1918) – member of RSDLP 1898; Bolshevik 1903; RSDLP Baku committee from 1904; soviet executive committee president and commissar of internal affairs of Baku Soviet government 1918; executed with twenty-six other Baku commissars at instigation of British intervention forces.

Ebenholz – Austrian prisoner of war in Russia; organizer of military commissariat and chairman of Bolshevik organization among German settlers on Volga.

Eberlein, Hugo (1887–1944) – joined SPD 1906; member of Spartacus and Communist Party of Germany central committees; delegate to first Comintern congress; played leading role in Comintern until stripped of leadership posts 1928; fled Germany 1933; Comintern Control Commission 1935; arrested in Soviet Union during Moscow purge trials 1937; died in prison.

Ebert, Friedrich (1871–1925) – SPD leader, close collaborator of Bebel from 1906; cochairman of SPD 1913–19; chauvinist during World War I; appointed imperial chancellor by Max von Baden 1918; led Council of People's Representatives government 1918–19; worked with army High Command to crush January uprising; German president 1919–25.

Eisner, Kurt (1867–1919) – German Social Democrat; *Vorwärts* editor 1900–1906; revisionist before World War I; opposed SPD pro-war policy and founded Munich USPD; led November 1918 revolution in Munich; prime minister of Bavarian republic November 1918–February 1919; helped organize right wing at Bern conference; assassinated by monarchist in February.

Enfiadjian, Artashes – Armenian tobacco manufacturer; finance minister in bourgeois Kachaznuni Armenian government from 1918.

Engels, Frederick (1820–1895) – lifelong collaborator of Karl Marx and cofounder with him of modern communist workers' movement; coauthor of *Communist Manifesto;* a leader of revolutionary democratic forces in 1848 German revolution; lived in England 1841–44 and again from 1849 to his death; in his last years the outstanding figure in Second International.

Eshche (Worker) – Communist Tatar newspaper published in Kazan.

Fabierkiewicz, Zbigniew (1882–1919) – Polish revolutionary; contributor to and editor of many socialist and communist papers; returned from Russia to Poland 1918 where he helped lead party work; shot by Polish police.

Faure, Paul (1878–1960) – leading figure in centrist opposition in French SP during World War I; opposition delegate to 1919 Bern conference; opposed SP affiliation to Comintern 1920; general secretary of French SP 1920–40; supported pro-Nazi Vichy government during World War II; expelled from SP 1944.

Federation of Foreign Groups of the Russian Communist Party – formed May 1918 by Russian CP to organize among prisoners of war and immigrant workers in Russia; dissolved 1920.

Filimonov, A.P. (b. 1866) – commander of Kuban Host, a counterrevolutionary Cossack organization; active in civil war in Transcaucasia 1917–19.

Fineberg, Joseph (1886–1957) – member of British SP 1908–18; moved to Russia, joined Russian CP; helped prepare Comintern founding congress 1919; subsequently worked for Soviet state publications.

First International (International Working Men's Association) – founded 1864; united working-class organizations in a number of European countries and North America; Marx became its central leader; campaigned to defend 1871 Paris Commune; faced stiff repression after defeat of Commune and went into decline; seat moved to New York 1872; dissolved 1876.

Fischer, Ruth (Elfriede Eisler, then Friedländer) (1895–1961) – member of Austrian SDP left wing from 1914; cofounder Austrian CP 1918; moved to Germany, joined German CP 1919; leader of its leftist faction; Comintern executive committee 1924–26; opposed Stalin's political course in latter half of 1920s; expelled 1926; briefly supported Trotsky after 1933; later anticommunist.

Die Forderung: Organ für Sozialistiche Endzielpolitik (The demand: organ for the politics of socialism, the final goal) – publication of group of Swiss communists led by J. Herzog; nine issues from October 1917 until banned March 1918.

Die Freiheit (Freedom) – daily organ of German USPD published in Berlin 1918–22.

French Communist Group – small group of French Communists resident in Russia; affiliated to Federation of Foreign Groups of Russian CP; carried out valuable educational work that helped prepare ground for mutinies among French intervention troops in 1919.

Freylikh, Moshe – member of Poale Zion in East Galicia before World War I; won to communism while prisoner of war in Russia; returned to Galicia 1918 and edited *Chervonyi prapor* (Red flag); Central Committee East Galician CP 1919; delegate to Comintern executive committee 1919; returned to East Galicia 1920; moved to Vienna and left Communist movement 1920.

Friedländer, Elfriede – see Ruth Fischer.

Frossard, Louis-Oscar (1889–1946) – a leader of centrist opposition in French SP during World War I; party general secretary from October 1918; opposition delegate to 1919 Bern conference; SP representative to second Comintern congress 1920; French CP general secretary 1920–23; split from CP 1923; SP member 1923–32; minister in several governments in 1930s and subsequently in pro-Nazi Pétain government 1940.

Gailis, Karl (1887–1960) – Latvian Social Democrat from 1906; soon joined Bolsheviks; Latvian CP Central Committee from 1917; delegate to first Comintern congress; Latvian Soviet republic people's commissar 1919; worked in Soviet administration in Moscow after overthrow of republic 1919; left politics 1940.

Galician Social Democratic Party – see Polish SDP of Galicia and Silesia.

Gazeta pechatnikov (Printers' newspaper) – newspaper of the Moscow printers' union, under Menshevik influence; appeared from December 8, 1918, until March 1919.

Gedris, Kazimir (1888–1926) – Lithuanian; emigrated and joined left wing of U.S. SP 1913; traveled to Russia after February revolution and joined Bolsheviks 1917; delegate for Lithuania and Belorussia at first Comintern congress; lived in Lithuania and active in underground Lithuanian CP after 1924; captured and killed.

Gegechkori, Yevgeni (1881–1954) – Georgian Menshevik; chairman of Transcaucasian government from November 1917, then member of Menshevik government of Georgia; emigrated after Soviet power established 1921.

German Sections of the Russian Communist Party – united Communists from among the 2 million ethnic Germans in Soviet territory and 160,000 German prisoners of war; maintained own Central Bureau until 1921; had relations with German and Austrian CPs; 1,285 German members in Russian CP 1919.

Gompers, Samuel (1850–1924) – founder and president of American Federation of Labor 1886–1924 (except 1895); advocated policy of collaboration with employers; supported U.S. entry into World War I; chairman of Labor Commission at 1919 Versailles conference; refused to attend Bern conference for chauvinist reasons.

Gopner, Serafima Il'inichna (1880–1966) – Bolshevik from 1903; held important party and government posts in the Ukraine after 1917; member of Comintern executive committee secretariat 1929–38; one of only two people to have been a delegate to all seven Comintern congresses.

Gorter, Hermann (1864–1927) – Social Democrat from 1897; expelled from Dutch Social Democratic Workers Party with left-wing *Tribune* group 1909; cofounder of Dutch SDP 1909; supported Zimmerwald Left during World War I; cofounder of Dutch CP; held ultraleft views, quit CP 1921; left politics 1922.

Grekov (Oleksander Hrekov) (1875–1958) – Ukrainian general in tsarist army; held various posts in Ukrainian army and government under Rada and Directory 1917–19; briefly commander of Ukrainian Galician Army summer 1919; emigrated to Austria 1920; arrested by Soviets in Vienna 1945; released 1956.

Greulich, Hermann (1842–1925) – helped establish Swiss section of First International; a founder of Swiss SDP; belonged to bourgeois reformist Grütli Association; member of parliament from 1902; supported Swiss government policies in World War I; opposed Zimmerwald movement.

Grimlund, Otto (1893–1969) – belonged to left wing of Swedish Social Democratic Workers Party; cofounder of Left Social Democratic Party 1917; delegate to first Comintern congress; Swedish CP Central Committee member until 1925; rejoined Social Democrats 1929.

Grimm, Robert (1881–1958) – leader of Swiss SDP and longtime editor of *Berner Tagwacht;* took centrist position during World War I; participated in Zimmerwald and Kienthal conferences; chairman of Zimmerwald International Socialist Committee in Bern 1915–17; helped organize Two-and-a-Half International 1920; later returned to Second International.

Gruber – see Steinhardt, Karl.

Grumbach, Solomon (Homo) (1884–1952) – German right-wing Social Democrat; joined French SP 1908; International Socialist Bureau member; lived in Switzerland during World War I; pro-Entente, sharp opponent of Zimmerwald movement; attended Bern conference.

Grünberg, Carl (1861–1940) – Austrian Social Democrat; edited *Archiv für die Geschichte des Sozialismus und der Arbeiterbewegung,* a prominent socialist historical journal.

Grusenberg, M.M. – see Borodin, Mikhail.

Grütli Association – founded 1838 in Switzerland to pursue bourgeois social reform and education; affiliated to SP 1901; constituted chauvinist right wing within party; expelled 1916.

Gruzman, Shulim Aizikovich (d. 1919) – Ukrainian revolutionary; Bolshevik from 1912; member Central Committee of Ukrainian CP 1918; died in combat against Petlyura forces.

Guesde, Jules (1845–1922) – veteran of Paris Commune; one of first Marxists in France; a founder of French socialist movement; a leader of Second International and opponent of revisionism until 1914; chauvinist and government minister during World War I.

Guilbeaux, Henri (1885–1938) – French anarcho-syndicalist before World War I; later joined SP; supported Zimmerwald Left at Kienthal; participated in first, second, and fifth Comintern congresses; broke with communism in 1930s and became extreme reactionary.

Gusseinov, Mirza Davud Bagir-Uglu (1894–1938) – Azerbaijani revolutionary; Bolshevik from 1918; from 1919 chairman of Azerbaijani CP, which he represented at first Comintern congress; held government posts in Transcaucasia and Azerbaijan 1920s.

Haase, Hugo (1863–1919) – SPD Reichstag member from 1897; with Kautsky in SPD center current before World War I; SPD cochairman 1911–16; voted in Reichstag against war credits 1916; cochairman of USPD from 1917; member Council of People's Representatives government November–December 1918; assassinated by monarchist.

Haikuni, Gurgen (1889–1966) – revolutionary from Turkish Armenia; joined RSDLP 1905; commissar of Caucasus refugees after Russian October revolution; central leader of Armenian CP; in Armenian Affairs Commissariat in Moscow from early 1919; delegate to first Comintern congress; left politics after 1922.

Handlir, Jaroslav (1888–1942) – won to communism as Czech prisoner of war in Russia; represented Czech Communist group in Russia at first Comintern congress; returned to Czechoslovakia 1920; CP founding member 1921; delegate to third Comintern congress; trade union leader; opposed party leadership from 1925; expelled 1929; joined Czech SDP.

Hanecki, Jakub (Firstenberg) (1879–1937) – joined Polish Social Democracy 1896; leader of Warsaw opposition in Social Democracy of the Kingdom of Poland and Lithuania 1911; member RSDLP Central Committee (Bolsheviks) 1913; Zimmerwald Left supporter; held posts in Soviet government after 1917; executed during Moscow trials.

Henderson, Arthur (1863–1935) – general secretary of British Labour Party 1911–34; chauvinist during World War I; cabinet minister 1916–17; central organizer of 1919 Bern conference; chairman of Second International 1925–29; British foreign secretary 1929–31.

Herzfeld, Josef (1853–1939) – long-time German SPD Reichstag deputy; opposed World War I from 1915; centrist at Zimmerwald conference; USPD founding member 1917; joined CP in fusion 1920; died in emigration after Nazi takeover.

Herzog, Jakob (1892–1931) – Swiss Social Democrat, influenced by anarchism; leader of Swiss Socialist youth during World War I; headed radical *Forderung* group; expelled from SP October 1918; founded Swiss CP ("Old Communists") October 1918; attended second Comintern congress; part of fusion that formed Swiss CP 1921; leader of CP through 1920s.

Hilferding, Rudolf (1877–1941) – Austro-Marxist and economic theorist; supported SPD centrist opposition during World War I; USPD member from 1917; *Freiheit* editor-in-chief 1918–22; anti-Bolshevik; returned to SPD 1922; German finance minister 1923, 1928–29; killed by Hitler's Gestapo.

Hillquit, Morris (1869–1933) – leader of U.S. SP; International Socialist Bureau member; centrist during World War I; opposed Comintern.

Hudec, Józef (1863–1915) – founding member of Galician SDP; later member of Polish SDP; elected to Austrian parliament 1907.

L'Humanité (Humanity) – founded 1904 by Jean Jaurès; newspaper of French SP until 1920; controlled by chauvinist majority SP leaders 1914–18, then by centrists (former minority); organ of CP from 1921.

Huysmans, Camille (1871–1968) – leader of Belgian Workers Party; secretary of International Socialist Bureau from 1904; chauvinist in World War I; helped organize 1919

Bern conference; subsequently served in Belgian government.

Hyndman, Henry (1842–1921) – cofounder Social Democratic Federation 1884 and British SP 1911; chauvinist during World War I; founded National Socialist Party, on extreme right of Labour Party, 1916.

Independent Labour Party – British reformist party founded 1893; affiliated to Second International and British Labour Party; 30,000 members 1912; pacifist stand during World War I, although some members voted for war credits; left-wing minority split to join CP 1921; majority remained in British Labour Party; broke to form centrist group 1932.

Independent Social Democratic Party of Germany (USPD) – formed with 120,000 members April 1917 by centrist opposition expelled from SPD; participated in provisional government under Friedrich Ebert November–December 1918; included Spartacus current until December 1918; grew to 300,000 members by March, 750,000 by November 1919; majority fused with CP 1920; minority retained name USPD until rejoining SPD 1922.

Industrial Workers of the World – founded in U.S. as revolutionary industrial union movement 1905; rejected electoral participation and work in American Federation of Labor; opposed U.S. participation in World War I and suffered severe repression; went into decline after formation of CP 1919; rejected affiliation to Comintern-led Red International of Labor Unions 1921; participated in attempt to set up anarcho-syndicalist rival to it 1922.

Internationale Group – see Spartacus League.

International Socialist Bureau (ISB) – Second International executive body formed 1900; headquartered in Brussels; its secretariat moved to The Hague with outbreak of World War I, but the bureau did not meet again.

International Socialist Committee in Bern – see Zimmerwald Association.

ISB – see International Socialist Bureau.

Itschner, Hans Heinrich (1887–1964) – Swiss Social Democrat; cofounder *Forderung* group 1917; belonged to "Old Communists" group and joined fused Swiss CP 1921; anarchist 1930s; later became reactionary.

IWW – see Industrial Workers of the World.

Izvestia (News) – daily organ of All-Russian Central Executive Committee of the soviets from 1917.

Janović – see Jovanović.

Japanese Socialist Group – socialist grouping around *Shin Shakai* (New society), founded 1915 by Toshihiko Sakai; early socialist groups launched 1901 and 1906 had been fiercely suppressed; *Shin Shakai* led revival of socialism during World War I; declared for Bolshevism May 1919; Socialist Federation of Japan founded August 1919; Japanese CP founded 1922.

Jaurès, Jean (1859–1914) – leader of French and international socialist movement; held reformist positions; founded *L'Humanité* 1904; central leader of French SP from its foundation 1905; strong antimilitarist; assassinated by right-wing fanatic at outbreak of World War I.

Jewish Social Democratic Party (ZPSD) – formed 1905 by split of Jewish members of Polish SDP; left wing helped found East Galician CP February 1919; politically aligned with Bund, which it joined 1919; left wing joined Comintern 1921.

Joffe, A.A. (1883–1927) – joined Russian Social Democracy before 1900; with Mezhrayontsi during World War I; joined Bolsheviks June 1917 and elected to Central Committee August 1917; member of Soviet delegation to Brest-Litovsk 1918; Soviet ambassador to Berlin April–November 1918; supported opposition led by Trotsky in Russian CP from 1923; committed suicide when refused visa to receive medical treatment.

Joseph (1872–1964) – Hungarian archduke; field marshal Austrian army; palatine of Hungary for Emperor Charles; appointed Count Károlyi Hungarian prime minister October 31, 1918.

Jouhaux, Léon (1879–1954) – French union leader; began as revolutionary syndicalist; head of General Confederation of Labor (CGT) 1909–40; chauvinist during World War I; opposed Bolshevik revolution; leader of international reformist trade union federation after World War I; founded anticommunist trade union federation Force Ouvrière 1948.

Jovanović, Risantije (Rista) (1885–1960) – Serbian Social Democrat and union leader; signer of opposition manifesto, expelled from Yugoslav CP 1920; joined SP.

Kachaznuni, Hovhannes – leader of Armenian Dashnaktsutiun Party; premier of bourgeois National Council Government 1918–19; broke with Dashnaks 1920.

Kaclerović, Triša (1879–1964) – cofounder of Serbian SP; member of parliament 1908–21; part of Zimmerwald Left at Kienthal conference; went to Stockholm for conference organized by social chauvinists 1917; Yugoslav CP secretary 1923–25; delegate to fifth Comintern congress and elected to Comintern executive committee 1924; withdrew from politics mid-1920s; member of Yugoslav Supreme Court after 1945.

Kamenev, L.B. (1883–1936) – joined RSDLP 1901; Bolshevik from 1903; arrested with Bolshevik Duma deputies 1914; elected to Central Committee 1917; member of Russian CP Political Bureau 1917–26; aligned with Stalin and Zinoviev 1923–25; joined Trotsky and Zinoviev in United Opposition to bureaucratic current led by Stalin 1926–27; expelled from CP 1927; capitulated 1928; twice readmitted and reexpelled; executed during Moscow frame-up trials.

Karakhan, L.M. (1889–1937) – joined RSDLP 1904; joined Bolshevik Party with Mezhrayontsi 1917; secretary of

Soviet Brest-Litovsk delegation 1918; held other diplomatic posts; executed during Moscow frame-up trials.

Karaulov, M.A. (1878–1917) – Cossack official; monarchist; leader of counterrevolution in Terek (North Caucasus) after October revolution 1917.

Karmir orer (Red days) – published in Tiflis by Armenian Communist Party March 1918; soon suppressed; replaced in April by *Karmir droshak* (Red banner), which was also suppressed but relaunched in Russian exile 1919.

Károlyi, Mihály (1875–1955) – Hungarian count and politician; headed bourgeois government after first Hungarian revolution 1918; resigned March 1919 and emigrated; collaborated with Comintern against Horthy dictatorship; returned to Hungary 1946 and held diplomatic post; emigrated again in protest against purge trials 1949.

Kascher, Leonie (b. 1890) – originally from Poland, joined Swiss Social Democratic youth organization as student; member of *Forderung* group; imprisoned several times for revolutionary activity; exiled from Switzerland 1919; delegate to first Comintern congress; returned to Switzerland 1921.

Kasimov, Kasim – Tatar Communist; delegate from United Group of the Eastern Peoples to first Comintern congress.

Kautsky, Karl (1854–1938) – born in Prague; a leader of German Social Democracy and of Socialist International; collaborator of Engels; author of many works on history and Marxist theory; a leader of "Marxist center" in SPD before 1914; adopted pacifist stand 1914; apologist for chauvinist SPD majority; founding member USPD and supporter of its right wing; undersecretary in foreign ministry after November 1918 revolution; vehement opponent of Russian October revolution; rejoined SPD 1922.

Kerensky, A.F. (1881–1970) – Russian SR; leader of peasant-based Trudovik group; prime minister of Russian Provisional Government overthrown by October 1917 revolution; emigrated 1918.

Khatisian, Alexandre I. (1876–1945) – Armenian Dashnak, mayor of Tiflis, 1909–17; premier of bourgeois National Council government of Armenia 1919–20.

Khatisov – see Khatisian.

Klinger, Gustav K. (b. 1876) – prisoner of war in Russia; joined Bolsheviks 1917; leader of Volga German Soviet government 1918; Comintern business manager 1919; attended first three Comintern congresses; held various government posts.

Klochko, Volodimir (1889–1918) – Ukrainian revolutionary; took part in 1905 revolution; Bolshevik from 1913; leader of Ekaterinoslav Bolsheviks 1917; candidate member Central Committee of Ukrainian CP 1918; executed in Ekaterinoslav by Petlyura forces.

Kohn, Gábor – see Mészáros, Gábor.

Kolchak, A.V. (1873–1920) – tsarist admiral; head of White armies in Siberia and "supreme ruler" of Russian White forces 1918–1919; defeated by Red Army; tried and executed for his role in armed counterrevolution.

Kollontai, Alexandra (1872–1952) – Russian Social Democrat in 1890s; Menshevik from 1906; joined Bolsheviks 1915; elected to Central Committee 1917; People's Commissar of Social Welfare 1917; head of women's department of Russian CP Central Committee 1920; supported Workers' Opposition in Russian CP 1920–21; secretary of Comintern International Women's Secretariat 1921–22; held diplomatic posts after 1923.

Konovalov, A.I. (1875–1948) – Russian capitalist and landowner, leader of bourgeois Progressist Party; chairman of Central War Industries Committee 1915–16; minister in several cabinets of Provisional Government 1917; White emigré after October revolution.

Korean Peoples Socialist Party – founded in Khabarovsk, in Soviet far east, under chairmanship of Yi Tong-hwi early 1918; was the major Korean revolutionary group, but did not receive notice of first Comintern congress; initiated relations with Comintern mid-1919; Korean Communists organized in Shanghai 1919, in Korea 1922; Korean CP organized 1925.

Korean Workers League – small group of Korean revolutionaries in European Russia. See also Korean Peoples Socialist Party.

Korganov, G.N. (1886–1918) – born in Georgia; expelled from university for revolutionary activities 1907; in army 1914; people's commissar for military affairs for Baku Soviet government April 1918; a commander of Baku Soviet armed forces; shot at instigation of British interventionists.

Krasnov, P.N. (1869–1947) – tsarist general; led Cossack troops on Don against October revolution 1918–19; emigrated and continued anti-Soviet activity; collaborated with Nazis in World War II; executed by Soviet authorities.

Kreitsberg, Isaak Mironovich (1898–1919) – Ukrainian revolutionary; Bolshevik from 1913; in tsarist army during World War I, where did underground political work; secretary Kiev Bolshevik executive committee 1917; Ukrainian CP Central Committee member 1918; executed at Poltava by Petlyura forces January 1919.

Küng, Emil (1889–1943) – Swiss Social Democrat; a leader of Zurich strike 1918; president of city union council and chairman of Zurich Workers' Union.

Kuusinen, Otto (1881–1964) – participated in 1905 revolution; led center faction of Finnish SDP; member of Finnish revolutionary government 1918; Finnish CP founding member 1918; member Comintern executive committee from 1921; Soviet CP Central Committee from 1941; signed dissolution of Comintern 1943; Secretary of Presidium of Soviet CP Central Committee from 1957.

Lafont, Ernest (1879–1946) – French SP deputy, chauvinist during World War I; joined CP 1920; expelled 1922; rejoined SP 1928.

Lapčević, Dragiša (1864–1939) – cofounder of Serbian SP; three times party president after 1905; expelled from CP for centrism 1920; later Yugoslav SP chairman.

Laval, Pierre (1883–1945) – French SP deputy 1914–19; first with centrist minority, then open chauvinist; quit SP 1920; frequent minister and twice premier in bourgeois cabinets of 1920s and 1930s; premier of pro-Nazi Vichy regime 1941–44; executed for treason 1945.

League of Nations – imperialist alliance created by Allied powers at 1919 Paris conference; aimed to defend division of world imposed by that conference; disappeared with World War II.

Ledebour, Georg (1850–1947) – German Social Democrat; longtime SPD leader; opposed SPD majority position during World War I; backed centrist wing of Zimmerwald movement; cochairman of USPD 1917–19; a leader of January 1919 Berlin uprising; opposed USPD majority's fusion with Communists 1920; refused to rejoin SPD and led a small left-wing group throughout 1920s; emigrated to Switzerland 1933.

Left Social Democratic Party of Sweden – founded by expelled left-wing minority of Social Democratic Workers Party May 1917; 17,000 members 1919; affiliated to Comintern June 1919; majority became CP 1921.

Left Socialist Revolutionary Party – see Socialist Revolutionary Party.

Legien, Carl (1861–1920) – Social Democratic head of German trade unions from 1890; avowed reformist; supported SPD right wing during World War I; backed crushing of revolutionary workers' movement 1918–19.

Lenin, V.I. (1870–1924) – founded St. Petersburg League for the Emancipation of the Working Class 1895; exiled to Siberia 1896; went abroad and helped publish *Iskra* 1900–1903; central leader of Bolsheviks from 1903; participated in 1905–7 Russian revolution; defended revolutionary organization against liquidationism after

1907; RSDLP representative on International Socialist Bureau 1908–12; issued call for new, revolutionary International 1914; organized Zimmerwald Left to fight for this goal 1915–17; returned to Russia and led Bolsheviks' struggle for Soviet power 1917; chairman of Council of People's Commissars government 1917–24; central leader of Comintern.

Lequis, Arnold – German general; commanded troops brought into Berlin December 1918 in unsuccessful attempt to put down revolution.

Leuthner, Karl (1869–1944) – leader of Austrian Social Democracy and an editor of its paper, *Arbeiter Zeitung;* chauvinist during World War I; leading SDP deputy after 1918.

Leviné, Eugen (1883–1919) – born in Russia and participated in 1905 revolution; member of German Spartacus current and founding leader of German CP; arrested en route to first Comintern congress; central leader of Bavarian council republic 1919; arrested, tried, and shot after its overthrow.

Lieberman, Herman (1870–1941) – joined Polish SDP in Galicia 1896; deputy in Austrian parliament 1907–18; leader of Polish SP and deputy in Polish parliament after 1918; opposed Pilsudski dictatorship 1926; jailed; emigrated 1931; later favored collaboration with Polish CP.

Liebknecht, Karl (1871–1919) – son of Wilhelm Liebknecht; helped found Socialist Youth International 1907; jailed same year for book *Militarism and Anti-Militarism;* only member of Reichstag to vote against war credits December 1914; helped found Spartacus current; jailed for antiwar activities 1916; released October 1918; a founding leader of German CP 1918; a leader of Berlin January 1919 uprising; arrested and murdered by SPD-instigated Freikorps.

Liebknecht, Wilhelm (1826–1900) – participated in German revolution of 1848; friend and collaborator of Marx and Engels; a leader of First International in Germany;

cofounder of German Social Democratic Workers Party 1869; central leader of party until death.

Lindhagen, Carl (1860–1946) – Swedish liberal, then Social Democrat from 1909; mayor of Stockholm 1903–1930; internationalist during World War I; cofounder of Left SDP 1917; joined Comintern 1919; expelled from CP 1921 for opposition to decisions of second Comintern congress; rejoined Social Democrats 1923.

Litvinov, Maxim M. (Wallach) (1876–1951) – joined RSDLP 1898; Bolshevik from 1903; Soviet representative in Britain after October revolution; held high posts in Soviet foreign ministry after 1921; People's Commissar of Foreign Affairs 1930–39.

Liu Shaozhou (1892–1970) – Chinese worker, lived in Russia from 1897; Bolshevik from 1917; chairman of Union of Chinese Workers in Russia; Chinese Socialist Workers Party delegate to first and second Comintern congresses; returned to China after 1949 and held diplomatic post.

Lloyd George, David (1863–1945) – British Liberal politician; prime minister 1916–22; coauthored Versailles treaty and organized British intervention against Soviet republic.

Lockhart, Bruce (1887–1970) – British diplomat in Russia 1912–18; organized plot to overthrow Soviet government, arrested September 1918; soon released and returned to England.

Longuet, Jean (1876–1938) – grandson of Karl Marx; leader of French SP centrist minority after 1916; leader of centrist opposition at 1919 Bern conference; opposed SP joining Comintern; when it did so 1920 he split along with right-wing minority that retained name SP.

Loriot, Fernand (1870–1932) – leader of revolutionary left in French SP during World War I; secretary of French Committee for the Third International; presented revolutionary viewpoint at 1919 Bern conference; French CP international secretary 1921; opposed bureaucratization of CP and quit party 1926; collaborated with left opposition currents.

Luxemburg, Rosa (1871–1919) – founding leader of Social Democracy of Kingdom of Poland 1893; later lived in Germany, joining SPD 1898; Polish representative to International Socialist Bureau from 1903; led left wing against revisionist right in SPD and, after 1910, against center current led by Kautsky; leader of Spartacus current during World War I; imprisoned by German government 1915; founding leader of German CP 1918; arrested and murdered by SPD-instigated Freikorps after January uprising.

MacDonald, James Ramsay (1866–1937) – leader of British Labour Party from 1906; forced to resign this post 1914 because of pacifist position on World War I; opposed to Bolshevik revolution; delegate to 1919 Bern conference; Labour prime minister 1924, 1929–31; split from party to found coalition government with Conservatives and Liberals 1931.

Maklakov, V.A. (1870–1959) – Cadet party Central Committee member from 1906; Russian ambassador to France for Provisional Government 1917; leading White emigré in Paris after October 1917 revolution.

Manner, Kullervo (1880–1937) – joined Finnish SDP 1905; party chairman 1917–18; headed Finnish revolutionary government 1918; leading figure in Finnish CP and Comintern 1920s; expelled from Finnish CP as "Trotskyist sympathizer" 1935; condemned in Soviet Union to hard labor 1935; disappeared in camps.

Mannerheim, K.G. (1867–1951) – baron and tsarist general; headed White forces in Finnish civil war and subsequent White Terror; president of Finland 1944–46.

Mansurov, Burhan (d. 1937) – Tatar Communist; member of the Muslim Socialist Committee of Kazan 1917; joined Russian CP early 1918; member of Central Bureau of the Communist Organizations of the Peoples of the

East 1919; chairman of the Central Executive Committee of the Tatar Republic 1920; removed 1928; victim of Stalin purge.

Marcu, Valeriu (1899–1942) – Romanian Social Democrat; active in Swiss socialist youth during World War I; imprisoned in Romania during World War I for revolutionary activity; joined German CP after World War I; left party with Paul Levi 1921.

Marnus – see Marcu, Valeriu.

Martov, L. (Julius) (1873–1923) – a central leader of Russian Social Democrats and, from 1903, of Mensheviks; leader of centrist "Menshevik-Internationalists" during Russian revolution; opposed October revolution; opposed anti-Soviet White Guards; led Menshevik opposition to Bolshevik-led government 1918–20; emigrated 1920.

Marx, Karl (1818–1883) – cofounder with Engels of modern commnist workers' movement; leader of Communist League 1847–52; coauthor of *Communist Manifesto;* editor of *Neue rheinische Zeitung* in 1848–49 German revolution; central leader of International Working Men's Association (First International) 1864–1876; published first volume of *Capital* 1867; partisan and defender of Paris Commune.

Mehring, Franz (1846–1919) – German Marxist historian and scholar; biographer of Marx; opposed revisionism; an editor of SPD magazine *Neue Zeit;* a leader of Spartacus current; imprisoned 1916; Spartacus League founder and Central Committee member; cofounder German CP.

Mensheviks – originated as minority faction of RSDLP at its second congress 1903; moved increasingly to right after 1907; during World War I contained centrist and openly chauvinist wings; participated in Provisional Government 1917; opposed October 1917 revolution; during civil war one wing openly supported White armies; the other, led by Martov, opposed White Guards and participated in soviets but took no clear stand in defense of Soviet rule; this wing placed itself outside Soviet legality during Kronstadt crisis that threatened to undermine workers' and peasants' power in 1921; thereafter functioned primarily in exile.

Merrheim, Alphonse (1871–1925) – leader of French syndicalist movement; attended Zimmerwald conference 1915; broke with Zimmerwald movement 1917 and moved toward reformism; worked with reformists in French union movement from 1918; raised syndicalist criticisms of reformists and ultimately broke with them.

Mészáros, Gábor (Gábor Kohn) (1896–1920) – Hungarian Communist; joined Bolsheviks while prisoner of war; returned to Hungary 1918; sent by Hungarian CP to first Comintern congress but arrived late; organizer of Red Army for Hungarian Soviet Republic 1919; emigrated after fall of republic; returned to Hungary and killed by Horthy dictatorship.

Mezhrayontsi – Russian Social Democratic group formed 1913 with position intermediate between Bolsheviks and Mensheviks; took internationalist stand during World War I; among its leaders were Trotsky, Uritsky, and A.V. Lunacharsky; fused with Bolsheviks 1917.

Milhaud, Edgard (1873–1964) – joined Jaurès wing of French Social Democratic movement 1893; adviser 1899–1901 to Millerand, SP minister in French bourgeois government; lived in Switzerland from 1902 but continued to be active in French SP; represented far right wing of Bern conference 1919.

Milkić, Iliya (1882–1968) – a founder and organizer of Serbian Social Democratic and union movements; lived in France and Switzerland during World War I, in Russia 1919–22; participated in first, second, and third Comintern congresses; elected to Comintern executive committee for Yugoslav CP 1920; lived in Vienna, active in Yugoslav CP 1922–26; returned to Belgrade and left politics 1926.

Minoritaires (Minority) – wing of French SP led by Longuet during World War I; sought negotiated end to World War I while maintaining policy of national defense; won majority 1918.

Moraczewski, Jedrzej (1870–1944) – a leader of Polish SDP of Galicia and Silesia (PPSD) from 1893; deputy in Austrian imperial parliament; PPSD deputy in Polish parliament 1919–27; expelled for supporting Pilsudski; head of progovernment trade union organization 1931–39.

Morgari, Oddino (1865–1929) – cofounder Italian SP; chief editor *Avanti!* 1908; member Zimmerwald International Socialist Committee in Bern; centrist; briefly supported Russian revolution and sympathetic to Bolsheviks; observer for Italian SP at 1919 Bern conference; subsequently moved to right; stayed in SP in 1920s.

Müller, Gustav (1860–1921) – Swiss Social Democrat; chauvinist during World War I; leader of party right wing; briefly party chairman 1918–19.

Musavat Party (Equality) – Azerbaijani party of nationalist bourgeoisie founded 1912; opposed Baku Soviet government; headed anti-Soviet government 1918–1920.

Mussolini, Benito (1883–1945) – a leader of left wing of Italian SP before 1914; coeditor *Avanti!* 1912–14; adopted chauvinist position and expelled from SP 1914; founded fascist movement 1919; dictator of Italy 1922–43; captured and executed by partisans.

Naine, Charles (1874–1926) – a leader of Swiss SDP; member of Zimmerwald International Socialist Committee in Bern; joined right wing of Swiss party 1917; helped form centrist Two-and-a-Half International 1919–1921.

National Democratic Party (National Democracy; Popular National Union) – a right-wing nationalist party of the Polish bourgeoisie; largest bourgeois party after World War I.

National Workers Association – right-wing Polish labor organization sponsored by National Democratic Party.

Neue zürcher Zeitung (New Zurich gazette) – leading Swiss bourgeois daily newspaper.

Norwegian Labor Party – founded 1887; left wing won majority 1918; 105,000 members 1919; affiliated to Comintern June 1919; minority of 3,000 split to form Social Democratic Labor Party 1921; majority disaffiliated from Comintern 1923; minority founded Norwegian CP with 15,000 members.

Noske, Gustav (1868–1946) – SPD leader; chauvinist during World War I; member Council of People's Representatives government 1918–19; organized suppression of Berlin January 1919 uprising; German war minister 1919–20.

Nubar-Pasha, Boghos – wealthy Armenian politician born in Egypt; founded Armenian General Benevolent Union 1906; headed "Armenian National Delegation" to Paris conference 1919; opposed Dashnaktsutiun as too revolutionary and socialist.

Obolensky – see Osinsky.

Osinsky, N. (Obolensky, V.V.) (1887–1938) – joined RSDLP 1907; Bolshevik; a leader of Left Communist opposition 1918; delegate at first and second Comintern congresses; Central Committee alternate 1921; supported opposition led by Trotsky in Russian CP from 1923; later aligned with Bukharin; arrested 1937 and shot.

Ostapchuk, Yatsko (1873–1961) – member of Ruthenian-Ukrainian Radical Party, later Ukrainian SDP; elected to Austrian parliament 1907.

Paderewski, Ignacy Jan (1860–1941) – Polish pianist and composer; prime minister under Pilsudski 1919.

Pannekoek, Anton (1873–1960) – joined Dutch Social Democrats 1902; leader of left-wing *Tribune* current from 1907; member Zimmerwald Left during World War I; cofounder Dutch CP 1918; part of 1921 ultraleft split; subsequently left political activity while continuing to consider himself a Marxist and write on theoretical questions.

Pascal, Pierre – member of French military mission and of French Communist Group in Russia; attended first Comintern congress.

People's Naval Division – sailors' detachment stationed in Berlin after November 9, 1918, to defend republican government; radicalized and came into conflict with SPD-led government; clashed with government forces December 24, 1918; formally neutral in January fighting 1919; defended workers in March 1919 fighting, then dissolved.

Pernerstorfer, Engelbert (1850–1918) – Austrian pan-German nationalist and liberal democrat; became Social Democrat while maintaining nationalist views 1896; revisionist; head of SP parliamentary fraction from 1901; chauvinist during World War I.

Petin, Karl Gustav (b. 1887) – Latvian origin; Austrian soldier during World War I; prisoner of war in Russia; joined Bolsheviks 1918; head of Cheka for Commissariat of Volga German Affairs 1918; following visit to Austria, delegate of German Austrian CP to first Comintern congress; no longer active in Comintern after the congress.

Petlyura, S.V. (Semen Petliura) (1877–1926) – Ukrainian bourgeois nationalist; leader of Ukrainian Social Democratic Labor Party; headed anti-Bolshevik forces in Ukraine 1918–19; notorious for organizing anti-Jewish pogroms; participated in Polish offensive against Soviet Ukraine 1920; assassinated in Paris exile.

Petrov, G.K. (1892–1918) – colonel in tsarist army; joined revolution; Left SR; commanded First Don Soviet Army in Ukraine December 1917 to early 1918; sent to Baku July 1918; commander in chief of Soviet military forces at Baku; one of twenty-six Soviet commissars shot at instigation of British intervention forces.

Pichon, Stéphane (1857–1933) – French foreign minister 1906–11 and 1917–20; supporter of Clemenceau.

Pilsudski, Józef (1867–1935) – cofounder of Polish SP 1892; led nationalist Revolutionary Faction from party's 1906 split until 1918; backed Central Powers in World War I; headed newly created Polish republic 1918; led invasion of Soviet republic 1920; resigned 1923; right-wing dictator of Poland 1926–35.

Platten, Fritz (1883–1942) – Swiss revolutionary; SDP secretary from 1912; led Swiss Zimmerwald Left; organized Lenin's return to Russia from exile April 1917; SDP representative to Olten committee until August 1918; delegate at Comintern founding congress and member of bureau; led founding of united Swiss CP 1921; party secretary 1921–23; in Soviet Union after 1923 except 1930–31; arrested in Stalin's purges 1938 and died in prison camp.

Plekhanov, Georgiy (1856–1918) – founder of Russian Marxism and of Emancipation of Labor group 1883; influential writer on questions of Marxist theory; leader of RSDLP from its formation; Menshevik after 1903; open chauvinist during World War I; opposed October revolution.

Pögelman, Hans (1875–1938) – active in Estonian socialist movement from its foundation; cofounder Estonian CP 1918; delegate to first and second Comintern congresses; member of Estonian Soviet government 1919–20; after its overthrow, lived in Soviet Union; Estonian representative to Comintern executive committee 1921–22; control commission 1924–28; arrested during Moscow trials and shot.

Polish Social Democratic Party of Galicia and Silesia (PPSD) – founded 1890 as Galician Workers Party; took name Galician SDP 1892; renamed Polish SDP when separate Ukrainian SDP formed 1899; merged with Polish SP 1904 but retained separate identity; backed Central Powers in World War I; dissolved into Polish SP April 1919.

Polish Socialist Party – founded 1892; strongly marked by nationalist and reformist tendencies; left-wing majority founded Polish Socialist Party–Left 1906, adopted internationalist position during World War I, and merged with Social Democracy of the Kingdom of Poland and Lithuania to form Polish CP 1918; right-wing Revolutionary Faction supported Central Powers during World War I and participated in formation of Polish capitalist state 1918.

Politiken (Politics) – daily organ of Swedish Left SDP.

Polovtsev, P.A. (b. 1874) – Russian general, commander of Petrograd military region summer 1917; led shooting on peaceful demonstration and attack on *Pravda* offices during July days; White emigré after October revolution 1917.

Popović, Dušan (1885–1918) – secretary of Serbian SDP 1911–12 and 1915–18; went to Stockholm for conference called by social chauvinists 1917.

PPSD – see Polish SDP of Galicia and Silesia.

Pravda (Truth) – Bolshevik party organ first published in Petrograd and Moscow 1912–14; repeatedly suppressed and republished under various names; resumed regular publication 1917.

Radek, Karl (1885–1939) – joined Social Democracy of the Kingdom of Poland and Lithuania 1904; moved to Germany 1908 and was active in SPD left; expelled from SPD in factional purge 1913; Zimmerwald Left bureau member with Lenin and Zinoviev 1915; joined Bolsheviks 1917; Bolshevik and Soviet emissary to Germany December 1918; arrested February 1919; released January 1920; elected to Bolshevik Central Committee 1919; Comintern executive committee member; with Trotsky, part of communist opposition to Stalin 1923–29; expelled from CP 1927; capitulated 1929; arrested 1937 during Moscow frame-up trials and died in prison.

Rahja, Eino (1886–1936) – joined RSDLP 1903; commanded Red Guard in Finnish revolution 1918; emigrated to Soviet Russia 1918; Finnish CP Central Committee member 1918–25 and its representative at first Comintern congress; headed opposition at party congress 1925; expelled from CP 1928; died in Russia in prison.

Rahja, Jukka (1887–1920) – Finnish Bolshevik from 1905; Finnish SP 1907–13; member of Petrograd Military Revolutionary Committee 1917; participated in Finnish revolution 1918; returned to Moscow and helped form Finnish CP 1918; assassinated in Petrograd by opponent current previously expelled from CP.

Rakovsky, Christian (1873–1941) – prominent Romanian Social Democrat since 1890s; organized antiwar conference of Balkan Socialist parties summer 1915; elected secretary of Balkan Revolutionary Social Democratic Federation 1915; attended Zimmerwald conference; joined Bolsheviks 1918; became head of Ukrainian Soviet government January 1919; elected to Bolshevik Central Committee 1919; supported opposition led by Trotsky in Russian CP from 1923; expelled from party and arrested 1927; capitulated 1934; died in prison following Moscow frame-up trials.

Ransome, Arthur (1884–1967) – British liberal journalist present at first Comintern congress.

Rappoport, Charles (1865–1941) – Russian revolutionary; active in France from late 1880s; with Guesde in French SP before 1914; with minority during World War I; rallied to Third International 1919; with centrist wing of CP 1921–22; broke with CP in protest against purge trials 1938; joined SP 1940.

Ravesteyn, Willem van (1876–1970) – Dutch Social Democrat from 1900; leader of *Tribune* current from its inception 1907; Zimmerwald Left supporter during World War I; Dutch CP 1918; spoke for ultralefts at fourth Comintern congress; expelled with Wijnkoop 1926 and retired from political activity.

Red Guards – armed units formed spontaneously by Petrograd factory workers after Russian February revolution; numbered 10,000 by July 1917; defended working class districts during July days and Kornilov coup; numbering 20,000, played decisive role in October revolution; similar forces elsewhere in Russia; integrated into Red Army 1918.

Red Soldiers' League – founded by German Spartacus League November 1918; carried out political education and organization among soldiers.

Reich, Y.S. (Thomas) (1886–1956) – Galician won to communism in Switzerland; important Comintern organizer in Petrograd 1919 and Berlin 1919–25; left Communist movement 1926.

Reinstein, Boris (1866–1947) – Russian Social Democrat; moved to U.S. 1901; joined Socialist Labor Party; sent to abortive Stockholm conference 1917; went to Russia and joined Bolsheviks April 1918; attended first Comintern congress as SLP delegate; subsequently worked in Comintern apparatus.

Renaudel, Pierre (1871–1935) – associate of Jean Jaurès before 1914; central leader of French SP right-wing majority during World War I; editor of *L'Humanité* 1914–18; delegate at 1919 Bern conference; opposed Comintern; part of 1920 right-wing split that retained name SP; led right-wing split from SP 1933.

Renner, Karl (1870–1950) – prominent revisionist in Austrian Social Democracy; chauvinist during World War I; Austrian chancellor 1919–20 and president 1931–33.

Resel, Johann (1861–1928) – Austrian Social Democrat from 1880s; led negotiations for party unification at Hainfeld congress 1888–89; parliamentary deputy 1897–1901, 1907–18, 1920–26.

Roland-Holst, Henriette (1869–1952) – joined Dutch Social Democratic Workers Party 1897; supported its left wing; with Zimmerwald Left; joined SDP *Tribune* group 1916;

founding member Dutch CP 1918; left CP 1927; later Christian socialist.

RSDLP – see Russian Social Democratic Labor Party.

Rubanovitch, I.A. (1860–1920) – Russian Narodnik in 1890s; later leader of SRs; International Socialist Bureau member; chauvinist during World War I; participated in Bern conference.

Rudas, László (1885–1950) – Hungarian revolutionary socialist; Hungarian CP Central Committee 1918; delegate to first Comintern congress but arrived late; lived in Moscow 1922–46; imprisoned 1937 but released; returned to Hungary after World War II and directed CP school.

Rudnyánszky, Endre (1885–1943) – Hungarian prisoner of war in Russia; joined Bolsheviks 1917; took part in founding Hungarian Communist Group; chairman of Federation of Foreign Communist Groups late 1918; attended first, second, and third Comintern congresses; elected to Comintern executive committee; Moscow representative of Hungarian Soviet republic; disappeared from Russia with Comintern funds and was expelled from Hungarian CP 1921.

Rüegg, Paul (b. 1898) – Swiss Social Democratic youth leader during World War I; part of "Old Communists" group; joined Swiss CP; expelled from CP 1924; went to Soviet Union and joined CP there; a Comintern agent using his passport was arrested in China by Kuomintang 1931 and sentenced to death, and an international campaign worked to save "Rüegg"; Rüegg himself, still in Russia, disappeared during Stalin purge trials.

Russian Communist Party (Bolsheviks) – originated as majority (Bolshevik) faction of RSDLP at second congress 1903; led 1917 October revolution and establishment of Soviet government; changed name to Russian CP March 1918.

Russian Social Democratic Labor Party (RSDLP) – founded 1898; divided at 1903 congress into Bolshevik (majority) and Menshevik (minority) factions. See also Mensheviks and Russian Communist Party.

Rutgers, Sebald Justius (1879–1961) – joined Dutch Social Democracy 1899; part of left-wing *Tribune* group 1909; during World War I helped organize U.S. Socialist Propaganda League; delegate at first Comintern congress; headed Comintern's Amsterdam bureau 1919–20; headed settlement of U.S. volunteer workers in Kuzbas, Soviet Union, 1922–25; continued to live in Soviet Union until 1938, then returned to the Netherlands.

Sadoul, Jacques (1881–1956) – part of French military mission to Russia 1917; won to communism and volunteered for Red Army; sentenced to death in France in absentia 1919; delegate at first and second Comintern congresses; returned to France 1924 and pardoned; remained with French CP until death.

Scheflo, Olav (1883–1959) – Norwegian left-wing Social Democrat during World War I; editor of *Social-Demokrat;* led struggle for Norwegian Labor Party to join Comintern; delegate to second and fourth Comintern congresses; stayed with Comintern when Labor Party split 1923; left CP 1928; rejoined SP.

Scheidemann, Philipp (1865–1939) – SPD member; elected to German Reichstag 1898; became a secretary of SPD executive committee 1911; with Ebert, a central leader of party after Bebel's death 1913; led SPD into support for World War I 1914; SPD cochairman from 1917; appointed minister without portfolio by kaiser October 1918; member of Ebert's Council of People's Representatives government; participated in suppression of 1918–19 revolution; chancellor 1919; forced into exile by Nazis 1933.

SDKPiL – see Communist Workers Party of Poland.

SDP – Social Democratic Party.

Second International – founded 1889 as international association of workers' parties; collapsed at outbreak of World War I when most constituent parties supported interests of own bourgeoisie; revolutionary left wing founded Communist International 1919; right wing formed Labor and Socialist International 1923.

Seitz, Karl (1869–1950) – right-wing Austrian Social Democrat; deputy in imperial parliament from 1901; chauvinist during World War I; president of Austria 1918–20; chairman of SDP 1920–34; mayor of Vienna 1923–34; arrested by Nazis 1934.

Sembat, Marcel (1862–1922) – leader of French SP; chauvinist and government minister during World War I.

Shaumyan, S.G. (1878–1918) – Armenian; joined RSDLP 1900; Bolshevik from 1903; directed Bolsheviks' work in Transcaucasia and Baku; Bolshevik Central Committee 1917; chairman of Baku Council of People's Commissars 1918; shot at instigation of British interventionists.

Shop stewards movement – originated in Clyde valley strike in Scotland 1915; grew with strike wave and by early 1917 was national organization opposed to official trade union leadership no-strike policy; advanced revolutionary demands; movement declined after 1918 but many militant stewards joined British CP.

Shvets, F. – leader of right wing of Ukrainian Social Democratic Labor Party; member of Ukrainian Directory government 1918–19.

Sinn Fein – Irish nationalist and republican movement founded 1901; led independence struggle after 1916 Easter Rebellion; won 73 of 105 Irish seats in British general elections 1918; its deputies met as Dáil and proclaimed Irish republic 1919; refused to recognize Irish partition 1921 and continued liberation struggle.

Sirola, Yrjö (1876–1936) – joined Finnish SDP 1903; foreign affairs commissar in revolutionary government 1918; founding leader of Finnish CP 1918; elected to Comintern control commission 1921, 1928, and 1935; Comintern emissary to U.S. CP 1925–27.

Skoropadsky, P.P. (1873–1945) – Ukrainian aristocrat and tsarist general; head of German puppet government of Ukraine 1918.

Skrypnik, N.A. (Mykola Skrypnyk) (1872–1933) – Ukrainian Bolshevik; joined RSDLP 1897; member *Pravda* editorial board 1914; member of Petrograd Military Revolutionary Committee 1917; chairman Ukrainian Soviet government 1918; represented Ukrainian CP in Comintern; backed Stalin wing of CP; accused of "nationalist deviation" and purged during Stalin's assault on Ukrainian national rights; committed suicide.

Social Democracy of the Kingdom of Poland and Lithuania – see Communist Workers Party of Poland.

Social Democratic Party of Bosnia-Herzegovina – founded 1909; joined in creating Yugoslav CP 1919.

Social Democratic Party of Bulgaria – founded 1891; known as Bulgarian Workers SDP from 1894; split into revolutionary Tesnyaki (Narrow) and opportunist Shiroki (Broad) wings 1903; Tesnyaki won mass support during World War I and had 35,000 members 1919; joined Comintern and changed name to CP May 1919. Shiroki voted to quit Second International 1919; voted against joining Comintern 1920; left wing split and joined CP; Shiroki then had 8,000 members.

Social Democratic Party of Croatia and Slavonia – founded 1894; joined bourgeois government of new Yugoslav state 1918; left wing joined in forming Socialist Workers Party of Yugoslavia (Communist) April 1919, which joined Comintern; right wing joined SDP of Yugoslavia, which looked to Second International.

Social Democratic Party of Germany (SPD) – founded 1875 as Social Democratic Workers Party from fusion of parties led by followers of Marx and Lassalle; changed name to SPD 1891; largest and most influential party in Second International; more than one million members 1914; majority leadership supported German imperialist war effort; expelled oppositionists 1917; 250,000 members March 1918; headed bourgeois government 1918–19; one million members 1919; opposed formation of Comintern, participated in Bern conference 1919.

Social Democratic Party of Hungary – founded 1890; initially chauvinist during World War I; shifted to pacifist stand 1915; fused with CP and participated in short-lived Hungarian Soviet republic 1919; refounded and functioned as legal reformist opposition party from 1921.

Social Democratic Party of Norway – see Norwegian Labor Party.

Social Democratic Party of Serbia – founded 1903; opposed war credits 1914; participated in Balkan Revolutionary Social Democratic Federation from 1915; called April 1919 conference that united all Yugoslav Socialist parties (except Slovenian) to form Socialist Workers Party (Communist) April 20–23, 1919, which joined Comintern; 50,000 members late 1919; changed name to CP of Yugoslavia June 1920.

Social Democratic Party of Switzerland – founded 1888; leadership took centrist position during World War I, helping initiate and lead Zimmerwald movement; withdrew from Second International 1919 with 52,000 members; voted for Comintern affiliation at 1919 congress, but membership referendum later that year reversed decision; left wing split and fused with other Communist groups to form Swiss CP March 1921.

Social Democratic Workers Party of Austria – formed 1874 as United SDP, but soon broke apart; refounded 1888–89; loose federation of six autonomous national parties from 1896, which broke up by 1912; then functioned solely within German Austria; led governmental coalition with bourgeois parties November 1918; 335,000 members November 1920.

Social Democratic Workers Party of the Netherlands – founded 1894; left-wing *Tribune* current expelled 1909; chauvinist during World War I; 47,000 members 1919; supported League of Nations; voted to stay in rump Second International March 1921.

Socialist Groups in Tokyo and Yokohama – see Japanese Socialist Group.

Socialist Labor Party (U.S.) – founded 1876; led by Daniel De Leon from 1890s, it adopted increasingly sectarian abstentionist positions; took antichauvinist stand during World War I; 2,000–3,000 members 1916; initially sympathetic to October revolution; part of left wing joined in forming CP 1919; SLP later turned against Soviet state; degenerated into sect.

Socialist Labour Party (Britain) – formed as split from Social Democratic Federation 1903; looked to U.S. SLP; antichauvinist during World War I; opposed to Labour Party; 1,000 members at end of World War I; voted to affiliate to Comintern 1919; many members later joined CP.

Socialist Party of America – formed in U.S. 1901; 1917 membership referendum denouncing U.S. entry into World War I ignored by most of leadership, whose views ranged from centrist to pro-war; more than 100,000 members January 1919; majority left wing split August 1919 to form Communist Party and Communist Labor Party, which united 1921; SP membership dropped to 11,000 1922.

Socialist Party of France (Section française de l'Internationale ouvrière, SFIO) – founded by merger of Guesde's Socialist Party of France and Jaurès's French Socialist Party 1905; deputies voted unanimously to support war credits August 1914; 72,000 members 1914; dropped to 17,000 December 1915; centrist *minoritaires* won majority July 1918; voted to join Comintern with over 120,000 members and changed name to French CP

December 1920; right-wing minority of 50,000 split, retaining name SFIO, affiliated to centrist Two-and-a-Half International February 1921.

Socialist Party of Italy – founded 1892; openly reformist and chauvinist wing expelled 1912; took centrist stand on Italy's entry into World War I 1915; initiated Zimmerwald conference; 81,000 members 1919, 216,000 in 1920; affiliated to Comintern 1919, but refused to exclude party's reformist wing; minority split to form Italian CP January 1921.

Socialist Propaganda League – formed in Boston by members of U.S. SP's Latvian Federation 1915; strongly influenced by ultraleft views of Pannekoek and Dutch *Tribune* current; supported Bolsheviks and formation of Third International; played important role in birth of U.S. communist movement 1919.

Socialist Revolutionary Party (SR) – formed 1901–2 by rightward-moving currents from populist Narodnik tradition; affiliated to Second International; had wings that supported and opposed war effort during World War I; had majority support of peasant delegates to soviets 1917; split between supporters and opponents of Soviet power on eve of October revolution; subsequently, Right SRs opposed October revolution and took up arms against Soviet government; Left SRs opposed World War I, supported immediate confiscation of landed estates, backed October revolution and Soviet power; joined Bolsheviks in coalition government November 28 (15), 1917; broke from Soviet government and organized attempted insurrection July 1918; minority currents split away and eventually joined Russian CP.

Socialist Youth International (International Union of Socialist Youth Organizations) – founded 1907; fell apart during World War I; reconstituted 1915 by left-wing forces; organized 1915 Bern International Socialist Youth Conference, which denounced war, chauvinism, and "civil peace"; published *Jugend-Internationale;* central leaders later aligned with Zimmerwald Left; formed Communist Youth International with 300,000 members November 1919.

Sonnino, Sidney (1847–1922) – Italian baron and politician; foreign minister 1914–19; advocated Italy's entry into World War I; Italian delegate to Paris conference 1919.

SP – Socialist Party.

Spartacus League – originated as revolutionary current in SPD opposed to majority support for World War I December 1914; organized as Internationale Group January 1916; known as Spartacus group from name of newsletter and leaflets; functioned as public faction of USPD April 1917–December 1918; formed Spartacus League November 11, 1918; split from USPD and formed German CP December 30, 1918.

SPD – see Social Democratic Party of Germany.

SR – see Socialist Revolutionary Party.

Stalin, Joseph (1879–1953) – joined RSDLP 1898; Bolshevik from 1903; member Central Committee 1912; People's Commissar of Nationalities after October revolution; general secretary of Russian CP Central Committee 1922; after Lenin's death presided over bureaucratic degeneration of Russian CP and Comintern and their rejection of revolutionary internationalist course; organized Moscow frame-up trials in 1930s and liquidation of majority of Bolshevik leaders of Lenin's time; dissolved Comintern as political gesture to imperialist allies 1943.

Stang, Emil (1882–1964) – joined Norwegian Labor Party 1911; pacifist in World War I; leader, with Tranmael, of party's left wing 1918; deputy party chairman 1918–23; attended first Comintern congress; left Labor Party to help found CP 1923; left CP 1928; later Norwegian Supreme Court chairman.

Steinhardt, Karl (J. Gruber) (1875–1963) – member of Austrian SDP from 1891; militant antichauvinist, expelled from party 1916; chairman of Austrian CP 1918; elected general secretary 1919; attended first Comintern congress 1919; arrested in Romania April 1919; returned to Austria after release January 1920; attended second and third Comintern congresses; still active in CP after World War II.

Steklov, Y.M. (1873–1941) – joined Russian Social Democratic movement 1893; Bolshevik from 1903; "revolutionary defensist" after February 1917, but soon returned to Bolsheviks; an editor of *Izvestia* after 1917; disappeared during Moscow purge trials.

Stormklockan (Storm bell) – founded 1908; newspaper of Swedish Socialist Youth League; defended views of Zimmerwald Left during World War I; later organ of Swedish Communist Youth League.

Stuchka, P.I. (1865–1932) – joined Bolsheviks 1903; Bolshevik Central Committee 1917; Commissar of Justice 1917–18; head of Latvian Soviet government 1918–19; chairman of Supreme Court of RSFSR 1923–32.

Studer, Friedrich (1873–1945) – Swiss Social Democrat; parliamentary deputy 1908–22; chairman of Swiss SDP 1911–16; member Swiss federal court 1932–42.

Stürgkh, Karl von (1859–1916) – Austrian count; reactionary prime minister 1911–16; assassinated by Friedrich Adler.

Subhi, Mustafa (1883–1921) – member of Turkish socialist group from 1910; arrested and expelled, went to Russia 1914; joined RSDLP 1915; organized Communist group among Turkish prisoners of war 1918; delegate to first Comintern congress; chairman of Turkish CP 1920; participated in Baku congress 1920; returned to Turkey 1921 and murdered by police along with entire leadership of Turkish CP.

Sun Yat-sen (Sun Ixian) (1866–1925) – Chinese revolutionary democrat; president of republic after first revolution

1911–12; founder of Kuomintang 1912; removed by Yuan Shikai 1912; after two failed attempts, established government in Canton 1923; accepted help of Soviet Russia from 1923.

Swiss Communist Group – left wing of Swiss SP and youth alliance formed around *Forderung* newspaper from late 1917; launched CP in Zurich October 6, 1918, and nationwide May 1919; had ultraleft tendencies; 800 members 1921; joined with SDP left wing to form united CP 1921.

Tesnyaki – see SDP of Bulgaria.

Thomas, Albert (1878–1932) – leader of French SP right wing; chauvinist during World War I; held key government posts 1914–17 organizing railroads, artillery, and munitions; visited Russia April 1917 to promote war effort; a leading organizer of 1919 Bern conference; first director of League of Nations' International Labour Organization.

Timofeyevna, Ganna Gavrilivna (Gali) (1896–1919) – born in Ukraine; active revolutionary from 1914; initially with Ukrainian SDP, then rallied to Bolsheviks; fought for Soviet power in Kharkov 1917; worked in underground against German occupation of Ukraine 1918; killed in Kiev by Petlyura forces February 1919.

Timotić, Miloš (1881–1931) – Yugoslav Social Democrat and trade union leader; executive committee of Serbian SDP 1914; joined CP 1919; backed centrist opposition, expelled 1920; executive committee secretary of Yugoslav SP from 1921.

Tomschik, Josef (1867–1945) – leader of Austrian railway workers union; member SDP executive committee from 1896; parliamentary deputy 1907–34.

Trades Union Congress – federation of British trade unions; took chauvinist position 1914 in support of British government during World War I and opposed workers' struggles during war.

De Tribune (The tribune) – founded 1907 by Pannekoek, Roland-Holst, and others as publication of left wing of Dutch Social Democratic Workers Party; became newspaper of SDP of Holland 1909 and of CP 1919.

Troelstra, P.J. (1860–1930) – right-wing leader of Dutch Social Democratic Workers Party from its foundation 1894; member of International Socialist Bureau; chauvinist during World War I; made revolutionary statements during November 1918, then resumed right-wing course.

Trotsky, Leon (1879–1940) – Russian revolutionary leader; aligned with Mensheviks 1903–4; president of St. Petersburg soviet 1905; took intermediate position between Bolsheviks and Mensheviks 1904–17; joined Bolsheviks 1917 and elected to Bolshevik Central Committee; Commissar of Foreign Affairs 1917–18; organized and led Red Army 1918–25; prominent leader of Comintern; from 1923 led opposition in Russian CP and Comintern to retreat from Leninist policies; expelled from party 1927; exiled abroad 1929; launched fight for Fourth International 1933, which was founded 1938; main defendant, in absentia, at 1936–38 Moscow frame-up trials; assassinated by agent of Stalin.

Tsereteli, I.G. (1882–1959) – Georgian Menshevik leader; minister in Provisional Government 1917; a leader of counterrevolutionary government in Georgia 1918–21; emigrated 1921; executive committee of Second International.

Turati, Filippo (1857–1932) – a founder of Italian SP; avowed reformist; voted against war credits during World War I but supported Woodrow Wilson's Fourteen Points; opposed Comintern; led right-wing split from SP 1922.

Two-and-a-Half International – derogatory name applied to the International Association of Socialist Parties; formed 1921 by centrist parties that opposed Soviet power but had left Second International, with which it reunited 1923.

Ukrainian Party of Socialist Revolutionaries – first formed 1903 or 1904; few members until relaunched April 1917; strongest party in Ukrainian Rada, where it supported Vinnichenko-Petlyura regime; right wing broke away when left wing (Borotbists) took leadership majority May 1918; fought against Skoropadsky and Directory governments under banner of Soviet power and Ukrainian federation with Soviet Russia; joined Ukrainian Soviet government April 1919; criticized Bolsheviks for insensitivity to demands of peasantry and Ukrainian national rights; formed Ukrainian CP (Borotbist) August 1919; applied to Comintern for recognition as its Ukrainian section August 1919 but was refused; fused with CP of the Ukraine March 1920.

Ukrainian Social Democratic Labor Party – founded 1905; called for Ukrainian autonomy in reshaped Russian Empire; opposed dictatorship of proletariat; was refused affiliation to RSDLP because of insistence on organizational independence; after October revolution called for Ukrainian independence; played leading role in Rada and Directory regimes 1917–19; left faction joined Ukrainian Bolsheviks July 1918; later left-wing split formed Ukrainian SDP (Independents) 1919, which fought both Whites and Bolshevik-led soviets; supported Soviet regime from late 1919; renamed Ukrainian CP (Ukapists) 1920; defended Soviet power while advocating an independent Soviet Ukraine and accusing the Bolsheviks of failing to respect Ukrainian national rights; its forces joined Bolsheviks in stages 1923–25.

Ukrainian Social Democratic Party – founded through break from Galician SDP 1899; backed Central Powers in World War I.

United Group of the Eastern Peoples of Russia – see Central Bureau of Communist Organizations of the Peoples of the East.

Unszlicht, Jozef (Jurowski) (1879–1938) – joined Social Democracy of the Kingdom of Poland and Lithuania (SDKPiL) 1900; with Warsaw opposition current allied with Bolsheviks 1911; published SDKPiL newspaper *Trybuna* in Petrograd 1917; member Petrograd Military Revolutionary Committee 1917; Central Committee CP of Lithuania and Belorussia 1918; represented Polish CP at first Comintern congress; member Polish provisional government 1920; deputy chairman of Cheka 1921–23; disappeared during purge trials of late 1930s.

Uritsky, M.S. (1873–1918) – Russian Social Democrat from 1890s; Menshevik from 1903; participated in 1905 revolution; antichauvinist during World War I; joined Bolsheviks with Mezhrayontsi 1917; member of Bolshevik Central Committee 1917; chairman of Petrograd Cheka; assassinated by terrorist close to Right SRs.

USPD – see Independent SDP of Germany.

Vandervelde, Émile (1866–1938) – Belgian Social Democrat; chairman of International Socialist Bureau from 1900; defended chauvinist positions during World War I; cabinet minister throughout World War I; an organizer of 1919 Bern conference; president of Second International 1929–36.

Van Kol, Hendrick (1851–1925) – member of First International; founding leader of Dutch Social Democratic Workers Party; prominent advocate of colonialism with reforms; opponent of Zimmerwald movement and October revolution.

Verfeuil, Raoul (1887–1927) – leader of centrist opposition within French SP; supported opposition at Bern conference; joined CP at Tours 1920; was expelled 1922 for collaborating with party's right-wing opponents.

Verkhovsky, A.I. (1886–1941) – colonel in tsarist army; minister of war in Provisional Government 1917; emigrated, returned and joined Red Army 1919; professor at military academy from 1920.

Vidnes, J.L. (1875–1940) – right-wing Norwegian Social Democrat; member of party executive committee 1912–18; edited *Social-Demokraten* from 1915; helped social-chauvinist forces in abortive attempt to organize Stockholm conference 1917.

Vinnichenko, V.K. (Volodymyr Vynnychenko) (1880–1951) – leader of Ukrainian Social Democratic Labor Party; a leader of counterrevolutionary Ukrainian Directory government 1918–19; emigrated after Soviet power established in Ukraine 1919; returned next year and briefly held posts in Soviet government; emigrated again 1920.

Vityk, Semen (1876–1937) – member of Ukrainian SDP; delegate to Second International 1907 congress; deputy to Austrian parliament; backed Central Powers during World War I; settled in Soviet Ukraine 1925; arrested early 1930s.

Das Volksrecht (The people's justice) – founded 1898; official newspaper of Swiss SDP; defended party's left wing during World War I.

Volodarsky, V. (Moshe Goldstein) (1891–1918) – began political activity with the Bund 1905; then a Menshevik; active in U.S. SP from 1913; antichauvinist during World War I, worked with revolutionary newspaper *Novyy Mir* in New York; returned to Russia, joined Mezhrayontsi, then Bolsheviks 1917; Commissar of Press, Propaganda, and Agitation; assassinated by Right SR terrorist.

Vorovsky, V.V. (1871–1923) – Social Democrat from 1894; Bolshevik from 1903; edited *Vpered* and *Proletary* with Lenin 1905; headed Bolshevik Odessa organization 1907–12; in Stockholm 1915; member of Central Committee abroad 1917; ambassador in Scandinavia 1917–19; secretary at first Comintern congress; member Comintern executive committee 1919–1920; ambassador to Italy 1921–23; assassinated by White emigré.

Vorwärts (Forward) – main daily newspaper of SPD from 1876; in hands of centrist opponents of German party's pro-war course during first part of World War I; closed by government October 1916 on request of SPD majority leadership and reopened under the latter's control.

Vrublevsky, Mikola Evtikhiyovich (1897–1918) – mobilized into army 1916, where he conduced revolutionary work; Bolshevik 1918; member Ukrainian Soviet government March 1918; editor *Kiev Communist* August 1918; arrested by Skoropadsky regime and tortured to death.

Wasilewski, Leon (1870–1936) – Polish politician; member of Polish SP from 1896; a leader of right-wing Revolutionary Faction from 1906; foreign minister under Pilsudski 1918–19; continued as SP leader into 1930s.

Wels, Otto (1873–1939) – German politician; member of SPD Executive Committee from 1913; leader of party's right wing during World War I; Berlin city commander November–December 1918; elected SPD chairman 1931.

Wesolowski, Bronislaw (1870–1919) – a founder of SDKPiL and collaborator of Luxemburg; participated in Russian October revolution; murdered by Polish police.

Wibaut, Florentinus Marinus (1859–1936) – joined Dutch Social Democratic Workers Party 1897; party executive committee from 1905; initially centrist during World War I, then extreme chauvinist; attended Bern conference 1919; chairman of Second International 1919.

Wijnkoop, David (1877–1941) – Dutch Social Democrat; chairman of left-wing Dutch SDP 1909; supported Zimmerwald Left during World War I; leader of Dutch CP from 1918; attended second Comintern congress and elected to Comintern executive committee 1920, 1924; expelled from Dutch CP 1926; reinstated 1930.

Wilson, Woodrow (1856–1924) – U.S. president 1913–21; led U.S. into World War I; announced "Fourteen Points" as alternative to Soviet program for democratic peace without annexations 1918; participated in organizing invasion of Soviet republic 1919.

Yenukidze, A.S. (1877–1937) – Georgian; joined RSDLP in Tiflis 1898; secretary of All-Russia Central Executive Committee 1918–35; arrested and shot during Stalin purges.

Yuan Shikai (1859–1916) – Chinese general; reformist minister 1901–8; president of China after 1911 revolution; ousted National Assembly and established dictatorial regime serving imperialist interests 1913; attempted unsuccessfully to establish new imperial dynasty 1915.

Yugoslav Communist Group – group of revolutionaries won to communism while in Russia; affiliated to Federation of Foreign Groups of Russian CP; 112 members at time of first Comintern congress.

Zetkin, Clara (1857–1933) – joined German Social Democracy 1878; reported on women's movement at Second International founding congress 1889; a leader of its Marxist wing; editor of SPD women's paper; secretary of International Bureau of Socialist Women; helped organize International Conference of Socialist Women in Bern 1915; Spartacus leader during World War I; joined German CP 1919; elected to Comintern executive committee 1921; remained prominent in German CP and Comintern until death.

Zhang Xun (1854–1923) – Chinese war lord, governor of Anhui, whose troops temporarily restored Manchu dynasty in Beijing 1917.

Zhang Yongkui – representative of the Socialist Workers Party of China at the first Comintern congress.

Zhgenti, Tengiz (1887–1937) – member RSDLP from 1903; delegate of Georgian Communists to first Comintern congress; arrested for political views 1937 and died in prison.

Zhordania, N.N. (1870–1953) – cofounder of Social Democracy in Georgia; led Mensheviks in Caucasus; chauvinist during World War I; chairman of Tiflis soviet 1917; headed Menshevik government in Georgia 1918–21; emigrated 1921.

Zimmerwald association – parties and currents supporting September 1915 Zimmerwald conference manifesto and affiliated with International Socialist Committee in Bern established by that conference; further conferences held at Kienthal 1916 and Stockholm 1917; secretary was Grimm until June 1917 and Balabanoff thereafter; dissolved by first Comintern congress.

Zimmerwald conference – first gathering of antiwar parties and currents from Second International after its collapse; held in Switzerland September 1915.

Zimmerwald Left – formed September 1915 by left-wing delegates who supported revolutionary resolution at Zimmerwald conference; precursor of Communist International.

Zinoviev, Gregory (1883–1936) – joined RSDLP 1901; supporter of Bolsheviks; elected to RSDLP Central Committee 1907; lived in exile in western Europe 1908–17; member of Zimmerwald Left bureau together with Lenin and Radek; chairman of Petrograd soviet 1917–26; president of Communist International 1919–26; aligned with Stalin and Kamenev 1923–25, joined Trotsky and Kamenev in United Opposition to bureaucratic current led by Stalin 1926–27; capitulated 1928; executed following first Moscow trial.

Zubatov, S.V. (1864–1917) – tsarist police official; organized police-sponsored trade unions to maintain control over workers; committed suicide at the beginning of Russian February revolution.

Index

THE COMMUNIST INTERNATIONAL IN LENIN'S TIME SERIES

To See the Dawn

Baku, 1920—First Congress of the Peoples of the East

How can peasants and workers in the colonial world achieve freedom from imperialist exploitation? By what means can working people overcome divisions incited by their national ruling classes and act together for their common class interests? These questions were addressed by 2,000 delegates to the 1920 Congress of the Peoples of the East. $17

Workers of the World and Oppressed Peoples, Unite!

Proceedings and Documents of the Second Congress of the Communist International, 1920

The debate among delegates from 37 countries takes up key questions of working-class strategy and program and offers a vivid portrait of social struggles in the era of the October Revolution. Two volume set. $45

Lenin's Struggle for a Revolutionary International

Documents, 1907–1916; the Preparatory Years

The debate among revolutionary working-class leaders, including V.I. Lenin and Leon Trotsky, on a socialist response to World War I. $30

The German Revolution and the Debate on Soviet Power

Documents, 1918–1919; Preparing the Founding Congress

A day-to-day account of the 1918–19 German revolution in the words of its main leaders, including Rosa Luxemburg and Karl Liebknecht. $27

PATHFINDERPRESS.COM

PROGRAM AND COMMUNIST CONTINUITY

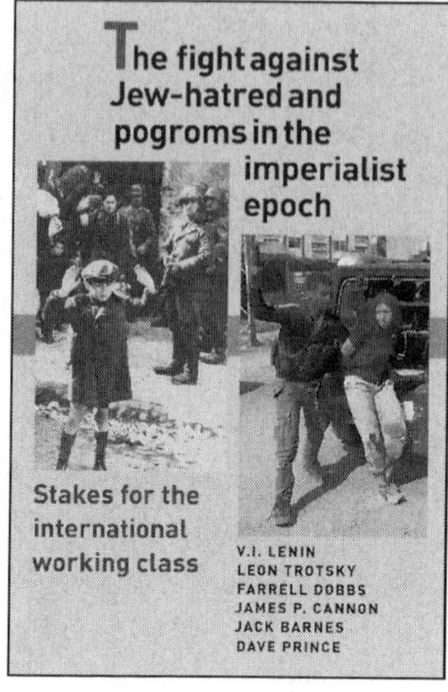

The Fight Against Jew-Hatred and Pogroms in the Imperialist Epoch

Stakes for the International Working Class

V.I. LENIN, LEON TROTSKY
FARRELL DOBBS, JAMES P. CANNON
JACK BARNES, DAVE PRINCE

Jew-hatred and pogroms—such as Hamas carried out on October 7, 2023—are part of the social convulsions and wars of the imperialist epoch. The authors explain why fighting Jew-hatred is decisive to the working class and oppressed nations of the world—and *what is to be done to end it*. $10. Also in Spanish, French, Greek.

The Communist Manifesto

KARL MARX AND FREDERICK ENGELS

Communism, say the founding leaders of the revolutionary workers movement, is not a set of ideas or preconceived "principles" but workers' line of march to power. It springs from a "movement going on under our very eyes." $5. Also in Spanish, French, Farsi, Arabic.

The Transitional Program for Socialist Revolution

LEON TROTSKY

The Socialist Workers Party program, drafted by Bolshevik leader Trotsky in 1938, still guides communists the world over. The party "uncompromisingly gives battle to all political groupings tied to the apron strings of the bourgeoisie. Its task—the abolition of capitalism's domination. Its aim—socialism. Its method—the proletarian revolution." $17. Also in Farsi.

The Low Point of Labor Resistance Is Behind Us

The Socialist Workers Party Looks Forward

JACK BARNES, MARY-ALICE WATERS
STEVE CLARK

The global order imposed by Washington is shattering. A long retreat by the working class and unions has come to an end. The bosses and their government are stepping up attacks on our wages, conditions, and constitutional rights. This book highlights opportunities for building a mass proletarian party able to lead the struggle to end capitalist rule, opening a socialist future for humanity. $10. Also in Spanish, French, Greek.

Revolutionary Continuity

Marxist Leadership in the U.S.

The Early Years, 1848–1917
Birth of the Communist Movement, 1918–1922

FARRELL DOBBS

"Successive generations of proletarian revolutionists have participated in the movements of the working class and its allies. . . . Marxists today owe them not only homage for their deeds. We also have a duty to learn what they did wrong as well as right so their errors are not repeated." —*Farrell Dobbs*. Two volumes, $17 each.

The Struggle for a Proletarian Party

JAMES P. CANNON

"The workers of America have power enough to topple the structure of capitalism at home and to lift the whole world with them when they rise," Cannon asserts. On the eve of World War II, a founder of the communist movement in the US and leader of the Communist International in Lenin's time defends the program and party-building norms of Bolshevism. $20. Also in Spanish and Farsi.

THE RUSSIAN REVOLUTION'S WORLD EXAMPLE

Lenin's Final Fight

Speeches and Writings, 1922–23

V.I. LENIN

In 1922 and 1923, V.I. Lenin, central leader of the world's first socialist revolution, waged what was to be his last political battle—one that was lost after his death. At stake was whether that revolutionary government and the world communist movement it led would remain on the revolutionary proletarian course that brought workers and peasants to power in Russia in 1917. $17. Also in Spanish, Farsi, Greek.

The Revolution Betrayed

What Is the Soviet Union and Where Is It Going?

LEON TROTSKY

In 1917 workers and peasants of Russia were the motor force of one of the deepest revolutions in history. Yet within ten years a political counterrevolution by a privileged social layer, whose chief spokesperson was Joseph Stalin, was being consolidated. The classic study of the Soviet workers state and its degeneration. $17. Also in Spanish, Farsi, Greek.

The History of the Russian Revolution

LEON TROTSKY

How, under Lenin's leadership, the Bolshevik Party led millions of workers and farmers to overthrow the state power of the landlords and capitalists in 1917 and bring to power a government that advanced their class interests at home and worldwide. Unabridged, 3 vols. in one. Written by one of the central leaders of that socialist revolution. $30. Also in French and Russian.

CUBA'S SOCIALIST REVOLUTION AND THE WORLD

New!

Cuba and the Independence War in Guinea-Bissau and Cape Verde

The Fall of the Last Colonial Empire in Africa

VÍCTOR DREKE

In 1974–75 the people of two West African countries, Guinea-Bissau and Cape Verde, put an end to 500 years of Portuguese colonial exploitation. Led by a popular movement forged by Amílcar Cabral, their struggle triggered the collapse of Portugal's entire colonial empire and brought down the 40-year fascist dictatorship in Portugal itself. Víctor Dreke's firsthand account brings to life this decisive victory. $12. Also in Spanish.

New!

Revolution and the Road to Peace in Colombia

The Example of the Cuban Revolution

FIDEL CASTRO

"No crime can be committed in the name of revolution," Fidel Castro declares, drawing from the example set by working people of Cuba as they took state power out of the hands of its capitalist rulers. In 2008, as part of efforts to end six decades of armed conflict in Colombia, he shared the exemplary record of Cuba's revolutionary struggle with the Revolutionary Armed Forces of Colombia (FARC) and the world. $10. Also in Spanish and French.

Cuba and Angola: The War for Freedom

HARRY VILLEGAS ("POMBO")

The story of Cuba's unparalleled contribution to the fight to free Africa from the scourge of apartheid. And how, in the doing, Cuba's socialist revolution was strengthened. $10. Also in Spanish, Farsi, Greek.

CAPITALIST CRISIS AND THE FIGHT FOR WORKERS POWER

Malcolm X, Black Liberation, and the Road to Workers Power

JACK BARNES

"The conquest of state power by a class-conscious vanguard of the working class is the mightiest weapon possible in the fight against Black oppression, the subjugation of women, Jew-hatred, and every form of human degradation inherited from class society." $20. Also in Spanish, French, Farsi, Arabic, Greek.

Is Socialist Revolution in the US Possible?

A Necessary Debate Among Working People

MARY-ALICE WATERS

Fighting for a society only working people can create, it is our own capacities we will discover. And we will answer the question posed here with a resounding "Yes." Revolution is possible but not inevitable. That depends on us. $7. Also in Spanish, French, Farsi.

Are They Rich Because They're Smart?

Class, Privilege, and Learning Under Capitalism

JACK BARNES

Exposes growing class inequalities in the US and the self-serving rationalizations of well-paid professionals who think their "brilliance" equips them to "regulate" working people, who don't know what's in our own best interest. $10. Also in Spanish, French, Farsi, Arabic, Greek.

The Teamster Series

FARRELL DOBBS

Four books on the 1930s strikes, organizing drives, and political campaigns that transformed the Teamsters into a militant industrial union movement. Written by the organizer of these battles and leader of the Socialist Workers Party. A tool for workers seeking to use union power and advance the fight for a party of labor. $16 each, series $50. Also in Spanish. *Teamster Rebellion* is also available in French, Farsi, Greek.

Capitalism's World Disorder

Working-Class Politics at the Millennium

JACK BARNES

The social devastation and financial panic, coarsening of politics, cop brutality, and imperialist aggression—all are products not of something gone wrong with capitalism but of its lawful workings. Yet the future can be changed by the united struggle of workers and farmers increasingly conscious of their capacity to wage revolutionary struggles for state power and to transform the world. $20. Also in Spanish and French.

The Clintons' Anti-Working-Class Record

Why Washington Fears Working People

JACK BARNES

What working people need to know about the profit-driven course of Democrats and Republicans alike over the last three decades. And the political awakening of workers seeking to understand and resist the capitalist rulers' assaults. $10. Also in Spanish, French, Farsi, Greek.

EXPAND YOUR REVOLUTIONARY LIBRARY

Labor, Nature, and the Evolution of Humanity

The Long View of History

FREDERICK ENGELS, KARL MARX
GEORGE NOVACK
MARY-ALICE WATERS

Without understanding that social labor, transforming nature, has driven humanity's evolution for millions of years, working people are unable to see beyond the capitalist epoch of class exploitation that warps all human relations, ideas, and values. Only the revolutionary conquest of state power by the working class can open the door to a world free of capitalist exploitation, degradation of nature, subjugation of women, racism, and war. A world built on human solidarity. A socialist world. $12. Also in Spanish and French.

Cuba and the Coming American Revolution

JACK BARNES

This is a book about the example set by the Cuban people that socialist revolution is not only necessary—it can be made. A book about the struggles of workers and other exploited producers in the imperialist heartland, and the youth attracted to them. About the class struggle in the US, where the revolutionary capacities of working people are as utterly discounted by the ruling powers as were those of the Cuban toilers. $10. Also in Spanish, French, Farsi.

The Third International After Lenin

LEON TROTSKY

Leon Trotsky's 1928 defense of the Marxist course that had guided the Communist International in its early years. Writing in the heat of political battle, Trotsky addresses the key challenge facing working people today: building communist parties throughout the world capable of leading workers and farmers to take power. $20. Also in Farsi.

Cosmetics, Fashion, and the Exploitation of Women

MARY-ALICE WATERS
JOSEPH HANSEN, EVELYN REED

"Norms of beauty and fashion are inseparable from the class struggle." That's the title of the opening chapter of this new expanded edition of a lively 1950s debate in the *Militant*, a socialist newsweekly. How cosmetics and fashion monopolies rake in profits from social insecurities of women and adolescents. Why women's integration into the workforce and unions is a major advance in the fight for emancipation. A Marxist classic on the origins of women's oppression and the working-class road forward. $15. Also in Spanish, French, Farsi, Greek.

Women's Liberation and the African Freedom Struggle

THOMAS SANKARA

"There is no true social revolution without the liberation of women," explains the leader of the 1983–87 revolution in the West African country of Burkina Faso. $5. Also in Spanish, French, Farsi, Arabic.

DEFENDING CONSTITUTIONAL FREEDOMS

Under the constitution "the power of censorship rests with the people over the government, not the government over the people."
—James Madison, *1794*

50 Years of Covert Operations in the US

Washington's Political Police and the American Working Class

LARRY SEIGLE, FARRELL DOBBS STEVE CLARK

How class-conscious workers have defended constitutional freedoms and fought the capitalists' drive to build the "national security" state essential to maintaining their rule. $10. Also in Spanish and Farsi.

Socialism on Trial

Testimony at Minneapolis Sedition Trial

JAMES P. CANNON

The revolutionary program of the working class presented in federal court in 1941 on the eve of US entry into World War II. The frame-up charges of "seditious conspiracy" targeted leaders of the Socialist Workers Party. $15. Also in Spanish, French, Farsi.

FBI on Trial

The Victory in the Socialist Workers Party Suit Against Government Spying

MARGARET JAYKO

The record of a historic victory in the fight for political rights, including the 1986 federal court ruling against government spying and excerpts from trial testimony by SWP leaders Farrell Dobbs and Jack Barnes. $17

PATHFINDER AROUND THE WORLD

UNITED STATES
(and Caribbean, Latin America, and East Asia)

Pathfinder Books, 306 W. 37th St., 13th Floor
New York, NY 10018

CANADA

Pathfinder Books, 7107 St. Denis, Suite 204
Montreal, QC H2S 2S5

UNITED KINGDOM
(and Europe, Africa, Middle East, and South Asia)

Pathfinder Books, 5 Norman Rd.
Seven Sisters, London N15 4ND

AUSTRALIA
(and New Zealand, Southeast Asia, and the Pacific)

Pathfinder Books, Suite 2, First floor, 275 George St.
Liverpool, Sydney, NSW 2170
Postal address: P.O. Box 73, Campsie, NSW 2194

BUILD YOUR LIBRARY!
JOIN THE PATHFINDER READERS CLUB

$10 / YEAR
25% DISCOUNT ON ALL PATHFINDER TITLES
30% OFF BOOKS OF THE MONTH
Valid at pathfinderpress.com and local Pathfinder book centers

Go to: pathfinderpress.com/products/pathfinder-readers-club

New International

A MAGAZINE OF MARXIST POLITICS AND THEORY

NEW INTERNATIONAL NO. 7

Opening Guns of World War III: Washington's Assault on Iraq

JACK BARNES

The murderous assault on Iraq in 1990–91 heralded increasingly sharp conflicts among imperialist powers, growing instability of capitalism, and more wars. Also includes:

1945: When US Troops Said 'No!'
by Mary-Alice Waters
Lessons from the Iran-Iraq War
by Samad Sharif

$14. Also in Spanish, French, Farsi.

NEW INTERNATIONAL NO. 11

U.S. Imperialism Has Lost the Cold War

JACK BARNES

The collapse of regimes across Eastern Europe and the USSR claiming to be communist did not mean workers and farmers there had been crushed. In today's sharpening class conflicts and wars, these toilers are joining working people the world over in the class struggle against capitalist exploitation. $14. Also in Spanish, French, Farsi, Greek.

NEW INTERNATIONAL NO. 12

Capitalism's Long Hot Winter Has Begun

JACK BARNES

Today's global capitalist crisis is but the opening stage of decades of economic, financial, and social convulsions and class battles. Class-conscious workers confront this historic turning point for imperialism with confidence, Jack Barnes writes, drawing satisfaction from being "in their face" as we chart a revolutionary course to take power. $14. Also in Spanish, French, Farsi, Arabic, Greek.

PATHFINDERPRESS.COM